Tom Read is a former member of the Parachute Regiment, Red Devils parachute display team and Special Air Service, and served in the Falklands, Central America and Northern Ireland.

FREEFALL

Tom Read

WARNER BOOKS

A *Warner* Book

First published in Great Britain in 1988
by Little, Brown and Company
This edition published in 1999 by Warner Books

A CIP catalogue record for this book
is available from the British Library.

ISBN: 0 7515 2659 2

Typeset by M Rules in Ehrhardt
Printed and bound in Great Britain by
Clays Ltd, St Ives plc

Warner Books
A Division of
Little, Brown and Company (UK)
Brettenham House
Lancaster Place
London WC2E 7EN

BOOK ONE

1

Thirty-four years ago, in the time before I went mad, a man looked down from the edge of space. Joe Kittinger Jr, a US Air Force captain, pulled himself upright, shuffled forwards and stepped from a balloon gondola 102,800 feet above New Mexico.

He looked like an over-stuffed teddy bear in his life-support suit, but without it, in the upper limits of our atmosphere, his blood would have boiled and his organs exploded. Thirty seconds after exiting the gondola he reached a speed of 614 mph – nine-tenths of the speed of sound at that altitude. He fell for another four minutes before his canopy opened – the longest freefall parachute descent in history.

Good old Joe. He's a colonel now – retired, of course. He doesn't seem to mind that I'm going to break his record; he actually wants it to happen. I've made that jump a thousand times in my mind. I've been there, more than twenty miles above the Earth, three and a half times higher than Mount Everest, twice as high as Concorde can fly, in that beautiful, quiet, near-vacuum stillness. I've stepped from that gondola in my dreams, and as I fall, dropping into silence – because there can be no sound in a vacuum – I open my arms, as if ready to embrace the entire planet.

Even now, as I gaze up at the snow-capped Alps from the window of my room, feeling the cold numbing my cheeks, I imagine every little manoeuvre that I'll make to keep myself from tumbling out of control.

Arched back, with my arms and legs acting like rudders, I accelerate to
Mach 1.2, faster than the speed of sound.

The dream is always the same; I can hear the oxygen pulsing through
my suit and see the swirls of abstract colour that stretch out beneath me
for 700 miles in every direction. But something happens to break my concentration and trespass on my dream – I hear the clatter of trolleys in the
corridor, or one of the loonies screaming in the garden. I can hear them
now, babbling in French.

The garden is criss-crossed by gravel pathways and dotted with winter
flowers. Maria is running up and down the paths with her arms outstretched and dressing-gown trailing in her slipstream. She thinks she's an
aeroplane, a bomber, and makes all the sound effects – '*Rrrrrrrrrrrrrrr*' for
the engines and '*Kaboom! Kaboom!*' for the bombs.

If she's not outside, then she's flying along the corridors inside and
dropping bombs in the dining-room. At night, when the others are trying
to watch television in the TV room, she flies in and out between the
chairs so that people have to look around her to see the screen. Some of
them start screaming and cursing and others keep staring as if they can
see right through her. Maybe they can. Here she comes again, making
another raid, scattering gravel with her slippers. '*Rrrrrrr. Kaboom!*'

I flick a burning cigarette stub on to the grass as she flies by. It lands
nowhere near her but she goes absolutely crazy anyway.

'*Merde! Merde!* Dangerous! Dangerous!' she screams, shaking her fists
at me. 'I have bombs and petrol, bombs and petrol. *Idiot!*'

There's nothing I can say to her; I don't speak French. All I can do is
smile apologetically as Maria gives me the 'evil eye' before setting off
through the garden again. '*Rrrrrrrrrrrr. Kaboom! Kaboom!*'

It depresses me when I look at the loonies. They're not really mad,
you know; they've been planted in this place to get close to me, just like
the orderlies and the doctors and the canteen staff. Most of them don't
even realise they're being controlled. I'm a pawn too, but the difference
is that I'm the only person who knows it. My destiny is being steered by
fate.

Who's steering me, though? Ask a religious person and he'll say it's
God; ask an actor and he'll say it's the director; ask a soldier and he'll say
it's the general. Go on dreaming.

It gets cold with the window open, but I won't go inside. I don't want to shut myself off. I like to smoke and look at the mountains. I don't know exactly where I am – somewhere near Chamonix, I guess, because that's where I stabbed Anna.

Unfortunately, no one speaks any English except for Dr Beirut. I don't know his real name, but I think he's Lebanese. He's either a psychiatrist or a drug pusher. So far he just pumps me full of stuff and I sleep most of the time. I'm waiting for him to give me one of those ink-blot tests where everything looks like a butterfly but you're supposed to say it looks like a vagina. Or better still, the word-association game – 'What's the first thing that comes into your head when I say "artichoke"?' – you know the sort of thing. Maybe that only happens in the movies.

The truth is, Dr Beirut doesn't seem that interested, and just goes through the motions with me. I think he's hoping someone will take me away, back to England, and I'll be someone else's problem. It would suit us both.

I don't know how long I've been here – it could be days or weeks. I've hardly had a conversation that stretched past '*Bonjour, comment allez-vous?*'

'*Ça va. Et vous?*'

'*Très bon, merci.*'

Et cetera, et cetera . . .

I can't even use the toilet or go to the dining-room without a chaperon. There's someone outside my room now because I'm regarded as such a dangerous loony. It's either Christian or Christiana, they take it in turns. I know their names because I've asked them, but my French couldn't stretch the conversation any further. It doesn't matter, of course, because they don't seem very interested in talking to me and I'm even less interested in talking to them. Never trust the enemy. Remember the 'big four' – name, rank, serial number and date of birth – that's all a prisoner of war can be compelled to give, according to the Geneva Convention.

My best mate Harry is coming to get me out – the SAS never leaves a man behind. We joined the Regiment together in 1981 and went to the Falklands. I took Harry on his first freefall and we were in Africa together and on the Everest expedition. I've never doubted *you*, Harry.

He and his wife Cath are the only two people who know I'm here. They were with me when I tried to kill Anna in Chamonix. I can't recall a great deal of what happened after the stabbing, it only comes back in brief flashes. By contrast, the build-up is amazingly vivid. I have a tape in my head of every hour of those last eight days – the dark days – and I can replay them at will. I lie awake at night going over the details and thinking about all the things I've done in my life and the people I've met. Was it all preordained, I wonder, this game between good and evil? Go on dreaming.

I have this memory of lying on the floor with people holding my arms and someone sitting on my back. I can hear Harry's voice, saying, 'It's all right, Tom. It's okay. Don't fight it.'

'Yeah. Okay, I'm calm,' I try to tell him.

The floor feels cold against my cheek and I can smell the polish and disinfectant. It's the same smell as the corridors and toilets at Depot Para I used to scrub as a raw army recruit until they gleamed.

Anna has gone, thank God – the evil has passed – but I can see the trail of blood on the white tiles where they dragged her away. Her ski shoes made two snaking red tracks that grow fainter as they reach the door. I can hear people running outside and the clatter of trolley wheels.

'I ca . . . ca . . . can't breathe, Harry.'

He doesn't hear me.

When the needle pierces my buttock, I flinch and strong hands squeeze tighter on my arms, pressing me into the floor. The sedative rushes through me and everything slips into soft focus. I feel drunk, people float, voices trail off and the blood slick shimmers like a river at sunset. My eyelids are so heavy. Please let me sleep . . . and then I'm falling . . .

Bug-eyed and thrilled to my toes, I dive out the door of the Cessna with my arms and legs stretched out. The ground is coming up to meet me.

It's my first pull of a live rip-cord. Until now, I've only done the standard military static-line jumps from 800 feet, where the parachute deploys automatically on exit and you drift down like a sack of spuds with no way of steering. Now I'm three times that high, with my velocity doubling every second. The slipstream of the Cessna gives me a kick and I start counting.

'Thousand and one. Thousand and two. Thousand and three.'

Four fingers grip the rip-cord. Pull! It locks and my hand rips off the handle. The pin isn't out of the cone – the chute won't open. Sixteen hundred feet and accelerating. The handle floats in the slipstream. Grab it! For God's sake, grab it!

My fingers close around the cable. I try again. Nothing. The fucking thing won't move.

One thousand feet, terminal velocity, five seconds to impact. My body position has broken and I'm on my back in a reverse arch, kicking and cursing. Grabbing the floating cable with my right hand, I slide it along to the handle. I can't get my fingers into the rip-cord handle; no leverage.

Bringing my left hand across, I smash it against my right fist. The pin rips out and the canopy flies up beneath my armpit. It blossoms above me and I'm gently rocking in the sky, 800 feet above Sibson Airfield near Peterborough.

The landing strip, hangars and trees are easily identified. On the edge of the drop zone I see my jump instructor, John Meacock, watching me through the telemeters – high-powered binoculars mounted on a tripod. He's a lovely old boy, who walks with a limp because one of his legs is shorter than the other after an accident years ago. Back in the 1960s he used to be a national parachute champion.

I come in to land – feet together, into the wind. The parachute flutters down and I start gathering the billowing cloth, cursing myself. The 400-yard walk seems much longer as I trudge towards John. At least my heart has stopped racing.

'What do you think you were doing up there?'

'Stiff pull,' I tell him.

'And what should you have done?'

'Pulled my reserve.'

'Damn right you should have pulled your reserve. That chute should have opened at two thousand feet.'

'Yeah. I'm sorry.'

He shakes his head. 'I've half a mind to put you back on the static line. You'll do it all again tomorrow. Same drill – a three-second pull. Don't mess it up.' He limps off and I follow him.

Later, in the shade of the Cessna, my jump-master Joe Foster jots down his remarks in my BPA (British Parachute Association) Log Book: 'Good exit and release. Counted and pulled but let go of the handle which floated. Looked for and pulled main r/cord with both hands and recovered position. A good jump done with presence of mind and determination.'

Washed out and waking again, I'm alone and crying. I see the double doors at the end of the corridor swinging open and shut. Outside is an ambulance loading bay. Red flashing lights illuminate the plastic doors. I'm lying on a hospital trolley, face-down with my chin hanging over the edge. The handcuffs are too tight, I can feel them cutting off the circulation to my fingers. Please, I want to go back to sleep. Why me? Why me? What is it they want to know?

I can't see Harry but I hear his voice. Cath is stroking my brow and running her fingers through my hair. She's a good girl – she's not evil. Harry leans closer. 'Tom,' he says. 'Do you realise what's happened? Do you know what you've done?'

He persuades a French gendarme to loosen the handcuffs. As the trolley starts to move, I hear their voices getting further away. I want to tell Harry, 'Don't leave me, mate. Make sure Anna is dead – she's evil. Believe me, Harry, the bitch has got to bleed.'

The trolley clatters through the doors and down a concrete ramp.

'Lift!'

'Push!'

The wheels fold beneath me. The ambulance has a clear narrow window above me, and as we start to move I can see stars or maybe street lights. All my military training tells me that I should get away now. The best chance of escape is to flee the moment you've been captured. If you wait, then every link in the chain as you are handed further back from the front line is stronger than the last. The first vehicle may have two guards, but then they take you somewhere that has six guards, and eventually you arrive at a top-security prison with dozens of guards and watchtowers and stuff, and then it's too late.

'Go now!' says a voice inside my head. Make a run for it, and hope the gendarmes miss when they open fire. They'll need time to organise a recapturing force.

'*But I have no money . . .*'

'Go now!'

'*. . . no passport . . .*'

'Go now!'

'. . . *I'm in a strange country* . . .'

Only Harry and Cath can help me, and this ambulance is taking me away from them. Anna is with them, she created all this. Harry doesn't realise that she's evil and controlling his mind. Please, God, let him be safe.

'Go now!'

No, please, I just want to sleep. I need to get my strength back if I'm going to fight the demons.

*

I'm fourteen and a half years old, living in the country near a small village called Holsworthy Beacon in north Devon. I take a car and go for a joy-ride with a mate of mine, Billy Peters. We don't steal the Mini; 'taking a vehicle without the owner's consent' is what the police call it. It's sitting in a car-park near the town centre with the door open, the internal light on and the keys in the ignition.

First up I do the driving because I've had more experience. My dad taught me to drive when I was about ten years old, when we were living on the Isle of Wight. He was a great believer in his children starting young, and it suited him because I could then chauffeur him back from the local pub when he'd had a few too many.

Billy and I head off along the back roads towards the Cornish coast, ten minutes away. I'm quite careful as we weave through the narrow lanes and B-roads in darkness. A few miles out of town, I get out and Billy has a turn. He kangaroo-hops for the first few hundred yards and then builds up a little speed.

'Let's turn round now,' I say. 'We can leave it back in the car-park.'

'Nah, c'mon – this is brilliant,' declares Billy, hunched up over the wheel.

'But we have to go back.'

'Just a bit further.'

'Turn left now, Billy. Take me back.'

'Not yet.'

'Go left!'

'Right.'

He goes straight ahead and puts the Mini through a hedge and into a grassy bank. His head hits the steering wheel, knocking him senseless and opening a gash on his brow. I shatter a kneecap and six teeth (three up and three down) when my chin hits my knees.

Crawling out of the door, I smell the petrol fumes and turn off the ignition. Then I drag Billy on to the grass and leave him sitting there while I go for help.

There's a house nearby, but for some reason I don't knock on the door. Instead, I keep walking along the road for about a mile, spitting out blood and pieces of broken tooth. I find another house and raise the alarm. A farmer and his wife take me inside and look after me until the police arrive. I look a real state with my blood-soaked shirt and swollen face.

In the back of the patrol car, I tell the police everything – I don't have the wherewithal to lie.

'What's your name, son?'

'Tom Read.'

'Where do you live?'

'In Holsworthy Beacon.' He's taking notes.

Billy is still sitting on the grass beside the Mini, holding his head to stop the bleeding. The police help him into the back seat and drive us to Plymouth Hospital. We say nothing to each other on the journey – we just contemplate silently the punishments that await us. As I slide out of the car the pain from my broken kneecap arrives in a screaming rush and I collapse.

The nurses patch me up and sit me up in bed. I look at the doorway, running my tongue over jagged half-teeth. 'Don't worry, your parents will be here soon,' a nurse says. It's not what I want to hear. I've been wondering how to keep my cracked kneecap and gappy mouth a secret from Dad; he can scare the hell out of me sometimes.

He's a huge, intimidating man who was a fighter pilot during the Second World War, flying Spitfires in 92 Squadron as well as other aircraft. He got shot down twice, and once had to bail out over the Mediterranean and paddle his dinghy for seventeen hours before being rescued.

Like a lot of blokes of that generation, he never really got over the war. He lost some good mates and there were some tough times, but they were also the greatest years of his life. He always refers to 1945 as the year 'when peace broke out', and I get the impression that he regretted when the fighting was over.

He met my mother, Penny, after he demobbed, and they married in the early 1950s. Because he injured his back in one of the bail-outs, Dad was eligible for a pension. Before the war he'd been an engineer in Canada, and afterwards he began inventing things, coming up with designs and asking local tradesmen to make prototypes for him. One of them is a particular type of pump that Sir Francis Chichester used on the *Gipsy Moth* when he sailed single-handed around the world.

I was born in the War Memorial Hospital in Chipping Norton on 8 August 1956, the middle of three brothers. Vince is eighteen months older and Andrew eighteen months younger. Growing up, we lived all over the place – in London for a while and then the Isle of Wight – but in between each move we always seemed to gravitate back to Cheltenham, where my grandmother (my father's mother) had a large house that could accommodate the whole family.

I didn't stay at any school long enough to sit exams or get a decent education, and I can't remember ever doing homework because I tried to stay away from the house as much as possible. Dad could be an enormously charming, polite and creative man, but as soon as I saw the bottle of whisky open on the kitchen table, I headed back into the woods. He had the verbal skills of a top-class advocate, and when I got in trouble he could use words to crush my defence and prove himself right – even when he was wrong. Fearful and humiliated, I just had to hold myself together, face against face, and show no sign of weakness. Years later I used to joke that I learned my E & E ('escape and evasion') skills well before I joined the SAS.

I hear his booming voice outside in the hospital corridor. He greets one of the doctors: 'Oh, how do you do, old chap. Awfully nice to meet you.' Then he walks through the door wearing his trademark ten-gallon hat. He's worn one ever since I can remember.

'Well, you bloody fool. I can see I wasted my time teaching you how to drive. All you can bloody do is wreck a car,' he says.

'I wasn't driving, Dad.'

'Oh! Well, ah, well . . .' He actually seems relieved.

Then Mum wades in. 'You stupid, stupid boy. Don't you realise that could have been a doctor's car? He could have been on an emergency call. Someone could have been taking their pregnant wife to hospital . . .'

She's in full flow when Dad turns round and says, 'That's enough, Pen.'

It surprises me. Of the two of them, I expected that he'd come down hardest, but he's a very practical and sensible man and can see that I've already been punished enough. I feel desperately sorry for having made Mum cry. She is the glue that binds my family together, and is totally devoted to us. She creates the harmony and keeps the peace in a household full of boys.

The police charge me, and for the next few weeks I stay at home with my kneecap in plaster. My friends come to visit and sign my cast, including Sheila Huggins, a girl I quite fancy who's a year or two older. My school-yard fame doesn't last, of course, and is quickly tempered by weekly visits to the dentist to have my shattered teeth removed, one at a time. Just as I'm getting over the pain in my mouth, and the inconvenience of having to eat nothing but boiled-egg sandwiches, Wednesday rolls round again and I'm back in the dentist's chair for another session.

My aunt, who has money, actually offers to send me up to London to have them capped, but she and my father are not on speaking terms so I'm stuck with the five-thumbed local dentist and false teeth that take ages to arrive.

A few months later I appear in the local Magistrates' Court and plead guilty to unlawfully taking a motor vehicle without the owner's consent. The prosecutor warns me that I might be sent to remand school, which may be a hollow threat but it certainly puts the fear of God into me.

Outside, my court-appointed solicitor has a heart-to-heart with me.

'Have you ever thought about a career in the army?' he asks.

'No.'

'Well, think about it now.'

Three elderly stalwarts of the community sit in judgement, peering down at me in my school uniform. The solicitor explains how I fell victim to a moment of madness – one which I wish had never happened. 'He has never been in trouble with the law,' he opines, 'and comes from a very fine upstanding family who are extremely upset by his actions and determined to make sure they are never repeated. The young lad is deeply remorseful and is hoping that this one foolish indiscretion will not jeopardise his future career in the army.'

Two years' probation is a good result, but it means I can't enlist until that time has elapsed. In the meantime, I leave home and work at a string of jobs on building sites and farms, earning good money. On my seventeenth birthday, 8 August 1973, I summon all my courage and walk into the Army Recruiting Office at Cheltenham.

'So you want to be a paratrooper? Sign on the dotted line. Son, we can make a man out of you. Welcome to Depot Para.'

*

When you fall asleep around the enemy, they strap you down with thick leather belts and buckles. I'm lying on my back in a trolley bed, with my arms pinned to my sides. A bottle of clear fluid hangs from a hook on a metal stand, and the snaking plastic tail is taped to the back of my hand.

I know the drill. I've seen men collapse from dehydration on punishing marches, their eyes rolling back into their heads. The patrol medic will arrive and slide a needle into their arm. Then the bag of fluid is attached and gently squeezed until the liquid begins to flow.

I'm at the centre of a room painted white that looks almost like an ice-cave except for a small window high up on a wall. I can see a snow-capped mountain. There's a shelf with a single book – an English–French dictionary. Although they've left me alone, I know they're watching me; they'll have spy-holes, or two-way mirrors.

There's a bubble suspended in the fluid inside the plastic tube. I wonder if I have the power to stop that drip going in? All I have to do is make my body pressure higher than the pressure in that bottle. Yes, I think I can do that, but I don't want them to know that I can.

Don't think about it, Tom, just go along with it. No one is going to hurt you; you're simply being used, like everybody else on this planet. Yes, but I *know* I'm being used.

For what purpose? Good must fight evil. What is good? Take nothing from 'good' and you have 'god'. Go on dreaming. It has to be a game. Children learn by playing games. Anna played games. But what is it? It has to be chess. Black and white . . . good and bad . . . pawns in the game.

There's an itch on my forehead that I can't scratch. I try to think about something else, but the itch grows worse. It feels like a beetle crawling on my skin. Don't think about it . . . mind over matter . . . it's just an itch. The beetle has started burrowing into my head. My fingers curl into fists, tugging at the straps. I have to scratch it. I feel like screaming in frustration, but I won't give them the satisfaction.

The door opens and I see Dr Beirut. He looks like a classic demon because he's got one of those hairline peaks on his forehead created by hair receding faster on the outer edges than at the centre. Yes, he's definitely one of them.

How are they going to extract information from me? I wonder. Mind probes? Hypnosis? Truth drugs? I know all about interrogation techniques. During Selection for the Regiment we had a Vietnam veteran tell us about how he'd been captured and tortured by the Viet Cong.

'I don't care how tough you think you are,' he told us. 'I don't care how high your threshold is for pain. Believe me, it isn't high enough.'

Just stories, I hear you saying. But if I could show you his eyes and let you hear the tremor in his voice, then you'd understand. There is no victory, only resistance and survival.

'Have faith in captivity,' he said. 'Remember your cover story and hold on to the memory of those you love and want to see again.'

That's what I'm doing now – resisting and surviving. These people want something from me but I don't know what it could be. Maybe it's some secret about the space-time continuum, or a formula for interstellar travel. Perhaps I've stumbled upon the answer without realising its significance. Think! Come on, think! What could it be?

Dr Beirut is pacing backwards and forwards beyond my head, where he knows I can't see him. I hear his leather shoes squeaking on the polished floor, like the sound a kitten makes when its eyes are still closed to the world. I know that a part of him is actually frightened of me. He might have the power to manipulate minds, change records and control people, but I can recognise his evil. I have the knowledge to stop him, if only I can find the key.

Yet even in the grip of this battle, occasionally something tells me that it's not quite right. It's as though I'm clinging to a tiny piece of my sanity in a world where nothing is what it seems. It's like flying in cloud – you must trust your instruments. Even though your body is telling you you're in a tight left turn and diving towards the ground, you believe the gyro and altimeter. That's how I hold on to reality – I trust my instruments. I have just enough sanity to realise that I'm insane; a tiny brain cell, still ticking over, going, 'Tom, you mad bastard, this is not reality.'

Dr Beirut has stopped pacing. I can't tell if he's gone or if he's still watching me.

'How long have I been here?' I ask.

There is no answer.

'What is this place?'

Still silence.

I hear his shoes squeaking as he leaves.

At some point they move me to this room overlooking the garden. The drugs have wiped out entire days and nights. When I'm awake, I never once think about Anna with any sense of remorse or regret. I tried to kill her, I want her dead, and it worries me to know that she's still alive. It doesn't even enter my head that I've broken the law or jeopardised my future. None of it matters.

'*Rrrrrrrrrr. Kaboom! Kaboom!*' Maria is bombing the corridor again, on her way to the dining-room.

I bring her in to land outside my room and smile my sweetest smile. She is willow-thin with untidy brown hair, hacked by careless scissors.

'*La bombe, bombe. Non, non, très mauvaise,*' I say, summoning up my best pidgin French.

'*Vous êtes très belle, très belle,*' I continue, stroking her face with my hands. She isn't at all, she's as ugly as sin.

'*Papillon. Vous êtes papillon.*' I know the French word for butterfly because I used to jump using an old Papillon parachute. '*Non petrol, essence. Seulement le vent.* Only the wind.' I blow softly on to her cheek and eyelids. '*Seulement le vent*, only the wind. *Avion sans moteur*, without an engine, a glider.'

'*Oui, oui,*' she says, her eyes shining. 'You think I am beautiful? You think so?'

'*Oui, très belle. Oui. Seulement le vent. Papillon.*'

Maria smiles and kisses me on the cheek. Then she floats silently down the corridor, fluttering her arms like a beautiful soft butterfly. She glides into the dining-room and the TV room and then back again past my door, whispering all the time, '*Seulement le vent . . .*'

The egg yolks are runny again. I try to tell the orderly serving the food, but she doesn't seem to care. '*Je voudrais prendre un oeuf* hard-boiled. *Comprenez-vous?* Not soft.' I dab at the watery, uncooked yolk.

She keeps serving the line.

'Hey, love, are you listening to me? *Oeuf* hard, not soft.' This time I put the plate under her nose. I see Christian, my minder, begin to stir at the corner table. What does he think I'm going to do, strangle the waitress because of a runny yoke?

I sigh and grab half a baguette. It seems strange to be eating after days of surviving on cigarettes and alcohol. Maybe my appetite is coming back, or maybe it's just the drugs they're giving me.

The only conversation I hear is in French, and people seem to stop talking when I walk past their tables. These loonies are lousy at surveillance. I sit opposite Christian, whose uniform is shining white and carefully starched, without a single crease or stain except for a dribble of spilled food that runs down alongside his shirt buttons. It looks like egg yoke.

How high are we above sea-level? I wonder. At sea-level it takes about four minutes ten seconds to cook a perfect boiled egg. You boil the water first, and when the bubbles start to form you slip in the egg and start the timer. However, if you were in Johannesburg, 5,000 feet above sea level, it would take a bit longer to cook the same egg. That's because at sea level water boils at 100°C, but in Johannesburg it boils at about 96°C. If the water isn't as hot, then it takes longer to cook your egg.

At 20,000 feet, water boils at 80°C, and by the time you get to 60,000 feet above the Earth, the outside temperature is -60°C but the blood will boil in your veins. It almost defies belief, doesn't it?

Air pressure is the reason. At sea level all the weight of the atmosphere above imposes a pressure of 14.7 lb. per square inch on any object. At 18,000 feet, more than half the Earth's atmosphere is beneath you, and the pressure per square inch is much less. At 102,000 feet, 99 per cent of the atmosphere lies below you, and the pressure is less than 0.2 lb. per square inch.

Now imagine boiling a saucepan of water on a beach, and having all that weight of atmosphere bearing down, trying to prevent those bubbles of water vapour breaking free. It takes a lot of heat for the vapour pressure inside the bubbles to equal the atmosphere pressure outside and make the bubbles burst forth. However, as you go higher, and the atmospheric pressure drops, it becomes easier for the bubbles to break free and the water boils at a lower temperature. Maybe that's why they can't cook a decent egg in this place. The chef doesn't realise we're in the bloody Alps.

I didn't know much about atmospheric pressure until I started researching Joe Kittinger's amazing leap. Now I'm an armchair expert on cosmic radiation, G-loads, rotational speeds, ballistic coefficients, Mach numbers at altitude and God knows what else. I know all about what it takes to sustain life in hostile skies on the edge of space.

Astronomers, astrophysicists and medics who specialise in aviation have debated for years about where outer space begins. Physiologically, it's not very high at all. At just 10,000 feet – that's less than the height of Mont Blanc – the amount of oxygen present and the pressure at which it enters the body is not enough to keep a climber operating at maximum efficiency. By 18,000 feet a condition known as hypoxia (lack of oxygen to the body) will render a person unconscious within thirty minutes. At 50,000 feet there is so little oxygen that human life cannot be sustained without supplementary supplies as well as a pressurised suit or cabin. At 63,000 feet the outside atmospheric pressure equals the vapour pressure of the human body, and bubbles of water and other gases begin to form as the body fluids begin to boil. At 80,000 feet an aircraft's pressurisation system no longer functions economically, because the lack of oxygen and nitrogen means it cannot be compressed to protect the crew from the outside elements. The ozone layer has begun to form, a substance poisonous to the human body.

By 150,000 feet the only propulsion system that will function is a rocket that provides its own oxygen as well as fuel. At 330,000 feet (62 miles) the stars no longer shimmer, but are hard points of light; there is no sound of sonic booms or explosions and the velvet blackness of space engulfs all trespassers.

If all of these environments are so hostile to human beings, where does space begin?

Hubertus Strughold, a German scientist known as the 'father of space medicine', developed the concept of medical outer space, or 'aeropause'. It began, he reasoned, as low as 80,000 feet above the Earth, because keeping a person alive at this altitude had the same logistical problems as keeping them alive at a height of 100 miles, or even 1,000 miles.

That's why when Joe Kittinger stepped from the balloon gondola above New Mexico in August 1960, he wore a pressure suit that was almost identical to the one used by the astronaut Alan Shepard, nine months later, when he became the first American in space.

'*Non-fumeurs,*' says Christian, blinking slowly. He's been looking at me all this time with his arms folded and fingers tucked under his armpits, with the thumbs pointing up to his shoulders. He's got me tagged as a loony for sure.

'*Endroit pour non-fumeurs,*' he says again. '*C'est interdit ici.*'

'What? This?' I motion to the cigarette hanging from my lips.

'*Oui.*'

I look closely at the offending item, rolling it between my yellowed fingertips. Then I tuck it behind my ear and smile at him. I'm going to be extra polite to people in here – then they might let me out.

The corridors are empty as I walk back to my room. The cleaners have just finished and they've done another lousy job.

*

The barracks at Depot Para in Aldershot are spotless and the air smells of floor wax and disinfectant. Windows are open the regulation number of inches; buckles and buttons gleam in the lockers; dress uniforms are immaculately pressed; shoes are like mirrors and my old-fashioned razor has been dismantled to show that the blade is immaculately clean. Shit, I haven't even started to shave yet.

Thirteen of us are straight from civvy street, while another eighty recruits have come from Junior Para and already know the drills. We look like boy scouts – most of us aren't old enough to vote or drink legally.

We're all responsible for our bed space as well as having room jobs – groups of two or three have to clean the toilets or the corridors, going up and down until the whole block is immaculate. It seems like bullshit, but I enjoy it because we're all in it together.

The platoon staff are absolute bastards. At the crack of dawn they start. We get beasted out of bed – sheets and grey army blankets neatly stacked in a perfect square at the end of the mattress – beasted into the shower, beasted to the cookhouse and then beasted on to the assault course. In a perverse sort of way I get used to being called a useless shit for the slightest mistake. It doesn't worry me at all.

I'm not particularly fit – too many cigarettes – but the Paras don't expect you to arrive in shape. That's why we spend the first month doing a long run every morning, as well as the bullshit like marching on the square and swab jobs. Then we go on to weapons, dry practising in the classroom first and then on to the range. I don't fire a round for the first month. I'm quite a good shot because of the air rifles I owned as a kid. The first was a little .177 Diana with a bent barrel that had to be held together when I fired. Then I bought a .22 air rifle and used to go out target shooting in the woods when I was avoiding going home. I fantasised about being a sniper, and could make the tennis players hop about on the courts near my grandmother's garden. I was a horrible little bastard back then.

One day my younger brother and I shot out all the windows in a derelict building that was about to be demolished. The police arrived at our house and forgot to close the front gate as they entered the yard. My father went off his head – 'Get out! Get out!' he screamed. 'If you can't close my front gate then you can't come into my garden!'

He made such a fuss that the local police inspector came round and apologised. Suddenly, Dad became charming and polite. 'Do come in, Inspector. Can I offer you a glass of something?'

'No, thank you, Mr Read. I just want to say how sorry I am for my officers' actions.'

'Quite all right. They were young and a little zealous. Too young for the war, I suppose. What can I do for you?'

The inspector mentioned the broken windows and I knew we were in heaps of trouble. Andrew and I were crouching on the landing, listening to them talk in the sitting-room. Dad's voice boomed loudly, and I could imagine his back growing even straighter in the chair.

'Is the building derelict?' he asked.

'Yes.'

'Will they be re-using the glass?'

'No.'

Dad was simply establishing all the facts before making his decision. Afterwards, he confiscated my air gun and gave me an earful. Andrew, being younger, got the benefit of the doubt, but I should have known better.

Part of our training for the Paras is in the Welsh mountains, and basically it means digging holes in the freezing ground and tabbing up and down hills with full bergens. Paras don't march, they 'tab' – only the Royal Marines 'yomp'. There's bugger-all difference, of course, but I did once hear a bloke on television say the difference between yomping and tabbing is that the Paras do it two miles an hour faster.

The weather is filthy, and after tabbing all day, we stop and dig defence trenches. The ground is all rock, so I never actually complete a trench – I just chip away all night long. In the meantime we have one hour on stag and two hours off. It's cold – nearly October – and the wind bites into exposed skin. I lie behind a machine-gun with my fingers numb. If I move a muscle, one of the DS staff will take off my helmet and hit me with a rifle butt or lean close and bite my ear.

This is what being a paratrooper is all about, they tell us – parachuting in, digging defensive positions and then launching operations. All I can say is it's bloody realistic – we've had ten lads go down with exposure and two with frostbite. At this rate, there'll be no one left to engage the 'enemy'.

If 'Basic Wales' is cold and miserable, then 'Advanced Wales' is ten times worse. January is always bitter in the Brecon Beacons. One night we collapse, near freezing, into old tin huts that look like pig-pens. There's a stove in the middle of the room and bunk-beds down each side. About two in the morning, the DS comes in and starts screaming, 'Get outta bed you shitheads! Up! Up! Up!'

He comes through the room, tipping up beds and swinging his boots at anyone who spends too long scrambling to their feet. I can tell he's been drinking.

'Five minutes! I want you all on the assault course!'

He shoves us outside and makes us go round the course twice. When I get to the pit of water covered with railway sleepers I start stepping across, trying not to fall, but he stops me.

'You go under them!' he screams.

The pool has frozen over and I think, 'You must be bloody joking!'

He makes me head-butt the ice with my steel helmet and I go under the sleepers and come up in between them. It's miserable, and for the first time I seriously think about jacking it in. A lot of the recruits have gone already, weeded out by the physical demands or the psychological abuse. I expect it to be hard; I want it to be hard. I'm not giving up.

About half-way through training, someone is silly enough to tell his parents about the beastings and his mother lodges a complaint. The newspapers have a field day, running headlines about army brutality and secret initiation ceremonies. The platoon staff start taking us out of camp on gentle jogs in nice clean fatigues because they know the press photographers are waiting. Once we're out of sight, they pick up sticks and start hitting anyone who drops off the pace. Nothing ever changes.

The Board of Inquiry is a farce. Instead of having a few days off, recruits are confined to barracks in case we have to give evidence. None of us is called, and we're pretty dirty on the lad who complained. He regrets it now, the poor bastard.

It's been six months since we started and we're building up to 'P Company', the final trial before we do parachute training. On the first day we line up in PT (physical training) kit, double march to the gymnasium (P Company runs everywhere) and are roughly matched up in terms of size and weight for some unarmed combat. If the DS is really sick, he puts a tiny lad with a man mountain.

I've done some boxing before, when I was a kid on the Isle of Wight, but this is a completely different ball-game. The army calls it 'milling', and basically you have one minute to beat the shit out of the other lad. These are the rules: if you win too easily, you go in again; if you lose too easily, you go in again; and if you back off or don't hold your ground . . . you guessed it.

I'm hit loads of times but I don't go down. I guess I must land a few punches because the bout is declared a tie. Thank God that's over!

The second event is a ten-mile tab with a heavy bergen, and it's a case of chin down, mind in neutral, thumb up arse and go for it. That's the thing about the Parachute Regiment, regardless of whether you fall, or sprain an ankle, or your bergen strap breaks and you're humping 70 lb. on one strap, you push on and keep going because there is no such thing as jacking it in. I'm neither particularly fit nor a great runner, but I have a good frame for tabbing – long legs and a light upper body. Put a weight on my back and point me at a mountain and I'll reach the top. If there's time I make a point of lighting up a cigarette, just to piss the others off.

After the 'trainasium' – an aerial obstacle course built from planks and scaffolding poles which can psych out any recruits who are afraid of heights – comes the log race, the worst part of P Company. We are

divided into teams of eight, and each team has to carry a cut-down telegraph pole for six miles across country, keeping it off the ground with
ropes wrapped around our wrists. If someone falls off, the rest just keep
going, carrying more of the load.

My wrist is bleeding and someone is screaming in my ear to run
harder. Don't look up, just stay on the log. Push! Push! Each time I stumble my arm is nearly wrenched out of my shoulder socket. I can taste the
blood in my mouth. Half a mile to go. Sprint!

I still have the blisters a week later, when I'm 800 feet above
Oxfordshire, hanging on to the edge of a balloon and waiting to do my
first parachute jump. The instructor seems to take a perverse pleasure out
of seeing four seventeen-year-old recruits looking so scared they can still
taste their breakfast.

We've done a week of PLFs (parachute landing falls), jumping off
ramps and landing with our legs together and rolling to the side. They
teach us about exits and emergency drills, although for a static-line jump
from 800 feet the average paratrooper isn't switched on enough to operate emergency procedures. The canopy doesn't engage until 400 feet, and
by the time you realise it hasn't opened properly, there isn't time to pull
the reserve. The world is about to rise up and smite thee.

The instructor lifts up the metal bar and hangs out, looking at the
people on the ground. Two lads who went up earlier refused to jump.
What a waste of six months! I shuffle forwards and look over the edge.

'You got butterflies, lad?' he asks me.

'Yes, Sergeant!'

'You may never get rid of them, but you can teach them how to fly in
formation.'

'Yes, Sergeant!'

Then he shoves me out. There's a dead drop of several seconds when
gravity takes hold and affects everything except my heart, which shoots
upwards and catches in my throat. The canopy opens and I look up and
make sure the rigging hasn't tangled.

Round parachutes drift with the breeze and can't be steered. That's
why paratroopers are put out so low, because it means they can't get into
trouble. Imagine a classic 'Crete' landing, with the sky full of white blossoms: if the paratroopers could steer, there'd be people crashing into each
other all over the place. It's best that we're baggage.

The next jump is from an Andover cargo plane, which is smaller than a C-130 Hercules. I'm jumping clean fatigue, with just a main chute, a reserve, a steel helmet and a Denison smock. The plane is noisy and stinks of aviation fuel and sweat.

Three minutes to go and we stand for an equipment check. I'm number one in line, so I face the jump-master and look down at my reserve parachute buckled on to a harness with a big box-release mechanism on my chest. The lad behind me checks my back and hits my shoulder. Thumbs up.

Two minutes to go. The door opens and air explodes inside as if filling a vacuum. It's cold, loud and violent. I can see the ground whizzing by. I think it's Salisbury Plain or Weston-on-the-Green in Oxfordshire. My heart is thumping.

'Action stations!'

I turn and face the door, standing just inside with my left arm across my reserve for protection and my right arm on the door frame. I try not to look at the ground; instead I concentrate on the two tiny light-bulbs near the door, one red and one green.

The jump-master has his hand across the door to prevent me going too early. He's watching the lights. The red bulb flashes on – we're over the drop zone. My right arm comes down and goes over my left arm. Five seconds . . . green!

I drive out the door as if trying to reach the wing-tip, but instantly get thrown sideways by the slipstream. My chin is tucked into my chest to stop the whiplash from the back of the helmet. I get two or three seconds before I feel the canopy deploy, and in that short time the sense of flying is amazing. I feel the jolt and look up. The canopy has inflated, but the lines from my left and right shoulders have twisted and spiral half-way up the rigging lines. I kick out with my legs until they unwind and I'm floating freely. Looking around, I see other lads around me. Some of them look dumbstruck, while others have these huge look-I'm-alive! grins.

Nothing else comes close to those first few seconds after leaving the plane, because once you take that last step there is no going back. A racing driver or a skier or climber can pull over and stop, have a rest, but with parachuting, once you cross that threshold, you have to see it through.

The fickle breeze makes my chute oscillate and swing. I have to be ready to come in forwards, backwards, left or right. I reach up on the rigging lines, assess my drift and land with my knees together, chin on chest and elbows tucked to my sides.

*

Another cigarette butt arcs towards the garden, shooting out sparks as it bounces on the gravel pathway. The wind has kept most of the loonies indoors, but Maria is still fluttering quietly between the flower-beds, pollinating the stamens and being pushed sideways by each gust.

Rhaffi is moon-walking across the lawn, wearing headphones that are plugged into thin air. When he gets below my window I can hear him singing, something about it not mattering what colour you are: 'Ooh, ooh, yea, yea, yea now . . . Ooh, ooh, yea, yea, yea now . . .'

I don't think it's meant to be sung in a French Algerian accent.

Rhaffi has broken teeth, black hair and a dark complexion. He looks a lot like a devil, or maybe I'm just into demons. He glances at me and then gives me an ankle-clicking, high-speed spin, striking a Michael Jackson pose in the gravel. Then he's off again, dancing down the path.

'*It's black, it's white, whoo . . .*'

And they think I'm crazy?

2

In the summer of 1991, I meet Joe Kittinger at Orlando Executive Airport and he strikes me as being too small to hold his own history. This guy is a legend, and I expect him to look like John Wayne. Instead I find a portly 64-year-old with red sandy hair and watery eyes.

He picks me up in his white London taxi, the only one in Florida, and proudly tells me how he had it shipped from England and has to import the spare parts or have a local mechanic make them for him. I'm sitting in the back seat, talking to him through the glass partition.

Joe chats easily and gives me a sort of guided tour and potted history of the Everglades as he reminisces about how his father used to take him fishing as a kid and how he used to muck about with boats. It sounds so all-American that I half expect him to tell me about his mom's home-made apple pie and how he married his college sweetheart.

I know all about Joe's career from my research at the Library of Congress in Washington, but I'm still stunned by the photographs and citations on his walls, which make the house seem like a museum of aviation history. Old Joe knew them all – Chuck Yeager, Alan Shepard, Neil Armstrong; he mixed with five-star generals, dined with movie stars and helped put man into space. The guy is obviously made of 'the right stuff'.

There he is shaking hands with President Eisenhower in 1959; and being inducted into the United States Air Force Hall of Fame in 1969. He won the Distinguished Flying Cross – twice adding Oak Leaf Clusters to it; a Silver Star, Legion of Merit, Bronze Star, Purple Heart and Presidential Unit Citation. There are seventeen military decorations, before you even start counting the civilian honours or the world records he holds.

Dominating everything else on his walls is an enormous photograph, about six feet by four feet, which is the most famous image of his record jump. Taken automatically from the gondola at the moment he stepped off, it shows him falling forwards, arms outstretched, with an ocean of rolling cloud 70,000 feet beneath him.

'Do you know how to fly, Tom?' he asks me.

'I've got a private fixed-wing licence and a helicopter licence.'

'That's good,' he says, pausing momentarily. I know he's going to continue. 'I don't know what I would have done if I didn't fly; it's such an adventure. I've been doing it for forty-six years and I've got 15,000 hours of flight time in seventy types of aircraft. Did you know I flew 483 combat missions during the Vietnam war? I downed a MiG-21 in a dogfight and two months later was shot down myself near Hanoi. I spent ten months as a POW.'

One story moves seamlessly into the next, and Joe tells me how he once bailed out of an F-100 jet at 800 feet when the engine disintegrated on take-off. He got just one swing under the parachute before he hit the ground. He's flown across the Atlantic five times, once in a Cessna 180, three times in a jet fighter, and in 1984 he became the first person to make a solo crossing in a helium balloon.

I start wondering where he's going with these stories, but don't want to interrupt. Finally, he pauses and says, 'Do you know something, Tom?'

'What's that?'

'It doesn't matter what else I've done in my life, I'm destined to be best remembered for that one leap.'

I don't know what to say. I can't tell if he's sad because I'm going to break the record, or if he wants to be remembered for something more.

'What you did was amazing,' I say. 'You lived more in those few minutes than some people live in a lifetime. Just look around you.'

Joe doesn't look up; he can see the photographs with his eyes closed.

We talk about flying in general, but what I really want to know about is the jump. There are so many missing pieces – how he handled his electrics, for example, and what he used to power the cameras, ventilator and gauges. How did they protect the batteries from the extreme temperatures and the pressure? What effect did the pressure have on the AOD (automatic opening device) on his parachute?

'Do you know how many times I've been contacted by people like you who want to beat that record?' he asks.

'How many?'

'At least a dozen letters a year. I ignore most of them. I'm only talking to you because you sound half-way serious. You've done your homework, whereas some of the others have half-baked, hare-brained schemes and I wouldn't trust them to fall out of bed, let alone to fall from way up there.' Joe glances out the window, as if studying the brilliant blue sky like a road map.

'What did it feel like?' I ask him.

'The jump?'

'To fall for that long. Did four minutes and thirty-six seconds seem like forever?'

'I don't know about forever, but it seemed like a long time.'

'Can you tell me about the drogue parachute?'

Joe explains how the stabilisation chute deployed, using a static line which activated as he exited from the gondola with a sixteen-second delay. This allowed him time to pick up enough speed to inflate the small parachute in the thin air at such an altitude.

'What made you decide to use one?' I ask.

Joe doesn't hesitate. 'Stability. I had to fall a long way before I could reach a liveable altitude where my main parachute could open. Without the drogue I'd have been spinning out of control for 80,000 feet. You know how dangerous that could be?'

'Flat spin' is a characteristic of any falling object that is aerodynamically unstable, like the human body. Even at low altitudes, a loss of stability can lead to a parachute deploying incorrectly or becoming tangled around the body, which is why modern freefall techniques are designed to maintain control.

During experiments in the 1950s, dummies were dropped from balloons at a height of 100,000 feet and they whirled like runaway propellers, attaining 200 revolutions per minute. Tests had shown that a rate of even 130 rpm could be harmful, possibly fatal.

'That's when they came up with the idea of the stabilisation chute,' Joe says, explaining how Francis Beaupre of the US Air Force's Aerospace Medical Division invented a small parachute that he hoped would stabilise a jumper, just like a sea anchor steadies a ship.

'It also slowed you down,' I point out.

'Yes, but that's not a bad thing. I still fell at over 600 miles per hour.'

'How wide was the canopy?'

'Six feet. My main parachute was twenty-eight feet and fairly conventional. It opened at 17,500 feet.'

After testing the Beaupre stabilisation chute at lower altitudes using a USAF Hercules, Joe took the system on a balloon jump from 76,400 feet in November 1959.

'That's when it all went wrong,' he says. 'The timer lanyard of the stabilisation unit was pulled prematurely, and the canopy and shrouds popped out after only two seconds of freefall instead of sixteen seconds. It fouled around me.'

'What did you do?'

'I went into a free spin. At first I thought I might be able to slow it down, but it got faster and faster. It was like being in a centrifuge. The Earth spun into a blur and I blacked out. I would have died if the main parachute hadn't opened automatically at 10,000 feet. When I regained consciousness, I was drifting down beneath the canopy. I want to tell you, I had a long thank-you session with the good Lord right there and then.'

I'd read the story in Joe's book, but I still wanted to hear him tell it to me face to face. He'd done fewer than fifty jumps in an era when very little was known about freefall techniques. You have to be impressed with the courage of someone with so little skydiving experience going up there again.

'I had faith in the people around me,' he explains, rubbing his eyes. 'The stabilisation unit worked the next time. It kept me face down and stable – but you know that already, don't you?'

'Yes.'

'So why are you asking?'

'I want to know about those fifteen or twenty seconds before you had enough speed for the drogue to deploy in your slipstream. How much stability did you have?'

'None. I just tumbled.'

'Did you try to remain stable?'

'I remember kicking out with my legs on one jump and it stopped me tumbling.'

I knew from experience that this couldn't be the case. More likely, Joe had unwittingly made another manoeuvre that had worked.

'Can the same jump be done without a stabilisation chute?' I ask.

Joe chuckles and looks at his hands, flexing his fingers as if shaking out the stiffness of age. 'I wouldn't have done the jump without one. We were testing high-altitude ejection systems.'

'I appreciate that, but can it be done?'

'Perhaps,' says Joe. 'If the skydiver is good enough.'

During freefall, subtle changes in body position can control a person's movement on the cushion of 'workable air' created by the speed of their descent. But where will I find workable air in the near-vacuum conditions of the stratosphere? Equally, there would be nothing to slow me down until I reached denser air at lower altitudes.

'I think you should seriously consider using a drogue,' Joe says, unable to hide his disquiet. He explains how his aluminium-coated nylon and rubber suit was quite cumbersome and inflexible. Pressurised at 5 lb. per square inch, it was like trying to adapt to life inside a pneumatic tyre. This explains why he went on to his back in a reversed-arch position until the drogue opened.

Slipping a cartridge into a video machine, Joe punches buttons on the remote control. The images that emerge seem to be from an old newsreel.

'*National Geographic* arranged the cameras,' says Joe, talking me through the documentary. 'It took two hours to reach altitude. It was brilliant sunshine when I took off, but just prior to the jump the cloud came in. That's why they couldn't film me from the ground.'

The onion-shaped balloon is seen rising from the Earth at 1,200 feet a minute. As it rises it swells to the diameter of a football field, standing out starkly against the darkness of the sky. Joe talks me through the ascent and his final preparations for the jump as he unhooks his life-support hoses and triggers the cameras. The images are captivating, and so is his commentary.

'At first it's like being in suspended animation,' he says of the jump, 'because apart from the balloon there's no real way of sensing that you're falling. Then the clouds that seemed so far away start rushing up towards you. I'd never entered clouds in freefall before, and had to persuade myself that they were mere vapour and not something solid.

'And at the same time I had to keep up a commentary because they had a microphone recording my voice. I had to give them readings from a stopwatch and an altimeter.'

Joe had entered the cloud belt at 21,000 feet, and his main parachute opened when he still couldn't see the ground. He escaped the clouds at 15,000 feet and could see two helicopters circling and waiting for him. The recovery trucks were coming.

I watch the video twice more, and we talk until late into the evening and again the next day. There are hundreds of tiny details that Joe elaborates upon, such as the electric socks and gloves he wore to protect his extremities, and how plastic water bottles and aluminium foil were used to shield the cameras and other equipment against the cold. A curtain of aluminium hung around the gondola had reduced his exposure to solar radiation and chamber tests had simulated aspects of the flight.

The logistics of the project are awesome, but Joe doesn't seem to get tired of answering my questions. His memory and his energy are astonishing. By the time I leave Orlando, I'm already thinking about suggesting Joe as a technical adviser, or perhaps even the Project Manager, for the 'Skydive from Space'.

On the drive to the airport we watch a twin-engined Cessna gain height above the runway. 'Nice day for it,' says Joe. 'As a kid I used to ride my push-bike down here and watch the planes land and take off. I guess you could call it my field of dreams.'

'We've all got one of those.'

*

I'm having a bad day, although I guess it's pretty good that I can recognise that. Occasionally, it's as if the clouds part and I get a glimpse of reality, a place where I'm psychotic and I need help. Then the clouds close in again.

In my madness, I see myself as being good and pure but nothing more. I desperately want to be able to touch people and heal them, but it's not a religious thing, and I don't believe that I'm Jesus Christ or some divine being. There must be half a dozen loonies in this place who float around forgiving people and blessing the baguettes at mealtimes.

My dad used to tell me that I was a dead ringer for my grandfather, who I never met. He died of the effects of gas in the First World War.

'Aged thirty-three – the same age as Jesus Christ,' Dad said.

From then on I told myself I probably wouldn't live past the age of thirty-three. It had nothing to do with religion and everything to do with my grandfather. We looked so alike that I imagined he had somehow been re-born within me.

Loonies keep wandering into my room and thanking me, sometimes with a nod or by shaking my hand. I've become quite popular since I convinced Maria the war was over. Some of them talk to their shadows and others clean themselves compulsively. One bloke keeps taking off his clothes and delivering them to the laundry because he says they're dirty.

Gérard, who lives across the corridor, is a mate of Rhaffi's and can speak a little broken English. We're chatting about the weather when, out of the blue, he tells me that he's the boy king of Egypt and his people are building a pyramid for him near Thebes.

'Good for you,' I say. 'Those things are really made to last.'

Strange thing is, Gérard doesn't actually seem that crazy – a little deluded maybe, but not loony tunes. He's actually amazingly well-read, and probably knows more about Ancient Egypt than a lot of the so-called experts.

There's a mirror opposite my bed, and I'm sure that it's a two-way because it backs on to the bathroom next door. I won't smash it because that would give the game away. They're waiting for me to do something like that. I've done surveillance operations and I know all about self-control and discipline. That's why I won't lash out at these people. I tell myself to be polite. It's all '*bonjour*' this and '*merci*' that – I must sound like a bloody tourist.

Outside my room the corridor is deserted. The night orderly lifts his eyes from a television and watches me turn right and open the next door along, a toilet. One of the cubicles backs on to my wall and I can smell burning. Crouching on the tiles, I look beside the bowl and find a small pile of grey ash. There are fingerprints at the edges, showing where someone has scooped it neatly together into a delicate pyramid that one breath would scatter. What did they burn? I wonder. Maybe they took strands of my hair or a piece of my clothing. But why would an enemy that has the power to manipulate minds and control people need to use black magic?

I kneel, with my face pressed to the cold tiles, thinking about Anna. In the entire planet we are the only two people who know what's going on. She had all the answers from the beginning, but it took me longer to piece the clues together.

Fucking good one, Tom, you told her your entire life story; you were sleeping with the enemy!

—But she knew it already; it was all preordained.

Is she the head of the opposing forces?

—No, but she must be a very senior agent to be privy to such a huge and complex plot.

Why me? Why was I chosen?

—Maybe because you passed a very difficult Selection to join the Regiment.

What do these people want from me?

—A secret.

What secret?

—I don't know.

I hear the door open. The orderly is checking on me. A tap is running. He's washing his hands in the sink. I pull myself upright, tie my dressing-gown and flush the toilet. His eyes follow me as I splash water on my face – I won't look at myself in the mirror – and wander back to my room.

Perched on my windowsill, I rub my wrists, massaging the bruised skin with fingertips that are still numb. I still have pins and needles where the handcuffs were snapped too tightly. I think the nerves are damaged.

Yesterday, I managed to fix north by studying the position of the sun, because I wanted to know if I have to cross the mountains to escape. With only pyjamas and a dressing-gown, I'll need to find shelter and warmer clothing. The next priority will be food and some form of transport. I won't be able to steal cars or use trains because they'll be expecting that. It means travelling at night and sleeping up during the day in hedges and forests. How far is it to the English Channel? Five hundred miles, I guess. I don't have a map, or money, or a passport. There's no underground network of friendly agents or emergency rendezvous points.

As it begins to grow light, the far wall in the garden takes shape and I can pick out individual leaves on the trees. The most beautiful sunrise I've ever seen was in Africa, when the acacia trees seemed to be on fire. The worst sunrise is today, but that'll only last until it rises again tomorrow.

At ten o'clock they let me make a phone call to Jackie Green in Hereford. She's in the office upstairs in my house, trying to field calls about the project and sort out my affairs. My car is at Heathrow Airport, Anna is in hospital, and our luggage is at the hotel in Chamonix.

'Get me out of here, Jackie, this place is awful,' I say tearfully.

'We're trying.'

'You can't lock the doors and there are real psychopaths wandering around.'

'Harry is working on it. He's talking to lawyers in Paris.'

'What's taking so long?' I must sound ungrateful.

'It's pretty serious. The police want to charge you,' says Jackie.

'Sorry. I know.'

We fall silent and for a moment I don't know what to say. Jackie asks me about Christine and Jason, my ex-wife and teenage son. No one has told them what happened.

'Maybe they don't have to find out,' I say, hopefully.

'Come on, Tom.'

'Yeah, I know, I just . . . I don't . . . let's wait . . . I'll tell them when I get back to England.'

Jackie has been telling people I'm on holiday, and trying to stall the Russian engineers who are waiting on the final specifications for the life-support suit. 'Harry said to keep your breakdown a secret. He said it might affect the project if it gets out.'

'Yeah, do what Harry says.'

Jackie keeps talking. 'Anna is out of hospital. I'm picking her up from the airport today. She's staying at a hotel at Heathrow tonight and then flying back to America in the morning.'

'Yeah, that's good.'

'She's not going to press charges; she knows you're sick.'

'Uh-huh. Now listen, Jackie, the party line is that I'm full of remorse, but as soon as I get out of here I'm going to finish her off.'

Jackie is shocked.

'Come on, Jackie, you've never liked her.'

'That isn't the point. I'm going to hang up now.'

'Please, don't!'

'Well, stop talking like that.'

'Okay. Whatever you say.'

'No more talk about Anna.'

'I'm sorry. I just want you to be careful around her.'

'I have to go now, anyway,' says Jackie.

'Have you got enough money?'

'I'm using your credit card.'

'Good girl. Be careful.'

*

I keep going over events in my life, trying to decide where particular people fit in and whether they were on my side or unwittingly working against me. It's not an easy thing to review a life. How many birthdays can you remember, or names of teachers you had at school, or who sat next to you in class?

Every time I try to think about events in a particular order, my mind races ahead or bounces between images. One second I'm remembering how Dad used to send us scrumping for apples so he could make cider; the next I'm thinking about Africa, and I picture a rhino on its knees with a bloody hole in its head where the horn has been hacked off by poachers.

Every incident has to be broken down; every character examined. What did they mean to me? Were they signs of things to come?

My first sight of a dead body is in an alleyway off Hillman Street in the New Lodge area of West Belfast. I'm on a regular foot patrol when we're called to a shooting incident. There's a man lying face-down in a pool of blood about sixty yards away.

Myself and a lad called Pip are told to check it out, so we head down the alley, covering each other. The derelict buildings on each side are ideal sniper locations for the IRA. They've been known to use killings as a 'come-on' so they can ambush the patrol sent to investigate.

The victim has been shot in the kneecaps and the head – a typical IRA punishment or revenge killing. I kneel down in the man's blood and feel for a pulse. His head rocks back and I see how they've shot away half his face. He's a young lad, probably only a few years older than me. I don't think about death or my own mortality. The scene is so unreal that it's almost like a comic-book picture from one of those 'true crime' magazines.

I'm eighteen years old, on my first tour of Northern Ireland with Rifle Company, 2 Para. We're the green army on the streets of West Belfast. A few bricks have been thrown and cars set alight, but mostly it's been quiet. Even so, it's unnerving to patrol roads that look little different from places where I grew up, knowing that some people inside the houses want to kill me. Not just adults, mind you, but also their kids. Youngsters of barely six and seven hurl abuse as we pass.

In spite of this, I'm quite fond of Belfast, because a lot of the people find something to smile about amid the barbed wire and barricades. Most of all I love being with the Paras. There's a camaraderie and a sense of being part of a family that has a glorious history. Even in the darkest moments, laughter is never far away.

Steve Chandler, the company's comedian, is always telling stories about how his family were so poor they'd huddle around a candle in winter – and how when it got really cold they'd light it. And how the only time his mother missed the stove was when she went to lean on it.

Chandler has become something of a legend in the Parachute Regiment ever since a visit by the Queen to present the colours. For the first time since anyone can remember, all three battalions, with 650 men in each, as well as the two Territorial Army units, had gathered together. More than 2,000 men had stood on the parade square, resplendent in their dress uniforms and brightly polished boots that had been inspected first by the corporal of each section, then the platoon sergeant, then the company sergeant major, then the regimental sergeant major . . . all the way up the line.

I'd never known inspections like it. Our boots had had to be bulled with spit and polish until they gleamed, which took hours – until someone discovered that a quick coat of industrial floor cleaner, put on like lacquer, produced a really brilliant shine.

The rehearsals had been going on for weeks on Montgomery Square at Aldershot. Everything had to be perfect. Standing at the top of the parade square, the RSM looked down on a sea of red berets. One look at his face and it was obvious that all his life had been so much bullshit until that moment. He'd been born to command the entire regiment. Puffing out his chest, he let loose, 'REGIMEEEENT – *'SHUN!'*

There was a deafening crack as two thousand feet hit the concrete in unison, snapping to attention. In absolute silence, nobody dared move amid the tide of berets because every man was convinced the RSM was looking directly at him. You didn't even squint your eyes off to look at him 100 metres away. Eyes to the front, chest out, chin up, with thumbs down the seams of our trousers, heels together and toes the regimental distance apart.

'REGIMEEEENT, STAND AAAT *EASE!*'

The left leg comes out, bangs down, arms shoot behind our backs, still rigidly straight with elbows locked and hands together. Everything happens instantly, and woe betide anyone who's even a fraction of a second too slow or too quick. Someone's left hand might betray them and it doesn't matter if they're three battalions deep, way back in D Company, four platoon – the RSM spots it.

'Third Battalion, D Company, four platoon, sixth from the left. YOU! GET OFF MY BLEEDIN' SQUARE!' he bellows.

The Regimental Police come to attention on the edges of the parade square, ready to herd off the poor sod. Meanwhile, everyone in four platoon is thinking, where am I? Am I sixth from the left? Please don't let it be me . . . No one can afford to look round because all eyes are to the front.

But the true culprit knows it's him – they always do – but he stands there praying anyway, '*Please let someone else have fucked up bigger than I did.*'

But the RSM is all-seeing, all-knowing. Losing patience, he roars, 'YES, YOU, YOU BLEEDIN' MORON. I'M LOOKING AT YOU!'

The offender comes to attention, does a smart left turn, dismisses himself from the parade square and marches off – the loneliest bastard on Earth. He'll spend the next week in jail polishing dustbins and running around the assault course every morning before breakfast carrying a wooden practice artillery shell.

The sacredness of the parade square is absolute. Unquestionably the most famous Parachute Regiment RSM, Nobby Arnold, once had his wife arrested and thrown in jail when she walked across his square. Another time he busted the Regimental mascot, a pony called Ringway, from sergeant down to corporal because it had shat where it shouldn't.

As the big day looms, the rehearsals for the Queen's arrival are even more intense. Over and over we practise every aspect of the ceremony. There's even a WRAC standing in for Her Majesty, riding in the highly polished open-top Land Rover.

The RSM's chest is getting bigger by the moment. He opens his lungs and lets loose with another command. Two thousand people move in harmony, perfectly synchronised, except for one man who misses the movement completely. He isn't just a fraction late, he doesn't move at all. It is Steve Chandler.

The RSM looks like he's about to explode. He launches into a verbal blitzkrieg that probably includes every bit of abuse he's picked up over twenty-five years of army service. After about five minutes he begins running out of steam, and he finishes, apoplectic, by saying, 'You . . . you . . . you're just bloody *donkey's bollocks!*'

There is complete silence, and then Steve Chandler pipes up, 'Donkey's bollocks, Sergeant-Major? Donkey's bollocks?'

The veins in the RSM's head turn dark purple, and I imagine his head taking off and going shooting around the parade square. Rather than marching off, though, Steve casually strolls away, and I remember thinking, 'They'll *execute* him for this.'

Three days later, the Queen arrives to present the colours to the regiment. It starts to rain as she inspects the troops, with the RSM and an entourage of brigadiers behind her. As she comes to me, out of the corner of my eye, I notice an odd chemical reaction caused by the downpour. Our boots have started to bubble with foam and turn blue. And it isn't just our company – almost the entire regiment has used the floor cleaner.

Afterwards, we are all banned from going out and have to spend a week polishing the camp. I don't think the RSM ever recovers from the shame.

If I'm breaking down my life, looking for signs, where should I start? How long ago was my destiny decided? Forget childhood – I don't want to think about that now. Stay with the Paras a little longer. Did something happen that changed the course of my life? But so *much* happened; how to pinpoint one thing?

I have this image in my head of RAF Lyneham, where dozens of C-130s are lined up with their engines roaring. I'm facing an open ramp with hundreds of other soldiers, most of them Territorial Army volunteers. We're about to do a night drop into West Germany on a NATO exercise codenamed 'Bold Guard', involving soldiers from Britain, Germany, France, America, Belgium and Holland.

Two waves of British soldiers have already jumped over the past two nights, including 2 Para. I should have been with them. We'd reached the drop zone, last night, got the green light and then someone had fallen over in the doorway because he had so much equipment. He couldn't stand up again, and by the time they'd cleared the door, the red light had come on and seven of us had missed the jump. In a military exercise you can't go round again for another attempt, so the Herc had flown us all the way back to England. It was actually the first time I'd landed in a plane.

So here I am again, twenty-four hours later, jumping in with the TA volunteers. The order is shouted over the engines and we trudge up the ramps. I can't believe how much gear I'm carrying. This bergen must weigh 100 lb., on top of 26 lb. for the main parachute and 20 lb. for the reserve.

Crammed into the nylon seats down each side of the plane, I watch the ramp close and the interior grow dark. All of us are nervous – night jumps have that effect. Somehow I manage to doze off. When I wake I can smell the sweat, oil and vomit. The RAF jump-master is climbing all over our containers because there isn't room to move on the floor.

'Prepare for action!' he screams above the noise. I hook my weapons container to the lower D-rings of the parachute harness just below my chest. Then I check the straps over my shoulders and under my arse that lock into the release box.

'Stand up!'

I reach up and snap my hook on to a wire running along the roof. I'm on the starboard side, facing the rear door.

'Tell off for equipment check!'

I check the main parachute of the man in front of me and hear the numbers being called out behind me.

'Thirty-two okay!'

'Thirty-one okay!'

'Thirty okay!' Each man slaps the back of the man in front.

We're now at low altitude, hugging the terrain to avoid radar. A dull red light illuminates the inside of the C-130 so as not to destroy our night vision. The pilots are in darkness. As the navigator approaches the drop zone he allows for the wind speed and direction and then gives us two minutes' warning.

'Action stations!'

I can see the silhouette of the jump-master standing near the door. We start shuffling towards him with each foot in unison. There's no question of pulling out. In the Parachute Regiment, refusing to jump on a green light is effectively disobeying a direct order – a court-martial offence.

As the doors open, the sudden in-rush of air threatens to suck out my eardrums. We're doing 125 knots, 750 feet above the German countryside.

'Red on!'

'Green on! Go!'

I drive out into the darkness, unsure of where the ground and sky begin and end as I tumble in the slipstream. My chin is tucked down in case I bang my head on the bottom of the aircraft – they call it 'checking the rivets'.

After 100 feet the canopy opens and I drift down into a black, seemingly bottomless pit. I start lowering my bergen on a fifteen-foot rope that uncoils from my harness. At least it's going to hit the ground a second before I am and give me some warning.

Suddenly, I hear the sound of splintering branches and crunching leaves. Shit, I've come down in trees! There's no time to react. I'm helpless. I smash through several upper branches and then seem to drag clear for a split-second before I find another tree. The chute collapses and I fall, certain that I'm going feel my legs shatter or my back break.

Twigs tear at my face and I throw my arms up as I fall. Suddenly the harness yanks me to a halt and I seem to bounce slightly. I can smell the pine needles and wet earth. The pressure from the straps between my legs tells me I'm suspended, but how high above the ground? As my body twists, I drop another six inches and stop with a jolt. I might be hanging from a twig that could snap at any moment.

My heart is thumping as I wonder what went wrong. How could I have missed the drop zone by so far? There shouldn't be any trees within a few hundred yards. To the left of me I hear a scream, then another. People have been hurt. A splashing sound indicates we're near water. I hear someone flailing around, drowning. They've dropped us in the wrong place!

The air is full of shouts and cries. People are calling for medics. Lads are still landing in the water with no chance. Their equipment must be dragging them straight under.

I can't feel the weight of my bergen on the rope beneath me, which means it may be lying on the ground. I might be less than fifteen feet from the base of the tree. It's worth the risk. Using my left hand, I hit the box on my chest and feel the straps whip over my clothes as I fall. Branches break and I hit the ground, rolling forward. Nothing is broken.

There's a crash above me! A huge wooden equipment palette is coming down through the trees, snapping thick branches like kindling. All our heavy kit is being parachuted on top of us – machine-guns, Land Rovers and artillery pieces. Unsure of where to run, I crouch down and hope that nothing falls on me.

When the crashing stops I start moving. It's so dark I can't see the hand in front of my face and I keep stumbling into tree trunks and snagging my feet on roots. Torchlights dance in front me through the dark shadows. A flare arcs into the night. It's a 'No Duff' – no longer an exercise, but a real emergency.

Some lights are rallying points, while the red flares signal a man down. I kick something with my feet. There's a bundle on the ground, moaning.

'Over here! Medic! Over here!'

Shadows crouch beside me. In the torchlight I can see cam-cream smeared on their faces.

'Are you hurt?' an officer asks me.

'No, sir.'

'Okay, the canal is that way. Help with the search?'

I almost tumble down the bank before I realise I'm next to the water. Nearby, torches are shining on a wooden palette. Some poor bastard had managed to get out of the canal, crawl on to the muddy bank and light a cigarette before being crushed by a falling Howitzer.

We're all wearing life-jackets with a zipped pocket at the top that holds a CO_2 bottle to inflate the vest. Because no one expected to jump near water, a lot of the lads removed the bottle and filled the pocket with extra rations like chocolate bars. It proved a fatal decision for some.

With a water jump, reactions have to be almost instantaneous. You have to unhitch the reserve parachute and ditch the container before landing. Then, just before your feet touch water, you hit the quick-release device and hold on to the shoulder straps of the main chute until the last moment. In this case, unfortunately, nobody knew about the canal until their containers hit the water a split-second before they did. After that, they were drowning.

The drop-zone safety officers and DS staff begin to take charge of the emergency. There are helicopters overhead and boats in the canal with searchlights. The local farmers come out to help with their tractors. Some time before dawn, I climb into a Land Rover with the rest of the 2 Para contingent, and we head to where the battalion has basha-ed up for the night. A full military inquiry is already under way to find out why seven soldiers have died and another eight were pulled out of Kiel Canal. Some paratroopers had landed on power lines, roads, rooftops, or been strung up in trees for up to twelve hours.

Later, at the inquest, it emerges that the C-130 crews mistook the lights of a ship in the canal for the drop zone, which was another ten miles further south. A German military commander responsible for keeping shipping out of the canal was found hanged in his barracks two days later.

'Bold Guard' took place in September 1974, just after my eighteenth birthday. Later, my dad told me a story about how he woke up that night, saying to himself, 'Lights on the water. Lights on the water.' It was only a few hours before we jumped. Now he thinks it was some kind of premonition. Who knows? I guess some things can't be explained.

Trouble seems to be following me. After Germany, I'm sent to Belfast and I get a nasty gash in my forehead from a flying brick during a riot. It's a good talking-point when I'm home in Cheltenham on my first break in four months. It feels great to be in civvies again.

I'm staying with a friend of mine called Al Steed, an Irish lad who has a flat near the centre of town. We hit the pubs before going to a disco that finishes at about midnight. On the way home we stop at Joe's Café for a coffee. It's a local landmark that's open twenty-four hours a day. Al is blind drunk and falls asleep at the table. 'Hey, Al, wake up. You're paying,' I say. He's almost lying on the floor.

I get another cup of coffee just as two girls and four blokes walk through the door. The girls are young and the lads are out to impress them. As I'm sitting at the table, minding my own business, one of them deliberately trips over my foot. I don't know why he picks on me, maybe because I've got short hair when most people are wearing it long.

'I'm sorry,' I tell him.

He's swearing at me and there's a little voice inside me saying, 'Shut up, Tom. He wants a fight. Don't say anything.'

Al is under the table, asleep. They haven't seen him yet. He's in no state to fight, or even defend himself. Maybe I can draw them away from the café.

'Come on then, let's take it outside.'

I expect to fight just one of them, but all four start circling me. At any moment, one of them will throw the first punch and they'll all pile in with knees, boots, fists, you name it. I haven't got a prayer.

My mind is racing. They haven't seen Al; I have to get them away; I can't be caught fighting with civilians or they'll kick me out of the army. So I run. The streets are dark and slick with rain. I'm fitter and faster than they are, but every so often I turn and let them catch up, trying to lead them away from the café. When they look like giving up, I taunt them. 'Come on then! Why don't you come and get me, you fat gits.'

'Whaaat!'

I lead them towards the park, thinking I can double back to Joe's Café and pick up Al before they catch up to me. In the darkness, I don't notice that a couple of them are missing. Then it's too late. They've done a left flanking manoeuvre and cut me off at a T-junction.

There's nowhere to run apart from a building site, surrounded by hoardings and scaffolding. It's dark inside and I stumble over rubble and into a drain. There are broken bricks and bits of scrap metal about the place.

Crouching in the shadows, I wait. They're standing at the entrance, silhouetted by the street light behind them. One of them picks up a bottle and smashes it against the pavement. I hear the sound of tinkling glass and see the jagged edge glinting in the half-light.

I pick up a piece of scaffolding but put it down. It's too long. I find a shorter piece – about two feet in length; it's full of hardened concrete.

They start moving forwards, staying close. What am I going to do? The pipe is heavy in my hands.

During riots in Northern Ireland, when we're lined up against a hateful mob, throwing bottles and bricks, the commander will say, 'The one in yellow.' We look at the crowd and the one in yellow is twenty lines back. Oh fuck!

We charge in arrow-head formation, with batons, boots, steel helmets and flak jackets. We focus on the one in yellow and steamroll through the whole front row, knocking them aside. They're punching and kicking and hurling bottles, but that doesn't matter. I want the one in yellow. I grab him and pull him back. We're battered and bruised, but we have the instigator of the trouble.

That's what I do now. There is no man in yellow, but I focus on a point beyond my assailants. Then, bellowing at the top of my lungs, I rush towards them, swinging the pipe around my head. Momentarily, they separate by just a few feet, enough for me to get through and I'm clear, running like hell. I don't even turn around, I just throw the pipe over my shoulder without looking.

I head straight for Al's flat but he's not there. I wait for an hour or two, getting worried, and then go back to the café. He's not under the table.

'The police have arrested him,' says the owner.

'What for?'

'Someone has been injured in a fight.'

At the local police station, the sergeant behind the desk takes one look at me and knows he's found the man they're looking for. My pursuers have described me as having stitches in my head. The police have apparently taken statements from everyone involved and arrested Al as being an accessory even though he slept through the whole thing. Typical fucking Irish luck.

'But what's the problem? Who got hurt?' I ask.

Eventually the sergeant explains that someone has been hit on the head by a piece of scaffolding pipe. It must have happened as I threw it over my shoulder.

'What the hell is going on?' asks Al as they lead me past his cell.

'Don't worry, they're letting you go,' I tell him.

The police pull fingerprints off the bottle to prove my story, but I'm still charged with causing grievous bodily harm. The injured local lad spends three days in a coma. I'm desperately sorry about that.

Now my whole army career is on the line. Even a suspended sentence will mean a conditional discharge, yet I have no choice but to plead guilty – I threw the pipe, simple as that.

I have to wait a month before the trial, and when the big day comes, I walk into the Crown Court in my best dress uniform, wearing the red beret and my Northern Ireland campaign medal. I notice the judge visibly stir when he sees the beret.

The three lads who give evidence claim they were innocent victims of an unprovoked attack. According to them, I waded into them with a concrete-filled pipe and smashed their mate over the head more than once. Thankfully, other witnesses tell a different story, and it comes out about the café and how police found fingerprints on the broken bottle.

Having pleaded guilty, my only hope is that mitigating circumstances can sway the judge. I can't argue self-defence because I was already running away when I threw the pipe. My court-appointed solicitor explains how deeply sorry I am for what happened.

'The accident occurred while my client was on leave from a difficult tour of Northern Ireland and still bore the scars of violent clashes in that province. Private Read has more than one hundred parachute jumps to his credit, and his ambition is to join the Parachute Regiment's freefall display team, the Red Devils. That ambition will certainly be ended, along with his military career, by any custodial sentence.'

He calls a character reference witness, a young rupert about my age. He's from 2 Para but I've never seen him before in my life. He stands up and says what a marvellous lad I am and how I have this great future in the army.

As I rise for sentencing, the judge peers over his glasses and tucks his double chin down on to his chest. 'As tax-payers, we are somewhat responsible for this offence,' he says. 'In the Parachute Regiment men are trained to get out of tight situations. This young man found himself under attack and cornered, and that's when his natural training came into play.'

He looks directly at me: 'In many ways you can consider yourself very fortunate, Mr Read. Even if I were to give you a suspended sentence, a promising army career would be over. Therefore, I feel the appropriate course of action is to give you a conditional discharge.'

That Sunday, one of the tabloid newspapers carries a front-page story with the headline, 'PARATROOPER SCARS YOUTH FOR LIFE AND WALKS FREE'. The judge is described as an ex-Parachute Regiment major.

For the next few months I keep clear of Cheltenham because the local thugs are pretty pissed off that I'm not in jail. I know that I scarred someone terribly and I wish I'd never thrown that pipe, but I was frightened and out-numbered. I have to live with that.

3

I'm allowed into the garden for the first time. There's a bitter wind blowing off the Alps and my dressing-gown is too thin, but at least I can stretch my legs. The gravel crunches underfoot as I stride along the pathways, trying to keep warm. Maria tries to stay with me, but my legs are too long for her butterfly wings. She drops away and waits for my next circuit.

I'm day-dreaming and listening to the sound of the gravel under my shoes. There's a voice inside my head saying, 'Squaaad – halt! Atteeeen*shun!*' I glance up and see six watchtowers around the perimeter walls, standing out starkly against the grey sky. I'm wearing Parachute Regiment dress uniform – immaculately pressed denims, polished boots and a red beret. The ammunition pouches on my belt are empty, but have little wooden blocks inside to keep them nicely square.

Six of us from the battalion are lined up in single file outside the guardroom at Spandau Prison. The corporal marches us through the walled garden, which is dotted with gnarled old trees in between spartan winter flower-beds. At the first watchtower he bellows, 'Squaaad – halt!' The rear soldier does a right turn and marches into the tower to take up his post for the next two hours. The guard going off duty briskly double steps and joins the line, making us six again.

'Squaaad – quick march!'

We head towards the next tower. Then I see the prisoner. He's wearing a long greatcoat with the collar turned up, and he's strolling along the gravel pathway with his arms behind his back. As we march closer he stops in the middle of the path and looks up quizzically. He has the deepest, blackest eyes I have ever seen.

'Squaaad – halt!'

We have to stop because the prisoner is standing in the way.

'Squad, side-step two paces to the right!' cries the corporal.

'Squad, quick march!'

Rudolf Hess watches as we pass, turning his head slowly. I can see wisps of grey hair on his eyebrows and creases that almost appear to be pencilled across his forehead.

'Squad, halt.'

'Squad, side-step two paces to the left.'

'Squad, quick march.'

We've just done a neat little box around him. It's the strangest drill in the British army, but a necessary one because it amuses Hess to put his jailers to this trouble. The war may be long gone, but the former deputy leader of the Nazi party treats Spandau like his own personal kingdom rather than a prison. Woe betide anyone who does their drill sloppily, for Hess will report them immediately. One afternoon, he asked a guard for a cigarette, lit up and then reported him to his superiors for fraternising with a prisoner. No wonder he's been the only inmate here since 1966 – any other prisoners would probably have killed him by now.

The British forces watch Hess for a month and then hand over to the Americans; the Americans do their bit and then hand over to the French; and finally the Soviets get their turn. In time it'll be only the Soviets who want Hess to stay in Spandau, but they have their reasons: for the Communists it's a toehold in West Berlin, which means they can slip a few more spies into their mission and, more importantly, go shopping for Western luxuries.

Thinking of Berlin always reminds me of Christine, because we became engaged while I was stationed there. Two Para were posted at Brook Barracks. We were the front line of defence if the Soviets invaded. Supposedly, we had to hold them for four hours until reinforcements arrived.

Most of our time is spent going for runs and training for close-quarter battles in derelict houses. In one exercise we used 40,000 sandbags to turn a house into a fortress. There were tunnels all over the place, with fire holes in the sandbag walls. It took a whole platoon a month to set it up, which is great if the Russians give us a call and say, 'We'll be invading four weeks from today.'

I call Chris every week in Cheltenham, just to say hello. That's where I met her, at a pub called the Sarah Siddons, when she was seventeen and I was nineteen. I'd hitch-hiked from Aldershot to spend a weekend at my grandmother's.

I remember hearing Chris laugh first. It made me turn, but I couldn't see her. I kept waiting to hear that laugh again. She was with a gang of her friends, sitting at some tables, and she looked up and smiled at me. I must have been staring.

She had dark hair and a slender figure, but most of all I loved her eyes; they're gorgeous. Later that first evening, I had to hitch-hike back to Aldershot to be on duty the next day. I asked Chris for a kiss goodnight and she gave me a quick peck on the cheek.

'Oh, come on, I get kisses like that from my father,' I told her.

I must have been keen because I hitch-hiked to Cheltenham to see her whenever I could in the following months. Later, when I'd bought myself an old Morris Oxford, we went away together for a weekend to Bournemouth. The only tape in the car was by Cat Stevens, and we listened to it over and over.

We had very little money, but managed to find a cheap self-catering place for seven quid a night. By the time we dropped the bags off it was already about 9.00 p.m., so we went looking for a drink. Strangely, Bournemouth boasts hundreds of restaurants but very few obvious pubs, and we drove all over the place until we eventually found one.

It was a good night, but come closing time, back in the car, I suddenly realised I didn't have a clue where we were staying. Neither of us had taken down the address, and Bournemouth was a mystery to us. I drove around for about an hour, hoping to recognise a familiar landmark. Eventually I asked a policeman. Chris remembered seeing an old night-club at the end of our road that had closed down – there had been a large sign. The policeman recognised the description and we followed him back to the hotel. It must have been three in the morning before we found the place.

When I telephone Chris I use a pay-phone in the barracks, waiting for my turn in the queue of lads.

'How are you, darling? What have you been doing?'

'Oh, you know – parties, balls, concerts, theatre . . .'

'Waiting for my call, huh?'

'How did you know?' she laughs.

We talk for a while and then she drops the bombshell. 'Tom, I'm pregnant.'

She's listening hard, waiting for my reaction. I imagine her biting her lip anxiously.

'That's great news, isn't it?' I say.

Now she's tearful. There's no doubt in my mind that Chris is the one, and so I tell her, 'I guess that wedding is going to be a little earlier.'

A week later, I buy the engagement ring on a day-trip to Communist East Berlin. The army insists we wear dress uniforms when we cross at Checkpoint Charlie, and we're supposed to keep in groups of four, never using public transport. Once across the border, it's like a scene from a Peter Sellers movie because a couple of East German Stasi agents immediately start following our group, each of them wearing a trademark trilby, greatcoat with the collar turned up and a folded newspaper in the pocket.

The rest of my foursome want to find a bar, because big steak dinners are available for less than a quid, but I drag them off to jewellery shops to buy a ring. There isn't a great deal of choice apart from plain gold bands.

Later we join another group of lads and spend the rest of the day in a bar. The spooks trailing us sit together and we take the mickey out of them, but neither of them cracks a smile. What a job!

Another person I always associate with Berlin is Popeye, a lad from 1 Para who got pissed one night and climbed from the West to the East. Bearing in mind how many people had been shot trying to go the other way, this was quite an achievement. Having successfully 'escaped' to the East, Popeye was kept for two or three days until the East Germans realised he was a pissed squaddie rather than a defector and sent him back again.

Chris and I are married on 17 June 1978 at a register office in Cheltenham. Chris is about three and a half months pregnant but it doesn't show. My mum and dad are there, as well as my brothers Andrew and Vince. There isn't the time or money for a honeymoon.

Rather than move straight down to Aldershot, Chris stays with her mother in Cheltenham because we need the separation allowance that married couples receive in the military when they're apart. In late October her waters break early and the hospital calls me at the barracks. By the time I arrive there's no sign of the baby, but the doctors want to admit Chris until the birth, which could still be weeks away.

I see her twice a day during visiting hours at St Paul's Hospital and spend the rest of the time at home, working on the Morris Oxford and trawling the local scrap-yards getting bits and pieces.

On a Friday night I arrange to go to a party and visit Chris at the hospital beforehand. She's not in her bed. She's gone into labour, but they won't let me in the delivery room for the birth. Instead I have to wait in a corridor, occasionally nipping outside for a cigarette. My local pub, the Caledonian, is just over the road, and I down a lightning-quick pint of lager and a whisky before rushing back to the hospital. I'm only gone for as long as it takes me to smoke the cigarette.

Jason isn't born until the early hours of the morning, and they keep the pub open for me, with a pint and a whisky waiting on the bar when I dash inside. I give the punters a running commentary on the breech-birth situation and then dash out again.

By the time Jason emerges I can hardly stand, but I manage to catch a glimpse of him as they rush him straight into an incubator. Chris looks shattered.

'It's a boy,' she says.

'I know.'

'You wanted a boy.'

'I didn't care.'

'Liar.'

Then she's asleep.

*

Familiar voices echo in the corridor. It's Harry and Cath – thank God, they've come for me! Des and Schwepsy are with them, two old mates from the SAS.

Des brushes past me. 'Good one, Big Nose, good one. Thank you *very*

much. I really wanted to come to fucking France.' He leaps on the bed
and spread-eagles himself. 'So, this is the nut-house you live in. Well,
you deserve it. You *should* be here. I've always said that!' He's grinning
at me.

Harry had called Des in the States and he'd immediately dropped
everything. America had been brought to a standstill by a blizzard and
Des spent two days snowed in at Dallas Airport before he could even get
to New York. Then he booked himself on more than twenty flights out
of JFK, willing to go via Singapore or Buenos Aires, as long as it meant
getting to Geneva.

God, it's good to see him. Des is from 1 Para and looks like a cartoon
character with all his tattoos. He's a barrack-room lawyer who never gets
stressed and can come up with an analogy for any situation.

Schwepsy is more formal, and shakes my hand. He used to be an
instructor down at Depot Para and he was perfect for the role. There's a
frustrated RSM inside him, and he loves running recruits around and
having them polish things. Everything has to be in order for Schwepsy,
which is why the asylum makes him uncomfortable.

Straight away, he's down to business. 'Right, Tom, we're working with
the top lawyers in Paris. These guys represent the French government,
you know, they're the dog's bollocks . . .'

Meanwhile, Des is saying, 'Listen to it, Big Nose, listen to it.'

I'm so zonked out on drugs, I can't understand a word Schwepsy is
telling me, but I don't care because I'm not frightened any more. I'm not
alone. The lads will get me home. I think of Dr Beirut and the nurses and
the patients who are all plants. The 'opposition' has finished with me and
they haven't been able to get what they want. They've thrown up lots of
difficulties like lawyers and police, but destiny has sent the lads to get me
out.

Schwepsy is still talking. 'A lot of people are working to get you
home, to get you better. We've got the best lawyers, the best medical
advice . . . We have to get an English doctor to take responsibility for
you . . .'

I'm listening and trying to focus on what he's telling me, but there are
too many details about phone calls and meetings with lawyers, doctors and
police. I look at Des, knowing that he'll break it down and explain it
simply.

'Look, Big Nose, bottom line is, we're getting you out of here. We are not leaving you here.'

Schwepsy is still talking. 'We need a private jet to get you home because no commercial airline will take you. Loel Guinness has offered us his plane . . .'

Des is in full flow, 'And we'll have two, no, make that three pretty nurses on board. There'll be lots of champagne. Cases of the stuff.'

Cath gives me a peck on the cheek. 'You look much better,' she says, lying.

Schwepsy has finished organising my future. 'I've brought you an English newspaper,' he says, handing me a copy of *The Times*.

I flinch.

'Why have you brought me *The Times*, Schweps? You know I read the *Telegraph*.'

'Force of habit. I read *The Times*.'

'But you haven't read this one.'

'No, I know how people hate reading a second-hand newspaper. This one is fresh off the news-stand.'

'What's the time?'

'I don't know, Tom, I don't wear a watch.'

My mind is racing. Schwepsy, where do you fit into my life? You didn't start SAS Selection with the rest of us. You came later, when we were in the jungle in Belize. Did the opposing forces recruit you then? Have you really been used by them all this time?

You, out of all of them, are probably the plant, Schwepsy. You never wear a watch. Anna gave me a Breitling watch as a present. I never wear it. The magazine advertisement I read on the plane to France was for a Breitling watch. Now you've brought me a copy of *The Times*. Are you one of them, Schwepsy?

He's staring at me strangely. Instantly, I realise that I've almost exposed myself to him. 'Oh, don't listen to me,' I say. 'I'm just being paranoid, you know.' Schwepsy shrugs. I'll have to be more careful in future and not raise any suspicions.

That's the beauty of this place – I don't have to appear sane because the lads have provided me with the perfect cover story. They keep telling me that I stabbed Anna because I'm a mad bastard. That's brilliant. Every soldier needs a cover story in case he's interrogated, and the closer the story is to the truth, the more believable it becomes to the enemy.

'This place is amazing,' says Des, looking out the window at the loonies. 'I didn't think places like this still existed. It's like something you see in the movies.'

'You've got to get me out of here,' I say. 'I'm sorry about Anna, but I can't get better in here. I need to be home.'

Cath gives my hand a squeeze and says, 'Won't be long now.'

The door to my room is open and Rhaffi wanders in. So little happens in the asylum that visitors become entertainment and loonies drop by to see who's arrived.

'This is Rhaffi, and Rhaffi is barking mad. Aren't you, Rhaffi?'

He's nodding to me.

'You think you're Michael Jackson, don't you, Rhaffi?'

He doesn't understand a word I've said until he hears 'Michael Jackson' and then he grins.

'We'll be your bodyguards,' announces Des, springing to his feet. '*Protection le corp.*'

Cath translates. 'Yes, Michael Jackson *has* to have bodyguards.'

Rhaffi's face lights up.

'No, even better, we can be the Jackson Five!' says Des. 'I'll be Jermaine, Harry can be Marlon, Schwepsy is Tito and Tom, you can be Jackie.'

Cath translates and Rhaffi tries to get his head around having suddenly been reunited with his 'brothers'.

More people arrive, including Gérard from across the corridor. 'He's been here twelve years,' I tell the others. 'He spends all day reading books, don't you, Gérard? You're probably a bloody genius.'

We have coffee and tea in the canteen and I know the lads are monitoring my behaviour, asking themselves if I'm okay. I'm doing exactly the same thing, trying to give nothing away because I know that patients are listening to our conversation.

Schwepsy and Harry are discussing the details of their meetings with lawyers and the police. All sorts of strings are being pulled and favours sought. My old boss, Saad Hariri, a wealthy Arab who Des and I used to bodyguard in Washington, has said, 'Whatever you need, just do it. I'll pick up the tab.'

Anna has been encouraged not to press charges against me. The others sound genuinely sorry for her, and Harry still can't believe I wanted to kill her. They don't seem to realise that I stabbed her because I had no choice. Obviously she has them all fooled, so I have to be careful.

It's time for them to leave.

'Don't go,' I say, almost in tears. If they go now the link will be severed and they'll never get back to me. Dr Beirut will find some way to stop them and I'll be detained for ever.

'We'll be back tomorrow,' says Harry. 'We're only an hour away.'

'Can't you check into a hotel that's closer?' I plead.

Harry grows impatient. 'Come on, Tom, pull yourself together. We've gone to a lot of trouble to get here. We'll be up in the morning.'

'But something is going to go wrong, I know it is. There's going to be a problem and you're not going to get me out. You can say what you like, but you won't because they'll stop you.'

'Who's going to stop us?'

Des is lying on the bed, pretending that his hands are strapped to his sides and he's rocking his head from side to side, saying, 'We are not leaving here without you, Big Nose. Not a chance. You're coming with us.'

My confidence collapses once they've gone. There's no one I can trust in here. I stare out the window all evening, wondering what it is I'm supposed to know.

Come on, Tom, think a little harder. What is it that these people want from you?

*

My first few sport parachute jumps are in Thruxton, down near Salisbury Plain. I hitch-hike down from Aldershot and kip overnight in a hangar in my sleeping-bag. It costs about two quid a jump – a lot of money for someone who only earns £90 a month.

The weather is changeable – jumps are cancelled if the wind is over 10 mph because it's too dangerous. The training parachutes are round, similar to the military, although they have a forward speed of about 5 mph.

Because of the strong winds I only get a few jumps, all of them static-line. I might not get back here for another month. What a waste of time! In the cookhouse back at camp, I start chatting to Scotty Milne, who's the

British National Freefall Champion and a member of the Red Devils.

'You're doing it all the wrong way,' he says. 'What you need is continuity.'

I tell Scotty that I'm off to Northern Ireland for four months, and then I have two weeks' leave.

'Wait until then,' he says. 'Save your money and go somewhere for a fortnight to do it properly.'

That's how I finish up at Sibson Airfield near Peterborough, with John Meacock as my jump instructor. I broke my right thumb in that first stiff pull, but it doesn't dissuade me. Nothing I've experienced can match the exhilaration of falling towards the Earth at 120 mph. Imagine travelling on a motorway at that sort of speed and standing up through the sun-roof of your car. Feel the way the rushing air tugs at your clothes and presses hollows in your cheeks. Hold out your arms and notice how the dynamic pressure affects them as you raise them higher or lower. It will give you some idea of how it feels to freefall, but not even an inkling of the adrenalin rush.

After getting my licence in Peterborough, every spare moment I can find is spent hitch-hiking to airfields and drop zones. I produce my log book and the instructors watch me through telemeters as I practise different manoeuvres and try to move up the categories from one to ten.

From the standard 'frog position' – flat and face-to-Earth, with knees bent at ninety degrees and arms outstretched level with my shoulders – I begin learning how to initiate turns. I pick up a heading on the horizon, dip a shoulder and turn either left or right before stopping 360° later. When that is mastered, I move on to the next skill.

I had never really had an ambition in my life until I decided to join the Parachute Regiment. And now that I'm here, I want to apply to join the Red Devils. I'm not good enough yet, but if I can get 200 jumps under my belt and reach Category 10, then I'll have a chance.

In the summer of 1976, a real scorcher, I move from Mortar Platoon to the Motor Transport Platoon because I've never had an official driving licence. It's a month-long course, and on the first day the instructor says, 'Right, can anyone drive?'

About five of us put up our hands.

'When did you learn to drive, soldier?' he asks me.

'My dad taught me,' I say, which is almost the truth – someone had to get him home from the pub.

The instructor points to a Land Rover. 'Those of you who can already drive will go and practise in that vehicle. The rest of you will stay here with me.'

We drive straight down to Brighton and sit on the beach all day. Meanwhile, the rest of the lads are kangaroo-hopping around the parade square, learning how to change gears. This became the routine for the next three weeks. We swanned around, improving our suntans, and then put in some practice during the last week before the driving test.

Having passed the exam I'm posted to Mortar Platoon, which has its own motor-pool detachment rather than using the Royal Corps of Transport. Before long I'm back in Northern Ireland, driving for my old rifle company, based at North Howard Street off the Falls Road.

One afternoon, soon after we arrive, the out-going regiment is giving us a familiarisation tour, showing us the trouble spots and no-go areas. I've got a mobile patrol of four or five lads in the Land Rover. There's an armoured personnel carrier in front of me and I'm the last but one Land Rover in the convoy. As we round a corner into White Rock Road, near the security force base, there's a loud explosion in front of me.

Hand-brake up, everybody out! We run to each side of the road, taking cover against a wall and in doorways, waiting for the inevitable snipers to open up. It's quiet. What was it?

Soldiers are running up the road, covering each other and going into doorways. Others are peering over walls and checking windows. It was probably a nail bomb thrown from a window and, thankfully, nobody was hurt.

Back in my open-top Land Rover, I glance up and notice the rear-view mirror has gone. Then the lead vehicle finds the tail fin of an RPG-7 grenade, an anti-tank weapon commonly used by the IRA. The grenade had been fired at the armoured personnel carrier, skimmed off the road, gone past my left ear and exploded ahead of me. Welcome back to Northern Ireland!

Most of the time I drive patrols around and wait outside while they search houses or derelict buildings. Our Land Rovers have been stripped down to the bare minimum, with just a windscreen above the dashboard, as well as a 'cheese-cutter' on the front, which is an angle iron that sits up like a pike about seven feet high and is designed to cut any wires that have been strung across the road to take our heads off.

We get a call to a house in the Clonnard, West Belfast. I drop the lads and park up on the corner with another Land Rover. A couple of lads are protecting us and there are more at the far end of the street, securing the whole area. An old bloke answers the door of the house and the boys go past him, searching for arms and ammunition. There are two sons in the family and one of them is in prison.

As the patrol searches inside, John Geddis and Ebo Flynn take up sentry positions outside the front door. Each of them has a rifle and a Federal Riot Gun that fires rubber bullets and can do quite a bit of damage at close quarters.

Upstairs, with perfect timing, the old man has a heart attack. He's just out of hospital and has a history of heart problems. One of the boys starts giving him CPR, the normal drill, and we call an ambulance.

Meanwhile, a crowd starts gathering in the street because they've seen the army vehicles. People start banging dustbin lids, which is the signal for everyone to come out of their houses and generally start spitting and swearing at the soldiers, trying to get a good riot going.

The local priest arrives and demands entry into the house. The old man is in a bad way, and might need the Last Rites. I'm keeping one eye on the house and the other on the crowd as people start picking up broken bricks and bottles.

The sash window slides up and the priest pokes his head out.

'He's dead, he's dead! The bastards have fockin' killed him!' he cries.

Talk about lighting a fuse. The crowd goes berserk.

Suddenly there's a whistle. Time to go.

The lads pile out of the house as bricks, bottles and metal bars come raining down. John and Ebo are the cover-men and the last two to go. The first vehicle roars away and leaves them, along with a dog-handler and his sniffer dog, a German shepherd. The crowd's anger is now focused on those who remain.

Under attack, they have to make a decision – to react or not react. I hear the shots and know John and Ebo have started firing rubber bullets. They're trying to manoeuvre towards the rendezvous point at the corner of the street, keeping the dog-handler between them, but they're trapped. The crowd is hanging back until they run out of bullets.

Shoving the Land Rover into reverse I come round the corner backwards, with the engine screaming. People are diving out of the way.

'Get in! Get in!' I cry.

They scramble on board and the crowd surges forward, sensing their quarry is about to escape. John and Ebo are running out of ammunition. I accelerate away but about fifty yards down the street the sniffer dog tumbles out the back of the Land Rover and rolls along the road, still attached to a long lead.

'My dog! My dog!' cries the handler.

'Bugger it, keep going,' says Ebo.

'No!'

Glancing over my shoulder, I see the crowd starting to surround the confused animal. Fuck it! I hit the brakes. John and Ebo put down their last rubber bullets and the handler starts wheeling the dog back on its lead and pulling it on board.

The windscreen has been shattered by bricks and a mob of teenagers now climbs on to the cheese-cutter, swinging on the pike until it bends down and looks like a metal lance. The engine is roaring and I'm feeding back on the clutch bite, edging forwards, making sure I don't stall it. As I turn, I see half a dozen lads cowering in a doorway as the cheese-cutter scrapes along a wall heading straight for them. I swerve just before it impales them.

'Everyone hang on,' I yell, wrenching the wheel and pulling the Land Rover back into the centre of the street. Bodies are throwing themselves out of the way. The road is clear, we're safe.

My best mate is a lad called Duke Allen, another driver for D Company who went through Para training a year before me, having been a junior. He's exactly two hours younger than me and I always say to him, 'When you get to my age, Duke, you'll appreciate what I'm saying.'

We both want to get out of Northern Ireland so we volunteer for the Parachute Regiment's Recruiting Team, which is looking for a couple of drivers. Basically, it means touring around the countryside visiting showgrounds and setting up a big scaffolding tower that is used to simulate parachute drops. People queue up to get dropped down a big cable known as 'the death slide'.

There are ten of us on the team, and it's a pretty sought-after job because of the allowances for food and accommodation. Normally we stay at local army camps and occasionally at hotels, although I'm more likely to pocket the money and sleep in the back of the lorry.

Duke is a fan of the other great fringe benefit of the job. The blonde he met in Luton yesterday is the third girl he's been out with this week. The uniform is a real come-on. I have Christine in Cheltenham, though, and I get home at every opportunity, either hitch-hiking or borrowing one of the Land Rovers.

I take Schitz with me, wrapped in my smock with just his head sticking out. He's a Labrador puppy that Duke and I found abandoned by the side of a road. We're not supposed to have animals, so we have to sneak Schitz into the army camps and hide him from the officers. He's a good dog – he never craps in my bed but jumps on to Duke's bunk instead. If he does it again, Duke says he'll kill him.

I don't know how much longer we can keep him hidden. Schitz is growing bigger every day and needs room to run about. Right now he's tied up in the shade of the tower with a length of paracord, playing with a couple of other Labradors.

'Does this dog belong to you?' asks a matronly type in a floral dress. She owns the other dogs.

'Sort of,' I say. 'We found him, anyway.'

'He's lovely, isn't he?'

'He's a bit of a nut-case.'

'No, you're lovely, aren't you? You're a sweetie.' She's not talking to me any more.

Duke and I have been discussing what we should do with Schitz, because sooner or later we're going to get caught. This lady seems nice. Her dogs look really happy and healthy.

'He needs a proper home,' I say, even though I don't want to lose him.

She doesn't hesitate. 'I'll take him.'

That afternoon, Duke and I go to her place – a nice house with a big garden.

'Do you think I could give Schitz another name?' she asks politely, as she pours another cup of tea and offers a scone.

'Sure, he's your dog.'

'Now any time you want to come and see him, you're quite welcome.'

The five-month-old puppy is playing in the garden when we leave. Duke is almost in tears, even though he's always pretended to hate Schitz. I tell him he's a big marshmallow and he threatens to knock my head off.

*

The lads promised to come and see me again today. I wonder what's taking them so long? I keep getting all these ideas about Anna and Dr Beirut keeping them away from me; watching from behind mirrors and creating new obstacles whenever they get close to freeing me. Is Anna really back in America? Or is she here, watching me?

It all seems so blindingly obvious, but then my one good brain cell tells me that I'm being paranoid, and that there's no conspiracy or global plot. I'm just twisting the facts to suit myself and drawing the wrong conclusions from coincidences. But how do I know what's real and not real? Trust your instruments.

'Big Nose, Big Nose, Big Nose!' Des bounces into the room and flings himself on to the bed. 'How's my favourite loony?'

'Are we going?'

'Not yet,' says Schwepsy.

'Come on, let's just go now. We can catch a plane and be back in England in a few hours.'

'No, no, no, Big Nose,' sighs Des. 'You're such a fucking loony that none of the nice airline people want to take you on their planes. Not even in a strait-jacket. There's some kind of Hannibal Lecter clause in the safety regulations.'

'But you can't leave me in here. I'm going to die. Someone is going to hurt me. Des, this is me, get me out of here!' I'm getting distraught.

'On Friday, Big Nose. Whatever happens, you'll be out by Friday.'

Schwepsy looks at Des as if to say, How can you tell him that?

They're arguing with each other and I hear Des say, 'I don't give a fuck about the lawyers! On Friday he either comes out legally or we'll break him out. I'm not going to let him rot here.'

Des turns to me. 'I could no more leave one of my children in this place than I could leave you. Believe me. I know you're scared, but hang on. You are coming out of here on Friday – that's two days from now. I promise you.'

Des has always managed to cheer me up; he's just so positive about life and so certain of himself. Schwepsy is very logical and rarely distracted by emotion, but Des sees the funny side of things and listens to his heart as well as his head.

My paranoia is easing, but I doubt if the lads realise how serious it is. On the way back from the canteen, I show Des into the toilet and he finds one of the little piles of grey ash on the tiles. He knows what it is immediately. It's not voodoo or black magic – some loony has been smoking roll-ups and rather than just flicking ash on the floor like any normal person, they've been making a small pile of ash and broken matches.

I can see it now. Why didn't I realise it before? I keep hoping that I'm going to wake from a dream and everything will be okay. I'll be home in Hereford and none of this will have happened. Let me sleep for years, but make me well again when I wake up.

4

'*Welcome to the show, ladies and gentlemen, boys and girls. My name is Tom Read and I'm your Red Devils commentator for this afternoon's display. In about three minutes from now the aircraft will appear overhead. I'll just see where they are now.*'

The radio handset crackles as I hit the button.

'*Hello Delta Hotel, this is the DZ. How far out are you?*'

'*DZ this is Delta Hotel. We're approaching from the north at two thousand feet. You should see us about now.*'

The twin-engined Islander is a speck in the distance. I'm standing in the middle of an arena, next to a large orange cross on the ground. Around me there are people staring skywards, shielding their eyes from the afternoon sun.

The 'Red Freds' won't let me take part in a display until I have 200 jumps under my belt. I know the ground commentary spiel like a bloody mantra, I've done it so often. I even did the odd commentary while I was on the Recruiting Team, when we bumped into the Red Devils at different showgrounds around the country. That was my foot in the door.

'*Today we have seven jumpers in the aircraft, and the jump-master is Corporal Sharky Sheridan. Sharky has done three thousand jumps while the newest member of the team, Rixie, has only a couple of hundred jumps and this is his first display.*'

If I stumble or run out of things to say, I make up stuff, like telling people it's one of the team's birthday. The kids love it, and so do the floozies. Sometimes the lads argue over whose turn it is to have a birthday.

I'm looking after John Meacock's young son, Chris. I made him a junior Red Fred for the day and he's been trailing me like a puppy dog ever since. He's a good little kid, and I imagine Jason at that age.

'Sharky will be looking out the open door of the aircraft and directing the pilot to take him immediately over the target area. Then he's going to drop a wind-drift indicator out the door, so don't think he's fallen out himself. It's actually a crepe paper streamer that's about eighteen feet long, and he'll be watching it drift down, plotting the direction and strength of the wind. That way he can judge exactly where to exit the aircraft. Now, boys and girls, Sharky's getting on a bit, he's long in the tooth and his eyesight isn't so good, so it might be a good idea if you keep an eye on the streamer for him.'

The Islander passes overhead and the streamer flutters downwards, drifting about 500 yards south of the arena.

'They're now going to begin climbing to the jump altitude, which today is seven thousand feet. That's going to take about ten minutes, which will give me some time to tell you about the Red Devils and what you are hopefully going to see today. The Parachute Regiment freefall team was formed in 1964. Since then some hundred and fifty members have passed through it. It's a great honour. The members are selected from the Parachute Regiment and are all trained soldiers who have served their battalions in various parts of the world . . .'

I only had about half the required jumps when I joined the Red Freds in February 1978, but it didn't take me long to build up the numbers. Jim Coffey, one of the senior instructors, drove me down to Netheravon, a bleak army camp on Salisbury Plain which is the headquarters of the Joint Service Parachute Centre.

'I'll be back in ten days,' he said. 'Just get on with it.'

The dormitories normally slept thirty people but I was there by myself, feeling bloody lonely. The weather deteriorated most afternoons, so I could only jump in the mornings.

The Red Devils has two teams, red and black, with about ten members in each, as well as a team sergeant-major and two jump-masters. I'm on the red team. We train on Queens Avenue in Aldershot, a huge recreation ground where the Islander, an old piston aeroplane that struggles to get over 7,000 feet, can land and take off again. There's a running track around the outside and a school at the top end.

I get to work about 8.30 a.m., load up the DZ van and put in the bollards to mark the runway, which is really just a grass strip. If the ground is too soft, the Islander takes off from RAE Farnborough, which is just next door. Our pilots are mainly commercial lads from British Airways, who enjoy occasionally flying by the seat of their pants again instead of having computers do it all for them.

If the weather is good we do as many lifts as possible. While one team repacks their parachutes, the other team will be airborne. I'm only a C Licence, and can't do a display until I have my D Licence, which is Category 10. This means showing that I can left turn, right turn, back loop, track horizontally, spin, separate, track turn and recover from any kind of unstable exit.

Another discipline is 'relative work' – being able to fall relative to others and to link up. We practise the manoeuvres beforehand on the ground, known as 'dirt-diving', holding each other's arms and legs, to make various formations such as 'snowflakes', 'diamonds' or 'donuts'.

Freefalling is a combination of balance and aerodynamic configuration. It's very similar to riding a bicycle in the sense that it relies on a combination of balance, speed and the tiny correcting movements that a person makes almost instinctively. These are things that can't be explained, they must be experienced.

Back flips are just like on a trampoline, you bring your knees into your chin, push your arms down in the air and throw your head back. Suddenly you see blue sky, then green, then blue again before you flare out back into your frog position.

Tracking is where you shape your body like an arrow, with your arms tilted back like a delta-winged aircraft. This gives you horizontal movement across the sky while falling. It also generates enormous speed, and means that relatively you are travelling much faster than someone descending in the frog position.

'Ladies and gentlemen, the Red Devils will now be making final adjustments to their equipment, checking each other off. From seven thousand feet, looking out the door, you can see the whole of Manchester, but the orange cross here allows them to pick up the drop zone.

'*Today, we have lovely conditions. Winds of only about ten knots. And they'll be exiting the aircraft – if you look where I'm pointing – just about five hundred yards north of the arena. Once they have exited, they will try to link up in the air while accelerating to a hundred and twenty miles per hour. Don't worry, you will see them; they'll be wearing red and blue smoke canisters and you'll see the smoke trails.*

'*They will have thirty seconds of freefall to get together and then to separate and find their own bit of space before opening their parachutes at two thousand feet. Once the parachutes are open, each jumper will be looking around to find the drop zone, because only Sharky has seen it and perhaps the lads who are lucky enough to be sitting by a window.*

'*The parachutes will be opening just above those trees you can see, and their aim will be to land in the arena. With a bit of luck we might get all seven in today. The cross I am standing next to is just a signal to the aircraft in case we lose radio communications – it is not a target, but there is always a little bit of competition among the lads to see who can get closest to the cross . . .*'

My whole first season is spent training and setting up drop zones. Normally it means leaving Aldershot at the crack of dawn to drive the old Bedford van to the venue. We call it the 'ice-cream van' because it's covered in flashing lights for going into airfields. Each new arena is checked out in advance, often months earlier, to make sure it fulfils certain requirements in terms of a minimum size and whether there are any obstacles.

Eventually, the sergeant-major, Ted Lewington, a hard-nosed Cockney, relents and lets me do a Red Devils display even though I only have 137 jumps. I think Ted figures I can't get into too much trouble because the drop zone is so big – we'll be landing in the English Channel for the opening of the new Brighton Marina.

Water jumps are a lot of hassle, especially sea water, because it means having to wash everything down afterwards with fresh water and then dry it out. To protect our best equipment we're jumping in the old round parachutes, without altimeters, which the water would ruin. Instead, we'll jump from 3,000 feet and count to five before pulling the rip-cord.

As the Islander takes off, next to me is Jim Coffey, the old man of the Freds, who has taken me under his wing and is teaching me accuracy. Behind me is Dixie, always laid-back and unflappable. The only time he moves fast is in freefall. Sharky is near the door, and gives me a wicked grin.

Most of them started freefalling at civilian centres in their own time and at their own expense. None of our training has a military use; the Red Devils are primarily a public relations vehicle for the Paras – and a very good one.

Water jumps can be more complicated because there's nothing to put yourself in perspective and judge altitude when you're falling towards something as featureless and flat as the sea or a lake. At least in Brighton we'll have reference points such as boats and the seafront.

Today we're doing a team stack because the cloud base is low and we're on round parachutes. Ted Lewington is the jump-master and will step out of the aircraft as it gets over the opening point. Sharky will give him three seconds and then go, followed by Jim Coffey in another three seconds. By the time the last man steps out, the other parachutes have either opened or are opening, separated by altitude and time.

I exit badly, fighting for control, and pull back into the frog position as the count reaches three. Below me, I see yachts in the marina and brightly coloured fishing boats further out to sea. There's a band on the pier in bright red uniforms and a merry-go-round nearby. There are hundreds of families on picnic rugs on the beach and people watching from the footpaths.

'Thousand and four . . . Thousand and five.'

Pull!

The round parachute blossoms and I'm drifting downwards, trying to judge my height and keeping an eye on the rest of the team. As I get lower I drop the dust covers and put my hand on the jettison ready to cut away the parachute as my feet touch the water. The timing has to be perfect or I risk becoming tangled in the lines.

On another jump into Brighton, a Red Fred called Billy Sharp jettisoned his parachute too early, and fell from about thirty feet. His life-jacket was inflated and it stopped him so suddenly they had to use a boat-hook to fish out his semi-conscious body.

Spearing into the water, I submerge completely, and the shock of the cold clears my head instantly. I kick for the surface, hoping the parachute has drifted clear. I'm not a particularly good swimmer, and even with a life-jacket it's a nervous wait for the inflatable boat.

There it is! I turn and wave. Why isn't it slowing down? At the last second, I dive clear as the driver roars over me, heading for someone else.

In my log book, I write: 'Water jump, unstable exit, great, got run over by the life-boat.'

The Red Freds are like an extended family, and Chris gets on well with the other wives. On a nice day the drop zone at Aldershot looks like a picnic area as the wives bring out baskets of food and sunbathe while the children play on the grass. Meanwhile we do seven to ten training jumps, stopping only for lunch.

Chris has a part-time job in a shoe shop and Jason is in a nursery. They stayed in Cheltenham until he was five months old and then moved into the married quarters in Aldershot. I see so much of Jason that I barely notice how quickly he's growing, and Chris is happy because I'm home most nights, rather than being away on long tours with the battalion.

During the summer, there are sometimes five or six displays a day, at race meetings, soccer games, fêtes and country fairs. One Bank Holiday weekend the two teams manage eighteen displays between them. The Red Devils always attract a lot of interest and the organisers tend to put us on late in the day to keep the crowds from going home.

At a mixed-team display in Aldershot one evening, the guest of honour is Prince Charles, the soon-to-be-married Colonel-in-Chief of the Parachute Regiment. We jump at dusk from 5,000 feet and land in a small drill square, surrounded by buildings. It's a tight drop zone and I come skimming over the rooftops, lifting my knees at the last second to just miss the edge. I sail across the square before landing about ten feet from a large fence.

In a well-practised drill, each member of the team collapses his parachute, kneels down, takes off his harness and headgear and slips on the red beret. On a nod from Ted Lewington, we run to the front and form a slick military line to be presented to Prince Charles. Ted brings us to attention and one by one introduces each member of the team.

'This is Lance-Corporal Sharky Sheridan.'

Prince Charles asks Sharky if it had been a static-line jump.

'No, sir, it was a twenty-second delay in freefall.'

Then he comes to me and recognises immediately that I'm the bloke who narrowly missed the roof.

'I bet you won't do that again in a hurry,' he says.

I grin and look at his longer-than-regulation hair, hanging out of his beret. 'And I bet the RSM doesn't ask you to get a haircut.'

The colonel of the battalion looks horrified; the RSM wants to shrivel up and die. There's a pause of a fraction of a second, and then the Prince laughs and everyone joins in.

Less than a fortnight later, we're jumping at Silverstone race-track and I meet him again in another line-up. He looks at me and says, 'Don't I know you?'

'Yes, sir. I've met you twice in the last two weeks, and if I meet you again I'm going to class you as a personal friend and expect an invitation to your wedding.'

The red team is envied by the black team, because we're younger and tend to have more fun. For one thing, we don't have Ted Lewington jumping with us on team displays. He's an old-time skydiver who just gets out and bores a big hole in the sky. He doesn't have a clue about body position and just waves at people to come and get him. Meanwhile, while he's waving, he's back-sliding like the demon from hell, making it very difficult for anyone to catch him.

Of course, no one dares mention this to Ted or they'd cop a back-hander. Because Ted is hopeless at relative work, Sharky convinces him to leave the plane with a four-way already linked up, so the others don't have to catch him. Ted likes this because all he has to do is sit in the door, while the others take certain grips on his arms and legs – then it's ready . . . set . . . go!

Trouble is, Ted possesses a death grip and enjoys going low. He likes to scare people and doesn't seem to realise that the lower you open the canopy, the less time you have to steer and land in the arena. He's also lousy at 'spotting', which means he often has the team exiting from the aircraft either too early or too late.

At the Manchester Flower Show the black team launched from 6,000 feet with Sharky, Rixie, Ted Lewington and Boxhead (Roy Wright), making up a four-way. The rest of the team dived out after them and tracked in different directions so their smoke trails looked like a bomb burst over the top.

Boxhead could break off at any time because Ted didn't have a grip on him, but poor old Sharky and Rixie were trapped in the SM's vice-like fists. Normally at 3,500 feet they should have broken, turned away from each other and been ready to open. They shot through this height and began gesticulating to Ted to let go. He'd stopped looking at them, though, and was staring at the altimeter on his chest. They sailed through 2,000 feet and were still linked in freefall.

It takes five seconds to cover 1,000 feet, and by the time you get below 2,000 feet you run into a time factor because you need time to turn away and find a clean piece of sky. Once you get below 1,000 feet you're pushing the limit as to whether you can get a canopy up in time.

Ted took them down to 1,200 feet, reached back and pulled his parachute. Sharky and Rixie couldn't suddenly dump in the same way or there'd be a mass of nylon. They had to turn away from each other, using up more time. They opened at 700 feet. Rixie landed on a pedestrian bridge over an electrified railway line; Sharky finished up in a holly tree in a psychiatric hospital; and Ted cut it so fine that he took a down-winder and straddled a fence that he didn't see. They needed a wheelbarrow to move him because his gonads were busted. Only two lads made the line-up – the rest were spread all over Manchester.

The red team is doing all sorts of new displays with smoke bombs, flags and 'cutaways'. It's been a few years since anyone in the team has done a cutaway and I adopt it because no one else seems very keen. The rigger has made up a new cutaway rig which can take three parachutes.

When the Islander reaches altitude, I squat in the open door, take hold of the left sill, and then push myself out into the slipstream, which is blowing me back. I pirouette on my left foot, still hanging on to the door, and push up with my right hand until I can grab hold of the VHF aerial on top of the aircraft fuselage. I am now known as the 'rear floater'.

The next lad backs out into the open door, sticking his backside out first and putting his hands on each sill and his toes on the edge of the doorway. He is the centre floater. Someone actually sits *on* the sill and reaches up to take hold of the centre floater's armpit with one hand. A fourth team member is squatting inside, with his head under the centre floater's chest strap, ready to dive out. Everyone is looking in to each other as the centre floater starts a rocking count – ready . . . set . . . go!

Hanging on in the slipstream, I can't hear the count, but I see the rocking and release at precisely the right moment, taking hold of the others as we fall away. By getting as many team members as possible outside the aircraft before jumping, we drop together and can move more quickly into formation. Otherwise, lads are always trying to catch up to those who have jumped a few seconds earlier.

For a cutaway demonstration, I deploy my first parachute early and the rest of the team track off to different points of the compass before opening, creating a bomb-burst effect with a lone parachute in the middle. I check there's no one else around me and then deliberately jettison one of the two risers that hook the canopy to my shoulders. The risers go up about two feet and then branch off into a dozen different lines that rise eighteen feet to the canopy. On the ground, the crowd suddenly sees half my parachute collapse, streaming out in a classic Roman candle malfunction. I can almost imagine the collective 'Oh!'

In the old days we used to do this without warning, but two women fainted and someone had a heart attack so now the ground commentator describes what's going to happen in advance.

I'm 3,000 feet and falling.

Because of the malfunction, I have to cut the collapsed canopy away or risk fouling my second parachute when it opens. Releasing the second of my risers, I let it go and suddenly accelerate back into clean air, freefalling through the middle of the others who are under their canopies.

At 2,000 feet I pull my second parachute and float downwards. Modern canopies have a forward speed of between 20 and 30 mph, which means I can come in very fast and pull up at the last second, hopefully, near the DZ marker.

I can hear the ground commentator telling the children in the crowd that whoever retrieves my jettisoned canopy gets a free T-shirt and a poster. They race off across the field and I start packing things away.

The parachute I always jettison is an old reserve which has taken a fair bit of wear and tear with half the lines missing around the canopy. This is rather unnerving, because if I can't release it, I'd have to land on it regardless.

The new rookie on the Freds is Deano, and one of his jobs is packing the cutaway parachute because I'm busy packing my own main and checking my reserve.

He comes over to me. 'Hi, Tom, got the cutaway rig back. One of the lines is broken.'

'Oh, it doesn't matter, just stuff it in the bag,' I say, knowing that a round parachute can open without a lot of the lines.

'But what if it doesn't deploy properly?'

'Then it becomes a real malfunction and I'm going to chop it anyway.'

Deano doesn't say exactly where the eighteen-foot nylon line has broken, but I assume he'll cut it off completely and throw it away because one of the big things about parachuting is making sure you don't have any loose ends on your clothing or equipment. In this case the 500 lb. breaking-strain line has snapped near the canopy, and Deano takes me at my word and lays it alongside the rest of the lines before stowing it into the bungees and stuffing it into the pack.

There's another display that evening, and the cutaway chute deploys correctly with a dozen suspension ropes leading from my shoulders to the inflated canopy. But unbeknown to me, a single line is now snaking out eighteen feet below me.

I deliberately malfunction the parachute and then perform the cutaway. As I accelerate into freefall, the trailing nylon line snatches around my neck like a lashing whip. It flicks off immediately, but I feel as though I've been sliced from ear to ear with a cut-throat razor. I'm afraid to lift my chin up in case my head falls off.

Under the canopy, I finally risk putting my hand to my neck. There's no blood, but the line has given me a friction burn which hurts like hell. When the cutaway comes back, I realise what's happened. 'You clever bastard,' I say to Deano. 'Why didn't you tell me?'

'I did, but you said don't bother about it.'

It's a lesson learned, and from now on, I check it myself.

I stand down for a few days because my neck swells up, and in my absence the sergeant-major gives the airborne commentary duties to Ken Campbell, an aggressive Glaswegian who sounds like Billy Connolly. On his first commentary, he begins: 'I'm over your fucking heads now and I'm looking down and seeing ya bastards. By Christ, it's a long way up . . .'

That's the last time Ken is asked to do any public speaking.

Apart from the cutaway, my other speciality is a 'diamond track' with John Street, another member of the team. The two of us leave the aircraft together, holding forearms as we accelerate. Smoke streams from canisters at our ankles. We separate and turn in opposite directions, tracking away from each other while falling. From the ground it looks like two tiny jets racing away from each other, leaving their tell-tale vapour trails.

At 5,000 feet, I suddenly perform a 180° turn and track back towards John, looking for his smoke trail. I can see a red blob in the distance. Meanwhile, John has done exactly the same manoeuvre and we're closing on each other at a combined speed of over 200 mph.

We're getting low. Can we complete the 'diamond' before we pull? Ted goes mad if we don't cross because it destroys the whole illusion from the ground.

I change course fractionally and aim at John. We're hurtling towards each other, and at the last possible second, when I see him smiling, I veer off and pass on the left. The smoke trails join and I pull the ripcord.

The displays don't always go to plan, and one Saturday, over London, we have trouble finding the arena. It's a hot summer's day and there are cricket matches, school fêtes, race meetings, gymkhanas and country fairs all over the place. The traffic is horrendous and the DZ van is caught in a tail-back, miles from the venue. As I'm looking out the door, I spot the Union Jack on the roof of the van and we make radio contact. They're not going to make the drop zone in time.

All we have is a six-figure grid reference, and when we arrive at the location, there are carnivals, polo games, cricket matches and vintage-car rallies all within the space of a mile. Which one is our venue?

The Islander circles overhead and we look for a clue. John Street is the jump-master and we have a discussion about what to do.

'I think it's the place with the beer tent,' I say, having noticed the Heineken logo on the roof.

'No, I reckon it's the horse show over there,' says John.

Boxhead pipes up, 'Well, we can't stay up here all day.'

'Tom, you've done commentary before, you want to give it a go?'

'Sure, what do you want me to do?'

'Jump.'

The Islander runs in up-wind and I jump out over a venue at 2,000 feet, opening straight away. I land inside a roped-off area, next to the beer tent, and a country gent in tweed jacket and wellingtons strides out to me.

'Excuse me, are the Red Devils supposed to be jumping here this afternoon?' I ask.

'No, I'm sorry, old chap, although I did see a poster outside. I think you're supposed to be up the road.'

Gathering my parachute, I hitch a ride to a large showground less than half a mile away. A relieved steward shakes my hand. 'Are you the commentator? We've been expecting the van.'

'Sorry, there's been a problem. Have you got a microphone?'

Walking to the centre of the arena, I set off my red smoke bomb. With no orange DZ cross, this becomes the signal that it's safe to jump. The Islander flies directly overhead and John throws out the wind-drift indicator.

'Welcome to the show, ladies and gentlemen, boys and girls. My name is Tom Read and I'm your Red Devils commentator for this afternoon's display . . .'

*

On a Monday afternoon in late August 1979, I'm waiting in the departure lounge at Exeter Airport, staring at the tea-leaves in a plastic cup. I still can't believe it – Earl Mountbatten is dead! According to the radio that morning, the IRA had planted a bomb on board his boat in Mullaghmore, County Sligo.

The Red Freds have a display planned and the Islander is being refuelled. Ian Marshall digs me in the ribs and motions to a TV. I see the words 'Northern Ireland' on the screen and pictures of bodies being loaded into ambulances.

'Turn it up! Turn it up!' someone shouts.

Another bomb had gone off at Warrenpoint, County Down, but the number of casualties is unknown.

'It's 2 Para,' I say, knowing it immediately.

One of the lads is straight on the phone to Aldershot, but they can't give us any details. Later we discover that A Company has lost a dozen men. They were going to Newry and the IRA had set up a bomb at the side of the road which triggered as the Bedford drove by. Rescuers sealed off the area and set up a control point behind an old gate-house, but the IRA had planted another bomb right under them and more soldiers died.

Mountbatten's death is probably a greater shock to me. Professional soldiers must live with the dangers of Northern Ireland, but Mountbatten was just a respectable old man, related to the royal family. For God's sake, he was seventy-nine years old – what threat did he pose to the IRA?

Sitting on board the aircraft as we set off for the display, I suddenly feel guilty that my battalion is on operations and I'm not with them. I know the Red Devils do an important job in raising the public profile of the Paras, but I seem to be having a great time while other soldiers are dying or putting their lives on the line.

'Enjoy it while you can,' Jim Coffey says to me. 'Your turn will come.'

A new concept in parachuting has arrived from America called 'canopy relative work' (CRW), which is still in its infancy. It's only really become possible since the advent of square parachutes, which have a forward speed of 20–30 mph and can be steered.

At team training on Queens Avenue, some of the younger lads have been experimenting. The normal formation is a CRW stack, which involves one parachutist flying into the back legs of another. The higher man grabs hold of the lines and slides down until he almost appears to be standing on the other skydiver's shoulders.

As more parachutists join the CRW stack, the forward speed slows but it begins falling much faster. Anyone closing late has to virtually fly into the stack as it plummets past them – a difficult manoeuvre and not without risk.

Having built bigger and bigger stacks, we grew bored and began looking for another challenge. One afternoon Ian Marshall suggests we try a CRW diamond.

'I've never heard of it,' I say.

'That's because no one's ever done it before.'

There's probably a good reason for that, I think to myself, but I go along with the plan. On the next lift, Graham Copestake, Ian, Ray Ellis and myself exit at 5,000 feet, well short of the drop zone, and open our chutes immediately. Dick Kalinski is filming the 'world first'.

We fly towards the drop zone and quickly build a CRW four-stack. I'm the last to join. Above me is Ian Marshall, and he begins sliding along the 200-square-foot surface of my canopy until he reaches the extreme left edge. Then he holds himself in place by hooking his feet through the lines that attach to my canopy.

Ray Ellis then climbs down and slides all the way along to the right edge of my canopy. Ray and Ian's canopies are now touching, side by side. Graham, at the very top, then hooks his feet into the lines of the two lower men, completing the diamond.

Almost immediately the formation starts becoming unstable. One canopy wants to fly left, another wants to go right, and a third tries to accelerate forwards. We each try to control our own chute, but the canopies are washing around, bouncing off each other. The whole formation is unstable and oscillating.

Flying in a straight line, we have now almost passed over the top of the drop zone. As soon as we've held the diamond for thirty seconds we decide to break off. That's long enough to prove we've done it and it's all on film.

Suddenly Ian, the madman on the team, says, 'Let's turn it!'

'No, no, we're breaking off,' shouts one of the lads.

'Oh, come on, let's give it a go.'

Ian pulls down on his left control line and his canopy tries to turn, but Graham's foot is caught in the lines. He manages to get it out and turn with him before bouncing back. The four canopies are now oscillating wildly and Ian clears and goes on his own.

Meanwhile, the oscillation becomes a pendulum effect. Ray starts washing left and right and completely wraps around my lines. His parachute collapses, pulling Graham down.

Ray and I are next to each other with our canopies hopelessly entangled. Graham's parachute is the only thing holding all three of us aloft. Our rate of descent has increased dramatically and we're falling at thirty feet per second. We're now at 1,100 feet.

'I can't hold you, I can't hold you,' Graham cries.

The cut-off point is 1,000 feet – if good canopy isn't open by then, a jumper should get the reserve out. But Ray and I can't risk opening a new chute until we cut away from the mess of nylon above us.

Ray's head is next to mine and our bodies are pressed close together. 'I'm going to cut away,' he says.

I watch him take hold of the orange cutaway pad and pull. His risers release and he dead drops away from me. I look down and watch him going . . . going . . . going. I see the container open on his back and the extractor of his reserve chute spring out. Go on Ray, go on! The canopy opens. He's safe.

I'm still wrapped in a mess, with Graham tangled above me. I look at the altimeter – 800 feet.

'That's much better, Big Nose,' says Graham. I can't see him above the red, white and blue mass of nylon.

'What do you reckon, should I cut away?' I shout.

'No, no. I can hold you.'

We're drifting down on one parachute, coming over the boundary to one side of the drop zone. The main road, Queens Avenue, is just beyond a line of trees. Graham begins turning into the wind ready for landing. Half-way around, I swing out slightly, directly over the trees.

'I can't hold you! I can't hold you!' he screams.

That's all I hear, but I know I'm going to die if I fall from this height.

The normal drill for a cutaway is for the right hand to pull the orange pad that jettisons the failed parachute and, once clear, the left hand pulls the reserve rip-cord. It's almost a 'one . . . two' movement – right hand, then left.

I don't have time. I put both hands to my chest and pull the handles together, wrenching them straight out. Instinctively my feet come up and I look between my knees and see trees slightly behind me and very close. I hold my hands right up, hoping I can backslide into the branches to break my fall.

There's a father teaching his son to play golf. I can see their horrified faces as they look up and see me falling. At that same instant the reserve bangs open above me. Thank God! It's hard but it's beautiful. I just have time to get my knees together before I land.

I lie on the ground, unzip my jump-suit pocket and pull out my cigarettes. There are ten left. I light one and stare up at the sky, ignoring the parachute fluttering behind me. The DZ van races across to me from the far side of the field.

'Bloody hell! Are you all right, Tom?' says Kenny Campbell.

'Piss off. I've still got nine cigarettes to get through.'

The new sergeant-major, Ken Yeoman, tells the lads to leave me in peace and the van departs. I quietly smoke the entire packet, contemplating my own mortality.

Afterwards, Ken Yeoman insists I repack my reserve and go straight back up again. 'I don't really agree with CRW,' I tell him. 'It's a waste of good freefall time.'

'No, don't think like that, Tom,' he says.

On the next lift, I close third on a CRW three-stack and everyone seems happy.

Apart from performing at British venues such as Cardiff Arms Park, Wembley Stadium and Hyde Park in London, the Red Devils are occasionally invited to jump overseas, for foreign dignitaries and at events such as a football international at the Olympic Stadium in Berlin and a Chinese New Year celebration in Hong Kong.

Although the red and black teams perform separately, we mix a lot in the winter months during team training. At least once a year we all go abroad, somewhere warm like Cyprus or the south of France. My first trip is to Dubai, and we're based in the middle of nowhere because the Queen is due to visit and the local military want us to keep a low profile. They tuck us away in old huts and try to pretend we're not here.

Early on the first morning, helicopters arrive to take us jumping. We're using American Hueys that can get up to 12,000 feet. The pilots are Arabs, and don't seem to appreciate that gas has a tendency to expand as you climb higher and flatulence is a fact of life for skydivers. The first time one of the pilots gets a whiff of the problem, that's it! He lands and orders us to get out.

'You have to be joking!' says Ted Lewington, unable to believe it.

They have a heated argument and reach a total impasse. Apparently, it's a Muslim thing. Finally Ted announces: 'Okay, nobody farts. And that's an order.'

The pilots go off and refuel at midday and tell us they'll be back in the afternoon. We wait and wait but they don't turn up. Later, we find out they've gone to the mosque and then taken the rest of the day off. It becomes the daily routine, so we only get the morning to jump.

One of those other rare occasions when both teams are together is during the annual Newcastle Show, when we're booked to jump twice a day for a week. The teams rotate, with one always available to shoot off and do a few displays elsewhere in the country.

We always stay in a nice hotel on the outskirts of Newcastle – one of those places where the plumbing is too noisy, the beds are too soft and there are a dozen pubs within spitting distance. Most of the lads are single and are a big hit with the local girls. They go out in their 'mincing kit' – grey pants, white shirt and blue blazer, with the Red Devils badge on the chest pocket.

At closing time we all go back to the hotel and have an impromptu party, with invited girls, keeping the barman busy until after two in the morning. It's in full swing when, pissed out of my skin, I wander out to the van and put on the gorilla suit. It's a novelty costume for the kids that looks incredibly life-like, although none of us likes jumping in it because there's no ventilation and every time you pull the rip-cord you get a fist-ful of fur.

Unfortunately, when I try to get back into the hotel, I've been locked out. The next thing I remember is waking up in a flower-bed opposite the hotel. As I open my eyes there are a dozen policemen staring at me, along with a primate expert from the local zoo and a vet. Two nuns on their way to the convent for five o'clock prayers had stumbled across me and fled in terror. The whole area has been sealed off, and they've even dis-cussed firing a tranquilliser into my furry arse.

Sitting up, I start talking to the police and trying to take off the head.

'Who's your commanding officer?' asks the police sergeant.

'Captain John Street,' I say, lying. I figure if John can come and get me, Captain Mickey Munn, the real team commander, might not have to find out.

The hotel manager is summoned from his bed. Unfortunately, he wakes Mickey instead of John. There are blue flashing lights up and down the street, as well as a fire engine. I'm in trouble, big-time, and Mickey reads me the riot act.

He's forever ranting or raving about something, but he's actually a good bloke. We have a team car, sponsored by Lucas Industries, a 2.3-litre Cortina that goes like shit off a shovel. Mickey is always complaining that we thrash it to death whenever someone takes it out. One afternoon in the packing room, he launches into a bollocking. 'I fucking know it's you, Read, you bastard.'

'But I drive it okay, boss.'

'No, you don't. There's always flies splattered on the windscreen and it's red hot when you get back. You're a maniac, do you hear me? We all know it does a hundred and ten miles an hour, but there's no excuse for driving it that fast.'

'Well, actually, you've got that slightly wrong, sir.'

'What do you mean I'm fucking wrong? You tell me why I'm wrong.'

'Well, actually, it does a hundred and thirty.'

The place just erupts and even Mickey laughs eventually.

There are some great characters in the Freds, people like Bob Harman, one of the older lads, who is absolutely fearless. One year in Newcastle, he says to me, 'Right, come on, Tom, let's go low. Chicken contest.'

'No way,' I tell him.

'What's the matter, lost your bottle?'

'Okay, Bob, if you want to go low, let's go low.'

I repack my parachute, ironing it in and wishing I'd never agreed. The plan is to hold hands and keep falling after the normal display finishes – the first to chicken out and pull his rip-cord loses the contest.

That afternoon, Bob throws the wind-drift indicator from the door and it lands more than 1,000 metres from the arena. This means we have to exit the same distance up-wind.

'Not this time, Bob,' I tell him. 'If we open lower than 2,000 feet, we're not going to have the altitude to get back into the arena.'

We do a normal display but, ironically, Bob has a rare malfunction and lands under his reserve parachute near a motorway. If we'd gone low on that jump, it's unlikely he would have had time to open a reserve.

A few hours later, on a lovely summer's evening, we take off for another display. The Islander climbs to 7,000 feet and I can see all of Newcastle spread out beneath us. John Street sits on my left, alongside Ken Campbell, who's been nicknamed 'the FISP' (fucking ignorant Scottish pig). Reaching down, I check the smoke canister on my ankle, making sure the ignition string isn't snagged on anything. One of the canisters had opened accidentally on Ted Lewington one day and almost suffocated the poor pilot.

The wind-drift indicator is thrown out, and for the first time in my life, it lands inside the arena. There is absolutely no wind, so we'll be getting out right over the top of the arena.

I look at Bob. After the earlier malfunction, I know he's going to be nervous. 'Okay, mate, you want to go low, let's go low.'

He doesn't even blink.

'You did pack your reserve properly, didn't you?' I say, winding him up.

'Don't you worry about me.'

Six of us exit at 7,000 feet and build a six-way in freefall. At 3,500 feet, everyone turns and breaks off except for me and Bob. We link together hand in hand and keep falling. Racing through 3,000 feet, I look down and see that we're right over the arena. At 2,500 feet, I look at Bob and hold out my hand, inviting him to pull his rip-cord. He shakes his head.

The needle on my altimeter goes through 2,000 feet and comes out the other side. We have less than ten seconds to impact.

At 1,500 feet Bob looks at me and holds out his hand, inviting me to pull. At 1,000 feet, I mouth the words to him, 'Well, are you going to open?'

The needle passes through 900 feet and Bob shakes his head. I don't break off. I reach back, grab my rip-cord and pull. Bob looks at me, gives me a wanker sign and does a back-loop in freefall. He accelerates away and I watch his canopy open at 400 feet.

Another one-off character is the team clerk, Jimmy Newbury, a jovial Scouser with a stutter and dyslexia, which is clearly why the army has him answering the phone and typing all the Ops orders.

Jim has never actually jumped out of a plane, but he likes to make out that he's a veteran. He's the sort of bloke who polishes the brass plaque on his door and answers the phone by barking, 'Red Devils, office manager, Staff Sergeant Newbury speaking, sir!'

Unfortunately, the stutter will either trip him up or he'll mispronounce words. One particular night, there's a big official dinner at the garrison mess at Aldershot and the Freds are designated to provide the transport from the train station as well as doing the valet parking for all the VIPs. Jim Newbury stands at the top of the stairs in his best uniform, greeting everyone with a salute and creeping outrageously.

'Sergeant Newbury, Red Devils. Good evening, sir and madam.'

This one gent turns up in a Rolls-Royce. Boxhead and I see the car pull up and a chap leans out the window. 'Oh, I say chaps, where do I park this wretched motor?'

'Over there, sir.'

'No, I can't possibly do that. Dicky battery, you know. Must park it on a hill.'

Sure enough, at that moment he stalls the car and we offer to give him a jump-start. 'I say, chaps, I'd be awfully grateful if you drove the old girl around for fifteen minutes, just to charge her up.'

'Yes, certainly, sir. Not a problem.'

I get the jump-leads from the team car and we get the engine started. Boxhead and I look at each other and grin. We've got a Rolls-Royce. I jump behind the wheel and Boxhead gets in the back. We've never even seen electric windows. Next minute we're roaring up the road and Boxhead says, 'Let's take it on the tank tracks and see what it can do.'

'Are you going to clean it afterwards?'

'Okay, let's go cruising in town. We have to impress someone.'

'I've got a better idea,' I say, and we spend the next fifteen minutes boosting the battery before heading back to camp.

Jim Newbury is standing at the base of the stairs as the Roller comes crunching along the gravel driveway and pulls up outside the posh Officers' Mess.

I hit the button for the electric window, which slowly descends.

'I say, old chap . . .'

Jim snaps to attention, his back ramrod straight and chest puffed out. 'Evening, sir.'

He glances down and gets this glazed look in his eyes and his jaw starts flapping up and down noiselessly. Eventually sound comes out. 'Fucking, Read, what are you doing in there?'

Boxhead is giggling in the back seat. 'Hiya Sarge! Aren't you going to open the door for me?'

Jim just explodes. 'What in Christ are you doing in that car?'

I tell him, 'Oh, some silly sod left his keys in the ignition, so we took it for a spin.'

'*You stole it!* That's it! You're on a charge, you bloody fools.'

By that stage nothing can calm him down. Jim is at 20,000 feet and climbing.

5

They're here! They're here!

'Okay, Big Nose, did I not promise Friday? Look at the calendar. What day is it?' Des is grinning in the doorway. Schwepsy, Harry and Cath are behind him.

They burst into laughter when they see me. I've been ready since five o'clock this morning. I've had a shower, a shave, combed my hair, packed and repacked my things. Since then I've been sitting on the windowsill like a kid waiting to be picked up from boarding school for the holidays.

'Is that all your kit?' asks Schwepsy.

'You must take one of the robes, Big Nose,' says Des. 'The only reason to stay in one of these posh places is so you can pinch the robes.' He's lying on the bed, looking exhausted. The boys have obviously been out celebrating their successful negotiations with the lawyers. It must have been a big night.

'We've got the plane waiting in Geneva,' says Harry. 'It's flown from England with a doctor and a nurse.'

'I'll be with you in a minute,' I say, heading for the bathroom.

Meanwhile, Des closes his eyes and tries to catch forty winks. The doctor, a New Zealand psychiatrist in her late thirties, arrives in the room looking very uptight. She casts a concerned look at the bed.

'Good morning, Mr Read, let me explain what's going to happen.'

'Oh, I'm not Mr Read,' says Des.

She shakes her long face. 'Very well, whoever you are today, do you think you need a sedative?'

'No, really, I'm not Mr Read,' says Des, looking at Harry and Schwepsy for support. They're too busy laughing.

As I walk back into the room, Des leaps to his feet. 'Here he is! Tom, say hello to the doctor . . .'

She looks at me and back at Des. I look as fresh and clean as a new pin; Des is unshaven, wearing the same clothes as yesterday and smelling like a brewery. The rest of them are laughing, but the psychiatrist can't figure out who she should be chaperoning.

While the paperwork is completed, I take a final walk around the asylum with Des and Schwepsy. Des has brought a camera because he wants to take photographs of the place – otherwise no one will believe him, he says.

The other loonies have heard that I'm leaving and a lot of them come up to me and say goodbye, patting me on the back. I want to feel sad for them but I'm just so happy about getting out of here. Maria gives me a hug and presses something cool into my hand, closing my fingers over it and pressing them into a fist.

'*Papillon,*' I say.

'*Oui, papillon.*'

Rhaffi offers to give me a high-five and Gérard waves from the window of his room.

Outside in the car-park, as Harry opens the car door, I turn back to see the asylum as a whole for the first time. It's only a few storeys high and looks remarkably ordinary. I had imagined the enemy would choose somewhere a little grander. Opening my fingers, I discover that Maria has given me a pebble from the garden. I slip it into my pocket and wave back at the windows.

The psychiatrist seems nervous. She's obviously been briefed about this dangerous psychopath, and all she wants to do is get me back to England and lock me up tightly so they can investigate.

The drive to the airport takes about an hour, and the lads are in great spirits. I can hear myself laughing at their jokes but I'm still so drugged up that everything is flat and colourless. A part of me is afraid that I'm dreaming and that I'll soon wake up and find I'm back in the asylum.

move on. I'm still a private soldier and there's little chance of being promoted in the Red Devils. Going back to 2 Para seems like a backward step – that part of my life is over. Instead I think about joining the Army Air Corps (AAC) and learning to fly helicopters, or perhaps trying out for the SAS. I'm twenty-six years old, and the cut-off for being a pilot is thirty. I figure that I could give SAS Selection my best shot, and if I don't get through, I can still apply to the Air Corps.

January Selection is six months away, so I should start getting fit. I haven't done any serious soldiering for nearly three years, and the Freds aren't famous for their physical training standards. Mickey Munn once tried to change this, when he assigned Dougie, a lance-corporal, to take us running every day. What a nightmare! Dougie was one of those zealots who thought that exercise had to hurt to be helpful.

A few months later he went on leave and I was assigned to take over. First morning, I took the lads running over the square, knowing Mickey Munn was watching. As soon as we were out of sight, I stopped and started walking – straight to the nearest café for a cup of tea and a glance at the morning paper. Then we walked back and sprinted the last 400 yards, arriving puffed, with hands on hips and breathing deeply.

'He's too hard on us, sir,' complained Boxhead, down on his haunches.

'He nearly killed us,' echoes the FISP. 'Bring back Dougie.'

Mickey beams proudly. 'Well done, Private Read.'

Ironically, by the time Dougie gets back, I've actually started a serious training programme for Selection. I'm in the pub one night, chatting to Scotty Milne, and I tell him my plan. He's working at Depot Para as an instructor, bringing the young officers through who come down from the military college at Sandhurst for a few weeks.

'You better get training,' he says.

'Yeah, I'm going to stop smoking and start soon.'

'Why don't you come out with me tomorrow? We've got a final march over the South Downs from Farnham to Petersfield. It's cross country, about forty miles. You're not that fit, so this will make you push yourself to see if you've got the mental strength.'

'Yeah, sure,' I say, a belly full of beer doing the talking.

Chris wakes me next morning at 5.30. 'There are two blokes outside in a Land Rover from Depot Para. They've come to get you.'

'Oh no!'

I drag myself out of bed, put on my old green army boots that haven't been worn for nearly three years and stagger outside. These two lads are laughing as they pour me in the back and drop me at the cookhouse so I can get some breakfast. Scotty helps me pack a bergen – it has to be 40 lb. – and I set off with about five officer trainees at 8.00 a.m.

All day and into the night we march, until my feet are blistered to hell and my back is rubbed raw. Scotty does the first half with me and then eggs me on from the back of a Land Rover. I don't stop to rest because I might not start again. Mercifully, the ground is easy going and we stick to bridle paths and farm tracks.

Two of the officers have dropped out, so there's only four of us left. In the last half-mile I'm stumbling all over the place and two corporals come down and offer to take my pack. I wave them away. I'll collapse if they take the pack off me; it's moulded to my back.

Somehow, I climb into the Land Rover at the finish and we drive back to Aldershot. When we reach the camp, I can't get out. My tendons have seized up and I can't straighten my knees. Scotty drives me back to the house and they have to carry me inside.

That decides it! My routine for the next three months is to get up at 6.30 a.m. and do a ten-mile run on Mondays, Wednesdays and Fridays. On Thursdays and Saturdays I run for six and a half miles. I clock the route in a car and make sure at least a mile of it is uphill.

During Christmas leave I head for the Brecon Beacons for two weeks of solid training before Selection begins. I'm planning to just doss in a sleeping bag in the forest, getting used to the cold and the terrain. About seven other lads have the same idea, and the army allocates us a Nissen hut. That's when I first meet Harry. He has some hair back then, but it's disappearing fast. He used to be a Marine, but the navy wouldn't let him apply for the SAS so he had to leave and become a civilian. He'd been on the dole in Hereford waiting for Selection.

Des is also in the hut, moaning about the cold and arguing about whether he snores. Then there's Doug, a former Red Devil who left the Paras and spent a few years flogging televisions in Australia before joining the Territorial Army. 'Hillbilly' (Paul Hill) is another ex-Para. He's about five foot ten, with a punched-in face and a background in the Merchant Navy.

We're up early, climbing the biggest hills we can find and practising mountain navigation. We take rucksacks with food, water, sleeping-bags and overnight gear just in case the weather turns bad. I team up with Hillbilly, and Harry and Des stick together. We might not see each other all day, but at night we all finish up at Fat Fred's pub in Brecon for pie and chips and a few pints of Guinness. Fred is a former CO's driver from the Paras who now runs The Wheatsheaf.

The Paras have never liked the Marines, so Harry gets a bit of blag-garding about being a 'bootneck', but we all seem to hit it off. The others are much more confident about passing Selection than I am. I'm so sure of failing that I don't even warn Christine about the possibility of having to move to Hereford if I get through. As far as she's concerned, I'm just going on another course.

After the pub, we all pile into my car for the drive back to the hut. The old Morris Oxford is pretty temperamental, and I have to crank her up with a starting-handle.

'This is a load of shit,' says Hillbilly.

'Why, what's wrong with it?' I say, defensively. 'So what if the wing mirrors bend in at sixty-five miles an hour and the bonnet flies up at seventy-five?'

Hillbilly continues: 'And don't forget the windscreen-wiper that doesn't work and the slug-like acceleration . . .'

'What's that?' asks Des, pointing to my 'tax disc'.

'It's a beer-bottle label,' I say. 'You think anyone's going to register this car?'

A fortnight later, I drive into Bradbury Lines, the headquarters of 22 SAS.

'Follow the signs to the accommodation block,' says an MoD police-man, looking closely at the car.

'It's a wonder he doesn't arrest you,' says Hillbilly in the passenger seat.

As we near the block, a soldier suddenly steps out in front of the car, holding up his hand. He's wearing olive-green trousers, American-style boots and a green and brown pullover with brown patches on the shoul-ders. More importantly, he has the sandy-coloured beret of the SAS.

Hillbilly mutters: 'Whatever it is, it's your fault.'

The soldier strides over to the driver's side window and motions me to wind it down. I need both hands to pull the glass down. We've heard all these stories about 'sickeners' in the Regiment, where they test the mettle of applicants by confronting them with the unexpected.

Crouching to peer inside the car, he says, 'Question: why is a giraffe's neck so long?'

I look at Hillbilly and he looks at me. Is this a test? Before we can answer, our interrogator barks, 'Because their heads are so far from their bodies!' He starts laughing and strides away.

That night we assemble in the gymnasium, 140 applicants all eyeing each other up and wondering who's going to last the course. The OC, Paddy B., is a quiet bloke with a southern Irish accent and a dry sense of humour.

'You are about to undertake the most punishing and difficult Selection course in the world,' he says, before reading the riot act about what we can and cannot do. 'You are allowed outside the camp of an evening, but certain pubs are off-limits. But let me warn you, don't think that you can go out at night hooting with the owls and come here in the morning and expect to scream with the eagles.'

I look across at Hillbilly and he winks.

Paddy continues: 'I wish you the best of luck, gentlemen, because you're going to need it. A four-ton lorry carries twenty people, and there are seven lorries outside. By the end of this course you'll be able to get what's left of you in a Land Rover.'

After the briefing, Hillbilly and I head down to the local for a pie and chips and a few pints of Guinness. It becomes an evening ritual, even when we're shattered by fatigue and comparing blisters.

People don't seriously start dropping off until the 'Fan Dance' at the end of week one. It's up and down the Pen y Fan, the highest mountain in the Brecon Beacons, with a 45 lb. bergen and the clock running. The four-tonner drops me at the Storey Arms, the site of a former pub on one side of Pen y Fan. From there we head straight up the Fan, around Windy Gap, contouring the hills and dropping down the old Roman road to the railway line and turnaround point. Then it's back up the mountain, retracing the route.

We're strung out by now, each fighting our own personal battle against the clock. The weather has started to deteriorate and I'm only wearing a sweat top underneath my smock. It's a mistake, and by the time I reach Windy Gap, the gale is cutting straight through me. My body furnace is dropping because I didn't eat enough this morning. I can feel myself going, and there's nothing I can do. I fall, then drag myself on to one knee, only to fall again. My head is spinning. Now I'm sitting in the mud, unable to feel my hands and feet. My sweat is starting to freeze.

Two years ago a soldier died of exposure during the Fan Dance, when he became disorientated and got lost in appalling weather. They found him propped up with his back to a rock.

'You all right, mate?'

I look up and see a bushy black moustache framed by the dark grey sky. It's Vince Phillips, a big runner who can do a marathon in under two and a half hours. He's a quiet lad who hardly says a word. Vince crouches next to me, making me take sips of water and unwrapping Mars bars. He forces about three into me and helps me up. He gets me started up towards the Fan. From there it's all downhill, with the bergen banging against my back.

The Fan Dance is a race against time and I will never forget Vince for what he did. No one knows exactly how much time we have to complete the course, but he sacrificed ten or fifteen minutes to help me. Thanks to him, I manage to survive Selection for another day.

I won't make the same mistakes again. I wear thermal underwear – the thin stuff that can breathe – and eat a huge breakfast every morning, eggs, bacon, sausages and toast, going back for more when that's finished. The cook makes up real doorstop sandwiches for lunch and I shove Mars bars in my smock pockets.

Paddy is right. After a fortnight, instead of seven four-tonners, they now only need five trucks to carry us each morning. We lose even more lads on the Sketch Map exercises in the Elan Valley and the night tab. The days get progressively harder, and as I reach each new checkpoint I want to collapse, exhausted. Do I really need it this much? I ask myself. Then I say, 'Just one more checkpoint. Then you can jack it in.'

I'm not living from day to day, I'm living from checkpoint to checkpoint, because a day is too long. I fight on for another six miles, positive the clock is winning, and arrive at the next rendezvous to see lads sitting there who have thrown their hand in. They look so dejected and broken that I decide not to give up just yet – I'll make it through the day and then quit. That's how I get through.

With fewer people in the barracks, those who remain move into rooms together. In a perverse way, this encourages me. Maybe I can get through this after all. My feet are okay and I have cream and masking tape all over my blistered back. I bathe in shallow water to keep it dry.

Test Week is in the Brecon Beacons, with longer and longer tabs each day carrying more and more weight. It culminates in an ordeal known as Endurance – a monster tab over mountains with weapons and 55 lb. bergens. This is non-stop for twenty-four hours.

The first ten miles are not too bad – I've peaked at the right time – but then the pain begins. After six hours my knees are shot, the blisters on my back are weeping. This isn't like walking up a road, these hills are made for mountain goats.

I can't remember the last twelve hours – the pain wipes away all trace. As I drop down towards a reservoir on the last leg, I catch up to Des. We're too exhausted to speak. My knees have gone and they can't take the strain on the steep slope. I bounce down on my arse like a kid. Des is next to me and suddenly we're laughing like idiots.

'Come on, let's finish this,' he says.

We're both hobbling and I'm eating painkillers like chewing-gum. The local medic had been handing them out at the last checkpoint. We've been tabbing since six o'clock yesterday morning, and now the sky is getting light again. It's amazing how much strength you find when you see the truck and the big dixie full of airborne stew, with bits of gristle and chunks of vegetables.

I lean back on a rock and finish two bowls while the truck slowly fills.

*

I wish I could remember more. I'm sure there's something important that I'm missing; some reason why I managed to survive the first hurdle in SAS Selection and others failed who were fitter, faster and more determined. Why didn't I twist my ankle, or pull a hamstring, or have my blisters turn septic?

You're not supposed to smoke in the Charter Clinic except in designated areas, but I'm lousy at following orders. At this sort of price they should have free cigars in every room. I find a suitable spot by the window and light up, watching last orders at the Chelsea Potter. A few regulars are dawdling over their pints, unwilling to surrender themselves to the cold outside.

The barman is putting chairs on to tables and cleaning ashtrays. He has a teatowel over his shoulder and another tucked into his belt. I watch him usher the reluctant few out the door and slide the bolt locks into place. A final wipe of the bar, a night-cap and then he turns off the lights.

In spite of the cold, there are still quite a few people on the King's Road. A handful are waiting at the bus shelter and I catch a glimpse of others as they cross the road, hurrying home from the theatre or the cinema. A convoy of red double-decker buses pulls up, and it's quite comforting because I know that I must be in England – not just because of the vehicles, but their frequency.

I've almost forgotten about France and the asylum. All that must have happened to someone else; a friend of mine. No, that's not right. What about Anna? Blood has been spilled and it can't be forgotten. Think, Tom, think; when did it start? Were you chosen to kill her?

*

Our jungle camp is little more than a series of makeshift lean-tos made of poles and Attap leaves in the rainforests of Belize in Central America. Separated into four-man patrols, each of us erects an A-frame using small trees and poles to support bedding and a poncho. It will be our home for the next six weeks.

'The jungle is your bread and butter,' RSM Taff R. shouts. 'This is why the SAS was born. Those of you who think it's all about black kit and swinging through embassy windows can leave now. This is where the real soldiering is done.'

There are forty-five of us left for the jungle phase of Selection, each of us sweltering in the humidity. Belize is a steaming, fetid, dirty place, crawling with things that bite or sting or suck. No sunlight pierces the canopy and the tree trunks, dotted with fungus, seem to close in at night, trying to swallow a person whole.

For the first week we stay at the main base camp doing classroom work on map-reading, camp attacks, ambushes, jungle navigation and patrol skills. We sit on logs, glancing up at the blackboard and keeping one eye out for scorpions. Soon the theory is put into practice and we go out on patrols, each of them longer than the last. There are four-man patrols dotted over a wide area, and each night we build hammocks and sleep wearing our boots, with webbing as a pillow and rifle within reach in case we come under attack.

An hour before first light we wake in total darkness, silently putting on wet kit and moving to a stand-to position about thirty feet from the basha. Braced against a tree, I peer into the jungle looking for an unseen 'enemy'. The real enemy is Don W., our patrol's DS, who basha's away from us each night and silently watches. The slightest noise as we wake or failure to remove all trace of our presence can mean failing Jungle Training.

The 'Stand Down' order passes quietly between the patrol and we grab everything and move off. An hour later we stop for breakfast, lighting up the hexy stove to make porridge from an oatmeal block and to fry Spam which we eat between hard tack biscuits and wash down with the customary brew.

Don W. is like the fifth man on patrol, but he does his own thing. He drifts back to see how we're doing and sometimes calls a break. Everyone looks gaunt and dishevelled. Dirt, gun oil and cam cream are ingrained in every pore.

A lot of the lads get frustrated in the jungle, because nothing is easy. Turn around twice and you're lost; there are thorns that can pierce a hand and wait-a-while vines that seem to reach out to drag you back. None of us knows how we're doing as individuals because we're members of a team. You might pretend you're a team player for a while, but eventually the jungle exposes the deception.

On one exercise our patrol gets lost, although the army prefers to call it 'temporarily misplaced'. We're running low on water and this is the dry season in Belize. We have to find a river but because we're temporarily misplaced the maps are useless without a landmark to fix our position. We're wandering in an ocean of green, looking for ridges or shapes of hills.

We should have made the river by yesterday afternoon. Don W. came to the camp last night and asked us how much water the patrol had left. We each carry four water bottles and we're down to half a bottle each. Don gave us one of his bottles. The bloke is amazing; he's so quiet and confident. He doesn't waffle or bullshit. He's the epitome of an SAS soldier.

'So where are you?' he asks John H., a crap-hat officer in charge of our patrol.

'We're lost.'

'Yes, I know that, but where do you think you might be?'

We're crouched around a map on the ground, pointing with twigs and discussing our next move. Don doesn't suggest a route, he lets us decide.

Next morning, we stand-to, have breakfast and then move off, hopefully in the direction of the river. All day we tab, sweating in the oppressive humidity and using up our precious supplies of water to avoid dehydration. Normally we drink it as tea to help quench the thirst and camouflage the taste of steriliser tablets.

'That's it,' says Doug as we finish the last dregs. 'Learn to be thirsty.'

The situation has become critical, but no one breaks with the SOPs (standard operating procedures). Our every action has to be guided by the belief that we are in enemy territory. Late that afternoon, Doug is lead scout when we reach the river. It's little more than a series of muddy pools joined by a trickle of water.

Doug and John slide down to the bank and stake out an area, watching closely for any sign of the enemy. After twenty minutes, we hand Doug our bottles and he slips into the water while we keep him covered. John is passing his bottles down when he says, 'Hang on.' He raises a canteen to his lips and we hear the *glug, glug, glug*. He's been holding out on us.

Don W. doesn't miss a thing. I can see him looking at the officer, thinking, 'You're gone, matey.' That's what I mean about being a team player – the jungle finds you out.

There's no letting up. Day after day we practise different skills, like contact drills, river crossings, demolitions and how to cache food and swap reports with other patrols. The stench of our bodies doesn't matter any more and neither do the bugs or the wet clothes. The cuts and sores will heal in time and even the hammocks feel like home.

Despite the hardships, I've grown quite fond of the jungle. I don't find it claustrophobic, like a lot of the lads; instead there is something very basic and primeval about it that appeals to me. Lying in my basha, I look up through a tiny break in the canopy and see the thin vapour trail of an aircraft against the blue sky. I think of all those people in their suits and fine clothes, sipping their gin and tonics, reading magazines and getting wine with their meals. I don't envy them.

After the final exercise – a full-scale camp attack – we helicopter back to Belize City. Our beards are shaved off, sores are tended and weapons are cleaned and packed away. A C-130 is coming to fly us to Washington and then home. I'm shaving away six weeks' growth when someone yells out, 'Has anyone heard of the Falkland Islands?'

No one replies.

'They're British and they've just been invaded.'

'Who by?' someone yells.

'Argentina!'

I have this picture in my mind of South American bandidos capturing the Orkneys and holding several thousand sheep hostage.

Soon the whole camp is huddled around various radios, listening to the BBC World Service. The details are sketchy, but a British outpost in the South Atlantic has been invaded. There is talk of a military task force being sent to recapture the Falklands.

None of us really thinks it will come to war. Surely the diplomats and politicians will sort it out before a shot is fired? But just in case, I'd better get through Selection. A distant campaign in difficult weather is just the sort of thing the SAS is trained to handle.

6

Dr Friedman looks like a Tory politician in his pinstripe suit and red tie. He's the psychiatrist who signed the papers to get me out of the asylum in France. We haven't exactly hit it off so far.

'We're going to start you on some medication, Mr Read,' he says, reading from a chart and not looking at me.

'What sort of medication?'

'Fairly standard psychiatric drugs – an anti-depressant and a neuroleptic drug. It will mean an injection once a week and tablets twice a day.'

'If I take the drugs, will you let me go home?'

'No, not just yet.'

'I'm a voluntary patient. I don't have to be here.'

'That's true, but you're an intelligent man and you will choose to stay here because you realise that you need my help.'

What a pompous arse. 'These drugs that you want to give me, what do they do?'

'Chlorpromazine is a stupefier. It's an anti-psychotic drug that has a few side-effects.'

'Like what?'

'Well, it can cause muscle spasms and shakiness; and some patients complain of feeling drowsy and lethargic. It can also cause faintness, dryness in the mouth, blurred vision, sensitivity to the sun, impotence and constipation.'

'Is that all?' The sarcasm is totally lost on him.

I don't like this man, but I put my Para head on and tell myself not to blow it. I'm almost home and dry; Hereford is only two hours up the road. It took a lot of hard work to get me out of France and now it's up to me. I can't give these people any reason to keep me here. I have to stick to my cover story, take their drugs and convince them that I'm okay. Then they'll let me go home.

Friedman doesn't stay very long. 'I'm a busy man,' he tells me. Twenty minutes later, a male nurse hands me a little paper cup with two pills inside. I feel like a five-year-old who has to take his vitamins or he won't grow up to be big and strong. I tip the cup up and swallow.

'Show me,' says the nurse.

I open wide, showing my empty mouth. Then I roll my tongue and the pills pop up.

'You have to take your medication, Mr Read.'

'Yeah, sure, I'm just sucking mine . . . making them last, you know.'

This place has room service like in a posh hotel, and I keep ordering sandwiches rather than going to the canteen. I don't want people to see me; I don't want to see their questioning eyes or have to explain myself to them. There's a small TV in my room and Jackie brings my video recorder from Hereford. Des goes to Harrods and buys the whole collection of *Fawlty Towers* and *Blackadder* tapes. I can't watch more than ten minutes before I get pacey and start to wander. It's the same when I visit the gymnasium in the basement – I can only last five minutes on the weights.

Harry doesn't seem surprised when I tell him about Dr Friedman. The lads had already tried to give the staff some background information about what happened in France, but they got the impression that the doctors would rather draw their own conclusions.

'We warned them that you could be extremely manipulative,' says Des.

'Who, me?' I say in mock surprise.

'Yeah, you're as cunning as a shit-house rat.'

Des knows that I'm trying to control the side-effects of the drugs and to appear normal. He even buys me a card that has a picture of a skyscraper with one broken window and a psychiatrist in a white coat flying out of it backwards, as if he's been punched in the stomach. The caption reads: 'Hey, I feel better already.'

On about the third day I make a mistake on the phone to Jackie. 'I think I've got everyone in here duped,' I tell her. 'They think I'm really sorry about what happened to Anna, but I'm not.'

She's straight on the phone to Harry and Schwepsy, who read the riot act to the doctors, telling them not to be fooled into letting me come home too early. It didn't take Einstein to realise that they are either tapping my phone calls or Jackie has dropped me right in it. From now on I'll be more careful.

Most of the other patients keep to themselves. There aren't many real loonies – not like in France. Instead, the Charter Clinic is full of rich coke-heads and skinny girls suffering from eating disorders. Occasionally I see one of them in the corridors, looking gaunt and prematurely old, but mostly they stay in their rooms or live upstairs.

The lads visit me every day and we have cups of tea in the canteen. Des is going back to the States soon, and Harry will return to France. Because Schwepsy lives in London they've made him my temporary guardian. He's perfect for the job because he's an expert at bossing people around.

Apart from their visits, I phone Jackie every day. She's been brilliant, fielding all the calls and looking after the house.

'How are things?' she asks.

'Bloody awful. I think they're trying to poison me. They give me these pills and I feel like a rat in a science experiment. Next they'll have me running through a maze.'

'I'm sure it's making you better,' says Jackie. 'Are you getting any sleep?'

'A little. I hate this place.'

'It's one of the best clinics in the country. They're trying to help you.'

'No. It's just a waste of money. I'd be far better off at home.'

'Don't worry about the money. Saad is picking up the bill.'

'That's not the point. I appreciate what Saad is doing, but I'm not going to get better in here. I should be at home.'

Jackie mentions Chris and Jason and the arrangements to bring them up to London to visit me.

'How about on Wednesday?' she asks.

I agree, although I'm nervous about it. I don't want Jason to see me like this . . . not in here. He's fifteen years old and quite the young man. He's talking about studying law and is a conscientious student.

Chris and I have been divorced for more than ten years now, but we've always stayed close. She's done a great job in bringing Jason up. Knowing what I know now, I might have tried harder to keep us together, but ultimately, like a lot of SAS marriages, ours was a victim of neglect and of long periods away from home. Who'd be a soldier's wife?

I remember hearing the news. I was in Northern Ireland when the final papers arrived, and various lads dropped by my room to say how sorry they were. They don't like divorce in the Regiment – it takes minds off the job at hand.

*

'Right, that's it!' says Hillbilly, seeing my long face. He opens my wardrobe and shakes his head in disgust. 'Hmm. These are Pad clothes' – married man's clothes – 'and they've got to go.'

Hillbilly has been divorced for years, and I think it's made him quite bitter about marriage. He starts tossing cardigans on the floor.

'Do you know what you need?' he says.

'What's that?'

'You need a good shag. We're going to change your wardrobe. Then we're going to do some serious training. You need some muscle to pull the birds.'

Hillbilly's favourite pastime is the wooing and bedding of women. He might not be much to look at, with his punched-in face, but he has the gift of the gab and when he truly starts romancing a girl, very few have the strength of will to deny him.

He makes it his mission in life to take my mind off Chris, by focusing it on all the other 'fish in the sea'.

The tour has been quiet, and we've spent most of our time training and going to the occasional private party with the police. Sometimes we go drinking in Belfast, but we have to be careful about who we meet and what we say. For example, I can't go back to a girl's place on the first night unless I've checked her out and made sure she has no known affiliations or links with the IRA.

I can't simply ask her, and neither can I give her any idea of what I'm doing in Northern Ireland. My cover story is that I work for an aircraft company, shipping and installing spare parts. I can describe the job in tremendous detail, and use the fact that I travel back and forth to England to avoid giving her a contact number.

She might be sweet as can be and giving me all the right signs, but unless I can get her surname and date of birth, I can't run a security check on her. Her name isn't difficult to get in the course of a conversation, but women can be very protective about revealing their age.

'I'll bet you were born on a Wednesday,' I say.

'What makes you say that?'

'Because you look like a Wednesday girl. Definitely.'

She laughs.

'Do you know what day of the week you were born? Don't tell me, just say yes or no.'

She nods. 'I think so.'

'Okay, just tell me the date, but not the day.'

'The 22nd of April, 1963.'

I do the calculations quickly in my head, using a simple mathematical formula. 'Oh, so you're not a Wednesday girl, are you? It was a Monday.'

'How did you know that?'

She's impressed, but more importantly, I've just managed to get her date of birth. Slipping out to the car, I call base on the radio. 'It's Tom here, I've got a P-check for you. Sally McLaughlin, date of birth 22 April 1963.'

'Okay, we'll get back to you.'

A few minutes later, the check is complete. 'Yeah, she's okay. Her father's a teacher. They have no known links with PIRA [the Provisional IRA].'

That's the all-clear – I can walk Sally home and see how things develop.

Hillbilly is incorrigible, and when we team up it becomes almost like a contest to see who can chat up the prettiest girl. After a barbecue in Hereford, when I manage to spirit off an angel in a white bikini, Hillbilly pesters me for weeks for her phone number. Eventually, we're on a firing range in Wales, aiming at targets across the valley, and Hillbilly lines up a flock of sheep below us.

'I know you're an animal lover, Tom, which is why I'm giving you a chance. You give me the number or I take out the sheep.'

I know that he'll do it, so I finally relent.

Even when he's on leave, Hillbilly will call me in the middle of the night while he has some new girl in bed with him. 'I just want you to say hello to Maggie,' he'll say. 'And Maggie, say hello to Tom.'

We're like two teenagers trying to outdo each other. While he's away, I train like crazy so that when he gets back and we go for a run I can beast him about being an unfit slob. And then when I go on leave, Hillbilly does exactly the same thing.

I remember how he tried to talk me out of buying my first guitar from a second-hand shop in Belfast. It came with a how-to book, and I practised 'House Of The Rising Sun' over and over until the lads threatened to kill me. Hillbilly still blames me for sending him tone-deaf. After that, I took to playing it in the sauna, always remembering to lock my room so no one could take revenge.

Hillbilly is a parent's nightmare and an out-and-out rogue, but he's the best mate I've got and I'll be forever grateful for how he helped me get on with my life since the divorce.

*

I'm waiting in the downstairs reception area when Chris and Jason arrive at the Charter Clinic. Chris looks wonderful, but as soon as she sees me her hand covers her mouth. I look gaunt and drawn, with sunken eyes deep in my skull. My hands are shaking and the drugs make my mouth so dry that I carry a bottle of water with me.

Chris holds my hand and tries to be cheerful. 'This place looks great.'

'I'd rather be home,' I tell her, smiling.

Jason is watching quietly, deciding how to react. He's almost as tall as me now and is playing football for his school.

'How long are you gonna be here, Dad?' he asks.

'I don't know, Jase. Not long I hope.'

'Are you going to be okay?'

'Oh, sure. I just need a rest. I drove myself into the deck by working too hard and not sleeping or eating. Once I get out of here and start exercising and looking after myself, I'll be better again in no time.'

'How's Anna?' asks Chris.

Although it's sensitive, I don't want to avoid the subject. You can't run away from the past when it haunts the present. 'It's all finished now, which is probably a good thing,' I say. 'Poor old Anna bore the brunt of things, but I don't think it was a particularly healthy relationship, do you? You didn't like her that much, did you, Jason?'

'She was all right, Dad.'

I have this fleeting image of Anna on the ski slopes above Chamonix. That's why I stabbed her; I thought she wanted to hurt Jason. 'It's come to this, Anna,' I said to her. 'It's going to be one of us. I don't really care what happens to me, but what's going to happen to Jason?'

She didn't answer straight away, so I asked her again. That's when she looked directly at me and said, 'I don't know. Maybe nothing.'

I had to stop her after that. I couldn't let her get back to England. She had to die in France.

My mind is racing again. Where did she first meet Jason? It was in Washington, when he came over during his school holidays. I can picture Anna dancing with him on a boat. A year later, we all flew down to Corsica in a light plane and arrived in time for Napoleon's birthday celebrations at his birthplace, Ajaccio. We hired the only car left on the island and got it hopelessly bogged on a beach. That night Jason and Anna slept in the car while I lay in the sand, looking at the stars and listening to the waves.

How did Anna treat Jason on that holiday? She's not the maternal sort, but I can't think of any sign of ill-will or malice.

Anna *did* panic on that trip. We were flying to Malta to see an old mate of mine, Steve Delia, when the electrics failed on the Cessna. We had just over-flown Sardinia and were half-way through the three-hour flight. Jason is in the right-hand seat wearing a headset and peering out the side window. Anna is behind us, reading. God knows why I take her anywhere, she never takes her nose out of a book. I tell them about the problem.

'Are we going to crash?' asks Jason.

'No,' I say firmly.

'We're empty, we're empty!' cries Anna, pointing at the gauges.

'No, we're not. Don't take any notice of those, we've got plenty of fuel.'

Most of the gauges work on electrical power, as do the wing flaps, radio, cockpit lights and landing lights. I've turned off everything that isn't essential, in order to save power.

The Mediterranean is 8,000 feet below us. When I filled out our flight plan it had asked for the markings of our life-raft (a prerequisite for flying over water). I didn't have one, so I went to a local shop and bought one of those inflatable children's dinghies. On the flight plan I described it as being purple with yellow dolphins and a nylon rope around the outside. The seas are warm at this time of year and I can always bring the plane down near a ship.

'I want you to get the hand-held radio out of my bag, Anna. Can you do that for me?'

'Uh-huh.'

I try the radio several times without success. Either the batteries are low or it doesn't have the range. The VHF radio is still working, but will quickly bleed the battery.

'Malta Approach this is Cessna November 84587.'

'November 84587 go ahead.'

'I have a slight problem. I have lost all of my electrics and am expecting total electrical failure shortly. Because of limited power I would like to restrict my transmissions to you but will remain on listening watch. Can you give me airport information at this time?'

'Roger that, November 84587. You are losing electrics and wish to restrict communications. Do you require diversion to Sardinia?'

'No, I wish to carry on.'

Sardinia is closer, but regardless of where I land, I'll face the same problems. I have plenty of fuel, the GPS (global positioning system) is working, I know my altitude, my air speed, the runway information and local weather in Malta – I can do this.

Steve Delia has a house on the island and he's been expecting us. We were supposed to arrive yesterday and I know Steve would have been there to meet us. Hopefully, he'll ask if anyone has lodged a flight plan and he'll know we're coming today.

Anna is silently flapping in the back seat as we fly onwards in the darkened cockpit. An hour later, the lights of Malta emerge on our left. 'Keep your eye out for the runway,' I tell Jason.

'Yeah, I've got it, Dad. Over there.'

I lean over him. 'Where?'

'There!'

'Got it.'

We're about eight miles out. 'Malta Approach, this is November 84587. I have the airport in sight. Request a straight-in landing.'

Sssshhh – the radio is starting to break up. I hit the pressle. 'Malta Approach, I'm losing the radio. If you can hear me I'm setting up for a direct approach on Runway 27. I have no flaps, no lights, estimate eight minutes from now.'

There is no reply – the radio is dead. Did they get my last message? There's nothing else I can do except hope that the control tower heard me. The runway is seven miles ahead and I'm looking all around us, trying to see if anything else is trying to land. Without lights, the plane might as well be invisible.

'You just keep your eyes on that runway, Jason. Tell me if you see any aircraft coming in or taking off.'

'Malta Approach, transmitting blind, I have the runway in sight. Will make a visual direct approach to Runway 27. Negative lights.'

There's no response.

I start my approach from five miles and have to adjust the angle because I have no wing flaps. These act as air brakes that slow an aircraft and allow it to come in at a steeper angle. Without them, the landing is going to be long, low and fast, but it's something I've practised.

Taking plenty of runway, I bring the Cessna down over the rooftops and touch down at 80 mph instead of the normal 60 mph. As the wheels grip and we start rolling, I notice two fire trucks and a van with flashing lights beside the runway.

Later, Steve tells the story of how he and his mates were sitting at a bar on the flight path, looking up between the buildings as different aircraft passed overhead.

'Is that Tom?' they'd ask occasionally, as they glanced up at the landing lights.

'No, he's got a small plane,' explained Steve.

Eventually, they heard the distinctive sound of a piston engine, coming in very low, without lights. Steve swallowed his beer and stood up. 'I'd better go. That *is* Tom.'

You weren't so clever, Anna, were you? That was one of your mistakes. Later, when I thought you could destroy me, I remembered Malta and how you panicked when you saw the fuel gauges. I knew then that you weren't so switched on. I had a chance.

I'm sad when Chris and Jason leave. Next time, they'll stay in London for a few days and visit more often. Although Chris and I have never laboured over what happened in our marriage or tried to dig up emotions and sentiment, I can't help missing her. I wonder if we might get back together again. A part of me still loves her.

Without even thinking about it, I have surrounded myself with things from home, like the video, my guitar and sheet music. Home is safe. Home is where I will get better. That's where the answer lies to what happened. And when I'm there, I'll be able to fix the back fence and redecorate the spare room. Lots of jobs need doing. Yes, I have to get home.

But every time I ask them when I might leave, they change my drugs and the dosages. I'm even on drugs to stop the side-effects of other drugs. The end result is that I can't focus on any subject for more than a few minutes. Colours aren't as bright and voices seem flat and monotonous. I can't concentrate on the television or read a book. Everything feels like it's happening in slow motion, and I'm always ten seconds behind every conversation. I find myself sweating when I shouldn't be hot, and my hands have started to tremble. There's a ringing in my head that sounds like the high-pitched hum of a gyro. I keep trying to work out whether it's in my right ear or left ear, but it's actually in the middle of my head. I've had it ever since I arrived from France.

'I want to see Friedman,' I say to a nurse.

'I'm sorry, but Dr Friedman isn't available.'

'Well, phone him up.'

She smiles reassuringly. 'He'll be in tomorrow.'

I hate this! I can walk out the door at any time, but I want the doctors to give me the green light. That way I don't let anyone down – not Harry or Des, or Schwepsy or Cath, or Jackie, or Saad, or Loel – all those people who got me out of France and smoothed things over with Anna. But I won't stay here for ever.

*

Doctors and drugs will not succeed where Anna failed. The demons may only exist inside my head but that doesn't worry me. I have passed the most rigorous military entrance test in the world and I know that I *can* defeat this.

Does that sound positive? It probably seems strange coming from someone whose fear of failure guarantees a negative approach to any challenge. I still find it hard to believe that I passed the jungle phase of Selection.

Of the original 140, only 15 of us remain. According to the CO, we have already been 'selected' by the SAS, and it's now up to us to justify that faith. The final hurdle, Combat Survival, is designed to give us a taste of life on the run.

Although compulsory for SAS applicants, Combat Survival is also offered as an optional course for other soldiers. Consequently, we are joined by about eighty senior NCOs and staff sergeants from crap-hat battalions and overseas. Those of us on Selection are broken up and each placed in a separate group. I finish up with a rupert from the Irish Guards who's so typically 'officer material' that there should be a life-size poster of him outside Sandhurst saying, 'This is what you must look like when you leave here.'

There are two Italian Special Forces recruits mincing around, combing their hair and looking arrogantly disinterested. Because they only speak a few words of English they're going to be kept together.

Paddy B. looks directly at me. 'You, young man, are taking the two Italians and I *want* to see them come back.' In other words, don't dump them straight away.

After being searched we're each given a greatcoat and told to remove the laces from our boots. We are to be dumped in the middle of nowhere with a sketch map, no money or supplies, and each with a survival kit that must fit into a tobacco tin (American Express cards are not allowed). I choose to take a button compass, a condom for carrying water, a snare, razor blade, wire saw and a basic first-aid kit.

Adding to the realism of the exercise, a hunter force of crap-hats with helicopters, dogs and motorbikes will be tracking us down, saturating the entire area. We have to avoid capture, make contact at a designated checkpoint each night, and use our training to survive.

On Sunday morning it begins, and within twenty-four hours my stomach thinks my throat has been cut. During daylight hours we hide under hedges and in ditches, and then at night we start moving, navigating to the next checkpoint. The rupert is awfully posh but not a bad bloke. I call him Captain Puttee, because he doesn't know how to wear his puttees without looking like a prat.

The Italians, however, are a bloody pain. Every time we climb a fence, or go past the hunter force, they jump around on the bloody wire, twanging it and compromising our position. They whinge about being hungry and keep suggesting we knock on farmhouse doors asking for food. These blokes think they're on holiday, but my future depends on getting through this.

'What's wrong with your foot?' asks Captain Puttee on the second morning.

'Nothing.'

'I've seen you limping.'

On Saturday night, Hillbilly and I had gone out drinking and arrived at the barracks late. During the night I had accidentally knocked over and broken a heavy ashtray. Next morning, I swung my legs out of bed, put them down, took the weight and a piece of glass pierced my heel.

'You shouldn't be here. That's gonna go septic,' says Captain Puttee.

'That's exactly what the medic told me.'

'So why didn't you listen?'

'Because I'm afraid they'll fail me.'

I limp onwards, hoping the wound will heal. On Wednesday, we're lying up under some fallen bracken in woodland when I hear the hunter force sweeping through with their dogs. We'd done a deception plan as we came into the woods, but something had obviously gone wrong.

I glance up at Captain Puttee, whose head is covered in leaves. Where are the Italians? Fuck them, we'll have to leg it!

The 'enemy' has surrounded the wood and as I break cover, running and hopping, I'm easily captured. Captain Puttee gets away, and so do the Italians, who'd compromised our position by wandering around in daylight. Blindfolded and roughed up, I sit all day on a hill without food or water, occasionally being interrogated. My foot is throbbing and I have a splitting headache. That night the DS arrives and I hear him arguing with the hunter force about their tactics of saturating the area, giving us no chance to break out.

Suddenly the blindfold is lifted. 'Right, you're back in the field,' he says. White dots swim before my eyes. I flinch as my right foot takes my weight.

'What's wrong with your leg?'

'Nothing, Staff.'

'You want to come off the course?'

'No, Staff.'

'Do you know where the RV is?'

'Yes, Staff. I can find it if they take me back to where I was captured.'

They drop me in a Land Rover and I make my way back up the hill to the wood. That night I reach the next checkpoint, and the agent says that one of my patrol is waiting for me. Captain Puttee emerges from the darkness. He'd given me a couple of extra hours to make the RV.

Others haven't been so lucky or committed. Some have been caught scavenging food and sleeping in barns and stables to escape the elements. We stay out of doors, but the Italians are slowing us down and I'm pissed off with their antics.

At daybreak we hide in a forest, sleeping under bracken and leaves. Just before last light, I wake Captain Puttee. 'Come on, we have to go,' I say. 'We're meeting the Italians at the bottom of the hill.'

Unbeknown to him, I had lit a small fire and put leaves on it to create smoke. A chopper came in and caught the Italians before they were even awake. Good riddance!

At each new checkpoint the agent gives us a new map reference and a piece of food – which could be a bag of tripe, a pig's trotter or an onion. Moving at night makes it difficult to use the snares, because you have to be around in the morning to pick them up.

My hunger is constant, and early one morning, near a farmhouse, I watch two schoolgirls throw some stale brown loaves over a fence into a paddock, feeding their horses. I leg it from the bushes, racing the horses to the feast. I beat them and scoop up the loaves before escaping. We spend the next three hours running like hell, knowing the farmer will report our position to the hunter force.

For six days we run, exhausted and hungry. At the final RV, the hunter force is waiting. Blindfolded and bundled into trucks, we are taken on a journey that seems to last for hours. The point of the exercise is no longer escape and evasion, but interrogation.

I count the stairs as my feet drag over them and feel the concrete floor against my cheek. I'm stripped naked and made to wear a boiler suit and plimsolls that are too small. Still blindfolded, I kneel on the floor with my hands on my head and my head tilted back so that it faces the ceiling. I hold the position for an hour, in agony, and then they lean me spread-eagled against the wall with my weight on my fingertips. After about fifteen minutes I can't feel my hands. In another fifteen my arms give way and I crash my head against the wall. White noise blares constantly in my ears.

Rough hands yank me upwards and run me blindly down a corridor. I'm forced into a chair and the blindfold is suddenly removed. Bright lights. Two men opposite – one sitting, the other pacing the floor. The closest offers me a cigarette.

'We haven't started yet. Do you fancy some tea?'

I nod my head.

'Is that a yes?'

'I cannot answer that question, sir.'

He looks at his watch. 'No, I mean it. We don't start for another five minutes.'

In the weeks before Combat Survival, we'd been briefed about inter-rogation techniques and the tricks they use. 'Forget all the bullshit from the classroom,' the DS instructor had said. 'The only thing that comes out of your mouth is name, number, rank and date of birth.' These are the 'Big Four', and we recited them over and over.

The only other response allowed is: 'I cannot answer that question.' Even uttering 'yes' to the offer of a cup of tea or a cigarette would mean instant failure, because it is seen as the thin edge of the wedge. An enemy can use doctored tape recordings and video footage to turn a simple 'yes' into a damaging confession or propaganda.

There are loads of stories about people who get this far and then fuck up. Like the Irish Ranger who was asked if he was comfortable. 'I cannot answer that question, sir,' he replied.

'Okay, do you need your glasses?'

'I cannot answer that question, sir.'

'Listen, we haven't started yet, you wanker. It's just a course, we don't want to hurt anybody. And we have to be very careful, medically, not to put candidates under too much pressure. Now do you need your glasses?'

'No thanks, I can do without them.'

He failed.

My favourite story is about a French Special Forces trooper who was down town every night, wooing the local girls. Pépé le Pew was a real ladies' man, so they put a beautiful female interrogator on his case.

'What is your name?' she asks.

'Er, 21499, Sergeant Pépé le Pew.'

'Okay, we've got that. What's your date of birth?'

'Ze second of ze tenth, nineteen fifty-five.'

'What's the name of your commanding officer?'

'I cannot answer zat question.'

'Why have you got a condom on you?'

'Whhhh—? I cannot answer zis question.'

'Do you always carry a condom with you?' she asks, smiling sweetly and leaning over the desk, letting her blouse gape open. The top button's undone.

'Ahh, I cannot answer zat question.'

This carries on for a while. And then she says, 'Well, look, you've done very well. We're coming to the end of the course now. I've seen you around and I was just wondering if we could get together. You know what I'd really like? To see that condom on the end of your cock just before you stick it in me.'

'*Oui, oui* – but I cannot talk to you now. Maybe later, hey?'

He failed too.

I've come too far to make any stupid mistakes. The British Task Force is already in the South Atlantic, nearing the Falklands. We might be at war in a few days and I don't want to miss out.

The man across the table is toying with his tie. 'You say you were born on the eighth of the eighth, is that in July or August?'

'I can't answer that question, sir.'

'Oh, come on. You must know the month?'

'I can't answer that question, sir.'

The 'nice guy' routine doesn't last. Pretty soon one of them is screaming abuse in my face, so close that I feel the spittle on my cheeks and see the blackheads on his nose. I keep repeating: 'Private Read. Serial number 24429893. Born eighth of the eighth, nineteen fifty-six.'

As soon as they hear the rank 'Private', they know I'm on Selection. 'Oh, so you want to join the SAS, do you? What makes you think a wanker like you is wanted in the Regiment? A private at your age?'

He tries to goad me into getting angry, but I find it quite amusing. After half an hour of this, the blindfold goes back on and I'm dragged down the corridor into the incessant white noise and made to kneel again. My back is killing me in the stress positions, and I actually prefer the interrogations to the waiting.

In the next session I get a real bastard who builds himself up into a crescendo of screaming rage and rabid fury. He tries three times to break me, dragging me back and forth into the tiny room, making me do press-ups and calling me names. I'm so tired I could sleep on a phone wire. My chin drops and hits my chest, double-tapping as it bounces back up again and I'm awake.

Forced against the wall, I keep thinking about all the lads who have failed. I never thought I'd get this far. Now all I have to do is hang on for a few more hours and I'm there! The SAS has selected me, now it's up to me. Just a few more hours.

I lose all sense of time as they interrogate me over and over again. Eventually I'm dragged back in front of the same pair who began the process.

'Listen, all we want from you is your parent unit and your commanding officer's name. Tell us that and we'll let you go – you're out of here, you're in the showers, you get a feed. We just need a crumb of info to keep our bosses happy. It's not as if it means much.'

'I cannot answer that question, sir.'

'All right, all right,' he sighs, getting frustrated. 'You look knackered, why don't you get your head down.'

Leaning forward, I fall asleep before my cheek touches the table . . .

'Wake up! Wake up, Read!' The interrogator is shaking me. 'Okay, this is the deal. I asked you when you were asleep if you were in the engineers, and you said, "No." Didn't you?'

'I can't answer that question, sir.'

'Well, you did, believe me. I then asked you if you were in the Paras, and you said, "Yes." I put several other questions to you using a special technique, and I know that you're from 2 Para.'

How could he know? My heart sinks. Chris always told me that I talk in my sleep. I've blown it.

'Listen, you're going to fail Selection when we tell your people you've given us this information. All I need to know is your commanding officer's name to keep my fucking boss happy. Tell us that and I'll say you're clean. No one need know who gave me the information.'

I keep thinking to myself, 'I've failed . . . I've failed.'

'So what's the name of your CO?' He puts his arm around me, but I'm so programmed that I still won't answer him. Some time later they drag me outside and let me curl up on the concrete floor. The blindfold is taken off.

'Congratulations, it's all over. How do you feel?'

'I cannot answer that question.' I sound like a broken record.

'What day do you think it is?'

'I cannot answer . . .'

Only when Hillbilly walks in with a cup of tea do I really believe it's all over. Emotion washes through me and the sense of relief is enormous, but at the same time I'm almost inconsolable. I wish I'd failed on the first day rather than come so close.

Outside I have a big bowl of stew and another cup of tea. One of the DS staff sits down beside me. For six months these blokes have been my worst enemies. 'Congratulations, very well done,' he says, shaking my hand.

'But I failed.'

'No, you didn't. I told the interrogators you were 2 Para to give them something to needle you with. You did the right thing. Get yourself to B Squadron.'

It's late on Saturday night by the time the debrief finishes. Des, Hillbilly and I go straight to the Paludrin Club and get pissed on two cans of beer. We haven't showered and are wearing borrowed clothes. Only eleven people have passed Selection and, remarkably, these include our entire gang who had trained beforehand in the Brecon Beacons. That's when we nickname ourselves 'the S Squad'.

7

I don't stare at the wallpaper or count the slats in the venetian blinds or wonder how many bolts there are in the bed-frame. I should know this room better than my own in Hereford, but the drugs have made it non-descript. It might as well be an ice-cave. The only view that registers with me is the Chelsea Potter. I watch it open in the morning and close at night. I know what times the bar staff change shifts and when the different regulars arrive, taking up positions on their favourite stools or at particular tables. I know when the kegs are delivered and the windows cleaned.

This is my life, now; I sit at this window, smoking myself to death and counting how many times the Number 22 bus passes every hour. I watch council street-sweepers come by and notice how one of them gets a coffee from over the road every morning and sits on the pub steps reading a copy of the *Sun*.

This is what it has come to. There has to be a reason.

Twice a week I have a session with a psychologist, an Australian bloke who's in his mid-forties and really laid-back. He asks me questions that I try not to answer because I think they have some hidden meaning.

Dr Oz doesn't have a couch or a stopwatch on his desk, but it sort of psychs you out when someone is trying to look inside your head and interpret every mannerism and pause. That's why I'm being extra careful with my answers, but Dr Oz seems a clever bloke. Every time I stumble or repeat myself, he doesn't correct me or interrupt. Instead he smiles, leans back and folds his arms over his chest as if to say, 'I'm listening. We have lots of time.'

'Tell me about the Falklands,' he says, toying with a scrap of paper.

'There's nothing to tell.'

'I can't believe that.'

Although I say nothing to him, I find myself thinking about things. Interrogation had finished on a Saturday night in May 1982. Chris barely has a day to pack up our quarters and load our things into the Red Devils' van. We don't have much furniture and most of it is on hire-purchase in Aldershot.

On Sunday afternoon she and Jason arrive in Hereford and move straight into new quarters. The family officer in the Regiment fixes them up with a TV from Rumbelows in town and makes sure they get settled. Meanwhile, I'm busy getting issued with equipment, zeroing weapons, night-firing at the ranges and going to briefings about a proposed mainland assault on Argentina.

Already the main Task Force has retaken South Georgia, but on 4 May it lost the destroyer HMS *Sheffield* to an Exocet missile fired by Super Etendard naval strike aircraft. Twenty men died, and the attack has put the plans to retake the Falklands in jeopardy. If an Exocet were to destroy a British aircraft-carrier it could mean the end of the war.

That's why the mainland option has been considered – the bosses want to know if it's possible to destroy the Etendards and Exocets on the ground. While I've been running around on Combat Survival, B Squadron has been training day and night for a mainland assault. One option being investigated is to fly two C-130s from Ascension Island directly into Argentina to drop off the Squadron, which would fan out and attack several major airfields. That's why they've been practising flying under radar at Heathrow Airport and doing mock attacks on airfields in northern Scotland and the Midlands. A lot of questions still have to be answered. Will we parachute or land? What are the potential targets? How do we escape?

There are four operational squadrons in the SAS – A, B, D and G – and each has four specialist troops – Air, Mountain, Boat and Mobility – with up to twelve men in each. To compensate for the fact that we missed the lead-up training, one new recruit is assigned to each troop in B Squadron. I logically go to Air Troop, while Harry, a great climber, goes to Mountain Troop along with Des, who isn't so happy. Hillbilly is sent to Boat Troop and Schwepsy joins Mobility Troop. Only Doug misses out and finishes up in A Squadron.

Chris and I have absolutely no money, but a sergeant at the pay office arranges a £100 advance. I've never seen so much money in my life. When I hand it to Chris, she asks me where I'm going, but I don't know how much I'm allowed to tell her.

'You're going to the Falklands, aren't you?'

'I don't know.'

'Oh, come on, Tom, tell me the truth.'

'If you don't ask me then I won't have to lie.'

We leave on Wednesday, and I'm not even 'badged' until that morning. To save time we have a group ceremony, with the Regiment's second-in-command handing each of us our sandy-coloured beret. 'Welcome to the Regiment, gentlemen, you come at a very exciting time,' he says.

As I'm packing my kit in the barracks, I meet the rest of Air Troop for the first time. Individually they come over and shake my hand. There's Tiny, so-called because he's six foot four; Cyril, the old man of the troop, who's a big runner and super-fit; Frank Collins, a soft-spoken ginger-nut; John P., the troop second-in-command and a former member of the Intelligence Corps; Bedlam, so-called because of his tortuous private life; John F., the troop sergeant, who everyone calls 'Dad'; Phil M., a red-faced northerner: Lou L., a corporal who takes everything too seriously; Chris, a blond-haired ex-Para; and Saddlebags, who's a year younger than me but has already been in the Regiment for almost five years.

Charlie, one of the 'Old and the Bold', takes me under his wing and gives me advice on how to pack my bergen properly. Charlie has been with the Regiment since the early 1970s and is a veteran of Storm, the secret desert war in Oman. He's a hard man, always scratching his balls and barking at people.

A few hours later, the buses arrive to take us to RAF Brize Norton. From there we catch a VC10 directly to Ascension Island and then settle into barracks. The British land forces, including my old mates from

2 Para, had landed at San Carlos Bay in the Falklands on 21 May. Troops are now starting to push across the island towards the capital, Port Stanley, coming under heavy air attack.

The mainland option can counter the threat, but we're still trying to sort out the problems. The prime targets are two airfields, Rio Grande and Rio Gallegos, either side of the Strait of Magellan, at the very tip of South America. Various forms of insertion are considered, including the possibility of landing the squadron by boat, submarine, or tabbing across the Chilean border.

Air Troop is pulled aside to look at the freefall option. Discussion centres on dropping a six-man patrol on to the mainland to set up a landing zone for a C-130. The patrol will cut down telegraph poles and trees along a dual carriageway with chainsaws and test the road surface using a special machine. Meanwhile, the C-130 will go back out to sea and circle until getting the all-clear. Then it will come in low to avoid radar, dropping into a black hole without lights. As it touches down the rear ramp will open and the motorbikes and Land Rovers drive out.

Because of my freefall experience, I get chosen as part of the advance patrol, although some eyebrows are raised by the decision because I'm so new and I don't have any additional skills like being a medic or knowing signals or demolitions. I sit quietly in the background.

The meteorological charts indicate that winds in the target area average about 40 mph at this time of year. That's why there are six men on the patrol – they don't expect everyone to get down in one piece, and you only need four men to set up an LZ (landing zone).

They want to close down Ascension airfield so we can practise the drop. A C-130 is going to fly in very low, pop up to its maximum height beneath the radar and we'll jump off the back of the tailgate at 600 feet.

I don't think anyone in Air Troop has ever jumped from so low, and I doubt if they have the experience to stay stable and open the rip-cord the instant they exit the aircraft. Most military freefall training provides just enough experience to get people out of a plane, fall, open the parachute and land fairly accurately. It doesn't guarantee a stable exit. From 600 feet, unless you pull immediately, the chute might not open in time. It's a real bottle job.

I've done a couple of thousand jumps, whereas most of these blokes have a few hundred, but I keep my mouth shut because I'm the new boy.

We're in the general accommodation room of the barracks, and there are maps and satellite photographs spread across tables and pinned to the walls.

Bertie Buchan, the RAF dispatcher, wants to shut the airfield and do a trial run.

'With or without equipment?' asks John F., the troop sergeant. 'Are we gonna carry all the kit – the chainsaws and road-testing machine?'

'Why not? It has to be realistic.'

John isn't happy. 'Are you sure the Hercs can't give us any more height?'

Bertie is adamant. 'Six hundred feet tops.'

John turns to me. 'You've said nothing, Tom. What do you think about it?'

The faces of Air Troop focus on mine and I feel myself redden a little. I've only been in the SAS less than a week.

'Well, I don't believe in practising something you can only fuck up once.'

There are nods of agreement. 'If you want to see how long it takes for the parachutes to open then let's get out at 3,000 feet and see if we can get off the tail and open our chutes straight away. That way we don't lose anyone if they make a mistake.'

Although I didn't voice all my concerns, I knew that the slipstream is often so violent on exit that people flip over and go unstable. Normally they have the height to sort themselves out before they pull, but from 600 feet they wouldn't have the luxury. At the same time, it's extremely dangerous to pull a square parachute from an unstable position because it can cause a malfunction.

From now on, my advice is sought on all freefall aspects of the operation. I keep stressing to the patrol not to become obsessed about sorting out their body position before pulling their rip-cord. 'Stand on the ramp, facing in, with one hand on the rip-cord. As soon as you step off, you dump. It won't make for the most comfortable of openings, but at least you should deploy okay.'

Discussing the details with John, I suggest that we might give ourselves more chance if the Herc runs in a bit faster. 'Instead of slowing down for the jump, it could come in at 120 knots. Because of the blow back, you'll find the parachutes will actually open more positively.'

Apart from the various troop briefings, we have larger squadron meetings to discuss the full operation. The initial patrol will set up the LZ on the dual carriageway, allowing the RAF pilots to bring in the C-130s.

The squadron will then brass-neck it, driving straight along the main road on motorbikes and in right-hand-drive Land Rovers. I like the audacity of that. Our intelligence lads have interviewed a Canadian who used to work at Rio Grande airfield. He's given us details of the layout and the location of the local military base. There are two guards on the security gate and Des has been assigned to take out one of them, while Harry McCallion takes care of the other.

The open-top Land Rovers have mounted machine-guns as well as Browning 30s and a handful of M-202s – American-made white phosphorous grenade-launchers that look like something out of a James Bond movie. They're only as long as a shotgun, but they have multi-barrels and when you squeeze the trigger there's a gentle explosion and a wall of flame. It can destroy an aircraft in seconds.

At H-hour we'll pour through the front gate and spread out, splitting into smaller groups and hitting different targets. One patrol will take out the control tower, another will blow the fuel tanks and a third will attack the accommodation bunkers and try to kill the pilots. My Land Rover is to head for the aircraft hangars and use the M-202 to destroy the Super Etendards.

'Okay, you're probably wondering what the enemy will be up to while we're doing all this,' says Ian C., the new OC of the squadron. 'Our intelligence says the airfield has a limited troop presence. About two miles away there's a military base with about 1,800 Marines. That's why one of the primary targets is the comms centre. Assuming these troops are alerted, hopefully by the time they get their shit together and weapons out of the armoury we'll have finished and gone.'

Discussion turns to our escape, but the options are limited. The nearest Task Force ship will be five hundred miles away, and the choppers on board have the fuel capacity to reach us but not get home again. This leaves us with a dash towards the Chilean border, forty miles away. Basically we'll have to drive as quickly as possible towards the border on one of two roads until we hit road-blocks or are compromised. After that, it may be a case of tabbing over the tundra.

'Take any vehicles you can get, but try not to kill any civilians,' says Ian C. 'Once you're across the border, surrender to the Chilean authorities.'

It's not much of an escape plan and Rhett, one of the older lads, pipes up, 'Boss, I think I should point out that I shouldn't be here, because I cheated on Combat Survival.' Everyone laughs.

Call it youthful enthusiasm, but I don't even contemplate failure. More experienced heads than mine are going to decide what's right. There are no escape maps or cover stories in case of capture. The Argies will doubtless seal off the roads and put up helicopter gunships. Once the element of surprise has gone, we'll be deep in hostile territory and vastly out-numbered.

Until the green light is given, we spend our time going on runs over Green Mountain and doing weapons training. I take the M-202 down to the beach, loading up the barrels and firing it at various rocks. A lot of the lads want to have a go because it's a new weapon. On another day, I go fishing with Charlie and we catch enough red snapper for a squadron barbecue.

A week later, the operation is confirmed. We leave in twelve hours. The compo boxes are opened and we sort out rations and ammunition. I'm jumping with the minimum of kit, just a chainsaw. The rest of my gear is in one of the Land Rovers.

After packing everything away and writing letters home, we get word of a hold-up. Twenty-four hours later it's on again and then off again. This happens all week, and each morning B Squadron goes for a run, trying to work off the frustration. Apparently, there's disquiet in Downing Street about the predicted 60 per cent casualty rate of a mainland operation. Prime Minister Thatcher isn't happy with the odds. Equally, the RAF isn't thrilled about abandoning a burning aircraft and leaving the crews to tag along with us.

The mainland option seems to be falling apart when, on 8 June, the *Sir Galahad* and *Sir Tristram*, both British transport ships, are hit by Argentinian Skyhawks and Mirages in Bluff Cove. The ships are torched and dozens of soldiers die, most of them Welsh Guards. Some of the injuries are truly horrific. Suddenly, the mainland operation is back on again. We are due to leave on a flight at 0700. I'm in the baggage party, humping all the gear into the cargo hold in the pre-dawn cold. The sky is growing light but I'm sweating. A lot of the younger lads like me are raring to go, but the older blokes are more circumspect. Maybe their instincts for self-preservation are more acute.

A Land Rover arrives beside the aircraft and the news is broken – the operation has been cancelled. Apparently, a British newspaper had published a story saying that an SAS squadron based on Ascension Island were practising for a mainland operation. Within hours the Argentinians had started moving their planes away from the airfields and scattering them about the countryside, parked under camouflage nets. The chance of striking a blow against the Super Etendards had been lost.

I feel gutted. For the first time I question whether I should have joined the SAS. Two Para had covered itself in glory during the battle for Goose Green on the Falklands, and my old platoon, Mortars, had played a crucial role. A number of the lads went down with broken bones in their feet from standing on mortar-base plates that couldn't be bedded properly because of the frozen ground.

The sense of anti-climax is enormous, but it quickly dissipates two days later when we get word that B Squadron is to lead an assault on Port Stanley airport. The war is reaching a climax, and by taking the airfield we tighten the noose and prevent the Argentinians from sending in fresh troops.

Ian C. breaks the news, looking like the cat who's swallowed the cream. 'We leave at 0600 hours tomorrow, 11 June, and will be parachuting into the ocean to rendezvous with the Task Force. The actual assault will be a helicopter insert.'

The airfield is on a peninsula to the east of Stanley. Initially, they consider landing a C-130 on the runway because we've been practising such a manoeuvre, but RAF bombers have peppered the area and intelligence reports indicate the runway is cratered. Later we discover the Argies have very cleverly emptied bags of sand on the runway to make it look damaged. Even so, there are hundreds of troops on either side, and a direct assault would be foolhardy.

Next morning, two C-130s carrying B Squadron leave Ascension for the Task Force flotilla in the South Atlantic. There's a huge fuel bladder right behind the cockpit running half-way down each of the planes. I'm sitting right on top of one, puffing away and dropping my cigarette ash into a cup of water. Our RAF dispatcher, Doomwatch Des – so-called because he's always flapping about things going wrong – has a fit about me smoking.

During mid-flight refuelling the pipe from our Victor tanker is shredded and fuel sprays wildly across the windshield. There isn't enough fuel for both Hercs to make it to the Task Force and then back to Ascension, so one will have to turn back immediately. Because we are deemed to be carrying more specialist equipment, we get the extra fuel and continue on. Harry is among those on the other C-130, and they finish up spending nearly forty hours on an aeroplane. They go back to Ascension, change their kit and take off again.

Meanwhile, we reach the convoy and quickly prepare for a static-line jump from 1,000 feet, directly off the ramp. Whitecaps stretch from horizon to horizon. My dry suit will give me about five minutes in the freezing water before I lose consciousness. It has a hood and feet, but no hands. I stuff my training shoes inside my leggings because the rest of my kit is already bundled and packed into huge boxes to be dropped after us.

There are twenty-one of us on board, and seven jump on each pass because there are a limited number of inflatable boats to pick us up and ferry us to the warships. Timing is crucial, because three ships have manoeuvred into a U-shape to act as a landing zone. The C-130 flies up through the middle and the green light flashes on. Another seven blokes go off the ramp. As I hook up my static line, Doomwatch Des is busy looking out the window, with his eyes bigger than portholes. He doesn't want to be here. Reports of enemy aircraft in the area have him totally spooked.

On the ramp, I can see lads in the water and inflatable boats moving towards them. The pilot doesn't want to make another pass because he's worried he won't have enough fuel to get back to Ascension. Come on, don't lose your bottle now, I think, as the C-130 does a sharp turn and heads back towards the convoy.

Red light . . .

Green light . . .

Go!

The canopy swirls upwards and opens. Looking up, I make sure none of the lines are twisted and then ditch the reserve chute, gone for ever in the sea. The last man is drifting dangerously close to one of the ships and almost bounces off the stern, unable to steer the round parachute.

A few feet from the water, I hit the release box on my chest and jettison the chute. I break the surface and let the water slow me down as my body surges under. The cold slaps me in the face like a punch and I get the worst ice-cream headache imaginable. From a thousand feet, the swells hadn't looked too bad, but now they're huge. One minute I'm in the bottom of a valley and the next I'm on top of a hill. Entire ships are disappearing in the troughs. Full credit to the marine coxswains, banging around in their dinghies – they surf off swells and risk capsizing to get to us within a few minutes. I feel the cold leaking through the suit and see the boat bouncing over the wash. Strong hands reach out and pull me on board.

The aircraft makes a final pass and drops the equipment. The boxes, wrapped in cargo nets, burst open on impact and the contents spill out. The seas are now so rough the navy won't risk sending the inflatables back out. Instead, they try using helicopters to winch boxes on board, but only manage to save a few.

As I climb the side nets on to the *Andromeda*, someone wraps a blanket around my shoulders. I turn to see my bergen, rifle and webbing flop through the side of a net and sink to the bottom. Everything I'd personalised, my letters from Chris, a painting that Jason had sent me . . . all of it gone.

Taken down below, I have a shower, a scoff and then head for the Warrant Officers' Mess for a beer. The assault on Port Stanley airport has been overtaken by events. The land forces are within striking distance of the capital, so we are to relieve D Squadron patrols in the West Falklands. We'll be choppered in within twenty-four hours to mop up isolated pockets of resistance and set up OPs (observation posts) to guard against any Argentinian attempt to retake the island.

Overnight we sail inside the 200-mile limit, and early the next morning, I cross-deck to the troop-carrier *Lancelot*, which is moored within sight of land. Some of the D Squadron lads are on board. I envy them. Colonel Mike Rose, the Regiment's commanding officer, gives us an update on the land campaign. He's an impressive man, well-respected by his troops.

Afterwards Bedlam and I are told to borrow a rifle and kit. We're being choppered to the West Falklands to go on patrol with two members of D Squadron. Soon I'm on deck waiting for the chopper, with cam cream on my face and the adrenalin starting to pump. The ship's tannoy suddenly crackles and buzzes. The broadcast competes with the howling wind, but the message is unmistakable: white flags have been seen over Port Stanley.

'That's the story of my fucking life,' I say out loud, and Dr Oz looks up from his desk. 'I get so close to things and then at the last minute, something happens . . .'

'Sorry? What was that?'

'Nothing.'

'So, Tom, are you going to tell me about the Falklands?'

'Well, I wasn't really there.'

'Did you lose any mates?'

'Don't you get tired of asking questions?'

What makes someone become a psychologist? I wonder. Most people have enough trouble keeping their own heads in order without living inside someone else's. There are some things you don't want to know about human nature because if you did, you might not like people any more.

'Did you get on to the Falklands?'

He's persistent, I'll give him that. Drifting back again, I remember hitching a ride on a chopper with Charlie and Bedlam, flying to Stanley to catch up with some old mates in the Parachute Regiment. Over a brew, Pip and Skelly tell me about Goose Green and start moaning about the Marines trying to claim they were the first into Stanley . . .

The Parachute Regiment had virtually led the attack every step of the way and, quite rightly, had been first into Port Stanley after a lot of fierce fighting. Yet the previous day everyone with a red beret had been told to get off the streets. Then a helicopter came in carrying senior-ranking Royal Marines who landed near Government House. The Para flag was taken down and the Marines were all photographed beneath their own flag, posing with machine-gun belts slung around their necks and blackened faces. They couldn't handle someone else getting the glory.

I go for a walk through town and there's debris all over the place – guns, clothing, webbing, helmets, magazines, compo tins, boxes – all abandoned when the Argies fled. There are POWs being shepherded in clean-up detachments, and they look terrified because their own propaganda machine had told them that the British torture and shoot prisoners.

A lot of them are young conscripts, but I can recognise a number of professional soldiers.

For the next few days, I hitch rides around the island, flying on choppers that are ferrying people and supplies. I walk up Wireless Ridge and Mount Tumbledown, where there are bodies still in the trenches and in places the ground is still smoking.

On the hospital ship *Uganda*, I catch up with Ned Kelly, who took a bullet in the stomach, and Chalkie White, a DS who terrified me in Depot Para. I hope to see Jim Coffey, but he's been evacuated to another ship.

As I walk through the crowded wards, I see Welsh Guardsmen wrapped up in plastic bags and Flammicine. They were on the *Sir Galahad* and now wouldn't be recognised by their own mothers. One of them is only about eighteen years old; he'd tried to commit suicide in hospital by cutting his own throat because he's so badly burned.

A week after the surrender, a couple of lads from D Squadron, Kiwi and Karl, suggest we do a jump.

'What have you got in mind?'

'Well, we have the rigs from the mainland operation, why not use them? We can give the lads a show at San Carlos Bay.'

Twenty minutes later we hitch a ride on a helicopter that is taking a dozen officers to the *Uganda*. It takes us up to 8,000 feet on a spectacular day with sunshine hitting Sussex Mountain and the ships in the bay.

The pilot gives me the thumbs-up and out we go, exiting upside-down and falling with our backs towards the sea. We link legs and then lean out, dropping fast in a formation known as a 'Horny Gorilla'. After forty seconds in freefall, we break and open the chutes, coming in to land on the cliff-tops overlooking the bay.

A day later I'm on my way home, feeling quite fragile after a wild party on the MV *Norland* with 2 Para and 3 Para. Our C-130 arrives at Brize Norton in the dead of night and there's no big welcome. The buses and Land Rovers drop us at Hereford and I dump my kit and head home. It's four in the morning and Chris and Jason are asleep. I don't have a key so I sit on the steps, smoking a cigarette, not wanting to wake them just yet.

*

I can hear Dr Friedman's voice from down the corridor. He's come to visit me again, all the way from Harley Street. He's such an arrogant bastard. He parks his Mercedes on double yellow lines on the narrow road outside, with two wheels up on the kerb. It means that mothers with prams have to wheel them on to the road to get past. From my window I can gob on to his windscreen. I wonder if he knows who's doing it.

Listen to him! He talks to people as he's walking away from them and treats the nurses like minions. 'Harley Street' gets mentioned in every second sentence. 'Traffic was absolutely awful. It's taken me forty minutes to get from Harley Street,' or, 'Sorry, I can't take appointments, I left my diary in Harley Street . . . blah, blah, blah.'

I lean out the window and gob on his car again.

'Good morning, Mr Read, how are we feeling today?'

'Drugged to the eyeballs.'

He doesn't look at me. I could have said I was Peter Pan and he wouldn't raise an eyebrow. In and out, sign the chart, collect another £200.

Then, as if reading my mind, he sits in a chair. 'Is there anything you want to ask me about?'

'Are you sure these drugs are working?'

'It will take at least a year, Mr Read.'

'A year! I'm not waiting a year. Do something! Find some other drug. I can't wait a year to get better.'

'I'm sorry, but there is no instant cure.'

The news is a shock to me. A year? I know the drugs are starting to tone things down. The paranoia hasn't totally gone, but I've stopped believing in friendly forces and opposition forces. I accept that I'm ill and what I did to Anna was wrong. I trust the doctors to make me better, but these drugs are a nightmare. The new one makes my mouth fill up with water as if I'm about to vomit. I'm dribbling everywhere and my hands are shaking uncontrollably. I've started to look like a proper loony.

'Isn't there something you can give me that doesn't make me twitch and dribble?'

Friedman tries to explain how individuals react differently to certain drugs. Some people require higher doses than others – not necessarily because they are sicker, but because they may be poor absorbers of drugs and very little gets into their bloodstream. Other people may need lower doses because the drug accumulates quickly in their bloodstream and can be toxic if it becomes too concentrated.

'By starting and stopping drugs slowly, the side-effects can be reduced,' says Friedman. 'We can also use other drugs to balance any unwanted effects.'

'When can I go home?' I ask.

Friedman doesn't look up from my file. 'We'll give you a new jab now and wait a couple of days and see if there is any adverse reaction.'

'Then can I go home?'

'When we've sorted out the drugs and they settle down a bit more.'

'When will that be?'

He shrugs. 'Hopefully, in a day or two.'

That's what he said last time. He's always shifting the goalposts. Just when I'm all psyched up to leave he'll say, 'Now we'll just try you on this and wait a few days to see if there's a reaction.'

I think he's dragging things out unnecessarily, shuffling the drugs and dosages because he's not sure what's wrong with me. There he goes, disappearing down the corridor in his shiny black shoes and classic tailored suit. What a deeply depressing man.

When I tell Dr Oz about what happened, he invites me to one of the group therapy sessions.

'No, I don't think so. It's just not me.'

'Come on, just try it once. There's no pressure.'

I keep thinking of the joke about how many psychologists it takes to change a light-bulb –only one, but the light-bulb has to really *want* to change.

At two o'clock I go upstairs and find about half a dozen people sitting in a semi-circle with a doctor in the middle. It looks like a firearms lesson, but a lot of these patients have been 'shooting' something else. The whole clinic is full or coke-heads and smack addicts with wealthy parents.

'Sit down, sit down, welcome,' says the doctor, gushing.

I pull up a chair and sit just outside the semi-circle.

'We have someone new, everyone. Let's give him a big welcome. Would you like to introduce yourself?'

'Tom.'

'Hello, Tom, I'm Barry. Everyone say hello to Tom.'

They go around the group, each person uttering his or her name with varying degrees of enthusiasm.

'Eugene.'

'Daphne.'

'Cecil.'

'Marcus.'

'Hugo.'

They sound like the cast of an Oscar Wilde play, with posh accents and an attitude that the world belongs to them.

'We were just talking to Daphne about why she feels so angry,' says the counsellor. 'Go on, Daphne . . .'

She's wearing hippy clothes and multi-coloured bangles. I listen to her moaning about how Daddy had threatened to cut off her allowance when she ran away to India and how her boyfriend Toby had left her stranded in Goa and run off with some American girl who bought Indian silks.

'I hope he dies of some *horrible* disease,' she says tearfully.

Cecil is picking at his toenails with a matchstick. 'You're such a silly tart!'

Marcus leaps to her defence. 'Listen here, it's not easy living without your allowance.' They're glaring at each other and posturing.

'I went to Goa once,' says Hugo, who's somewhere over the rainbow.

I know exactly what Des would say if he were here. He'd say they all suffer from NBPE (not being punched enough). The counsellor sees me blowing air through my cheeks. 'Tom, is there something you want to comment upon?'

My chair scrapes back. 'Look, I don't think I can add to this discussion. Perhaps it's better if you continue without me and I'll just wander off.'

Later, I get talking to a couple of the hoorays in the drug rehab programme. They actually seem to enjoy it here. They come to the Charter Clinic every year to dry out, treating it like an upmarket health farm where they can catch up with old friends. 'See you again next year, Jasper!' 'Ciao, Humphrey!'

Jimmy is the only sane person in this joint. He's a little bloke just down the hall who's famous for being the 'Birdman from Berkeley Square'. They brought him in a few days ago, whistling and garbling like a bird. God, he stank! They had a fearful time getting him out of his clothes and shampooing his hair.

Jimmy is a tramp who feeds the pigeons and sleeps rough in doorways or on park benches. The police picked him up for shouting obscenities in the street, and he finished up in Charter Clinic because there wasn't any room in an NHS hospital. He's clean now, but he doesn't like it here at all. He won't talk to anyone except me, and even then he doesn't say much.

He's Irish and about fifty years of age, although he looks a lot older. Twenty years he's been sleeping in Berkeley Square, which is a pretty salubrious address to have. He cleans up the litter and is a one-man neighbourhood-watch scheme, but the residents don't like him because he's an eyesore and attracts the birds. I guess there's a law against being ugly in some places, and that's why he's in here.

We play chess in the canteen every day, which isn't very successful. For one thing, we're both on chlorpromazine which means we look like a pair of dribbling idiots whose hands are shaking so much that each time we make a move the pieces go flying. There goes the bishop and black knight, bouncing across the tiles.

'Whose move is it, Jimmy?'

He shrugs.

'Okay, I forgot, so you have a move.'

Jimmy takes a rook off the board and shoves it into the pocket of his dressing-gown.

'Jimmy, you're cheating.'

He opens the palms of his hands as if to say, 'Who, me?'

This is ridiculous, we haven't finished a single game!

I try to explain the rules, which is pretty silly when you think Jimmy has never abided by rules. Later I buy him a little computerised chess set so he can practise.

Chris and Jason are coming up to visit me again today. I don't want Jason to see me looking like a dribbling invalid – not in this place. 'I was sort of hoping I might see him outside,' I say to Liz, an Australian nurse.

'You really shouldn't leave . . .'

'I know, I know, but we could go to the pub over the road, the Chelsea Potter. It's only a few yards away.'

'I don't think the doctors will let you out by yourself.'

'But I won't be by myself. My ex-wife will be there, and Jackie.'

Liz goes to speak to the senior nurse and comes back with a compromise plan. I can go to the pub, but only with a male nurse as a chaperon and only if I agree not to drink alcohol. My minder is a black guy carrying too much weight, but he has one of those jolly smiles you often associate with fat people.

I've been staring at the Chelsea Potter for so long that it's quite odd walking inside. It's not a big pub, but the large clear-glass windows make it seem larger, and you can sit inside and watch the Number 22 bus go backwards and forwards along the King's Road.

There are heavy drapes framing the windows and wooden panels on the walls. The floorboards have gone dark over the years and seem to soak up the light. Propped against the bar is a blackboard announcing the 'Specials', which include the ubiquitous pub favourites Chilli con Carne and Vegetarian Bake.

I'm still eating like a horse, so we order meals and I get a round of drinks. Chris has her usual gin and tonic, Jason a soft drink, Jackie a beer and I order a bottle of alcohol-free beer which tastes like water.

Next round, I pull the Aussie barman to one side. 'Listen, nobody's drinking alcohol-free beer except me, mate, so if anyone from our table orders a round, I want you to fill this bottle from the lager tap.'

'In there?' he says, pointing at my bottle.

'Yeah. It's our little secret.'

He gives me an odd look and glances at our table. The male nurse is sitting with his arms folded, keeping one eye on me. 'Are you from over the road?'

'Yeah, a fully fledged loony.'

He grins. 'Okay, mate, whatever you want.'

From then on, I get full-strength beer in an alcohol-free 'package', and my new Aussie friend keeps the bottle behind the bar so I can use it whenever I come over.

Jason asks me what will happen with the Skydive from Space project.

'It's on hold for the moment.'

'So you're still going to do it?'

'We'll see what happens.'

The truth is I don't have a clue what's happening. Harry and Jackie keep telling me it's on hold. Loel Guinness has already spent a small fortune, but a lot depends on sponsorship and marketing, which hasn't started yet.

'Maybe we can take another holiday together, Jase,' I say. 'How would you like to go back to Spain?'

'Only if you take me freefalling.'

'Not a chance,' says Chris.

I try to take Jason on a holiday every year, and during training for the Skydive from Space in Spain, I took him on a tandem freefall when he was about thirteen years old. The jump was captured on film, and Chris had no idea until Jason got home to England and showed her the video. She always said I was irresponsible, and that just confirmed it for her.

'Maybe we should just go fishing, Dad,' he suggests diplomatically.

'Remember when you caught that pike?'

'Sure.'

Jason had been just a lad, and I'd taken him fishing down to the River Wye. He was forever getting his line tangled up in the overhead branches or reeds, and I'd let him hold my rod while I untangled the line or baited his hook. His line was dangling only about a foot from the river-bank when I noticed the float had disappeared. 'Go and sort it out,' I suggested.

As he picked up the rod it started to bend. I thought it had snagged on the reeds, but suddenly the line took off, screaming through the reel. I dropped everything, ready to grab Jason and stop him being pulled into the river.

'Reel it in,' I said, 'but if it wants to run, give it some line.'

It took a long while to land the fish – a bloody great pike that came up to Jason's chest. We'd been letting the other fish go, but this one had swallowed the hook so badly, it couldn't be saved. We carried it home and ate fish for a week.

8

The rules have been relaxed a little since my outing to the Chelsea Potter – a chaperon is no longer required – and I'm getting quite good at finding excuses to nip across the road whenever I have a visitor. Schwepsy is a regular. I tell Liz I'll be gone for fifteen minutes and wander back three hours later.

'No alcohol,' she says sternly.

'Who, me?'

My Aussie barman is still filling up the same bottle, although the label is getting a bit tatty. 'Man's got to have a drink,' I tell him, 'otherwise he'd go mad.'

I still get edgy if I'm inside too long, and occasionally I take a walk around the block or wander along King's Road towards Sloane Square, past all the trendy shops and outdoor cafés. Music videos are playing inside and the window displays have so much chrome and glass, I don't know what they're selling. There are leather shops with SALE signs permanently stuck to the windows. My favourite place is a shoe-shop called 'R. Soles'.

I walk past Wellington Square and Royal Avenue, where all the tourists are eating lunch under the trees. Occasionally, I stop at a nearby Territorial Army unit. Saddlebags is a Permanent Staff Instructor there, and we have a cup of tea in his office upstairs.

It's nice to get out and stretch my legs, but as soon as I turn the corner and lose sight of the clinic, I get nervous. That's why I won't take any longer excursions into the West End. It's ironic, isn't it? I desperately want to get away from this place, but I get scared when I'm outside. I watch the faces of people in the street and I wonder if they know what I've done; does it show on my face? Is madness like a badge?

Today, I thought I might go as far as Knightsbridge, but as I reach an intersection near Sloane Square, I almost lock up in fear. I stand on the kerb, afraid to step off. There are no cars coming, but everything around me is moving so fast and the noise . . . Where am I? So much noise and movement – the pedestrians, the car horns, the laughter, the footsteps, coffee cups clattering in saucers. I'm too scared to cross the road. For Christ's sake, I'm thirty-seven years old! What's happening to me?

I look left and right – the street is empty. Still I can't bring myself to step off the kerb. I wait, breathing deeply. Here comes someone. I shuffle out as they walk past, tucking myself in beside them as they cross the road.

It has to be the drugs. I'm a dribbling wreck, afraid of strangers, unable to cross a road, restlessly pacing the corridors and dreaming of home. I have to get out of here.

*

Air Troop, B Squadron, are called 'the Sun Gods' or 'the Ice-cream Boys' because we always seem to go where the sun is shining. While we train in some exotic location like Cyprus or Texas, Mountain Troop are clinging to an icy rock-face in North Wales, Boat Troop are deep-diving off the south coast of England, and Mobility Troop are up to their armpits in axle grease and engine oil.

And while the others have to carry truck-loads of equipment and spend hours on preparation, we don't even pack our own chutes. The RAF controls military parachuting and they do it for us. We even get put up in hotels occasionally and given a bit of extra cash, because that's the treatment given to air crews and jump-masters.

I've been all over the place this last year, training in Germany and Cyprus and doing skills courses like signals and demolitions. Air Troop is on a squadron training exercise in Oman, and we have a new troop commander. I can't believe who it is – Captain Puttee, the Irish Guardsman who was with me on Combat Survival. Apparently he got a taste for the Regiment and decided to tackle all of Selection. He doesn't wear puttees any more so I've changed his nickname to 'Dunderhead' because he's so accident-prone. He busts his foot on one of our first jumps and I put him on the back of a motorbike and ferry him to the hospital in Muscat, about an hour away. It's quite a modern place but the emergency room is packed with people, many of them sitting on the floor and in the corridors.

'There's nothing wrong with half of them,' says the doctor. 'The Arabs love their medical attention.'

Dunderhead is taken straight into the X-ray room and his foot is put into plaster. Meanwhile, I'm waiting outside when another doctor appears and says, 'Are you here to give blood?'

'No, what makes you think that?'

He points to the sign above my head, which says 'BLOOD DONORS'.

'Sorry, I'm waiting for a friend.'

'Listen, since you're waiting, why don't you give some blood?'

'Do I get a cup of tea and biscuits?'

'No, but you get eighty rials.'

'Bloody hell, that's about thirty quid. How many pints do you need?' I roll up my sleeve.

As I'm chatting to the doctor, he asks what I'm doing in Oman. 'Would there be any more lads willing to give blood?' he says.

'On our salary, I'd say that's a certainty.'

He gives me his phone number and I pick up Dunderhead, who moans every time I hit a bump on the ride back to camp. At the squadron briefing that night, the major asks if anyone has anything they'd like to add, and I put my hand up. I mention the hospital and giving blood.

The air resounds with a chorus of 'Fuck off, Big Nose', 'Who do you think you are, Florence bloody Nightingale?' and suchlike.

'Hang on, hang on – not so fast. They pay thirty quid a pint.'

That shuts them up.

Next morning I ring the doctor. 'I've got thirty volunteers.'

We make an appointment and a few days later, two truck-loads of lads head off to Muscat. Schwepsy is among them but he's already flapping because he hates needles. Prior to going to Belize during Selection, he fainted during the inoculations.

At the hospital we form a queue, but Schwepsy keeps moving further and further back. Every time someone comes out of the donation room, he asks, 'What was it like?'

'Fucking awful,' says Bedlam. 'You should have seen the size of the needle.'

Schwepsy is turning different shades of white and green and getting nearer and nearer the back of the queue.

Finally I ask him, 'Why do it? Is it worth it?'

'I might be a coward, but I'm a greedy coward,' he says, forcing himself to go inside.

Dunderhead takes the brunt of our practical jokes because Air Troop hasn't had an officer for four or five years, and it's traditional to target the rupert even if he's a nice bloke. One time during squadron training in the Middle East we get him good and proper.

We'd set up a tented camp on the shores of the Red Sea, and, as usual, one of the first things we do is dig a big hole known as the shit-pit. The thunderbox goes on top of this pit, which even has a toilet seat. To seal it properly, we pack sandbags around the base and then erect a hessian wall for privacy, held up with sticks and several guy ropes.

Every morning Dunderhead pokes his head out of his tent and then strides up to the thunderbox wearing his very rupert-like pyjamas and army boots. The opportunity for mischief is too much for me. I tape four thunderflashes together which simulate the sound of a hand grenade and then wire up a shrike (detonator).

'Where are you going to put them?' asks Roy T., the squadron sergeant-major.

'What about straight down the shit-pit?'

'No, you can't do that. You might kill him. It'll be like a gun barrel.'

He's right. With all that methane gas down there, channelling through smaller and smaller holes, I'll blow him to kingdom come. Instead I put the flashes behind the thunderbox, hidden by sandbags, and then run the wire down to our makeshift weight-training area, which has an old Land Rover axle as the weight bar.

Soon the whole squadron is in on the joke, and they start arriving the next morning with cameras to record the big event. In typically rupert-like fashion, however, Dunderhead disappoints by choosing not to go for his morning constitutional.

'Do you think he's sussed it?' I ask Tiny.

'Nah. He just needs his bran.'

After three days of no-shows, I'm beginning to wonder if Dunderhead does actually go for 'number twos'. We've got him under surveillance to make sure he isn't sneaking out during the middle of the night. On the fourth morning, he emerges from his tent with a book tucked under one arm and heads for the thunderbox.

In the weight-training area, Lou L. is pretending to be pumping iron, ready to give the signal when Dunderhead is sitting in his most exposed position. At the same time, the pegs have been loosened on the hessian privacy screen and the guy lines are hooked up with string. One pull and the wall will come down.

Lou gives me the thumbs up, I hit the button and Chris pulls the string.

Dunderhead is just reaching forward for the toilet paper hanging on the hessian wall when he grasps at thin air. An orange fireball frames him against the backdrop of the Red Sea. The noise is astonishing, and for a split-second my heart stops – I think I've killed him.

Then I hear him shouting, 'For God's sake, somebody put the screen up!'

His pyjamas are smoking and his hair is standing on end, but the upper lip is as stiff as ever.

I like demolitions; it must be the little boy in me who likes to blow things up. It's a two-month course and we spend a lot of time in the classroom studying the theory before they let us handle explosives in the field. Then we learn how to create bombs that can do specific tasks, such as felling trees in the jungle for a landing zone, or blowing up railway lines and bridges. We're also taught how to manufacture home-made explosives out of general household items.

Bomb-making is only one aspect of demolitions. The aim is to cause maximum damage with the minimum amount of explosives, which means targeting the key components. It might be a fuse-box in a factory or a certain component of an engine which will cause it to be immobilised very quickly.

In the Middle East the squadron is practising an A-type ambush, an SAS speciality, which means rigging up a line of 81mm mortar shells, linked together with det cord, and setting them up alongside a track. A triggering wire is run a distance away behind cover. When set off, the booby trap blows a 360° frag, sending lethal shards of metal flying through the air and cutting down the enemy.

Each troop has a turn setting up the ambush and running the wire down to the main charge. But every time it blows, about twenty feet of wire disappears. By the time Boat Troop has a turn, the wire is getting very short. Harry McCallion is setting it up – he's a real hard-case who used to be in 2 Para mortars and then joined the South African Special Forces because it offered more opportunities to kill people. Although he got a lot of this out of his system in the Rhodesian independence wars, McCallion's special interest still lies in killing. His philosophy is that any organisation such as the IRA is dependent upon a handful of key personnel. They're the people he wants to kill.

Having set up the A-type ambush, McCallion lies down behind a little hill. The wire is now so short that he can't get far enough away to find proper cover, and he doesn't realise one of his legs is unprotected. He hits the tip, the mortar line explodes and I hear his scream. A lump of metal has gone straight into his shin.

It's a rough ride back to camp in a Land Rover, and McCallion is totally delirious on morphine when he gets to the field doctor. All of us have come to watch because McCallion isn't the most popular man in the squadron, and we want to see him in pain.

Mick is holding a drip and the rest of us help lift him on to a table that is still littered with bacon rinds from breakfast.

'Could you remove his socks?' the doctors asks Johnno.

We look at each other. Apart from having a big thing about people touching him and his 'personal space', McCallion is notorious for his poor hygiene. In Northern Ireland he would dry his gym kit in the sauna and throw his toenail clippings on the hot stones. None of us would go in there.

The doctor is getting impatient. 'What's the matter?'

'I'm not touching him,' says Johnno.

'But this man is in pain.'

'This man is a psychopath.'

The doctor finally coaxes some co-operation out of us, and McCallion is evacuated to a hospital in the UK. Meanwhile, an Army Air Corps engineer who witnesses the incident writes a letter to his boss complaining about how McCallion had been treated. Harry laughs it off. As I said, he's a hard man.

Although Air Troop is considered to have the cushiest life in the squadron, there's little difference between ourselves and other troops. Specialist skills like freefalling, mountaineering or scuba-diving are only modes of infiltration; once we're on the ground the soldiering requires all the same training and discipline.

Jumping on squadron training we always begin afresh because a lot of the lads haven't jumped since the last trip. We start off at 12,000 feet and work our way up to 25,000 feet, where we have to use oxygen. The troop members have a mixed range of experience, and few have done a great deal of relative work. I start coaching them because it's important for a four-man patrol to stay together, and if they can link up in the air it ensures they will land near each other.

Jumping in full kit with a heavy bergen strapped to your backside is a lot more difficult than a normal freefall, because the weight tends to make the body sit up and restrict leg movements. Even so, relative work is still possible with some practice.

It's actually far safer to carry equipment on the front, because it helps you fall face to Earth and gives you a lower centre of gravity, but the RAF packs the kits and they're slow to change. They use methods and tactics that civilian parachuting bodies have banned years ago because they're unsafe.

Their latest toy is a device that is designed to drop heavier equipment with a freefall team. It's a large cardboard box that is thrown out of the aircraft with a parachute attached, and has an AOD (automatic opening device) set for a specific height. It's a pain in the arse because we can't do any relative work or have any fun; instead we have to get near this thing and follow it down as it skids all over the Middle Eastern sky.

After four jumps I've had enough, but the RAF rupert wants us to go up again.

'What's actually in the box?' I ask him.

'For training purposes it's full of sand and rubbish,' he says disdainfully.

The AOD is armed by a small red knob known as a 'cherry', which is inserted into the height-finder. Once it is removed, the device is activated.

When jumping with a bergen we all carry AODs and only remove the cherry at altitude because the height-finders are controlled by barometric pressure. If it's set for 3,000 feet and I pulled the cherry at ground level, the parachute would open instantly.

Just before we jump, each of us pulls the cherry and holds it in the air for confirmation. Meanwhile the RAF jump-master pulls the cherry for the cardboard container and kicks it out of the plane. This time, instead of just trailing our 'cargo', I dock on it and use my cherry to disarm its AOD. The parachute doesn't open at 2,000 feet and the box hits the ground and smashes into pieces. I land a few feet away and quickly collect my cherry from the AOD before the RAF ground-crew arrives. They're scratching their heads, trying to work out why the mechanism failed, when the rupert arrives in his Land Rover.

'Out of my way, let me through,' he bellows.

He wants to hold a Farnborough-type inquest over the destruction of a cardboard box.

Meanwhile a handful of locals have appeared. They start picking through the remains of the box.

The rupert barks, 'Get them away from there! That's military property.'

'But it's rubbish,' I point out.

'It's evidence.' Just then, he puts down his briefcase and I automatically hand it to one of the urchins, whispering, 'Here you go!' He scampers off.

The rupert turns around. 'Where's my briefcase?'

'Actually, sir, I just saw one of those local lads running off with it.'

The last we see of the rupert is a cloud of dust from his Land Rover as he tears off into the desert pursuing his case.

I don't begrudge the locals anything they can scavenge or steal from us. Years of civil war have taken a heavy toll, and the poverty and hunger is inescapable. There's precious little food in the markets, as we discover when our cook seriously screws up our rations. In the first week we ate like kings – steak every night with all the trimmings. Unfortunately, by the second week we've run out of food. I take a Land Rover down to the local souk, looking for meat, and find the butchers trading in the open, with blood running down the gutters and a stench that makes the eyes water. Crows and desert vultures sit on poles waiting for scraps, and the animal carcasses appear to be black until I move closer and the flies rise like a dark puff of smoke.

'No fucking way am I eating that!' says Bedlam. 'As of now I'm officially a vegetarian.'

'I might join you, but we're not exactly spoilt for choice in that department either.'

The vegetable market had yielded a few beans and a large amount of aubergines. For the next week we eat aubergine fritters, aubergine omelettes, aubergine mash, aubergine surprise – anything the cook can invent. Mercifully, Boat Troop manages to catch some fish, but once their scuba tanks are empty there's no more diving.

By now we're quite weak with hunger, and activity is kept to a minimum for the final few days. The new boy in Air Troop, Al Slater, has a nap every afternoon, avoiding the sun because he's quite fair. I use a knife to make a little hole in his tent so the sunlight beams directly through on to his nose. Every ten minutes, I widen the hole a little more and use masking tape to seal it up after he wakes. Al can't work out why his nose is always sunburnt.

Al used to be an instructor down at Depot Para, and became one of the stars of a television documentary series called *The Paras*. By the time the show went to air, he'd joined the SAS and had to endure the embarrassment of seeing himself on TV every week and having the rest of us poke fun at him.

In one particular programme, the interviewer asked, 'What happens when the lads have done all this training?'

Al pondered this for a moment and, always well-spoken, said, 'Well, I suppose they just go down town and fill in a few crap-hats.'

Watching the scene on TV, Al buried his head in his hands, saying, 'Oh, no.'

Half our troop are crap-hats, including the troop sergeant. That evening during scoff, lads would wander past him, saying, 'Sorry, Al, you're not going to bash me just because I'm a crap-hat, are you?'

Our food problems seem to get worse, but limited training continues. The squadron has been asked to do some tests with microlights, to find out if they could be used in insertions. Apparently the Palestinians had recently used them for a terrorist attack against Israel. The Army Air Corps had taught four of us to fly the delta-winged microlights in England before we came out here, and our job is to decide if they have any operational value. Flying them is a real buzz, but is it possible to parachute from one?

I let Biggles, an Air Corps pilot, do the flying as we take off in a tandem microlight and climb to 2,000 feet. It's painfully slow, and every so often Biggles has to go into a shallow dive to let the engine cool. He drops down, gets a bit of speed and pulls up again. After twenty minutes we finally reach altitude and I climb out carefully, hanging over the side using an overgrip. The propeller is actually behind us and I want to make sure I clear it quickly.

Because of the weight shift, the microlight starts veering all over the place and Biggles is hollering, 'Let go! Let go!'

I drop away and see the aircraft swinging violently, with Biggles trying to regain control. I pull the rip-cord immediately and get down safely but Biggles isn't keen on doing it again. As far as he's concerned we've proved it can be done – mission accomplished.

Having the microlights gives me an idea – we could use one of them as a spotter plane for shoals of fish.

'But how are we going to catch them?' asks Andy M. from Boat Troop, who is better known as 'Tomato Splat'.

'We could blow them up!'

Putting our heads together, we thrash out a plan that involves lowering explosives into the water on det cord and attaching them to a branch sticking out of the water. I will be up above in a microlight, and when the fish are in range I'll signal on the radio.

'Aren't we going to need some sort of bait?' asks Hillbilly.

'Yeah, but I'm leaving that to Bateye. He says he has a plan.'

Everyone looks nervous. Bateye is a fanatical shark fisherman, and whenever we travel anywhere near the ocean he rigs up fifty-gallon drums with wire and bait, trying to catch a man-eater.

That night, I'm sleeping peacefully when a small explosion rips through the cookhouse. I roll over and go back to sleep. Next morning, Bateye turns up with a bucket of burly to attract the fish.

'What the hell is it?'

'Cat.'

'What?'

'There were these two strays who were hanging around the cookhouse, scrounging through the bins and driving the cook mad. I booby-trapped a bin and BOOM!' He tosses his hands in the air to illustrate the explosion.

I'm furious about it, but there's nothing I can do – the deed is done. Hillbilly and Tomato Splat set the explosives and start scooping out the burly and then clear out to a safe distance. I'm up above and I can see the fish moving closer.

'That'll do,' I say.

The explosion is muffled by the water and creates only a small cascade. About a minute later, fish start bobbing to the surface – dozens of them. The lads are scooping them into boats and Hillbilly dives down to get more from the bottom.

For the next few days we eat fish morning, noon and night. I swear I'll never touch another aubergine in my life.

Just before the final exercise, Air Troop is assigned to set up a strip landing in the capital, bringing in an RAF plane at night with four torches. It's more for the air crews to practise than for our benefit. Myself, Al Slater, John P. and Dunderhead are assigned to the task, and we get permission to use the main runway, which gets very little traffic at night.

Arriving at the airfield after dark, the white landing lights and blue taxi-way lights are already turned off. Because Al and Dunderhead have never set up an LZ, John P. puts me in charge of the exercise. Two minutes before the designated time, we set up the 1,000-yard LZ using infra-red torches that the pilot can see through his PNG goggles. The C-130 drops through the blackness and seems to be almost on top of me when I dive to one side. Suddenly all the aircraft lights come on. I hear the brakes squealing and the reverse thrust of the engines. The fuselage is sliding from left to right.

'What the hell!'

In the aircraft headlights I can see other aeroplanes. I've landed him on the taxi-way instead of the main runway. Somehow the pilot picked up shapes ahead of him in the darkness and realised something was wrong. Instead of having scope for overshoot on our landing strip, he has no room for mistakes. He wrestles with the controls and brings the aircraft to a stop as the wing tip almost brushes the local flying club.

A year later, I'm in Africa, setting up another strip, when I hear the RAF pilot say, 'Oh yeah, one of my mates was doing this last year and some fucking idiot landed him on the taxi-way.'

I shake my head, say, 'How brainless is that?' and slip away.

The final exercise is a full-scale camp attack. Air Troop is jumping in with full equipment from 25,000 feet at 0400 hours. The day before, we drive to the capital and stay with the RAF crews in the Hilton hotel, because like typical Biggles they like their creature comforts.

Straight down to the pool, we swim a few laps and monopolise the sun-loungers. It's just our luck that the country has outlawed alcohol and the hotel bars are all shuttered and locked. The police and navy are supposedly getting rid of all the booze by tipping it into the Nile, which is why you see a lot of pissed people in uniform. What a waste! I've been in the desert for six weeks and have started to dream beer commercials.

A British Airways crew is staying at the hotel, and we get chatting about the pitfalls of a dry Islamic state. It's amazing how the lack of alcohol takes away all the social life of a hotel, because everyone just has a meal and then retires to their room. During the conversation two stewardesses mention that their flight is leaving at the same time as ours the next morning. They're taking an empty Boeing 747 to Addis Ababa and then picking up passengers for the return leg to London.

'I'd rather be on your flight,' I tell them, feeling rather homesick at the sight of these pretty girls who'll be back in England within a few hours. 'I haven't seen a newspaper in six weeks.'

'Hey, listen!' says the pilot. 'We've got a load of stuff on the plane and we're flying the next leg empty. We can't take them off, but if you drop by we can give you newspapers, magazines, booze, all sorts of bits and pieces. You're welcome to it.'

Next morning, we load up the C-130 with bergens packed for the final exercise and then check our watches. We've got about fifteen minutes. Legging it from the military zone of the airport to the civilian side, Chris T. and I find the British Airways jet. The doors are open and the cabin is lit up. Inside the girls are sweeping up, but they recognise us immediately. They give us big plastic bags full of mini bottles of champagne, gin, scotch, bourbon, vodka – you name it. There are magazines, newspapers and packets of peanuts. We grab as many bags as we can carry and arrive back at the C-130, panting heavily.

'Where the fuck have you been?' asks Bertie Buchan. The engines are roaring and we've been given clearance to take off.

'Hang on, we can't go yet,' I say.

We start sharing the booze around between the troop to distribute the weight evenly in our bergens. Once we get back to camp, we'll share it with the squadron.

'If you're quite ready,' says Bertie, annoyed at the delay. He starts giving the briefing for the drop.

'Right, we're jumping from twenty-five thousand feet—'

'No, no, hang on, we can't do that,' I say.

'What's wrong now?'

'We can't go that high. The booze will bloody explode.' I have this image in my head of landing in the desert smelling like a distillery.

'It's supposed to be an oxygen jump,' he says, exasperated.

'Yeah, I know, but the booze!'

He glances from face to face and can see our look of expectancy. It's been a long time between drinks, and these are free. 'Okay, we do a simulated oxygen jump, wearing full equipment from twelve thousand feet. Are you lot happy with that?'

Grins all round.

Our bergens are loaded with booze as we touch down in the desert. We get picked up by Mobility Troop in Land Rovers. After the camp attack, we share the bottles out and toast British Airways. It's amazing how quickly you get pissed when you've been eating nothing but fish and aubergines.

*

A walk around the block takes me about ten minutes. I turn left out the door of the clinic and head down Radnor Walk, away from the Chelsea Potter and towards the Thames. Then I turn left into Tedworth Street and left again into Smith Street, which brings me back to King's Road. On the side-roads there are people walking their dogs and clipping their hedges. Some of them look up expectantly as I approach, wanting to smile and exchange 'hellos', but I keep my head down as if preoccupied with my own thoughts.

I don't want people to see me. I want to become grey and nondescript. I want to blend in with the background so completely that no one gives me a second glance. This is what they taught us in surveillance training in the Regiment.

When I first arrived at the clinic I overheard some of the cleaners talking in Irish accents. My paranoia hadn't totally disappeared, but I had some right to be concerned. When you've been in the SAS and worked in Northern Ireland you remain a possible target for the IRA.

The cleaners are harmless. I'm more scared of getting lost on my walks or having a panic attack. I don't want to meet anyone or discuss the weather. It's enough for me to get outside the door and back again. A hundred and eighty-five paces to Tedworth Street . . . turn left . . . one . . . two . . . three . . . four . . .

*

The surveillance course for the Regiment is run by the Intelligence Corps. It's nine to five every day, and afterwards, Hillbilly and I go out and practise. Normally, we choose someone and follow them, which is a difficult thing to do when you take into account third-party awareness. For example, when Customs and Excise do a drug operation, following a courier back from Amsterdam, they mustn't let the target see them. At the same time, however, they don't have to worry about a third party, like the granny standing by the side of the road, noticing them. It's different in Northern Ireland, because when you're watching or following a suspect, you have to be aware of the impression you're creating in the minds of by-standers and passers-by. One of them might be a 'dicker' – a look-out – or an IRA sympathiser, and they'll quickly tip off your target. That's third-party awareness.

Surveillance isn't about ducking into doorways and hiding behind newspapers. There's a science to it. Certain people are better at it than others, because they have learned how to blend into their surroundings and not be noticed by anyone. An attractive woman is useless because she stands out in a crowd. I have problems because I'm big and I have an unusual gait and stance.

So much depends upon what draws the eye to a particular person or scene. It might be a piece of clothing, or the way someone walks, or the speed at which they move. To identify these things about myself, I have to be totally objective and uninhibited. I study myself by watching other people. Take that girl over there. Does her walk attract attention? No, it's doing the job, just at the right pace. But her hair is pushed up high on her head, making her seem taller.

'Look at that group of people over there – which one of them stands out?' I ask Hillbilly.

'Him.'

'Why?'

'Because he's wearing that stupid orange anorak.'

'But that woman also stands out.'

'Yeah. Maybe it's the red lipstick. No, it's something else.'

We watch her a little longer, trying to pick what it is.

Movement is the biggest reason people attract attention. During camouflage and sniper training we learned the five key elements – shape, shine, shadow, silhouette and movement. All these things give you away, but 'movement' is the biggest one because it can be picked up by someone's peripheral vision, whereas the others are normally only picked up by someone focusing directly on you.

Hillbilly and I are sitting in a bar and we concentrate on how people enter. This is a nice bar, it could be our local, and it has a swing door which opens in or out. We notice some people come in by pulling the door towards them while others push it inwards. The first type tend to have more humility, as if they're saying, 'Is it all right if I come in?', while the second type, the pushers, enters with more confidence, as if they're saying, 'Okay, you lucky bastards, I've arrived.'

What does this teach us? Do we pull or push? This is about human nature and being aware of your environment. Oddly enough, there are many similarities between surveillance and tracking in the jungle. Again, it comes down to knowing your surroundings and being able to read the signs – which side of that leaf is crushed? See that mark on the tree; someone has propped a rifle here and the foresight touched the bark. It's probably an AK-47.

Air Troop has been in Ulster for about three weeks and it's been pretty boring, although I'm not supposed to say that because it's bad luck. The difference in being across the water with the Regiment rather than 2 Para is enormous. We only get summoned for special operations rather than doing routine patrols. We react to information and intelligence, making difficult arrests.

John P., the staff sergeant, calls us together for a briefing. Some of the lads are in the gym and others are watching TV. I'm fixing myself a snack.

We gather in the briefing room, pulling up chairs, while John sorts out the maps with Dunderhead. I sit down next to Al Slater, who I've nicknamed 'Mr Grumpy', and start snacking on my Marmite soldiers. Al is a big lad, six foot one, who only has to look at a cake to put on weight. It really pisses him off how I can eat anything and never put on an ounce.

'That's the one you pick your nose with,' he mutters as I lick my fingers.

'You know what your problem is, Al?' I say.

'Slow metabolism.'

'Nah. You dream about food while the rest of us dream about sex. It'll put on weight every time.'

John P. clears his throat. 'We believe that a very prominent UDR major – a well-known political and social figure in Northern Ireland and on the mainland – has been targeted for assassination by the Provisional IRA. His death would be a major victory for them.' He lets the statement sink in and continues: 'The information comes from the target himself, who has noticed suspicious cars following him to work. He varies his route occasionally and is quite sure he's being targeted. We don't know when the hit will take place, so we have to be ready within forty-eight hours. It's likely to happen on his way to work, so we're looking at a mobile arrest.'

Leaning forward, I rest my chin on my forearms. A mobile arrest is unusual and creates all sorts of complications. Generally, the SAS is used when the arrest is likely to be particularly difficult, and a mobile intercept has hundreds of different variables that can't be planned for or predicted.

John continues: 'There are six phases to the operation. Phase one – low-level protection at the home location; phase two – move to target area; phase three – on target; phase four – follow up; phase five – move out; and phase six – post-operative procedure.'

He looks up from his notes. 'The location is the area of Tamnamore and we're going to use a substitute. Al, how do you feel about being the target? You're the nearest lookalike.'

Al doesn't hesitate. 'Fine by me.'

'Good lad.'

'Shit job – need someone called Mr Grumpy to do it,' says Cyril, and everyone laughs. It's a tradition in Air Troop that the new boy gets blaggarded and given the worst tasks. In this case, none of us envies Al, because by pretending to be the target he might be putting himself directly in the firing line. He has to rely on the rest of us to keep him safe.

John continues: 'The target normally travels to work between 8.20 and 8.30 a.m. Al and Frank will go into the house the night before at 2200 hours. We'll have comms in the target's car and extra metal put in the doors. You'll come out in the morning, get in the car and head off to work – the same route and routine as the target. Frank, you'll be lying in the back seat out of sight, operating the radio.

'Saddlebags will do route clearance and be a couple of minutes ahead of you. Anything suspicious, he'll let us know. I'll be following in a back-up car with Chris and Jocky. Tom, you'll drive the second back-up car stationed along the route with Ernie and Cyril. Any questions?'

'Are we going to have a chopper?' I ask.

He shakes his head. 'According to the police the only helicopters normally seen in that area are in transit, and that's only one every two or three days. It's a Republican stronghold and PIRA will know within minutes if we put a chopper anywhere in there – even in a farmer's field with the rotors running.'

'There must be some way we can do it.'

'If we can't do the job without a chopper, the whole thing is off, according to the police. They'll simply saturate the area until PIRA stand down.'

We all knew the ramifications of that. The UDR major would still be a target and the local ASU (Active Service Unit) would simply wait a few months for the heat to die down and then try again.

John looks to the floor for any more questions. The lads shake their heads.

'Okay, let's look at the maps.'

For the next three hours we discuss the fine details of the operation, identifying critical intersections and landmarks on the route from the target's house to his workplace. These have to become second nature, because each member of the troop has to know where the other cars are at any given time. We have to be singing off the same hymn-sheet.

When the briefing breaks up we all have particular tasks.

The vehicles we use in Northern Ireland are 'sterile cars' – no different from ordinary civilian cars except for the run-flat tyres and a little extra zip in the engines. To guard against identification, they get replaced quite often if they've been used on sensitive jobs.

Among the new batch is a classy-looking Renault with power windows and an electric sun-roof. Tiny snaffled it straight away, but since he's on leave in the UK I decide to use it for the op. He'll be pissed off because it's his pride and joy. Not long after the Renault arrived, Tiny took it shopping and someone put a dent in a rear panel in the car-park. Although it wasn't his fault, we fined him a case of beer.

Not having driven it before, I take the Renault out that night and thrash it around the country lanes, getting used to the steering and handling. Most of us have done fast driving courses which involve defensive and pursuit driving, learning how to do hand-brake turns, J-turns and quick getaways.

Having got used to the Renault, I take it out next morning and do a recce of the route with Ernie and Cyril. Ernie is doing his first stint on the counter-terrorist team. A nice lad from the Queen's Regiment, he's been posted to us from a different troop to get a taste of Northern Ireland. Cyril is in his late thirties and super-fit. He's one of those lads who always looks as though he's about to collapse with exhaustion on the hard tabs, but as soon as he finishes, he'll light up a cigar.

As we drive over the route, keeping a low profile, Ernie spots a blue Fiat, three-up, with a number plate that doesn't fit with the area. We do a quick check and it comes back as belonging to a known PIRA operative.

'Cheeky bastards,' says Cyril. 'They're doing a recce of the route as well.'

In a situation like this we can't arrest them because they've done nothing wrong. They're unlikely to be carrying weapons and there's no law against driving around in your own car. Equally, if we make ourselves known, they'll certainly call off the job but then simply go for a different target or wait a few weeks and try again.

On Thursday afternoon we sit down and go over the details again. The UDR major has been interviewed extensively by the TCG (Tasking and Co-ordination Group) in Armagh. We have to know precisely what he's seen to raise his suspicions. From his descriptions of being followed to work, it suggests that PIRA will strike somewhere along the route.

'The local ASU that we're up against is particularly switched on,' says John. 'From their previous MO we know they're almost certain to use dickers who'll come into the area beforehand looking for any unusual police or army activity. They'll also be scanning for any increase in radio transmissions. They've clocked his routine and know his car, but we don't know exactly how they plan to do it.'

'The route is too busy for an illegal VCP [vehicle checkpoint],' I say, knowing that PIRA sometimes pose as police and set up dummy road-blocks.

'Maybe they'll take over a house alongside the road,' suggests Cyril.

'Or it could be a fake accident or a breakdown,' echoes Frank.

John turns to Saddlebags, who's on route clearance. 'If you see any-thing out of the ordinary, I want to know.'

The two back-up cars will enter the area only minutes before Al and Frank leave the target's house in his Saab. John, Chris and Jocky are in a Lancia, call-sign Romeo. They'll be a few hundred metres behind the Saab. Meanwhile, the Renault, call-sign Quebec, will be parked along the route at a Tamnamore roundabout above the M1 where the old Dungannon Road crosses over the motorway.

Finally, John says, 'Okay, I think we're ready. Good luck.'

Under cover of darkness, Frank and Al enter the UDR major's house at 2200 hours and set up low-level protection. Meanwhile, the mechanics put extra metal in the doors of the Saab, along with the comms equipment. All the radios are checked and re-checked.

Apart from wearing a bullet-proof vest, Al has a piece of bullet-proof material to rest on the passenger seat next to him. He can use it to pro-tect his face if they open fire on the car.

Back at the camp, the rest of us sort out our weapons. Cyril has gone for an MP-5, the standard weapon used in the team, which is lightweight and easy to conceal in the car. Ernie opts for the more powerful HK-53, better over long range. I'll drive with my pistol in a shoulder-holster. We sit chatting in the bar until quite late, going over the possible scenarios, knowing there is no way to cover every eventuality.

Because Tiny is away I've got a room to myself, but it takes me an age to fall asleep. I'm up before dawn, sipping a brew and going over the maps again. Cyril pokes his head around the door, saying, 'Nice day for a drive.' I'm sitting on my bunk dressed in a suit and tie, smoking a cig-arette. 'Never seen you looking so smart.'

'Yeah, this tie is killing me.' I loosen the knot and undo a shirt button.

This is my cover. A lot of businessmen who commute into Belfast pool their cars and pick up their colleagues. Because the IRA will most likely have dickers securing the area and checking for signs of an ambush, I need a reason to park near the roundabout without attracting attention.

Cyril and Ernie will keep out of sight on the floor of the Renault.

By 0800 hours we're in position at the roundabout. I have a tiny receiver in my ear and a radio hidden in my clothing. It has a wire running up inside my shirt-sleeve to a microphone inside my collar.

'Tom, are you in?' The question is picked up by my earpiece and I give two squeezes on the pressle.

Dunderhead is monitoring all communications and liaising with the police, but John has overall command of the operation on the ground.

Shortly before 0830 Saddlebags sets off along the route, one-up in his car, looking for anything suspicious. He rattles off car number plates, which are checked within eight seconds. As he nears the entrance to the house he gets a radio message from Al, who is about to leave. There's a suspicious-looking Mini at the end of the drive.

Saddlebags drives past and reads the number plate in his rear-view mirror, getting a single digit wrong. It means the car comes back as having a fake plate. Has it been booby-trapped?

The driveway entrance is overlooked by woodland and we've had a bloke sitting up there all night. He's convinced that no one has rigged up a bomb in the Mini or run a command wire back. All clear, keep going.

Al is already moving, with Frank lying across the back seat. They drive past the Mini, hoping we're right and the IRA aren't hiding inside ready to open fire, or haven't packed it full of explosives. This is where the unknown can prey on the strongest nerves.

We're about a mile away, facing the roundabout, knowing that Saddlebags will soon emerge from our left. A couple of cars pull up behind me, including a brown Cortina, one-up, with a CB radio aerial on the roof. It could be a dicker. I get out of the car and stretch my legs, leaning over the motorway bridge and watching the occupant out of the corner of my eye. I get the car registration and whisper it over the radio. It comes back within eight seconds as being from out of the area. Dickers have moved in – the job is on!

Saddlebags is three or four minutes ahead of Al, heading towards us. I can hear his radio messages as he drives along Dungannon Road.

'Yellow Escort van in a garage forecourt. It's definitely two-up but I can't see what's in the back. The windows are covered.' He gives the number plate and within seconds the reply comes back from Dunderhead, 'Not reported stolen.'

This doesn't remove the danger. The IRA are known to hold someone hostage and steal their car so the theft can't be reported until the job is completed.

As the Saab approaches, the yellow van pulls out in front and moves away slowly. Al eases off on the accelerator, trying not to close the gap.

'They're slowing down,' he mutters through clenched teeth.

From the back seat, Frank relays the message over the radio.

'They're indicating a right turn,' says Al.

'We're closing in behind you,' radios John.

There's still no way of knowing if the van poses a threat. With the indicator flashing, it slows almost to a standstill. Al has nowhere to go.

'Why don't they turn, nothing's coming the other way.'

'Don't close up,' says Frank.

The van has almost stopped completely and Al does the same, twenty metres behind it.

'It's gone right,' he says, breathing a sigh of relief. He accelerates and goes past the junction with Washingbay Road. By now, John and the lads are right behind him in the Lancia. It appears to be a false alarm.

John: 'Okay, let's continue as planned, we're dropping back.'

Saddlebags crosses over the roundabout, giving me a quick glance. The dicker's car is still parked up behind me.

Two minutes later, the Saab comes into view, with the Lancia about 100 metres back. Then I see it – the yellow van closing at speed.

'Suspect vehicle behind you, John. It's the yellow van.'

The suspects have done a U-turn and rejoined Dungannon Road. The Escort van has double doors at the back with rear windows covered in what looks like silver paper. I pull away and slip in behind it, putting it between myself and John's car. The dicker sees me leave and gets on his radio – the game is up!

Suddenly the van spears off to the left, giving up on the target. As they take the turn, they drop the galvanised tin covering the rear windows and open fire.

'Contact! Contact!'

I can see black masks and the muzzle flashes of an automatic rifle.

Within seconds we are hurtling along a narrow country road at 70 mph. I fight with every corner in the low gears. The van is much faster around the bends and keeps disappearing from view and then reappearing. Beside me, Cyril opens up with the MP-5 and punches a dozen neat holes in the laminated glass. He's trying to aim at the target at the same time as holding on as we swerve around corners.

Ernie is leaning over my shoulder, with his elbows braced against the two front seats and the HK-53 pointing directly out through the windscreen. When he opens up with his cannon I think my head has exploded. I half expect to see the van disappear in a ball of flames.

He keeps firing and the red-hot cases spit out of the breach, bouncing off my left ear. Two of them fall down the front of my shirt where I've loosened my tie. Shit, they hurt!

The Renault leans heavily on the bends and surges over dips as I try to create a stable platform for the lads to shoot. Trees and hedges flash past in a blur, but all I care about is not losing sight of the van.

At the same time, I'm constantly trying to transmit our location and direction, but part of the windscreen has been shot out and the noise of the rushing air and gun-fire means I can't hear any incoming calls. Each time we swing into view, the terrorists keep firing with what seems to be an Armalite and a shotgun. One round hits the dashboard and severs the electrics for the Renault's windows and sun-roof. Another goes straight through the windscreen and hits the back window, passing between Ernie's head and mine.

They're edging ahead . . . thirty metres, then forty. The IRA have selected a good vehicle. I could thrash them on a motorway, but the Renault doesn't like the tight corners and I'm hammering the low gears.

The van keeps weaving from side to side; it only needs something to be coming the other way.

'Where's a tractor when you need one?' yells Cyril.

Ernie: 'Don't lose them, Tom. Don't lose them.'

The windscreen is a mass of holes and cracked glass. I lean back and kick it with my left foot. My side flies out, but the other half blows back into Cyril's lap. A wall of rushing air explodes into the car, lifting debris from the floor.

Suddenly, we emerge back on to Dungannon Road, taking a sharp right. I see uniforms and a bus-stop. A half-dozen schoolchildren are crawling out of a ditch where they've thrown themselves to get away from the van.

'Oh, shit!' Wrenching at the wheel, I feel the weight of the Renault shift beneath me. For a split-second, I think I've lost it. I drop a gear and accelerate. Everything happens in slow motion – a young girl with muddy knees looks at me; she's got a red ribbon in her hair and her school books are scattered at her feet.

With every fibre, I will the Renault to turn. The tail-end is sliding. At the last instant, the wheels grip and the Renault responds. We go hurtling past the bus-stop and along the old Dungannon Road.

It's a long straight stretch running parallel to the motorway. Now the Renault has the advantage. Flooring the accelerator we begin closing the gap. The van is weaving from side to side as Cyril and Ernie open up.

Fifty metres . . . forty metres . . . thirty metres . . . twenty . . .

Recognising where we are, I call in our position. John's car is on the same road, up ahead of us, with the van heading directly towards them.

Fastening his seat-belt, John yells at Chris behind the wheel: 'Ram it!'

'You must be fucking joking,' he says. It doesn't make sense – at a closing speed of 170 mph they'd all die.

Chris slams on the brakes and throws the Lancia around, side on, trying to block the road. The van is almost on top of them and swerves up a right bank around them, like a wall-of-death stunt. John tries to get out of the front passenger seat with his seat-belt still buckled. It forces him backwards at the precise moment that two PIRA rounds hit the window of his door. If not for the seat-belt, he'd certainly have been hit.

Chris is out of the driver's side and takes up a firing position, kneeling down near the front right headlight. Jocky scrambles out a back door and also opens fire. I aim the Renault directly at Chris with my foot to the floor and just before I hit him I tweak the wheel and send the car into the ditch and up the bank, riding on the same near vertical wall as the PIRA van.

Again I close the gap, but the van is zigzagging from side to side. I keep a steady line, giving Ernie and Cyril a platform, even though it makes the Renault an easier target. The van is now on the wrong side of the road, risking a head-on collision with anything coming the other way. I can't understand why. Suddenly, it brakes and spears across in front of me, taking a sharp left turn into Washingbay Road. In a fraction of a second, I realise my mistake – the PIRA driver had been setting himself for the corner. He almost rolls the van but makes the turn. I start pulling the wheel, but at my speed from the left side of the road I have no chance. At the precise moment that I decide not to go for it, Cyril screams, 'No way!'

I hit the brakes in a controlled skid, overshooting the junction.

'John, it's gone left! John, it's gone left!'

The Lancia makes the turn but we've lost a crucial twenty seconds. Over the road, turn right, then left, where's it gone? The van has simply vanished. There's a Cortina with a single occupant parked opposite a muddy farm track.

'Which way did the yellow van go?' asks Jocky. The driver motions down the road and the Lancia takes off in pursuit.

They've been sent the wrong way by a dicker. The van has turned off along a gravel farm track. We scour the area for twenty minutes but all of us know it's too late – the terrorists have gone.

The RUC find the van later, full of empty shell cases, abandoned at the back of a farm. The IRA had taken a hostage, cut the phone lines and made their way on foot across several fields to Derryavena before taking another car. That's how they avoid the police road-blocks.

I'm exhausted and bitterly disappointed, but the news is about to get far worse. An innocent civilian has been killed in the operation. Frederick Jackson had been pulling out of a lumber yard in his car, with his foot propped on the clutch as he looked left and right. One of our rounds had ricocheted off the road and gone through the car door. It hit Mr Jackson in his body and exited through his neck. The car rolled back and re-parked itself.

As we head back to base, the RUC takes control of the scene, collecting bullet cases and interviewing witnesses. Our weapons are handed to the SOCO (scene of crime officer), the vehicles undergo forensic analysis and we all provide statements.

That night, the job is mentioned on the TV news bulletins. Tiny phones from England and I tell him about the chase and his precious Renault. He'd been fined a case of beer for a mere scratch and I'd managed to destroy the car in eight minutes.

9

Friedman is definitely playing the psychiatrist this morning – he's wearing his white coat. I've been practising what I'm going to say to him. No more bullshit excuses allowed, no more shifting the goalposts. I'm going to tell him, 'Listen, if it's the money, just charge me for the room until the weekend and let me go now.'

I deliver the ultimatum with all the authority I can muster, but the psychiatrist is totally unfazed. 'What are you going to do when you get home?' he asks.

'I'm going to fix my back fence.'

'And after that?'

'It's a big fence.'

I haven't really thought about what I'm going to do except find out what happened to me. I wanted to give Friedman a nice simple answer like washing the car or watching *Match of the Day* on TV. I know the back fence needs fixing and the house needs redecorating.

'If you do go home, you'll have to stay on these drugs,' he says.

'I accept that,' I reply, although really I'm thinking, 'Not for bloody long.' If I can get home, eat properly, become fit and get plenty of sleep, then I'll show them that I don't need drugs.

Friedman is jotting notes on a chart. 'I'll be writing a letter for your GP and he'll probably refer you to a local psychiatrist in Hereford.'

'Does that mean I can go?'

'Yes, you can leave tomorrow.'

I don't know what to say. 'How long do I have to stay on the medication?'

Friedman looks directly at me. 'Mr Read, you have a chemical imbalance in your brain. We don't know what caused it, but that is why you experienced a psychotic breakdown.'

He explains how the chemical processes in my body have been thrown out of whack and how the drugs are designed to speed up certain effects and slow down others. Unfortunately, the problem area of my brain is likely to be infinitesimally small, and not enough is known about the brain for drugs to be able to localise and target very specific areas. Instead they affect the whole of the body and create the unwanted side-effects.

I think about this for a while. 'But you're happy now? I can go home?'

'Yes, but don't make the mistake of thinking you're cured. You may be on these drugs for a very long while, perhaps indefinitely.'

I'm not even listening now. I'm determined to prove him wrong. I phone Jackie and tell her to pick me up in the morning. 'Come early, I don't want to give them time to change their minds.'

Despite Friedman's explanation of my illness, he can't tell me why I cracked up or what caused this chemical imbalance. Why did a 37-year-old man with no history of mental illness suddenly become psychotic? That's what I have to find out. I want to talk to people who were with me during the dark days before I stabbed Anna. And there are things in the house like photographs, books and notes that I'm yet to see the significance of. Did I miss some of the signs?

I'm so excited that I barely sleep. Early in the morning I go looking for Jimmy to say goodbye, but I can't find him. He's done a runner during the night. I feel like cheering. Go, Jimmy, go!

There's a post-mortem being conducted among the staff, who are trying to find out who left the door open. Jimmy had taken his pyjamas and dressing-gown, as well as the little electronic chess set I gave him. I can picture him on a park bench in Berkeley Square, feeding the pigeons and always playing white. I hope they leave him alone. He's a happy madman who doesn't hurt anyone.

Jackie arrives at 10 a.m. and we drive straight along the M40 past Oxford and on towards Cheltenham. As we near Hereford, the landmarks become more and more familiar, and I feel a surge of elation as we park outside my small terraced cottage, with its front garden full of weeds and the creaking front gate.

Jackie has put milk in the fridge and stocked up the larder. All the 'get well' cards are in a neat pile and the indoor plants have been watered. As soon as I get in the door, I sit in a colourful garden chair that's in the kitchen, beside the bench, where I can put my cup of tea, cigarettes and ashtray within easy reach. The refrigerator is in front of me and the small dining-table to my right.

I sit there for hours, enormously relieved to be home, but unsure of what to do next. Meanwhile, Jackie potters around, fussing after me. Eventually, she says, 'Okay, I'm off now, Tom. I'll be here early in the morning.' She's putting on her coat.

I don't want her to leave. I don't want to be by myself. 'Can't you stay a bit longer?'

'It's late. I should get home to Steve.' That's her boyfriend.

'You can sleep upstairs in the spare room,' I say.

She's looking at me closely, trying to decide if I'm putting on a little-boy-lost act so she'll stay, or if I'm really upset. She gives me a peck on the cheek. 'I'll see you tomorrow for breakfast. Then we have to see the new doctor.'

After she's gone I flop down on the brown sofa in front of the television and the gas fire. I'm not actually watching the programmes, but the noise and flickering images prevent me from thinking too deeply about things.

That's the dilemma I face. One part of me desperately wants to know what happened, but another is scared to death of going back to the days before I stabbed Anna. Something happened to me in the weeks or months before I picked up that pair of scissors; something so powerful and frightening that it screwed up my head. The answer is here, in this house, because this is where it started. Every piece of furniture, photograph, picture, letter, book, memento or stain on the carpet has a story behind it, and those stories make up my life.

But where do I start?

This room will do. Look around you – what can you see? What things are important to you? Do they represent something good and positive, or are they tainted?

I'm tired. I want to do this tomorrow.

No, you start now.

Most of my photographs and mementos are kept in a shoe-box in the attic. There's lots of bric-à-brac up there, like my diplomatic ID card from Washington and my campaign medals. There's a watch given to me for bodyguarding King Hussein of Jordan and an old newspaper clipping showing me instructing a Member of Parliament for a parachute jump.

I bring the box downstairs and begin sorting through the photographs on the kitchen table, deciding which ones I treasure and which ones I can put to one side. Here's one of Harry and me smeared with cam cream in the jungle. That's Saddlebags in the background. A dog-eared series of larger prints shows a counter-terrorist exercise, practising a mobile arrest. I'm wearing civilian clothes and have a handgun pointed at a car.

Each picture slips out of my fingers as I pick up a new one. This is me shirtless and sunbathing on a Welsh mountain after setting up a helicopter LZ. And here I am doing a tandem skydive with Harry in Spain. I'm sure I have a video of that somewhere.

What's this? I pick up a sheet of paper that is folded in half. As I open it, I remember what it is – a pencil sketch of Al Slater that was drawn by my old SSM in the Regiment, who became an artist after he left. It's a good drawing, and Mr Grumpy would have been flattered. I don't want to think about you, Al, but I guess it has to happen sooner or later.

*

Air Troop is still in Northern Ireland and I'm having this running battle with Tiny over who can come up with the best practical jokes. Normally we target each other, unless someone new arrives. Fortunately there's a new guy in the form of Minky, who's been attached to the troop as a liaison with the police. He used to be a DS when I was on Selection.

Poor old Minky, he's so on edge he's scared to go to the bathroom because he expects the toilet to explode or the roof to collapse. Yesterday I caught him sniffing his shaving cream, convinced it had been doctored.

'I need a volunteer for a job. You'll do, Big Nose,' says John P. It's amazing how the army can pick a volunteer when he doesn't even move a muscle.

'What's the job?'

'You have to drive a few head scheds down to South Armagh and show them around. You know the area. Give them a tour of the hot spots and local "attractions".'

I pick them up in the early evening. The new CO of the Regiment sits in the front seat while Andy, a senior NCO from Regional HQ, is in the back. I'm driving a 'sterile car' and we're all armed, although the weapons are well concealed.

From the base we head towards South Armagh and the conversation is pretty sober. Occasionally they ask me a question about the situation – how the tour is going, various jobs we've done. I tell them it's been pretty quiet.

I offer the CO a cigarette. 'Do you mind if I smoke, sir?'

'No.'

The conversation lapses into silence and the headlights cut through the darkened country lanes of South Armagh, known as bandit country. I take a long puff and suddenly the inside of the car lights up. BANG! Andy reaches for his gun and the CO grabs hold of his seat. I'm just sitting there, stony-faced, with a torn cigarette hanging out of my mouth and gunpowder fumes up my nose.

Instantly, I realise that someone has booby-trapped my cigarette with an exploding cap in the tobacco, most likely Tiny. I can see Andy's face in the rear-view mirror, and he's wondering what the fuck happened. My heart sinks.

I toss the butt out the window. 'As I said, sir, the lads get a bit bored occasionally and we try to keep each other on our toes.'

On a bitterly cold night in early December, we get a call-out from the RUC. There's been a tip-off that the IRA are going to detonate a bomb, but we don't know who or what the target will be. As a precaution, we decide to cover likely targets over a broad area, co-opting the help of 2 Para, which is the resident battalion in the region.

We drive down to St Angelo Barracks, a UDR base where the Paras are waiting, taking most of our operational equipment in the cars because we'll dispatch from there. Having gathered in the cookhouse, we decide that one member of Air Troop will take three paratroopers and form a patrol which will keep a security watch on each possible target. So as not to attract attention, each patrol leaves separately, driving out the gates and heading to their location.

Most of the teams have been dispatched when a call comes through from Special Branch on a secure line, saying the target has been identified. The duty officer at the RUC police station in Kesh, County Donegal, had received a phone call shortly after midnight from a woman with a cultured Northern Irish accent. 'Listen carefully,' she said. 'This is the Fermanagh Brigade of the IRA; there is a number of blast incendiaries in the Drumrush Lodge, Kesh. The reason for this is that they serve the bastard security forces.'

Drumrush Lodge is a restaurant on the Kesh–Beleek road, not far from the Bannagh river. Two separate pieces of intelligence also suggest the threat might be genuine. A blue Toyota van had been reported stolen earlier in the evening from a nearby village, and elsewhere, a policeman on his beat had become suspicious of a van being loaded with beer kegs.

Back at our HQ Dunderhead has detailed ordnance maps of the area, whereas we possess only basic road maps. We rely on him to provide us with directions and describe any landmarks and features of the terrain. It's a thirty-minute drive away.

'Right, we're going to check it out,' says John P., addressing the six members of Air Troop who remain. 'We have to assume that PIRA are going to plant a bomb or have already planted one. They have already made the phone call to the police, so it's a "come-on" aimed at the RUC.'

History shows that it's common practice for the IRA to lure the police and security forces into an area before detonating a bomb, and this can often include having an armed hit squad ready to ambush any survivors.

'The bomb, we're going to assume, is still being loaded,' says John. 'Flexible heads on. We have very limited information. Hopefully, we'll get updated by the boss on the way down. Let's go.'

The nature of the job has changed, which means getting into our bags to redistribute kit. I swap my MP-5 for an Armalite with a night-sight, until I realise there's so little ambient light that the night-sight won't work. I change my mind and opt for the HK-53. We then take off our top halves and put on civilian shirts and pullovers, leaving our army trousers and boots.

Tiny slips behind the wheel of one car, with John beside him and Jocky and me in the back. The second 'sterile' car contains Saddlebags, Cyril and Al Slater.

Meanwhile, an unmarked RUC car cruises past Drumrush Lodge and does a U-turn. Thankfully, it doesn't enter the hotel car-park or use its indicators, because this would have signalled the IRA to detonate a 'land-mine'. Nine beer kegs packed with explosives are hidden in a culvert beside the entrance to the driveway. A command wire runs up a telegraph pole and then across the entrance to another pole and down again. From there, it trails up into a hilly field to a firing point more than 300 yards away. A 1,000 lb. bomb is enough to ensure that there won't be a car left, let alone any survivors.

Unaware of the set-up, we move into the area where freezing fog has cut visibility to only a few feet. Tiny slows to a crawl and we have the windows open to stop them misting over.

Dunderhead has identified a link road about 100 yards from the hotel that joins up with the Kesh–Pettigo road. 'There's a side-road that inter-sects with the link road, and you should be getting close to that,' he radios.

John hits the pressle. 'Did you copy that, Cyril?'

In the other car, Cyril hits the pressle twice in confirmation.

Tiny is leaning over the wheel, pressing his face close to the wind-screen. 'We'll never find the side-road. I can't see a thing.' The headlights seem to bounce straight back at us, creating a white-out effect.

'I think we passed it,' says Jocky.

Tiny reverses slowly back along the main road, putting his head out the window and watching the asphalt beneath his door. 'This is it!' he says, turning up a side-road.

He stops the car.

'Tom, cover the front; Jocky, the back,' says John.

I'm out of the car, moving forwards alongside the wet road. The frost is so heavy it's like walking on crisp packets, and every sound is amplified by the darkness. After twenty feet, I look back and can't see the car in the fog. We're not carrying personal radios and the only comms are between the vehicles.

Crouching on my haunches in a ditch, I peer into the fog. I'm near a junction that must be the link road. Suddenly, a van door slides open. It's ahead of me, hidden by fog. Almost at the same moment headlights appear to my right. It might be the other lads, but I can't be sure. I quickly climb over a gate into a field and kneel behind a hedge. There are no leaves and I can see directly along the barrel of the HK-53 pushed through the branches.

At that moment, the gate rattles next to me and a dark figure jumps over. I hear his feet land in the soft earth about three feet away, and see his breath condense in the air. Who the fuck is it? I want to whisper, 'Is that you, Tiny?', but something stops me. Because my weapon is pointed through the hedge, I can't pull it back without making a noise. What if it isn't Tiny?

Whoever it is, he doesn't appear armed. I can hear his rasping breath and see his dark outline. What's that? It's a faint yet unmistakable *shhhh-hiss* of a radio carrier wave. He's carrying a hand-held radio. If I confront him now, he'll hit the pressle and alert his friends. I might compromise the lads if they're in that other car.

As the car headlights disappear slowly into the fog, the dark figure jumps back over the gate. Almost immediately, another shape moves directly in line with my muzzle.

'Tom, Tom!'

'Yeah, Tiny, here. Somebody just crossed the gate. He's right by you.'

The headlights had belonged to the other SAS car carrying Cyril, Saddlebags and Al. Driving slowly down the link road, they spotted a stationary Toyota van on the left side of the road.

'Confirm the van is parked up. Driver's side door slightly open,' radios Cyril. Edging slowly past without stopping, they reach the Kesh–Beleek road and turn, blocking the link road.

John has joined Tiny and me and together we move forward towards the location of the van, aware that someone is out there. We don't want to walk past him in the fog.

Suddenly, I hear Cyril's voice, echoing through the darkness.

'Stop right there! Put your hands in the air.'

'It's all right, it's only me,' comes the reply.

Cyril calls out again, 'Stop. Stand still. Put your hands in the air. I want to see them. Police.'

Someone starts running and I hear Cyril yelling, 'Stop or I'll shoot! Stop or I'll shoot!'

Deep within the fog, I see a pale burst of light. Someone has fired a flare but it soaks into the whiteness, barely casting a shadow. There's a long burst of automatic fire from more than one weapon. Rounds are zipping over my head. I dive into a ditch with Jocky, pressing my cheek into the ground. We're diagonally opposite the farm gate.

'Did you hear the Armalite?' I mutter.

Jocky nods.

None of the lads is carrying an Armalite. Which means someone has opened up on them, but from where? As the noise dies, I hear Cyril's voice: 'Stay down, d'you hear? Stay down!'

Saddlebags is with him. 'Hey, Al, bring us the plasticuffs.'

Seconds tick by.

'Al, can you hear me? Bring us the plasticuffs. They're in the boot.'

Al must have stayed with the car while the others chased the suspect.

They move back towards the vehicle, still calling for Al through the fog. Something is wrong! Why didn't they hear the Armalite? Maybe their own gunfire drowned out the sound. Although I'm only about fifty yards away, I've never felt so isolated and helpless. Tactically, John, Jocky and I are supposed to sit tight, and with a bit of luck the terrorists might come through us as they try to escape. If we move forwards we risk being shot by our own lads. My knees and elbows are wet with frost and I feel the cold of the stock against my cheek.

There's another commotion. 'Stop! Stop!' Cyril is shouting again. 'He's armed!'

People are running and I hear the familiar bark of a pistol and then a short burst from an HK-53. Then silence.

Each minute that passes feels like a life sentence. I want to get out of the ditch to find out what's happened, but our job is to secure one end of the road and hold our position. After fifteen minutes, John moves back to our vehicle to find out what's going on. He returns twenty minutes later. 'C'mon, we're pulling out.'

'What's happened?'

'We've got one down.'

'Who is it?'

'Al.'

I want to stay, but the SOPs are clear. After such an incident, the Quick Reaction Force from the RUC moves in to take over the scene. The area has to be sealed off and thoroughly searched. Bullet cases are bagged and labelled, tracker dogs scour the fields and the bomb disposal squad will examine the van for booby-traps.

The large bomb at the hotel entrance isn't discovered until first light. A pistol and radio transmitter are found next to a wire fence near the gate where I jumped into the field. Al Slater is dead along with the suspect – Antoin Mac Giolla Bride, a 26-year-old Irish Army deserter with strong links to the IRA.

Feeling absolutely devastated, we retire to the bar at base camp and have a drink for Al – a tradition in the Regiment when a member dies. But it's not until Cyril and Saddlebags join us that we can piece together all the disparate events and details.

Mac Giolla Bride had been the driver of the van, hijacked earlier that evening from a family in Pettigo. The van and an IRA scout car dropped off the terrorist unit and the beer kegs full of explosives. The van then parked up on open ground at the side of the narrow link road. If not for the fog, it would have had a clear view of the hotel entrance. At least two terrorists were at the firing point in the hilly field, ready to detonate the 'landmine'. Another group, having planted the bomb, took cover in a ditch at the junction of the link road and the main road.

Mac Giolla Bride heard a car coming and slid open the van door. When he saw the headlights, he took cover in the darkness, choosing the same hiding-place as me. He had a pistol stuffed down his trousers and a two-way radio.

The other SAS vehicle disappeared into the fog and cruised past the van before turning and blocking the road. Unknowingly, it parked directly opposite the ditch in which the IRA were hiding. Cyril told Saddlebags and Al to take up positions by the side of the road. Al put caltrops on the tarmac to puncture the tyres of any vehicle that tried to pass.

After about ten minutes, Cyril heard someone walking towards them. Mac Giolla Bride had jumped back over the gate and slowly made his way along the road. Cyril waited until he walked to within twenty yards and then called on him to stop.

'It's all right, it's only me,' said Mac Giolla Bride, still invisible in the fog. He didn't realise the car had stopped and he was talking to the security forces. He thought he was talking to his own mates in the ditch.

When he realised his mistake, he turned to run and Cyril yelled three or four warnings before he and Saddlebags opened fire, aiming wide.

Al put up a flare and stayed with the car. At that same instant the IRA opened fire on him from only a few feet away with an Armalite and a .303. Al tried to return fire, putting a couple of rounds down as he fell. Saddlebags and Cyril didn't hear the gunfight because of the noise of their own weapons.

Mac Giolla Bride ran back down the road, jumped a ditch and managed to climb a barbed-wire fence before the lads stopped him. Cyril and Saddlebags dragged him back on to the road and laid him face down while they searched him, calling for Al to bring the plasticuffs. When he didn't answer, they went back.

'I saw him lying by the car in a pool of blood,' says Saddlebags. 'Straight away, I handed my rifle to Cyril and checked for a pulse, but I knew Al was gone. I figured it had to be one of our rounds because no one else had fired. I didn't even think . . .' Saddlebags lets the sentence trail off and then rages, 'He didn't have a chance! They were only feet away.'

John P. tries to reassure him that there's nothing we could have done.

'What happened to the terrorist?' I ask.

Cyril answers, 'He tried to run. I was holding two HK-53s and suddenly he lunged for one of them. I tried to push him back but dropped a rifle. He charged, knocking me into the ditch. As I got up, I couldn't see both guns so I figured he had one of them. I yelled, "He's armed! He's armed!"'

Crouching beside Al, Saddlebags took out his pistol and fired into the fog at the fleeing shadow. He hit Mac Giolla Bride in the back and dropped him. Cyril had given chase and saw the terrorist try to stand and turn, as if about to open fire.

'That's when I shot him,' he says. There's a genuine sadness in his voice, but no hint of remorse. I don't expect any. We'd lost one of our own to the IRA and they deserved no sympathy.

Further details emerged in the coming days. Two armed men were picked up at a checkpoint across the border in a stolen car a few hours after the shooting and became suspects. It also became clear that the IRA bomb had failed to explode. The two terrorists on the hill must have seen the flare and heard the gunfight. They tried to detonate the bomb and then fled south towards the border, getting as far as the Bannagh river, where they entered the water, trying to cross. Although only twenty feet wide, the river had deep pools and was in flood. One of the terrorists reached the other side and couldn't find his companion. The body of Kieran Fleming was washed up three weeks later.

Much later, it transpired that the IRA had a tout at St Angelo Barracks who'd seen us getting changed and driving out the gate. He alerted the terrorists to the possibility that we might be on to them, giving them advance warning.

In the days that follow there is a lot of soul-searching. I keep replaying what happened in my mind, over and over like a video recording. I rewind and see it all in slow-motion, freezing the frame when Mac Giolla Bride jumped over the gate and crouched beside me. Who knows, if I'd challenged him then things might have been different.

Every Monday, Al and I had been doing an education course which might help us with promotion, but it had become a bit of a standing joke because whenever the teacher asked us why we didn't turn up to a class, we answered, 'We can't divulge that information, sir.'

Two days after the shooting, I visit the class and hand in Al's calculator and books. 'I apologise, sir, but Al Slater won't be coming in again.' As I'm saying the words, I can see the *Sun* newspaper in the staff room with the headline, 'SAS SOLDIER KILLED IN NORTHERN IRELAND'.

Afterwards, back at the base, I find a quiet room and write a letter to Al's parents. It's the first letter I've written since I was twenty years old and wooing Christine. I can't tell them the operational details of the job, but I include things that I think they'd want to hear about their son. It's such an emotional letter that I ask Frank Collins to read it because he, too, was close to Al.

'That's fine, Tom, send it,' he says.

'Are you sure, Frank? You don't think it's too heavy?'

'No, no. It's a good letter. Send it.'

Air Troop fly back from Ireland for the funeral at Hereford. It's a very moving ceremony surrounded by tight security. Afterwards, there's a wake in the Paludrin Club, and Al's father finds me at the bar and shakes my hand, holding it for a long time.

'I want to thank you for the letter you wrote to us,' he says. 'It meant a lot.'

I want to say how sorry I am and how much Al's friendship meant to me, but the words are caught in my throat. His father smiles sadly and seems to understand.

*

The shoe-box is still sitting on the table and the photographs are scattered under my arms. It's four in the morning – the worst time of the night. I must have fallen asleep still holding the sketch of Al Slater, clutching the edges a little too tightly.

Staring down I see a collage of images, photographs and letters lying haphazardly on top of each other, cutting off heads, dividing couples and removing rows of people from group shots. Isn't it amazing how much emotion can be contained in a single snapshot or a few words scrawled on a postcard?

As I look around me, every little detail triggers a memory or a new thought. During the dark days leading up to Chamonix, there were thousands of signs bombarding my consciousness. Everything around me seemed to stimulate my imagination. Now I want to find out why. I'm going to 'sterilise' this house, by deciding the significance of every bit of bric-à-brac, photograph, picture, book, letter and piece of furniture. It's going to take me a long while because everything is significant; I just have to work out *how* it is significant. How did it get here? Who gave it to me? Is it contaminated?

No, no, I'm wrong! I have to forget about the SAS, the Falklands and Northern Ireland. Forget about old photographs and tin medals in battered shoe-boxes. *Anna* is behind all this. She was the architect of my downfall; the puppeteer pulling the strings. Everything else is peripheral, just a piece of scenery on the stage. Who *is* Anna? What did she want from me?

BOOK TWO

10

It's a Sunday night in Washington, DC, and I've just finished work. The only thing in the fridge in the apartment is a packet of streaky bacon, two cans of cola and half a tub of ice-cream. There's a wine bar next door to my building and I go down in the elevator, turn left, walk ten yards and I'm through the front door.

The kitchen stops serving at nine o'clock and I'm fifteen minutes late. I pull the old favoured-customer routine and the chef fixes me up with a plate of spaghetti bolognese. That's when these two girls walk in and ask if the kitchen is closed. Anna is the quiet one; her girlfriend does most of the talking.

'Aw, come on, Henry! I can't eat alone,' I say. Henry is the chef, a huge black guy with forearms thicker than his legs. He disappears through the saloon doors and comes back with two more bowls of spaghetti. The place is pretty crowded, and I offer Anna my seat. She must think I'm a real English gentleman.

'You don't remember me, do you?' she says.

I look hard at her face.

'We met about two months ago.'

'Here?'

'No, another bar. You were with a friend of yours, Harry.'

I remember Harry coming to visit and how I took him out on the town, but I don't remember Anna. 'It must have been late,' I say apologetically.

Anna is only twenty-two years old, and has that exotic, quite fragile beauty of many Eurasian women. Her father was Russian and her mother Filipino. He died when she was young and her mother had since remarried.

She invites me to a nightclub and afterwards I take her back to my place. Next morning, I leave early for work. I've been in America for six months, bodyguarding Saad Hariri, the son of a wealthy Arab family, whose father Rafik is tipped to be the next Prime Minister of Lebanon.

I start my shift at 7 a.m. and Anna phones up within two hours. She just keeps talking, giving me her entire life story and telling me about her love for poetry and passion for ballet; about how her father came to America and how many times her heart has been broken. Although she doesn't say so in as many words, I know she's trying to tell me what a big bad world it is and how she wants me to protect her.

After a while I put her on speaker-phone because my ear starts to hurt and I keep marvelling at how anyone can have so much weird shit in their heads. Anna is studying to improve her SAT scores so she can go to medical school and be a doctor. She's very well-read and can speak Russian and play classical music on the piano. She's extremely sensual and at the same time very private. During the day she goes to her classes; I see her of an evening or at weekends.

The job is perfect. It means working four days on and four days off, which gives me time to research Joe Kittinger's record and keep flying. Saad is in his early twenties and goes to Georgetown University. He doesn't like high-profile security, but his father has given us the word to keep an eye on him. The main danger is kidnapping, and that means being a 'close escort' whenever he goes to university or ventures out of the house.

I've only met his father once, and he struck me as a very honourable man. He set up the Hariri Foundation, which pays for thousands of Lebanese students to attend university in America in the hope that as doctors, teachers, lawyers and engineers they will return to Lebanon and help the war-torn country get back on its feet.

Saad lives in a big house in Georgetown, where he has the top three floors and the bodyguard on duty has a basement apartment. It's basically just a bed, telephone, office chair and en suite. It's nicknamed 'the dungeon' and Des has put a Union Jack on the door and claimed it as British territory. My apartment is round the corner, and Des has a house for his family outside Washington. We don't see a lot of each other except when we're swapping over.

It was Des who managed to get me this job. I'd just finished an eighteen-month assignment in Africa where I learned how to fly helicopters and fixed-wing aircraft in my spare time. I'd come to America to get my commercial licence and instrument rating, which meant building up flight time. That's why I spent six weeks 'flying cables' in the south, following telecommunications lines that ran for hundreds of miles and looking for any potential problems such as erosion, flooding or illegal excavations. Des phoned me just before I was about to head home and told me about the job in Washington.

Looking after Saad is fairly relaxed, and I feel as if I've become like an older brother to him. His girlfriend Sarah is Egyptian, and looks like a princess. Saad hasn't been spoilt by money, but he has no concept of what it's worth. For instance, he gets really chuffed if he can run up a $30,000 monthly bill on his AmEx card.

I fill out all his cheques for him, and at the end of each month try to pin him down to sign them. Normally it means waiting until he's watching TV. Then he simply signs twenty or thirty cheques without even looking at what they're for or the amounts involved. Des and I both figure he should pay more attention to what he's signing.

This one time, we go out for a meal and Saad orders veal. I tell him how I worked in a veal farm for six months in between finishing school and joining the army, and how I got to know all the baby calves by name. When they were sixteen weeks old, they were loaded on to a truck and sent off to the slaughterhouse.

Saad makes a joke about it. 'Ah, my bodyguard is a big softie,' he says. 'Did they take away your little play-mates?'

A few days later the mail arrives, and among the dozens of letters is a pamphlet from the American equivalent of the RSPCA. I fill out a cheque for $100 and put it into the pile with the rest that Saad has to sign. At the end of the month, I corner him upstairs with the cheques and he starts scribbling his signature to pay for the gas, electricity, telephone, credit cards . . .

'I want you to look at what you're signing,' I tell him.

'I trust you,' he sighs.

'No, don't trust me, look!'

Reluctantly, he looks at the cheques. 'What's this one?'

'Every time you eat veal, Saad, I'm going to send a hundred dollars to an animal charity.'

He laughs and signs with a flourish. 'Okay, you do that.'

Another day there's a knock at the door and it's a bloke from Greenpeace collecting donations. We get talking and I discover that he's actually been in the field, rescuing dolphins from the drift nets used by Japanese tuna boats.

Eventually, I give him $50 out of my own pocket.

'Who was that at the door?' asks Saad.

'Just someone asking for money.'

'But why did you listen to him?'

'Because he was genuine, Saad. I gave him fifty dollars.'

Saad can't believe that I've given a 'beggar' fifty bucks. 'Catch up with him quickly.'

So I open the door and call the guy back. Saad gives him a cheque for $1,500 because I tell him that Greenpeace is a good cause.

Anna and I seem to be getting on pretty well together and we see each two or three times a week. Occasionally, when we're out, her bleeper goes off and she has to make a phone call. She then apologises and says that she has to go. At first I don't think anything of it, but then it dawns on me and I ask her, 'Why do you carry a bleeper?'

'I have to tell you something,' she says. 'I do some part-time work for an agency — escort work. It's not a big deal — simply a way of making money so I can get into medical school. I only have four regular clients.'

'Escort work?'

'Uh-huh.'

I don't ask her if that involves having sex. I don't want to know.

'A lot of girls do it to get through college,' she says. 'I'm very careful.'

It's not a case of being hurt or offended. I don't care what Anna does in her spare time. She's attractive, sensual and a lot of fun, but I'm not looking for a long-term relationship. Although she seems very young and insecure, Anna is quite street-wise and knows about the darker side of

Aged one, in 1957, with Mum and my older brother Vince.

Me (right), with 2 Para in Northern Ireland in 1975.

Training in Ulster: I am kneeling in the middle of the road, Schwepsy is running back, Harry and Des take up positions on the far side.

Malaya: resting on pole beds with 'Father Frank' Collins.

Africa: helping a local clean his gun during a jungle trip with the Regiment.

Killing time in a C-130 Hercules prior to a HALO (high altitude, low opening) jump.

With Al Slater and Frank Collins near Peterborough, August 1984.

Over Ampuria Brava with Jason, getting ready for a tandem. Anna looks on.

Training with High Adventure for the Skydive from Space.

Training jump for the fifty-way organised by Tim Mace, who later went on to become a cosmonaut with the Russians.

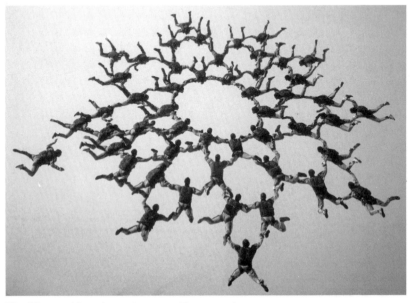

The fifty-way (almost) complete – a military record.

Thirteen thousand feet over Ampuria Brava – and naked!

Tandem jump over Spain with Livvy and Jackie (right).

On the second trip to Zvezda, the Russian space agency in Moscow. Joe Kittinger (right) watches as I try on one of their high-altitude pressure suits.

Zephyr, the Cessna 172 I flew across the Atlantic in July 1992. Here we're in Canada, just before making the hop over the Gulf of St Lawrence.

The Everest expedition, October 1993. With Harry (left), and with a group of local villagers near Base Camp.

Karl Henize, the NASA scientist who came with us on the Everest trip and, tragically, died there. He'd flown on the space shuttle Challenger, but the lack of oxygen on the mountain proved too much.

Arriving in the UK after my breakdown, with Harry (left), Schwepsy and Des, and a friendly stewardess.

With Livvy, at home in Hereford.

Washington and the drug culture. It's as if she hasn't decided yet whether she wants to be a girl or a woman, so she swings between both.

Sometimes she can seem so worldly and experienced that she appears almost bored by life, and at other times she's a lonely waif who wants someone to keep her safe from danger. She's right into fantasies and loves thinking of me as the cool, quiet British mercenary, or a moody French poet. She invents stories about me, trying to fill in the blanks in my life because she complains that I don't tell her things.

In my spare time I go flying, and Anna comes with me because her mother lives in Virginia, about an hour out of Washington, near the flying club where I hire the plane. My apartment lease is up for renewal and Anna suggests I move closer to the airfield. If I move out of the city I can get a two-bedroom apartment for the same price.

Anna is always complaining about being short of money and how she wouldn't have to work as an escort if she could save on rent. Because my new apartment is closer to Georgetown High, where she's studying, I suggest she takes over the spare room. 'We'll both have our own space,' I say. 'We can try it for a few weeks and see how things work out.'

Her wardrobe duly arrives, along with her piano, which is put into the spare room. She plays classical music whenever she needs a break from her books. It's nice to have someone here when I get home, although I find it strange that Anna has so few friends. When we're alone she talks endlessly, but in company she becomes introverted.

I know she's angry that I've never said I love her. She thinks I'm frightened of the words.

One morning she says to me, 'Last night you told me that you loved me.'

'I'm not being defensive, Anna, but I don't think I did.'

'Yes, you did. You'd had a few drinks and got very sentimental.'

I know she's wrong. Anna says she loves me all the time and it makes me want to run a mile. I ban her from saying it.

'If you want me to run, just say that again.'

Saad respects his father enormously and mimics him a little. He's even taken to smoking cigars – although not inhaling – because Rafik smokes them. His brothers, Bahar and Hassan, are both at school in Boston, and occasionally the three boys meet up in New York, particularly when their dad is in town for a diplomatic function.

The whole family seems very close, which makes the death of Hassan even harder on them. He dies in a car accident in Boston. Major figures from all over the Middle East are coming for the funeral.

Hassan is to be buried in Medina, Saudi Arabia, and one of the family's private jets arrives in Boston to pick up the body. I have to go down to the airport and put the coffin on board. Several of the French-based bodyguards are helping me – one of them is an ex-Legionnaire and the other two are Rhodesians.

The four of us turn up at Boston airport, wearing black suits, in black limousines, following a black hearse. Hassan is in a temporary aluminium casket which is pretty heavy. The 727 has a passenger door at the side and another door at the rear, reached by a ladder at a steep angle. This leads directly into the galley, and from there a narrow corridor leads around the bulkhead and further up the plane.

'Spare no expense – just get it on board,' Des had said to me. 'Call me on the mobile if there's a problem.'

We carry the coffin up the rear stairs, which are so narrow there's only room for one person at the front and another at the back. I'm at the front, all stooped over, trying not to lose my grip. Lots of people have gathered at the observation windows of the terminal, watching the sombre task. It must look like a scene out of *The Godfather*.

We get the coffin into the galley, but it won't fit around the sharp right and then left turn into the corridor. We rest it on the kitchen floor, and I have a word with the two British stewardesses, Debbie and Helen, who work for the family. 'Is it okay if we leave him just here?' I say. 'We'll cover it up.'

'Sure, we can work around that,' says Debbie.

I phone Des: 'Yeah, we got him on board the aircraft, everything is fine.'

'Where is he?'

'He's on the kitchen floor.'

'Fine.'

Five minutes later Des rings back. 'No, Tom, let's have a little more dignity that that. His father doesn't want him on the kitchen floor.'

So we pick up the coffin and try once more to get it around the corner. Then we carry it back down the ladder, straining under the weight, unaware that the number of on-lookers is increasing by the minute. We carry the coffin under the port wing to the normal passenger stairs.

'I don't think it's going to fit,' I say, eyeing the door.

'Come on, we'll give it a try,' says the Frenchman, and we shoulder the load again. There's a beautiful oak trim around the door and we take out a sizeable chunk before the Australian pilot pipes up, 'There's no bloody way that's going to go!'

Down the stairs we head, sweating in our shirts and ties. We carry the coffin under the starboard wing to the cargo bay doors. I call Des on the mobile, 'Look, mate, there's no way it's going anywhere inside this aircraft unless it's the cargo bay or on the galley floor.'

'He wants him in the master suite.' Des is adamant.

'There's no way this coffin is going around the corridor. It's not possible.'

'Tom, Tom – you have to completely erase the money question from your head. How long will it take to cut a hole in the side of the aeroplane and put him in through there?'

'That's ridiculous, you can't do that.'

'Well, have you considered it? Forget about how much it costs. The aeroplane doesn't leave until tomorrow morning, the engineers can work all night.'

This is crazy. Nothing is a problem to Des, but I try to explain that the jet will fall out of the sky if anyone tries cutting a hole in the fuselage. 'The only way to do it would be to take the body out of the coffin.'

'Wait a minute,' says Des.

He comes back on the line. 'I've just spoken to Mr Hariri. Do what you have to do, but he expects you to treat the body with dignity.'

We carry the coffin up the ladder into the galley and I carefully undo the screws. Then we carry Hassan along the corridor to the master suite and gingerly lay him on a sofa where people can come and pay their last respects.

The empty coffin is still in the galley. I nudge it out the door and the watching crowd is gobsmacked as they see it bouncing all the way down the stairs. We pick it up, toss the aluminium shell between hands and throw it straight into the cargo hold. Suddenly, there's a huge round of applause from the observation deck. There must be a thousand people watching us.

*

It has been three years since I left the SAS, and nearly six years since I first contemplated breaking Joe Kittinger's record.

I was on a training course in Kelang, Malaysia, when Harry asked me what I planned to do when I left the Regiment. The question surprised me because I hadn't thought that far ahead. Technically, I could stay with the SAS until the age of forty, and that seemed like an age away.

I knew what Harry wanted to do with his life. He'd just come back from Everest – a trip he'd been talking about ever since I'd known him. He seemed so animated and excited that I envied him – not for his dream, because I hate climbing – but for his certitude. That's when I remembered Joe Kittinger and his record jump.

'How high?' Harry asked, incredulously.

'Something like twenty miles.'

He whistled softly between his teeth. 'And he lived?'

'Yes.'

'Who in their right mind . . .' Harry didn't finish the sentence, because he knew how many people had perished trying to reach the summit of Mount Everest. Isn't it strange how one man's challenge will seem crazy to another?

Up until then, I had never considered breaking Kittinger's record. Truth is, I knew very little about it, apart from stories told in skydiving circles. It was a throwaway remark that became a whim and then a dream.

Four years passed before I thought seriously about it again. It was Harry who brought it up. We were both out of the Regiment by then and working on 'the circuit', bodyguarding VIPs and advising companies on security.

'Are you still interested in breaking that skydiving record?' Harry asked. We were in a bar in Johannesburg and Harry had just stepped off the plane from London. He'd been working for Sir Ralph Halpern, the Burton's boss, until three days previously when I convinced him to drop everything for a job in South Africa.

'Joe Kittinger's record?'

'Yeah. It's just that I might know someone who can help. He's one of the Guinness banking family.'

Harry explained his links with Loel Guinness and 'High Adventure', a company set up to support professional sportsmen and women involved in testing human performance and endurance. Already, it had successfully challenged several climbing and paragliding records.

'Freefalling is something entirely different,' I reminded him.

'Yes, but just imagine breaking that record. That would be something.'

Harry promised to set up a meeting with Loel as soon as we got back to Europe, but the six-month assignment in Africa stretched to nearly eighteen months, and it wasn't until early 1990 that I arrived in Normandy to meet the wealthy banker.

Loel Guinness was younger than I expected. Although probably my age, he had a boyish energy and desire for excitement. 'Tell me about this jump,' he asked. 'Can it actually be done?'

I tried to sound authoritative, but actually knew very little about the logistics. All I'd managed to get my hands on was a curriculum vitae for Joe Kittinger by writing to *The Guinness Book of Records*. 'He wrote a book about the jump called *The Long Lonely Leap*,' I said. 'It's out of print, but I'm going to America and I'll try to find a copy.'

'Good idea,' announced Loel. 'Is Kittinger still alive?'

'Yes. He lives in Florida. I want to see him.'

'How did he get up there?'

'In a helium balloon.'

I knew this seemed odd to Loel. In an age when aircraft had broken the sound barrier and rockets had put satellites into orbit, it was hard to believe that the best device for putting somebody on the edge of space was the oldest flight vehicle in the world – a lighter-than-air balloon.

'Small scientific payloads are launched all the time,' I told him. 'Mainly to measure weather conditions, but a balloon to carry a man would have to be much larger.'

'How big?'

'To be honest, I have no idea.'

The more we talked, the less I realised I knew. All I had was a concept, with absolutely no idea of the logistics or the cost. High Adventure was looking for a new challenge, but a skydive from the edge of space to break a thirty-year-old record was far more complicated and potentially dangerous than anything it had tackled before.

'Will you do a feasibility study for us?' Loel asked. 'Try to get some rough costings together and we can do a more detailed budget later if we go ahead.'

I nodded in agreement.

'And if it is possible, would you be prepared to do the jump?'

I grinned. 'That's why I'm here.'

I've been doing a lot of research since I arrived in Washington, visiting libraries and archives. In particular, I'm interested in high-altitude balloon jumps dating back to the 1950s, when America first entered the space race.

The Soviet Union had launched the first man-made Earth satellite, *Sputnik I*, in 1957, and suddenly the possibility of putting a man into space became a matter of national pride and competing doctrines. Dozens of experimental rockets were fired, reaching higher and higher above the Earth, discovering more about the composition of the atmosphere, pressure, temperature and radiation belts. Hundreds of new studies were conducted into rocket propulsion, G-loads, life-support systems, cosmic radiation, magnetic fields and satellite guidance systems.

Among the experiments were a series of balloon flights high above Minnesota called 'Project Man High', which were designed to test man's ability to live for prolonged periods in a sealed cabin similar to that of a spacecraft. Joe Kittinger was one of the test pilots, and on 2 June 1957 he took the first solo balloon flight into the stratosphere. He stayed aloft for nearly seven hours in a sealed gondola, breathing pure oxygen and making visual observations to doctors on the ground. His maximum altitude during the flight was 96,000 feet.

About nine weeks later, David Simons, the project officer for the Man High, exceeded Joe's mark and stayed aloft for thirty-two hours in a sealed capsule, remaining at 101,100 feet for about five hours. Simons became the first man in history to see the sun set and then rise again from the edge of space.

Both these ascents proved that a sealed cabin could be used to sustain human life in hostile skies. Ultimately, the environmental control system of the Man High capsule and the instrumentation for monitoring physiological conditions were almost identical to those used in the

Mercury spacecraft that carried the first American into space three years later.

Records continued to tumble – faster, further, higher and longer seemed to be the buzz words, and the boundaries were pushed back almost monthly. On 16 April 1958, an F11F-1F Super Tiger aircraft reached 76,828 feet, a world altitude record for a ground-launched plane. The record stood for only three weeks before a Lockheed F-104A Starfighter reached 91,249 feet. A year later the mark had been pushed to 103,389 feet.

At the same time, studies were under way into the behaviour of crews during the long confinement of a simulated space flight; rocket-propelled sleds reaching speeds of more than 2,700 mph were testing G-loads; and a centrifuge had subjected a human to over twenty times the force of gravity. Everything was aimed at 'Project Mercury' – NASA's plan to put a manned space capsule in orbit around the Earth.

By the end of 1958, Joe Kittinger had begun working on another balloon-based study. Known as 'Project Excelsior' (meaning 'ever upwards'), it aimed to develop an escape system that would allow someone to survive an escape at extreme altitudes. Until then, any pilot of a damaged aircraft would have to drop to at least 30,000 feet before ejecting. In the case of fire or structural damage this wasn't always possible. Even then, anyone who bailed out of a speeding aircraft above 20,000 feet and tried to open a parachute faced probable death from the canopy's opening shock, the lack of oxygen or the severe cold. Having invested millions of dollars in training a pilot or an astronaut, America didn't want to lose them.

Joe was to test a drogue parachute design that would allow him to freefall, maintaining stability, until he reached a safe height to deploy his main canopy.

On the first Excelsior jump from 76,400 feet in November 1959, his drogue chute tangled and he lost consciousness in a wild spin. Three weeks later, he successfully jumped from 74,700 feet, maintaining stability using the drogue. Then he set *the* record, on 16 August 1960.

I try everywhere to get a copy of his book, without success, and eventually visit the Library of Congress in Washington. The librarian behind the counter has a set of half-moon glasses that must be mandatory to work in this place. She looks at the computer as if it has teeth and gingerly punches in Joe Kittinger's name.

'Yes, we do have a copy, but only one. It can't be taken out.'

'Can I photocopy it?'

'The machines are over to the left. It's ten cents a page. This is the reference number. You can place your request in that box over there.'

The Long Lonely Leap is an ageing bound volume, published in 1960, with black and white pictures taken by *National Geographic*. I feed the photocopier with tubes of ten-cent pieces from a money-changing machine, doing two pages at a time.

The librarian also mentioned a *National Geographic* article, but when I telephoned the company and asked about getting a back issue, the archivist had only one copy of the December 1960 issue and it couldn't be released.

Two days later, sitting in a dentist's waiting room, I glance down at the coffee table and notice about half a dozen *National Geographic* magazines. There it is – December 1960. What are the odds of that?

The story is by-lined 'Captain Joseph W. Kittinger, Jr, USAF', and it begins:

Overhead my onion-shaped balloon spread its 200-foot diameter against a black daytime sky. More than 18½ miles below lay the cloud-hidden New Mexico desert to which I shortly would parachute.

Sitting in my gondola, which gently twisted with the balloon's slow turnings, I had begun to sweat lightly, though the temperature read 36° below zero Fahrenheit. Sunlight burned in on me under the edge of an aluminised anti-glare curtain and through the gondola's open door.

In my earphones crackled the voice of Capt. Marvin Feldstein, one of our project's two doctors, from ground control at Holloman Air Force Base: 'Three minutes till jump, Joe.'

Kittinger's first-hand account of the jump is quite astonishing. It isn't just the sheer audacity of the feat, but the logistics of the entire operation – the creation of the pressure suit, the altitude chamber tests, the mental and physical hazards, the size of the balloon. Hundreds of technicians worked on the launch, testing every tiny piece of equipment and overseeing check lists. Every detail, right down to Joe's diet, had been carefully controlled.

During the ascent Joe had reached 43,000 feet when he noticed that the air bladder in his right pressure glove had failed to inflate. He knew that his hand would swell and lose most of its circulation, causing extreme pain, but he didn't tell anyone. He kept going, because he was confident that he could still operate the gondola because the controls involved flicking switches that could be nudged with his hand.

It took one hour and forty-three minutes to reach 102,800 feet. Joe spent about ten minutes at altitude and made several important discoveries for the future space programme. His pulse rate hit 156, which meant a healthy man, properly equipped, could expend tremendous energy in space for brief periods. At the same time, the solar radiation caused him to perspire even though the temperature outside was -36°F. According to Joe, this supported evidence that temperature definitions break down in space. 'You can bake on one side, freeze on the other, regardless of what the thermometer says.'

As for the actual jump, Kittinger had written:

At zero count I step into space. No wind whistles or billows my clothing. I have absolutely no sensation of the increasing speed with which I fall. I drop facing the clouds. Then I roll over on my back and find an eerie sight. The silver balloon contrasts starkly with a sky as black as night . . . Again I look for stars, but see none.

When the six-foot stabilisation canopy pops out, I already have dropped to about 96,000 feet. I am delighted to find myself perfectly anchored against the dreaded flat spin. I turn with ease by sticking out an arm and leg. However, a new danger threatens. Soon after I become stabilised, I feel a choking sensation. I had experienced the same thing on a previous jump, and we had devoted countless tests to eliminating it. As I plummet lower, the sensation eases but worry remains.

Later the engineers arranged a 'hanging', where someone donned the equipment and was suspended from overhead hooks. Although they couldn't be positive, it looked as though the steel cable that anchored Joe's helmet to the pressure suit had been riding up, forcing the front of the neck ring against his throat. I make a note to ask Joe about it, if he agrees to see me.

According to the graphs monitoring heart rate and respiration, Joe had made one breath last through the first fifteen seconds of freefall – the period of instability prior to the drogue chute opening. A sharp intake of breath marked the deployment and by then his pulse had risen to 156 beats a minute. Static had blurred the electrocardiogram's measure of exertion.

Sixteen seconds after leaving the gondola the timer had fired perfectly and released the drogue parachute. Initially Joe felt nothing and wondered if it was working. He considered whether to use the manual override. Then he felt the gentle tugging and he stabilised, face to Earth. He spoke into a tape recorder as he fell, giving readings from the stopwatch and altimeter and making remarks on the overall situation, his feelings and the functioning of the automatic equipment. His chute deployed automatically at 17,500 feet, and he landed 13 minutes, 45 seconds after bailing out, more than twenty miles from the launch site.

Digging even further through the archives, I discover more articles about the jump, including one in *Life* magazine on 29 August 1960. Joe's jump is on the front cover – 'FANTASTIC CATCH IN THE SKY, RECORD LEAP TOWARD EARTH'.

Inside it begins:

Space Race Soars With a Vengeance

The space race went on with a vengeance last week. The US produced a new space hero, Air Force Captain Joseph Kittinger, who jumped from an open balloon gondola at 102,800 feet – the highest man has ever gone in an unpowered flight. He plummeted toward earth for sixteen miles before his main chute opened, in the longest freefall in history. As Kittinger fell, automatic cameras in the gondola caught some of the most exciting pictures of a man's daring ever made.

From the gondola, Kittinger had radioed back the message: 'There is a hostile sky above me. Man will never conquer space. He may live in it, but he will never conquer it.'

Among the notes I gather is an explanation of why Joe's jump isn't mentioned among many official balloon or parachute records. Apparently, to get an official balloon record, the occupant has to go up and come down with the balloon. Equally, for parachute records, a designated representative of the FAI (*Fédération Aéronautique Nationale*) must witness the jump and special recording equipment has to be carried on the drop – neither of which happened because Joe didn't set out to break any records. That's why the official holder of the highest parachute jump is a Russian, Eugene Andreev, who leapt from 83,523 feet in November 1962, near Volsk.

As I study Joe's book and gather together articles on the jump, it's clear that hundreds of scientists, researchers, technicians and engineers had been responsible. The staggering size of such an operation raises the obvious question of whether a civilian organisation such as High Adventure can possibly hope to beat the record. After all, Joe had the backing of the US Air Force and the newly formed national space administration, NASA.

When I report to Loel, though, he isn't daunted. With sponsorship and marketing agreements, along with TV, film and documentary rights, the cost can hopefully be covered. Admittedly, we face a problem because of the short duration of the jump. Events such as the Formula 1 Grand Prix are held over days, with practice sessions, qualifying laps and then the race itself. This makes for large crowds, lots of cameras and the sort of television exposure that brings in big sponsorship.

A skydive from high altitude, although visually dynamic and exciting, will last only a fraction of this time unless we can make use of the build-up. On the positive side, it's reassuring to know that the technology has been in place for thirty years and some of it will have improved. The major concern is the life-support system, which is so specialised that very few companies, or countries for that matter, are capable of building one.

According to the Royal Aerospace Establishment at Farnborough, the British have only partial pressure suits used by military pilots in the event of an emergency. These only function for short periods such as an ejection and descent. I need something that will keep me alive during the two-hour ascent.

Only the Russians and the Americans have the technology, because of their space programmes. John Parker, the chief executive of High Adventure, contacts NASA and meetings are arranged at the Johnson

Space Centre, about twenty miles south-east of Houston, Texas. Just getting through the security screening should have told us that these people jealously guard their secrets.

John Stanley, a NASA scientist, gives us the standard museum tour before getting down to business. Immediately, he makes it clear that the administration can't officially give us any assistance because its charter does not allow it to become involved in civilian projects. The law can only be changed by the US Congress. Even so, NASA is extremely interested in the Skydive from Space – particularly the effect of a human being going supersonic after a bail-out.

'It's a question we are planning to look at in the near future,' says Stanley, explaining the need for a better escape system for the US space shuttle. In the *Challenger* disaster on 28 January 1986, the rocket carrying the shuttle had exploded seventy-three seconds into the flight at 46,000 feet, going twice the speed of sound. The cabin had broken off the shuttle and it had plunged into the sea, killing all seven astronauts. The fact that there was no escape system to give the crew even a slim chance of surviving such an accident had angered the American public.

Since then, new procedures had been adopted which might allow one or more crew to bail out, equipped with oxygen tanks and parachutes. Unfortunately, few astronauts are likely to have the freefall experience to be able to maintain stability if they exit at high altitude. Nor is it known what effect going supersonic will have on them.

When Stanley shows us the normal pressure suit used in the ascent phase of a shuttle flight, it is obvious that it would have to be modified extensively for the skydive. The crucial joints in the arms, legs and shoulders are designed for someone in a sitting position, whereas I'll need far more flexibility in the arms and shoulders to maintain stability.

A civilian company makes the suits under contract for the American space programme, and they don't just hand them out to anyone. When I contact the company, it's suggested that things might be different if a well-known American aeronautical company such as Lockheed Missiles became associated with the project.

Following this up, I speak to the chairman of Lockheed, but again he explains the amount of red tape that would have to be shredded to grant us permission to use certain equipment. Free enterprise doesn't apply to the American space programme.

It's a similar story when I begin investigating the balloon. The National Scientific Balloon Facility near Palestine, Texas, has launched, tracked and recovered more than 1,700 balloons over the last twenty-two years. I decide I have to go and see them, and hire a helicopter to fly the last leg of the journey from Houston with John Parker. We're met by the operational manager, Danny Ball, who explains the research being done using the balloons.

'We've got a ninety-nine per cent success rate,' he says proudly of the launches.

'What's the average payload?' I ask.

'About three thousand pounds. The average balloon size is twenty million cubic feet.'

'And what's the heaviest payload?'

'We've taken eight thousand pounds to a hundred and thirty thousand feet. That's about the size of three small cars.'

Justifiably proud, Danny shows us videos of a launch taking place, and explains that ruptures are most likely at two points: as the balloon is being inflated, and when it passes through the tropopause – this is an atmospheric boundary between the troposphere and stratosphere, about seven miles above the Earth, where the coldest temperatures are encountered during any high-altitude flight, reaching as low as -94°F.

By this stage of a flight, the helium in the polyethylene balloon has expanded and stretched the fabric to less than two-thousandths of an inch thick – like a piece of cellophane. In the extreme cold it becomes brittle, and even a tiny object colliding with the skin will shatter it like a Christmas tree ornament.

Another critical area to avoid is the jet stream belt, where rivers of air race at upwards of 100 mph through the upper atmosphere. These increase the danger of a wind shear and can carry a balloon off course and into storm clouds.

The jet streams move north and south towards the poles at different times of the year and will affect what date we choose for the launch.

The NSBF has all the technology we need to launch and track the balloon, yet none of it is available to us. The facility comes under the same umbrella as NASA. 'We can't have any involvement with a manned balloon flight,' says Danny, genuinely sorry because the project fascinates him. 'But if you need any advice, I'd be more than happy to help.'

He hands me his card and mentions several former colleagues – now working for civilian organisations – who he says have the expertise and experience to get our balloon off the ground.

A fortnight later, I fly to Florida to meet Joe Kittinger. We're sitting at his house in Orlando, browsing through his photographs, when he first mentions the name of Nick Piantaniea.

'You haven't heard of him?' Joe raises an eyebrow.

'No.'

'Well you should. A lot of people have talked about breaking the record, but most of them have never left *terra firma*. Nick Piantaniea did. I worked on that project.'

'What happened?'

Joe lowers his voice. 'To tell you the truth, I didn't think Nick was ready for it or up to it, but he was determined. Nobody really had the experience, because sports parachuting was in its infancy. You see, Nick became interested in high-altitude bail-outs and started doing some testing on his own. He wanted to prove – just like you do – that ordinary sky-diving techniques could control a jumper from that altitude without any stabilisation chute.'

'How many jumps had he done?'

'Nowhere near as many as you.'

Joe tells me the story, pausing occasionally to answer my questions or sip on a drink. Piantaniea was thirty-three years old, six foot two inches tall and weighed 200 lb. He wasn't a trained astronaut or a military test jumper, but he had more than 400 parachute jumps under his belt.

He, too, wanted to break the sound barrier, and aeronautical engineers had estimated that by freefalling from 120,000 feet he would reach a maximum speed of approximately Mach 1.1 – 750 mph at 90,000 feet.

'He didn't have a drogue chute?'

'Yes, he did, but only in case of an emergency. If he couldn't maintain control in freefall he planned to deploy it.'

Joe explains how Piantaniea's first attempt began on 22 October 1965, when the 3,700,000 cubic foot balloon burst over St Paul, Minnesota, just after it passed 22,700 feet. A six-knot wind shear had shredded the balloon. A ground signal fired a small explosive charge that released the gondola from the stricken balloon and it fell for several seconds before a large parachute deployed. At 10,000 feet Piantaniea bailed out and pulled his own parachute, landing safely.

He made his next attempt on 2 February 1966, from Sioux Falls, South Dakota. Launched just after midday, the polyethylene balloon took an hour and forty minutes to reach 120,500 feet. Piantaniea began his five-minute countdown to the jump. With three minutes to go he activated his GE oscillator – an instrument to record his rate of descent. At jump minus two minutes he unclipped his seat-belt, activated his personal oxygen unit and reached forward and set the automatic timer that would release the gondola from the balloon fifteen minutes after he exited.

With a minute to go, he tried to disconnect his last link with the gondola – the main oxygen supply hose that sustained him during the ascent. The connection had frozen in the -96°F temperatures. Piantaniea's pressure suit had heavy mittens, with little movement in the joints once fully inflated. He had no tools. For ten minutes he struggled, trying to get the hose loose. Meanwhile, he continued rising to 123,500 feet – the highest a man had ever been in a balloon.

'He had no choice but to stay with the gondola,' says Joe. 'We were listening on the ground.'

'What did you do?'

'We had to get him down quickly. We told Nick we were going to release the gondola from the balloon. We gave him a countdown. He had to get seated and re-fasten his seat-belt. Only he couldn't do up the belt because of the heavy gloves.

'Sending a signal from the ground, they released the gondola at 2.12 p.m. and it began falling with Piantaniea inside, desperately hanging on. We had no idea if the gondola would fall in an upright position or tumble out of control, hurling him outside, ripping the oxygen hose loose and killing him within seconds. Nor did we know if the opening shock of the gondola's huge parachute at high speed could be survived by a human being.'

For thirty-five seconds the gondola plummeted, accelerating through a near-vacuum to 600 mph. Miraculously, it remained upright, and at 98,000 feet the streaming canopy caught enough air to inflate. Rather than being an enormous shock, the opening was no different than a normal terminal-velocity opening in freefall.

Until then I had never heard of anyone opening a parachute that high. The gondola still had to negotiate the high winds of the tropopause, which must have caused the parachute to oscillate violently.

'It took more than half an hour for him to get down,' says Joe. 'He wanted to bail out at a lower altitude, but he still couldn't get the oxygen hose loose. He came down inside the gondola, standing on his main parachute to cushion the landing shock.'

Silently, I'm taking notes. First, the gondola had remained stable during the freefall descent, which suggested that an object could fall from extreme altitude without spinning out of control. More importantly, I have to make sure that my pressure suit has flexibility in the fingers and hands.

Nick Piantaniea waited until May 1966 before he tried again. The balloon was launched early in the morning and an hour later had reached 57,000 feet. The ground crew, listening over the intercom, heard a sudden rush of air and a choked cry.

'They released the gondola instantly, but it took nearly half an hour to reach the ground. Nick was still alive, but in a coma from oxygen starvation.'

It appeared as if the visor had blown out of his helmet, exposing him to the hostile environment. He immediately tried to tear the connections and throw himself out of the gondola, hoping to freefall to where he could breathe.

Joe mentions that Piantaniea had a habit of lifting his face-plate to clear his nose. He thinks that maybe he became disorientated and opened his own visor, not realising he was so high. The effect was catastrophic. He died four months later without regaining consciousness.

11

Jackie arrives at 8 a.m. and I'm lying on the sofa, still dressed in the same clothes as yesterday. She knows that it's been a bad night. I sit in the garden chair in the kitchen, watching her fry up bacon and eggs for breakfast. The sun is shining and the first daffodils are out – my only flowers. There are weeds coming up in the lawn and sprouting near the garden shed.

'I brought you a copy of the *Telegraph*,' says Jackie. 'Do you want a cup of tea?'

'Yeah.'

She chats about local news and the number of cards people have sent me. 'I can help you write the replies,' she suggests.

I try to concentrate on the crossword, never leaving my chair as I swallow tea and smoke cigarettes. Later, when she goes upstairs to the office, I follow her and fidget, sometimes pacing up and down, or sitting down with my back against the door throwing scraps of paper at the waste bin. I ask her questions because the sound of her voice is comforting.

At 2 p.m. I have an appointment with my new shrink, Dr Allman. He's a psychiatrist from Stonebow Unit in the grounds of Hereford Hospital, about half a mile from where I live. He's younger than I expect, in his mid-thirties, slightly built with brown hair. Like a lot of these blokes, he seems to be in a hurry. They don't have time for small talk, and even a simple question like 'How are you?' is designed to assess how the drugs are working, rather than being an attempt at polite conversation.

Jackie is with me and she tries to be positive while I'm being negative and depressed. Allman jokes that I'm the only patient he knows who brings along a secretary to appointments. He's reading my case notes and the letter from Dr Friedman. I can see he doesn't agree with something.

'I'm going to put you on some new medication,' he says.

Bloody marvellous! They're moving the goalposts again. I spend four weeks being jabbed by doctors in London and now it's starting again.

'We'll just try you on this,' he says, arranging the injection, 'and then I want you to come and see me every day. If things start to improve, we'll make it twice a week and then weekly.'

'Can I stop taking the dribbling drug?'

'No, I wouldn't advise that.'

Another expert I have to prove wrong, I think to myself, as the needle slides home. Afterwards, Jackie asks if I want to go for a coffee but I've had enough of the outside world for one day – I want to get back so I can keep 'sterilising' the house, searching for answers.

That night I sleep on the sofa again, serenaded by the TV and wrapped in a duvet. I don't want to go upstairs to my own bed; I can't sleep in that room. I don't know why, I haven't worked that out yet. Right now it's not on top of my list of questions that I need to answer – I'm more concerned about Anna in Washington and the Skydive from Space.

*

Saad is finishing university and the job in Washington will end in a few months. I've done all the research I can do in the States and I really need to be nearer to Geneva, where High Adventure is based. We're approaching the Russian space agency, Zvezda, about a pressure suit and life-support system, which may mean having to visit Moscow.

I've bought myself a Cessna 172 and nicknamed her 'Zephyr'. I'm going to fly her back to Britain across the Atlantic. Des thinks I'm crazy, and Anna isn't exactly over the moon.

'It only has one engine,' she says, as if I've forgotten the fact. 'What happens if it suddenly stops?'

'I get wet.'

'Don't make jokes, this is serious.'

'I am being serious. People fly across the Atlantic all the time.'

'Yes, on 747s where they have meals on plastic trays and watch in-flight movies.'

'In light planes.'

'With only one engine?'

Anna has a point, of course, but Zephyr is a sturdy old girl. She was built in 1967, but the age doesn't matter because airframes last for years. She used to do forestry work in Arizona – a dry state, which means there's less chance of metal fatigue and corrosion. And I checked her history before I handed over the $14,000.

Light planes are cheaper in America and I'll have no trouble finding a buyer in Britain. I thought about shipping her home, but apart from being expensive it means taking the wings off and having them reassembled in England. From then on, the plane is treated as though it has a damaged history. Doing it this way I save money and show any future buyers how much faith I have in her.

First priority is to get my 'instrument rating' because I'm not licensed to fly in low visibility. Basically it means passing a test where they put a hood over my head which looks like a welder's visor and which blocks any view of the windscreen or side windows. I have to rely totally on my instrument panel and maps.

Bill, the instructor, looks just like a driving-test examiner, nursing a clip-board. He climbs into the passenger seat and looks over his shoulder. 'What the bloody hell is that?'

Zephyr is normally a four-seater but I've removed the two rear seats and replaced them with a big square aluminium tank. It's going to increase the Cessna's flying range from about three and a half hours to seventeen hours. Bill seems pretty impressed.

'Okay, show me your documents.'

I show him my papers.

'But where's your American private pilot's licence?'

'I haven't got one.'

My fixed-wing licence is from South Africa. The Americans don't recognise it, although the English do, which is rather complicated but somehow the system works. Bill agrees to continue, although he's not entirely happy. Once in the air, I don the hood and we fly around

Washington. With a map on my lap, I have to rely on my artificial horizon and direction indicator to navigate as we simulate flying in cloud.

During the next hour, I do a few controlled descents into imaginary
airports and then climb again. Not a problem.

'Okay, fine, take the hood off,' he says. 'But I'm not happy with this
licence business. I want you to do the basic VFR test [visual flight rules].'

That's like being asked to do your driving test again, when everyone
knows that you've forgotten most of the road rules. He gets me to do all
the set procedures – slow flight, stalls, descending into a place, cutting the
engine and gliding.

I manage to get through and then he says, 'Okay, basic VFR map-
reading. Take me back to W32.'

I haven't a clue where we are and he wants me to take him back to
Washington Executive using only the map. Scanning the countryside, I
look for a prominent road, river – anything that can give me a fix on my
location. Just my luck that Virginia has so much woodland.

Bill is getting impatient. 'Okay, just tell me what you should be looking for now.'

'Well, ah, first I want to establish where I am . . . I'm looking for a
prominent landmark to relate to the map.'

'Okay.' He's flown over this countryside thousands of times – it's like
his back yard.

On the dashboard of the Cessna I have a GPS (global positioning
system) that can instantly give my location, but it's not a standard piece
of equipment. Washington Executive Airport is programmed into the
GPS. By punching one button it would automatically give me a heading
and a distance.

Bill is glancing out the starboard window, his patience wearing thin.
Without him seeing, I hit the GPS. W32 flashes on to the screen. I hit
'Yes'.

'Twenty-seven miles, bearing 230.'

I glance down at the map, calculate a back-bearing on 230° for twenty-
seven miles and then say, 'Well, Bill, I think I'm some place about here,'
pointing to the map.

'Well done,' he says.

'In which case I want to be heading on about two hundred and thirty-
five degrees for about twenty-five miles.'

'Yes, not bad at all.'

When we land Bill gives me a ticket for my instrument rating. I'm set to go.

Unfortunately, the engine is shot. During a regular service, mechanics find nearly thirty faults, and the repairs will delay me for at least a fortnight. Saad is worried about me flying back, and when he hears about the engine he insists on buying me a new one.

I've been researching the flight for three months, reading books, writing letters and getting special dispensations. I've studied the radio procedures and call signs so I can rattle them off in my sleep. My VHF radio can only transmit 'line of sight', which isn't too bad from 9,000 feet when the range is up to 200 miles, but crossing the Atlantic I'll need something far more powerful to speak to Shannon in Ireland or Reykjavik in Iceland – between them they control traffic in the North Atlantic.

I rent a long-range HF radio for the flight and put it behind me on the fuel tank. This bounces signals off the ionosphere, and I know from my SAS signals training that you can change the reception by adjusting the length of the aerial. I rig up a makeshift aerial using a brick tied to a long piece of wire. The plan is to lower the brick out the window and unroll the wire until I tune into the strongest signal. It might not sound very scientific, but the aerial seems to work.

From the outset I've been planning to have a co-pilot, Jacob, a nice young lad who's good company and very keen. Unfortunately, the two-week delay for the engine means he can't make the trip. All my calculations for fuel use and the layout of the plane are based on two people. Unless I can find someone else, I'll have to use sandbags to re-create the 160 lb. weight of a passenger.

At the flying club one morning a Dutch student pilot approaches me. 'My name is Erik. I want to come with you. You will take me?' It sounds more like a hijack than a request, but it solves the problem. Erik is in his early twenties and thinks he's God's gift to aviation. He's going home to Europe after finishing college in Washington.

'There's no room for luggage. You can't bring anything other than the bare minimum,' I tell him. 'I'm not even taking a washing and shaving kit – just a toothbrush cut in half and a small tube of toothpaste. Do you have a survival suit?'

He nods.

'Okay, we leave on Monday morning at eight o'clock.'

'Yah.'

I should have known there'd be a problem. Erik turns up on Monday carrying a briefcase that weighs a ton and a blazer on a coat-hanger.

'What's this?'

'I have a job interview in Amsterdam. I must look good.'

For Chrissake!

The blazer can stay, but I make Erik go through the briefcase, tossing out pens and other crap. He's in a strop.

Saying goodbye to Anna is fairly painless and without tears; she's known for months that I'm leaving. I don't know if I'll see her again, but she says that she's going to visit me and there's a possibility that she might continue her medical studies in the UK. We've had fun together, but it's never been true love.

Zephyr takes off from Washington Executive and we head north. I've managed to get permission to fly straight over La Guardia airport and New York City at 10,000 feet. What a sight! Erik is moaning already about my smoking. He keeps eyeing the fuel tank and thinks he's going to perish in a ball of flames. If he doesn't shut up I'll make him get out and walk.

In calm, cold conditions we land in Bangor, Maine, and stay overnight. Next morning we cross the Canadian border, heading for Moncton near the Gulf of St Lawrence, two hours away. In the middle of nowhere we strike a thunderstorm with lightning slashing from the heavy grey clouds and rain cutting visibility to only a few feet. Zephyr is being buffeted fiercely and I hit the GPS, hoping to find an airfield nearby. There's one about fifteen miles to the east.

As I descend from the cloud on my final approach, I can see the horizon and the sides of the storm. I decide I can fly around it and keep going.

From Moncton we head north on a six-hour flight across the Gulf of St Lawrence and a wilderness of frozen tundra to Goose Bay in Newfoundland – my last landfall in North America. In case I have to ditch in this wasteland, I'm carrying knives, fire-lighting equipment, a compass, fishing line, cigarettes, rations and a small-shafted steel axe for cutting wood and ice holes. My only luxury is a jar of Marmite.

Goose Bay is a frontier outpost, full of fishermen, fur trappers and bar owners. Zephyr feels like a time machine that has landed in the last century until reality roars overhead in the shape of several fighter jets from the nearby Canadian Air Force base.

Over a drink that night, I befriend a couple of British RAF pilots who are training in Canada. They're fascinated by the Atlantic flight and one of them asks, 'Are you carrying a parachute?'

'No. If anything goes wrong I'll stay with the plane.'

I tell them about the inflatable life-raft, emergency radio beacons and ration pack. 'I've undone the bolts on the outer hinges of my door and made a mark on the inside of the airframe. Just before ditching, I'll use the axe to smash the remaining bolts and jettison the door so I don't get trapped inside by the pressure of the water. Of course, I'll have to be low enough to make sure the door doesn't blow back into the tail.'

'What about your passenger?'

'Oh, I'll hit him over the head with the axe first.'

I see the look of horror on their faces.

'He's a big clumsy bloke who's certain to bloody panic and kill us both. It's best to knock him out early.' For obvious reasons, I haven't told Erik the plan.

The Canadians have strict regulations on air safety, and the next morning someone from the Civil Aviation Authority checks all my survival equipment and asks me questions, inventing various scenarios to test how I'd react in an emergency.

The weather has closed in and I delay departure for another twenty-four hours, but the next morning – 24 July 1992 – is cold and clear. I'm up before 6 a.m., running my eye over Zephyr and filling the tanks. A couple of the British pilots have come down to say goodbye. The journey to Iceland is 1,400 miles, the longest leg. I've had to get special dispensation from Cessna, because normally the maximum take-off weight is 2,300 lb. and I'm nearly a thousand pounds heavier than that. Every extra gallon weighs 7 lb. – Zephyr has become a huge flying fuel tank.

She sits heavily on the ground, with the tyres splayed out. I start the engine, give her full throttle and she doesn't move for five seconds. I hit the brakes a few times and she nudges forward, slowly rolling towards the taxi-way. It takes me an age to reach the end of the 12,000-foot runway, but I'm going to need every inch of it.

I open the throttle and point her down the broken white line.

'Come on, Zephyr! Get a move on.'

Erik's head has disappeared somewhere up his arse. I'm watching the air-speed indicator as I race along the runway. Normally Zephyr will lift off at 60 mph, but I keep her down until she's doing about 85 mph and then ease back on the control column. She lifts off very sluggishly and flies better once she's lost the friction of the runway.

I have to climb to altitude before I set out over the sea, but it takes me forty minutes to reach 7,000 feet because of the weight. Every time I ease back on the elevator, Zephyr balloons up a little and I bleed off my speed. That's when the stall warning alarm sounds and I have to level her off again. Zephyr wants to descend, but I can't do that. Instead I nose her upwards, a few hundred feet at a time, finding it harder as the air grows thinner.

'Goose Bay approach, this is Cessna November 84587. Thanks for your help. Departing your area as per flight plan.'

The skies are blue and the horizon is clear as I head out across the Labrador Sea at 65 mph. Erik has opened his eyes again but he doesn't say much. A moose would be better company.

Two hours later, I'm starting to relax a little when two air force jets blast past me, one on either side. A voice crackles over the radio: 'Hey, how's it going?'

'Great.'

The jets are sitting right up, with the flaps down, trying hard to fly as slowly as possible, yet they still scream past in the blink of an eye.

'Hey, you're going kind of slow there,' one of them says.

'Yeah, I'm having trouble with my afterburner.'

'Well, I thought you might like to know that we're out from Goose Bay and our ETE [estimated time en route] is eight minutes.'

'Yeah, well at least I own it!'

They make a final pass before heading back. Zephyr is on her own again.

Normally aircraft have to report their exact location every ten degrees of longitude, but I'm travelling so slowly that I do it every five degrees, giving the time, my altitude, next location and expected time of arrival. I'm flying into a slight headwind at 9,000 feet, staying underneath the clouds. The sea is so rough it's hard to spot any shipping.

Erik has fallen asleep again, so I light a cigarette. The heater is operating at full blast. I've been pratting about with the HF radio, lowering my brick out the window. I manage to pick up Shannon, although the reception isn't good. It also costs a bloody fortune because they charge about £30 when all I say is, 'Hello, I'm here.'

The whole point of this exercise is to save money, so I switch back to the VHF radio and every few hours I find a friendly commercial airliner in the area.

'Hello, any traffic in the North Atlantic copy this message?' I'm transmitting on the emergency frequency 121.5, which isn't exactly encouraged.

'This is speedjet TWA Flight 105 out from London Heathrow en route to New York, we copy your message, go ahead.'

'Can you switch to talk frequency 123.4?'

'Roger. Switching now.'

'Speedjet TWA Flight 105, this is Cessna November 84587 over.'

'Roger. Receiving you strength five.'

'Can you relay a position report for me to Goose Bay?'

'Yeah, go ahead.'

Because the airliner is 26,000 feet above me it can use their standard radio because the greater height gives it a bigger range. I relay my latitude, longitude, flight level, expected time of arrival in Iceland and when I'll next report my location.

'Roger that. Wait out.'

A few minutes later the captain of the speedjet comes back to me and confirms the message has been delivered. Then he gets all friendly. 'Hey, what's your air speed? You must be flying a balloon.'

'A Cessna 172, Skyhawk.'

'Gee whiz, what are you doing way out here?'

Turns out that the pilot and a mate once flew a plane across the Atlantic. 'We've got you plotted and you're dead on track,' he says.

'It's the old GPS.'

'Ah, I see, we didn't have those in my day.'

Before wishing me good luck, he scans the radar and gives me a weather report on what lies ahead. This slight headwind is beginning to worry me because I'm using more fuel than I expected. I want to reach Reykjavik with two hours' worth of fuel in reserve, in case I'm delayed in landing. According to the GPS I'm a third of the way into the flight. At this rate, I'm cutting it fine, and if the wind gets any stronger Zephyr will be landing on empty or with her wheels in the water.

Checking the map, I do some calculations. Within twenty minutes I have to make a decision. Do I detour to Greenland or push ahead for Reykjavik? Before leaving Washington, I researched the likelihood of going to Greenland. There's an airfield at Narssaq, on the southern tip of the island, and it's manned by a single air-traffic controller. The bloke must have seriously pissed someone off to get this posting.

Okay, that's it, we'll pay him a visit, I decide, changing course. Erik is still sleeping. The airstrip at Narssaq is at the end of a long, narrow fjord and pilots have to be instrument-rated to attempt a landing. I soon discover the reason. Looking out the window, I see mountains that appear to be no more than five miles ahead of me, yet the map says they're four times that distance. They seem closer because of sheer size and the fact that the landscape has so few visual reference points.

'Trust your instruments,' I keep whispering. I turn and the runway is ahead of me. I'm flying over icebergs and fighting the urge to put down too early because I know the runway is further away than I think.

I'm still carrying a lot of fuel, and when I pull the column back to flare Zephyr, the tremendous weight at the back creates instability. I quickly readjust and trim it out before touching down. Because the runway is uphill I have to throttle on instead of off so as not to roll backwards and finish up with the fish.

The lone air-traffic controller is from Denmark and he lets me kip in the tower for a few hours, which is the only structure to be seen except for a few old sheds. He says we can stay longer, but I want to keep ahead of the bad weather following us.

We chat about the flight to Iceland, studying the map. The logical route is to head directly north-east across Greenland.

'Don't be tempted to try it,' he says. 'The icepack on the peninsula is about 12,000 feet – you won't make it. Fly south, back out of the fjord and then follow the coastline.'

After refuelling, I point Zephyr down the hill and gravity makes the take-off a little easier this time. The sky is blue and clear as we soar over the fjord. By contouring around the coastline I'm adding about two hours to the flight time, but looking left I can see the peninsula and the towering icepack. There seems to be a gap in the middle.

'Sod it,' I say, 'let's go for it.'

I turn north-east, aiming at the break in the distant mountains. Forty-five minutes later, the icy peaks are much closer, but cloud suddenly appears all around us. At 9,000 feet, in these temperatures, it can be fatal flying into cloud and picking up ice. I can't see a thing. How close are the mountains?

Erik is harping, 'Climb! Climb! Climb!'

'Shut up! We're not going further into cloud.' The nose pitches down as I push forward on the control column, going into a steep descent.

'What are you doing?' screams Erik. 'You'll kill us!'

The seconds tick by and the air-speed indicator climbs. The wings are going to come off unless I slow down.

Seven thousand feet . . . 6,500 . . . 6,000 . . . 5,500. Erik has eyes the size of saucers.

I'm relying on a belief that the mountain is further away than it looks. Zephyr hurtles from the clouds and all I can see is a complete white-out. The snow-covered ground and the clouds are the same colour. Staring downwards, I manage to pick up faint contours and level her out. We stay under the cloud at low level for half an hour and head back towards the ocean. I wait until there's a break in the cloud before climbing back to 9,000 feet.

The controller had been right. I should have taken his advice and followed the coastline rather than trying to cross the peninsula. Always listen to the locals.

Reykjavik is nine and a half hours away. I'm flying above the cloud in a crisp, beautiful blue sky. The cold air gets maximum power out of the engine and better airflow over the wings. Warm air is less dense.

To keep myself alert, I snack on chocolate bars and biscuits. There's no toilet on board and no opportunity to step outside, so I urinate inside my survival suit. The warm wet feeling soon disappears and my legs become cold. I use the little tricks I learned on OPs (observation posts) to stay warm and alert – moving my toes, flexing each muscle in turn.

Some of the cloud formations are astonishing – huge swirling whirlpools that look like miniature hurricanes and explosions of white that reach up like fingers into the sky and slowly close into fists. It feels as though I've found the source of the world's weather, and have been allowed inside even though Zephyr is little more than a wind-blown leaf when set against such an awesome canvas.

Reykjavik is a welcome sight because I'm exhausted. Erik hasn't offered to take the controls once – mostly he sleeps and whinges. I book into a hotel at the airport and peel off the immersion suit in the shower. It's time to sleep.

Two days later, on 27 July, I set off for Scotland, seven and a half hours away. My honeymoon with the weather finally ends, and the closer I get to Glasgow the filthier it becomes. Rain, sleet, high winds – the works. Approaching the airport I have to climb into cloud, picking up a lot of ice. It collects on the wing struts and creeps up from the bottom corners of the windscreen, spidery glass, edging out in splinters. I can also see it building up on the leading edge of the wings, adding weight to Zephyr and upsetting the aerodynamics. I'm losing lift. The only way to get rid of the ice is to descend, looking for warmer air.

Glasgow Airport is under heavy cloud, and the main runway is being lashed by a twenty-knot cross-wind. It's an IFR approach (instrument flight rules), relying on a chart on my lap and the information on the cockpit console. They don't recommend a single-pilot IFR into a strange airport because there's too much to do in the aircraft – reading maps, setting the stopwatch, watching the instruments and operating the radio.

Locked within cloud, I descend. As I break through at 4,000 feet, I feel like cheering. What a beautiful sight! The landing lights are blazing through the gloom and a commercial airliner is sitting on the taxi-way waiting for me to land. Now I realise that Zephyr is flying near sideways to counter the fierce cross-wind. I aim out to the right edge of the runway, keep descending and then, at about fifteen feet, kick left rudder and begin my flare. Immediately, Zephyr starts drifting across with the wind. One wheel touches first, almost on the centre line, and then the other wheel touches down. Hold the flare, hold the flare. Let the nose come forward. I'm down.

Erik is leaving to catch a commercial flight, but I spend a few hours putting Zephyr to bed. I'm tying down her wings when a customs officer arrives, wrapped in foul-weather gear and shouting into the wind. As he shakes my hand I notice a tattoo.

'You were never 3 Para, mate?'

'Yeah. Why?'

'I was 2 Para.'

'Well, fuck it! Get inside and let's have a cup of tea.'

Over a brew I complete all the paperwork for customs declarations and export certificates. The ground servicing manager, an old boy called Charlie, asks me if I want to hangar my plane. It costs £20 a day.

'Yeah, put her inside, she deserves it,' I say.

Afterwards, Charlie takes me through the airport and shows me where I can get a cheap hotel room for the night. He's very formal and keeps calling me 'Captain Read', even though I'm wearing an old tracksuit and I pilot a Cessna.

Next morning, Charlie picks me up from the hotel. The weather is still filthy, but I go straight out on IFR, climbing up through the cloud. The weather forecast says the ceiling is only 5,000 feet. Breaking through into sunshine, I fly south over Liverpool where the weather begins to clear. By the time I land in Shobdon, outside Hereford, the patchwork fields and picturesque hamlets stretch to the horizon. I've spent forty-two hours flying since leaving Washington, and I realise I don't want to sell Zephyr any more – we've been through too much together.

12

The Skydive from Space is taking over my life. I've been working full-time on the project and have set up an office upstairs in the house with a computer, fax machine and filing cabinets. Already there is paperwork up to my ankles because office management isn't one of my strong points.

Apart from liaising with High Adventure in Geneva, I'm keeping in touch with Joe Kittinger in Florida, Harry in France and also Loel Guinness, who never seems to stay in one place for more than a few weeks at a time.

There were two possible suppliers of a life-support suit – the Russians and the Americans – and since the Americans can't or won't co-operate, I'm now trying to sell the idea to Zvezda, the Russian space agency. I'm not a scientist, and I can't teach their aeronautical experts about aerodynamics and drag co-efficients; nor can I teach their life-support engineers about the extremes of pressure and temperature at high altitude. But I do know about freefall. I have to convince them that the jump can be done.

Dave Hirst is another important contact. He's the chief engineer for GQ Parachutes, a company which designs canopies for specialised tasks such as the escape systems on military aircraft. I'd been introduced to Dave through Rixie, my old mate from the Red Freds, who's now a test jumper for GQ.

Arranging to meet Dave in a pub in Woking, I explain that I need information on drogue parachutes and whether it is feasible to carry one on the record jump.

'How high are you going to go?' he asks.

'About a hundred and thirty thousand feet.'

'Well, to start with, a drogue isn't going to open at that height unless it's the size of a marquee tent. There isn't enough atmosphere to inflate it.'

Dave has done about 200 freefall jumps and knows about Joe Kittinger's record. 'You want to break the sound barrier, don't you?'

'Yes, but the altitude record is the first priority. If I can go supersonic at the same time, it's a bonus . . .' I let the sentence trail off and ask a new question: 'What are the likely physical effects of a body breaking the sound barrier?'

Dave ponders this for a moment. 'The overall effect of being supersonic doesn't cause injury. It's actually remarkably smooth, which is why you get such a nice ride on Concorde.'

'But that's not a human body in freefall. I've heard a story about the French doing some high-altitude tests with dummies and having the arms and legs ripped off.'

'Well, that's possible, I suppose. Being supersonic doesn't cause injury, but getting there is the problem. Do you know the reason it took so long for someone to break the sound barrier?'

I shake my head.

Dave pulls a pen out of his breast pocket and starts drawing lines on a notepad.

'For years people imagined that the sound barrier was this invisible wall in the sky that no aircraft could smash through without disintegrating. That's because planes weren't built to withstand that sort of speed.'

I've read a little about this. During dog-fights in the Second World War, pilots would sometimes gamble on shaking off their pursuers by going into a steep dive. This meant pushing the aircraft to speeds where the dynamic pressure of the air threatened to tear off the wings or the flaps. Shock waves would build up on the control surfaces until the plane started to shudder. The controls became locked and the pilot was helpless. Boom!

'But it's not a wall, is it?' I say.

Dave sips his pint. 'No. There's no definitive line or barrier – it's actually a band of speed that's called the transonic region. The buffeting effect begins at about Mach 0.95 – when an object is still subsonic – and continues until you reach a speed of about Mach 1.1, which is supersonic. Once you're there, it's as smooth as a millpond.'

'What causes the buffeting?'

'The shock wave of highly compressed air that forms at the front of a fast-moving object, like a jet, and moves back at a sharp angle as the speed increases.'

'So what would this buffeting do to a human body in freefall?'

Dave smiles and opens his palms. 'That, Tom, is the $64,000 question.'

'No one knows?'

'No one knows.'

I'm sure Dave thinks I'm crazy, but he's fascinated by the logistics of the project and we discuss ways of answering some of the unknowns. Wind-tunnel tests aren't feasible because they can't re-create the rapidly changing atmospheric pressure during the descent.

'It might be possible to do a computer simulation,' suggests Dave. 'We could come up with a mathematical model of a human, something made up of five cylinders – the torso and head, arms and legs. Then we plot the speeds, Mach numbers and altitude against time and calculate the figures.'

'How accurate would it be?'

'I don't know. We have a lot of information about the conventional aerodynamics of supersonic aircraft, but as far as I know, no one has ever looked at a human being.'

Dave agrees to work on a mathematical model looking at two basic body positions – the delta-shape and the reverse arch. GQ will also investigate using a drogue system. Once he has some facts and figures on paper, he'll get back to me.

In the meantime, I continue my research, concentrating on the sound barrier because I still have so much to learn. Years ago my father taught me that sound travels at 750 mph at sea level, but I didn't realise that it varies depending on altitude, temperature and the dryness of the air. At 20,000 feet, where the atmosphere is only half as dense, the speed of sound is 707 mph. At 90,000 feet it's approximately 675 mph.

Until Chuck Yeager first broke the speed of sound in the Bell X-1 on

14 October 1947, no one actually knew whether a pilot could successfully control a plane under the battering effects of the shock waves produced as it approached Mach 1.

Over a dry lake-bed in California, Yeager strapped himself into the experimental plane and took off beneath the belly of a B-29 that carried him to 25,000 feet. When released, he rocketed to 40,000 feet and 700 mph – faster than the speed of sound at that altitude. In his autobiography, *Yeager*, he describes the moment when the Bell X-1 broke through:

Suddenly the Mach needle began to fluctuate. It went up to 0.965 Mach – then tipped right off the scale. I thought I was seeing things! We were flying supersonic! And it was as smooth as a baby's bottom: Grandma could be sitting up there sipping lemonade. I kept the speed off the scale for about twenty seconds, then raised the nose to slow down.

I was thunderstruck. After all the anxiety, breaking through the sound barrier turned out to be a perfectly paved speedway. I radioed Jack in the B-29. 'Hey, Ridley, that Machmeter is acting screwy. It just went off the scale on me.'

'Fluctuated off?'

'Yeah, at nine-six-five.'

'Son, you is imagining things.'

'Must be. I'm still wearing my ears and nothing else fell off, neither.'

The guys in the NACA tracking van interrupted to report that they heard what sounded like a distant rumble of thunder: my sonic boom! The first one by an aeroplane ever heard on Earth. The X-1 was supposedly capable of reaching nearly twice the speed of sound, but the Machmeter aboard only registered to 1.0 Mach, which showed how much confidence they had; I estimated I had reached 1.05 Mach (later data showed it was 1.07 Mach – 700 mph).

And that was it. I sat up there feeling kind of numb, but elated. After all the anticipation to achieve this moment, it really was a let-down. It took a damned instrument meter to tell me what I'd done. There should've been a bump on the road, something to let you know you had just punched a nice clean hole through that sonic barrier.

Several months pass before I hear from Dave Hirst again. I'm about to fly to Moscow to discuss the life-support suit when he calls to say that he has some figures for me on the parachute-related aspects of the record attempt. We arrange to meet at the headquarters of GQ Parachutes in Bridgend, Wales.

'You've been working hard,' I say admiringly, as I flick through pages of diagrams and graphs that plot every second of the proposed jump, showing speed, acceleration, dynamic pressure, air density, maximum rotational speed and the effects of a drogue parachute. 'I think you'd better explain some of this to me.'

As promised, he'd constructed a mathematical model of the human form which regarded the body as being made up of five cylinders – the torso and head were considered to be one cylinder, while the arms and legs made up the other four.

'The big problem is the transonic zone,' says Dave. 'We know what happens to Concorde when it reaches this zone – it minimises the buffeting by traversing the region as quickly as possible. The faster it gets to Mach 1.1, the less buffeting.'

As he's talking, I'm thinking about the possibility of going into a head-down dive during freefall, so I can pass through the region much quicker. I don't know how much effect this would have, given the air is so thin and I'll already be accelerating at a phenomenal rate.

Dave continues: 'The trouble is that the human body is far more complex and less aerodynamically stable than Concorde. An object such as a cylinder undergoes roughly a doubling in drag co-efficient through Mach 1, which doesn't reduce at higher Mach numbers. Imagine what that will do to you. Even in a pressure suit, if the drag doubles, your limbs are going to flex. I seriously doubt if you can maintain stability.'

It's not what I want to hear. At the same time, there's something reassuring about the knowledge that the most dangerous time during the freefall might only last a matter of seconds if I can get through the transonic zone quickly.

Then Dave reminds me of something I hadn't even considered. If something breaks the speed of sound and becomes supersonic, at some point it has to slow down again and become subsonic.

'It's the same deal, only in reverse,' he says.

'The buffeting?'

He nods. 'Only this time, if you want to limit the effect, the quicker you decelerate and become subsonic, the quicker you'll pop out of the zone and reduce any buffeting. Ideally, you'd pull a parachute to slow yourself down, but you'll be travelling far too quickly for that. The opening shock would tear you apart.'

'So that means flaring out into a reverse arch.'

'That's the idea. Make yourself as big as possible so you're falling in the slowest possible configuration.'

'How long am I likely to be in the transonic zone?' I ask.

'Falling in a face-down, stable position, based on the model, I'd estimate about thirteen seconds in the first instance. It's harder to estimate how quickly you'll decelerate and come out again.'

Dave stresses again that the figures he's come up with are provisional. The unknown factors that could affect his projections are things like local weather conditions and temperature at the time of the jump, as well as the true final weight and drag figures of the pressure suit.

'We have to run the model again with those figures if you want it to be accurate,' he says. 'But I can tell you now that if it comes back as low mass, high drag and high temperature, it could mean that you'll be in the transonic region for an intolerable period.'

I nod my head. It's understood.

'If things get too bad, can I use a drogue?' I ask.

Dave has researched this and identified two main problem areas. One is the lack of atmosphere at high altitude to inflate such a parachute, and the other is the opening shock that I would experience if it opens while I'm supersonic. Based on his calculations, by the time I have enough dynamic pressure to deploy a drogue, I will already have gone supersonic. However, it may help me decelerate when I want to become subsonic again.

'Let me talk you through the whole jump,' he says, turning to the graphs.

'On leaving the balloon the dynamic pressure will be zero. You will be dropping through a near-vacuum and any rotation you might accidentally impart on exit will continue. If you knock the side of the gondola and start spinning, for instance, you won't be able to stop because there'll be no air flow for you to use.'

'How long will it take for the dynamic pressure to increase?'

'It's going to be below that of a normal freefall until about fifty seconds into the jump. That's why it's difficult to predict how much control you'll have.'

Fifty seconds might not seem like long, but a great deal is going to happen in that time. Based on the model, ten seconds after leaving the balloon I will be falling at 170 mph. At twenty seconds it will be 430 mph, and at thirty-five seconds I will break the sound barrier. Even then, I will continue to accelerate for another ten seconds, until reaching a maximum speed of between 840 and 900 mph – Mach 1.2 at that altitude.

Then, as the air density increases, I will begin slowing down – again quite rapidly. A minute after exit I will become subsonic, and after eighty seconds I will have slowed to 500 mph. This deceleration will continue until I reach opening height.

Twice I have to pass through the transonic zone, and each time my body position will have to be different. Initially, I will try to dive head-first towards the Earth in a delta-wing configuration that should hopefully help minimise the buffeting of the transonic region. Then, once I start slowing down in the denser air, I will flare out in a reverse-arch position and try to decelerate as quickly as possible, again avoiding the buffeting.

There's another problem that no amount of computer models and calculations can answer. As I approach the sound barrier, certain parts of my body – like the curvature of my head – will have air accelerating over the top of them like the camber of an aircraft wing. As that happens, these parts of my body might go supersonic before other parts – for example, my head might go supersonic before my legs. As soon as I punch through the sound barrier, the increase in drag suddenly doubles, and for a fraction of a second my head will slow to subsonic before punching through again. What effect will this have on me? I have this image in my mind of a bug hitting the windscreen of a car and its arse disappearing through its brain.

The weak winter sunshine provides no warmth on the twenty-minute drive from the airport into the centre of Moscow. Mounds of grey snow line the road and pedestrians slide on icy footpaths.

George Rykoff, the chief engineer of Zvezda, had been waiting for me at the airport, grasping my hand and welcoming me to Moscow. His

English is extremely good and he speaks very slowly and deliberately, as if choosing each word with care.

As we cross over the Moscow river, I see people fishing through holes in the ice.

'They're catching their dinner,' says Rykoff.

'They must be keen,' I say.

'No, they're hungry.'

The buildings are so grey and bleak they remind me of East Germany. But whereas Berlin had seemed exciting – a small Soviet enclave infused with tension and a sense of drama – Moscow is very tired and sad. It's also quite poignant to think of all the training I did to prepare for a Soviet invasion, when now I'm driving into the heartland of the old enemy.

As I check into my hotel and a bellboy delivers my bags to my room, I think of that old joke about a Western visitor asking his Russian concierge whether the hotel rooms are bugged. 'Of course not, sir, but if you have any complaints please speak into the end of your hot-water bottle.'

My concierge is equally worrying when he warns me not to walk the streets alone at night and to always order a taxi. Street crime is apparently a growing problem and Westerners are prime targets.

At eight the next morning a car arrives to take me to Zvezda's headquarters, just outside Moscow. This is the life-support and survival department of the Russian space agency. Rykoff takes me on a tour of the facility, including the museum, which has the capsules used to send dogs into orbit during trials on the life-support system later used by Yuri Gagarin.

The professionalism and skill of these people is immediately evident, and so are the stark differences between NASA and the Russian agency. The Americans are surrounded by pristine, high-tech, dust-free laboratories, with ergonomic furniture and lighting, the very latest computer systems and air conditioning. By comparison, the Russian vacuum chambers look like they've just been dropped off a lorry, with wires hanging all over them and snaking across the floor. There's an old guy smoking a cigarette and sitting in front of a lone computer screen beneath a dangling light-bulb.

This is why I've always had a sneaking respect for the Russians. On a shoestring budget compared to the Americans', and without the dozens of

Nazi rocket scientists the US spirited out of Germany at the end of the war, the Russians still managed to put the first human into space. That's some achievement.

Unlike in America, where NASA issues contracts to outside companies, the Russian space programme keeps everything in-house. From my point of view, this has the added advantage of having all the technology and experts in one place. For instance, Zvezda has a supersonic wind tunnel capable of simulating speeds equivalent to Mach 2.2. It also has an altitude chamber, centrifuge, load-impact test capabilities and doctors specialising in aerospace medicine.

Over lunch, Rykoff explains that he's been approached in the past with similar requests, from Australia, Europe and America, all of which had been turned down. For obvious reasons, Zvezda didn't want to be associated with a project that failed.

Apparently, I'm to meet the main man, Dr G. I. Severin, whose name is whispered in awe around this place because as a young apprentice he worked on the life-support system for Yuri Gagarin, and even helped dress him for the historic flight.

'Dr Severin wants to meet you face to face,' says Rykoff.

I'm quite flattered, but very aware that Severin is the key. If I can answer his questions and satisfy his concerns, then half the battle will be over. A conference room has been set up and there are half a dozen people with notebooks sitting around the table. Dr Severin enters like royalty and everyone stands. I'm conscious of the fact that one night at my hotel would probably cost these eminent scientists three months in wages.

Severin begins asking questions – what research have I done? What experience do I have? What are the danger areas? What emergency contingencies will be in place? I have all the timings at my fingertips because of the GQ report, and can tell them how far, how fast and how long the freefall will take.

'Joe Kittinger has offered his assistance as a technical adviser and possible project manager. On my next trip to Moscow – if we go further – I'd like to bring Joe with me so he can see the life-support suit and discuss the specifications.'

'Excellent,' says Severin, to murmurs of agreement around the table. They've all heard of Kittinger's jump and are quite excited about the prospect of meeting him.

'So you are not going to use a drogue,' says Severin. 'How do you know it can be done? How do you know you're not going to just black out?'

This is the key question, because I know that none of the men around the table are experts in freefall. At the same time, it is virtually impossible to explain how a skydiver maintains stability and balance.

'Captain Kittinger couldn't maintain stability without a drogue,' continues Severin, tapping a pencil against his lips.

'Yes, but Joe only had about forty jumps behind him; I have three and a half thousand. In 1959 not a great deal was known about freefall, and skydivers basically got out of an aeroplane, counted to ten and pulled a rip-cord. It was quite common for someone to be unstable for the whole descent. Some would tumble, holding a stopwatch, and when they got to the required number of seconds they pulled the rip-cord and the parachute would deploy through their legs or under their arms. Using a round parachute they didn't have to be stable, or at least it wasn't as critical. Freefall techniques have come a long way since then.'

Severin isn't convinced. 'That is all very well, Mr Read, but from a hundred and thirty thousand feet you will not have the air flow or dynamic pressure to make such corrections. How are you going to be able to control yourself? What sort of rudder or steering device are you going to use?'

'None, apart from my body.'

'Surely not!'

Another scientist suggests that I could squeeze gas canisters to move myself left and right, similar to those used on space walks. Most of them favour a drogue chute. I hold my ground, insisting that I can adjust once I have the air speed.

'Let me explain. On leaving the balloon the dynamic pressure will be zero, and I will have to wait fifty seconds to get the same dynamic pressure as in a normal freefall. But it must be relative because although I won't have the same amount of air to work on, I'll be travelling much faster at the higher altitudes and it may be that any small input in terms of movement will have a much bigger effect because of my speed.'

It's like that old riddle of why people run when they're caught outside in the rain. Obviously, they think that by running they won't get as wet, yet the truth is that the faster you move the more raindrops you come into contact with. I'm hoping that the faster I fall, the more air particles I will come into contact with and the more control this will give me.

Another possibility for making adjustments early in the jump may be using my mass rather than aerodynamic movements. By shoving my left hand out, for example, that transfer of weight may have the effect of sending me towards the right. Admittedly, the chances of making any major correction are minimal, but it might help.

'That's why the exit will be of paramount importance,' I stress. 'All the research and expert opinion agrees that if I exit cleanly from the gondola, there should be no tendency for me to become unstable. If I leave at slightly the wrong angle, or receive a knock, I will spin out of control. For that reason, we haven't ruled out using a drogue chute in an emergency.'

Severin pauses and looks around the table for any further questions.

Rykoff speaks up. 'Am I right in thinking you will have an AOD on your parachute?'

'Yes, in all likelihood, but I do see it as a potential danger.'

'Why is that?'

'An AOD is a complex mechanical device and we'll be subjecting it to extremes of temperature and pressure, as well as a shock-wave coming over the body as I pass through the transonic zone. If the AOD were to fail and prematurely open the parachute at terminal velocity, it would exert about twenty-six times the normal force of a parachute opening. The canopy is likely to disintegrate and the pressure suit would be ripped open.'

Severin had only intended to stay for twenty minutes, but we've been talking for an hour and a half. He makes his apologies and leaves, handing over to his deputy. Rykoff smiles across at me – it's a good sign.

Until now, I haven't asked about the pressure suit, but Rykoff hasn't forgotten why I'm here.

'Would you like to try one on?' he asks.

'Yes.'

'They're fetching one now.'

Several of the engineers help dress me as I sit on a chair, tugging a leather helmet over my head and plugging in a microphone so we can talk when the main helmet is lowered and sealed. Once this happens I'm completely cut off, and feel as though I'm in a different room. The internal bladder is sealed and the boots are laced. Rykoff explains how the pressure gauge works.

'We're going to pressurise the suit, taking you up to a simulated thirty-nine thousand feet. Then you can get up and try to move around.'

There's a pipe attachment on the floor and the suit is plugged into it. I'm breathing ambient air as they pump it up to 400 millibars – about half the atmosphere – or the equivalent of 18,000 feet.

Slowly the needle turns until the suit is fully pressurised and sealed at 39,000 feet. This is the pressure that it will maintain for the whole of the ascent and descent through the upper atmosphere.

I feel like a Michelin man and realise the amount of restrictive pressure created by the air circulating in the suit.

'Can you stand up?' asks Rykoff.

'Not without help.'

Two engineers help me upright. That's one problem identified. On the gondola platform, I'll have to be on a stool which keeps me in a semi-standing position, with some kind of bar in front of me so I can pull myself up.

The suit is lighter than I expect, weighing about 17 lb., but on top of this I will have the ancillaries such as oxygen, cameras, radios, a microwave aerial and, of course, a main parachute and reserve.

'Try to move around,' says Rykoff.

I lift my arms and take two steps forward. The knee and elbow joints have very little flexibility and every movement has to be positive and deliberate. I feel like a robot in a science-fiction movie.

I try to adopt various freefall positions, pulling my arms and knees back, but the joints won't allow it. The suit has been designed for a pilot in a basic sitting position, which is the reverse of what I need. I can't get my arms back behind my shoulders to arch my chest. The only classic freefall position it allows is a maximum track pose, with my head down and arms slanting back like a delta-wing aircraft. Other than this, the only possible configuration is a reverse arch, falling on my back.

'I need more mobility,' I explain to Rykoff. 'Can the joints be modified?'

He puffs out his cheeks in concern. 'Yes, of course, but any change will have to be researched, engineered and tested. It will take months.'

The mechanical joints are critical to the pressure suit, and the entire outfit has been built around them because they are the most vulnerable component. A balance has to be struck between flexibility and maintaining the airtight seal to prevent a disaster.

Rykoff is taking measurements of my hands and feet, making notes of how much dexterity the suit allows and what I need to make corrections and adjustments. We also discuss the thermal requirements to keep my hands and feet warm in the extreme temperatures.

I agree to write a proposal, giving detailed specifications for the suit, and Rykoff will do a preliminary budget. He also promises to research the balloon jump by Eugene Andreev, the Russian who holds the official world record.

If we agree on all the details, Zvezda will design, build and test a pressure suit with an autonomous life-support system. It will also provide all the necessary hardware, test facilities and technical advice for the jump.

In the meantime, Harry and I are planning to do some training in Spain, including some balloon jumps. Sharky had recommended the parachute centre at Ampuria Brava – one of the biggest in Europe – because the weather conditions are normally perfect and the backdrop of the Mediterranean will look great on the promotional video for the Skydive from Space. It's about two hours' drive from Barcelona in the foothills of the Pyrenees.

Harry has volunteered to be my back-up jumper on the project, even though he's completed only a handful of freefalls – everything else had been military static-line. It's my job to get him up to speed.

After he does a basic AFF course like a normal trainee, we set about doing some hard-core jumping, doing as many as ten lifts a day. I'm experimenting flying in a reverse arch and deliberately putting myself into spins so I can practise my recovery skills.

Because of the weight of the suit and ancillary equipment, I'm proposing to use a tandem-type parachute, which has the added advantage of having a drogue facility if I decide to go that way. To break in the parachute, I start doing tandem jumps to simulate the weight, choosing dossers who are hanging around the drop zone and are unable to afford a jump.

Harry has improved quickly and we've arranged for Andy Elson, a leading hot-air balloonist from Bristol, to bring his rig down to Spain. The plan is to start jumping from 12,000 feet and then build up to 38,000 feet, although we may have to lower the ceiling if our oxygen equipment doesn't allow us that sort of height.

We drive down to Badajoz in the south of Spain – tumbleweed country, where they filmed a lot of the spaghetti westerns and where brothels and bars appear in the middle of nowhere. Getting up early, Andy fills the bright red balloon and takes us aloft. There are four of us in the basket, including Harry and a freefall cameraman.

Experienced parachutists tend to enjoy balloon jumps because they offer something different, but for the inexperienced jumper they have a certain chilling quality because of the quietness. There's no wind-noise in a balloon, because it travels at the same speed as any breeze. In addition, when you step off, there's a dead drop that creates a rising feeling in your stomach. A plane has a slipstream, and a jumper is immediately surfing on a cushion of air because of the aircraft's forward speed. With a balloon it's like stepping off a building, and the novice jumper has to fight the tendency to immediately start waving their arms and legs.

On a tandem with Harry one day, the balloon envelope suddenly catches fire at about 6,000 feet. There are holes beginning to appear in the fabric.

'I have to descend,' says Andy. 'You'll have to jump.'

'But we need more height.' I'm not even hooked up to Harry and I've never done a tandem below 12,000 feet. The cameraman has bailed out, leaving three of us in the basket. Above us the rips are getting longer. Andy fires the burner, trying to give us more height, while I hook Harry to the front of me. Andy gets us to 8,000 feet and shakes his head. That's it. Unless he gets the balloon down quickly, he risks losing it completely.

I'm sitting on the edge of the basket, with Harry strapped on the front. The back of his head is in front of my mouth. I cock my head to the right and say, 'Okay, Harry, this looks like it.'

There's no need to shout into a slipstream, because only the creaking of the basket interrupts the silence. I rock back and forth. 'Ready . . . set . . . go!'

My stomach comes up as we drop away.

'Well, that seemed okay, Harry.'

'Yeah.'

After seven seconds of dead drop comes the *sssshhhhhhSSSHHHH!* as wind begins screaming past our ears, making conversation impossible.

I open the main canopy at 5,000 feet and we land near the trailer. Andy manages to get the balloon down safely and starts making repairs. We do a dozen jumps over the next six days, culminating in a tandem from 26,000 feet, with oxygen – the highest tandem ever attempted.

The balloon jumps have given me a better idea of what to expect, but the dead drop from 130,000 feet will be as long as thirty-five seconds, and I'll have to wait almost a minute to get the same dynamic pressure as in a normal freefall. For this reason, along with other safety concerns, I've decided that I want to do a full rehearsal, testing all the equipment and personnel. There are certain to be teething problems, and I want them sorted out.

I mention this to George Rykoff on my next trip to Moscow, this time accompanied by Loel Guinness and Joe Kittinger. I propose a jump where we practise everything except going supersonic. We can aim for 85,000 feet, so that we'll break Andreev's existing record as well as identify any problems.

The Russians agree with this approach, and also suggest controlled helicopter jumps from lesser heights and vacuum-chamber training that will re-create each different stage of the ascent and freefall.

Back in England, Kittinger spends five days with me in Hereford, staying at the house, as we put the specifications together for Zvezda. He keeps insisting I stop smoking for the project – pure of body, pure of mind, that sort of thing. The jump is at least a year away, probably two years, and I know I can quit smoking and get fit before then.

To keep him happy, I tell him I'm going for a run and lace up my training shoes on the stairs. I run straight to a friend's house for a cup of tea and light up a cigarette as soon as I'm in the door. It reminds me of what I used to do to Al Slater. He was always complaining about my smoking, and whenever we went for a run together he'd say, 'You're not taking any fags.'

'Of course not, Al.'

But I'd have been out earlier and put a packet of cigarettes and matches in a hedge at the top of a hill. When I got there before him, I'd light up and be casually puffing as he staggered up the rise. 'Come on, Al. Can't you hurry up?' It was guaranteed to wind him up.

Heading back to Joe, I make sure that I'm breathing hard when I arrive at the house.

'Good on you, Tom,' he says. 'You're a fit young buck.'

While he's in England we arrange to visit Slim McDonald at his workshop in Andover, Hampshire. Slim is a photographic genius, who can put cameras inside everything from racing cars to the pockets of snooker tables. The Skydive from Space is a totally new challenge.

The plan is to broadcast the jump live around the world, and Slim suggests putting small wide-angle cameras on one or both of my wrists so that with my arms outspread it will look as if someone is alongside me, filming the freefall. Another camera beneath my chin would film the ground. In each case, microwave transmitters would beam the pictures to a ground receiver, along with images from more cameras attached to the gondola.

A normal airliner travelling at 35,000 feet appears as only a silver glimmer and a vapour trail when viewed from the ground. At 130,000 feet, the balloon will be invisible to the naked eye. Even so, we decide to investigate the possibility of using the latest technology to film from the ground. During a recent space shuttle mission, the loss of a small heat shield concerned NASA but engineers were apparently able to investigate the problem from the ground using a powerful camera. The Russians have cast doubt on whether such technology exists, but we're checking it out.

13

I'm still waking at four in the morning, wrapped in a duvet and watching the TV throw shadows on the ceiling and walls. Then I wander from room to room trying to work out where different belongings fit into my life. I've been through all my photographs and letters – I could cram all of them into one shoe-box. Time to move on – what else is significant?

Everything.

But where do I start?

There's a painting in the living-room depicting the balcony scene from the Iranian Embassy siege, when the SAS swung through the front windows. Most of the guys have their faces covered by gas masks, but Tommy Palmer is clearly recognisable because he'd been killed afterwards in Northern Ireland, and once you're dead there's no need for anonymity.

Hillbilly had bought two of the paintings as an investment, but I took one off his wall after he died. I wish you were here now, Hillbilly. What would you have made of all this, eh?

I remember when you died. I was gutted. I'd just left the Regiment – it was September 1988, and I hadn't even handed my kit back into stores. I headed straight off on a quick bodyguarding job in Rio de Janeiro, standing in for someone else. Afterwards, back in Hereford, the ex-SAS officer running the job asked me if I wanted to do it full-time.

'Can I give you an answer on Friday?'

'Sure, Tom, but don't leave it any longer.'

I wanted to talk to you first, Hillbilly, but you were away on a trip – something very hush-hush in the Far East. I knew were coming back that day, so I phoned up at 7 p.m. and got your answering machine.

'Right, Hill, where are you? It's seven o'clock, Tuesday night. Give us a ring if you get in before nine. If not, I'll meet you down at the pub.'

I put the phone down and there's a knock on the door. I half expect it to be you, but Andy D. from B Squadron walks in with a hang-dog look on his face. 'I've got some bad news for you, Tom.'

'Yeah?'

'I'm afraid Hill's dead.'

I look past him, genuinely expecting you to walk in behind him. It's just some stupid joke.

Andy tries to convince me. 'No, it's genuine, Tom. I've just come from the camp. The boss wanted me to tell you.'

I still think he's winding me up, so I pick up the phone and call the camp. The squadron sergeant-major confirms that it's true. They know very little. You were on your way home from a very sensitive job in Asia and had stopped off somewhere. Because of the nature of the operation, they didn't want to put the whole team on one flight, so you came back in dribs and drabs. The married guys went first because they were keener to get home to their families, but I know what you'd have said, Hillbilly: 'I'm all right – leave me to the end.'

But you didn't turn up for your flight, did you? They found you dead in a hotel room. The official report said it was a massive heart attack, but I've never been satisfied with that. There are too many unanswered questions. Why did it take six weeks to get your body back? Why was nobody allowed to see it?

I hope you don't mind me taking one of your paintings, Hillbilly. I wanted something to remember you by. I'm going to leave it on the wall because you meant so much to me.

Glancing along the bookshelf, I make a mental note of which books I've read and which I haven't. There are half a dozen on space exploration, as well as my flying manuals, an illustrated history of the Red Devils, a book on the Parachute Regiment, my guitar music, two almost empty photograph albums, a few dog-eared thrillers and a very old copy of *Lord of the Rings* which I've never read. I don't know where it came from.

On the top shelf is a hardback copy of Frederick Forsyth's novel, *Fist of God*. I should sit down and read it, but my mind won't let me. I don't need the messages that are in there.

Freddy sent me a copy because I helped him with some of the research. He'd come up with a story about a vast gun called Babylon, hidden in a mountain range in Iraq, with a bore of one metre and a barrel 186 metres long. This is Saddam Hussein's secret weapon and it has to be destroyed, so they drop four SAS men into the mountains from high altitude.

Freddy is a stickler for accuracy, but his normal contact for SAS research was one of the 'old and the bold', and wasn't up to date on the latest techniques. That's why he came to me. I wrote him fifteen pages of notes describing a typical SAS HALO (high altitude, low opening) jump.

Since then Freddy has become a key supporter of the Skydive from Space project, and he's agreed to write some articles or perhaps narrate the documentary. Last summer I hired a helicopter and picked him up from Luton Airport, near his farm, and flew him to Stirling Lines on the outskirts of Hereford for a live-firing display by an anti-terrorist team. Occasionally, VIPs are allowed to watch the SAS drills at a purpose-built training area that features a block of flats and several other buildings. Various scenarios involving armed sieges and hostage-taking are practised, including fast-roping from helicopters and room clearing.

Afterwards I flew him home again and, although it was the middle of July, a real pea-souper fog descended, cutting visibility to only a few yards. We were about half a mile short of the runway at Luton, but it was too dangerous to continue and almost impossible to see what lay beneath us.

Hovering and edging forwards a few feet at a time, I spied the top of a set of rugby goal posts and could just make out the open side.

'I'm taking us down,' I told Freddy, who seemed pretty happy with the idea. We landed and he caught a taxi home, while I stayed overnight in a hotel and flew the chopper back next morning. There's a note upstairs – framed and hung in the office – dated 20 January 1994, less than a fortnight before I went to Chamonix with Anna:

> *Dear Tom,*
>
> *I hope this reaches you without being subjected to a controlled explosion! Actually, current publication is not until 28 April, but I thought an advance proof copy might amuse you. At any rate, it is something you can browse through while stranded in dense fog at alien airports after trying to fly authors home in the chopper.*
>
> *All the best,*
>
> *Freddy*

This letter can stay, I decide, because Freddy is a gentleman. I'm not so fond of Tom Clancy, who I've also met. He's another high-profile supporter of the Skydive from Space, and while I was working in Washington, I visited him at his house.

As soon as I walked in the door Clancy gave me a photograph of himself. 'Hi, I'm Tom Clancy. Here, have one of these,' he said. I felt like a groupie who'd been allowed back-stage.

The photograph was a PR shot that was typically right-over-the-top American. Clancy was pictured in a GI's uniform with a steel helmet, holding an Armalite rifle, butt on hip, and grinning at the camera with cigar clenched between his teeth. In the background, slightly out of focus, was an old burning car. I figured he must enjoy giving the impression that he's been in some sort of action.

He scrawled his signature across the bottom, along with a line from an annoying little jingle used in an advertising campaign for beer: 'It's Miller Time.'

I've never read any of Clancy's books, but before I met him I rented *The Hunt for Red October* from my local video store just so I'd have something to say if he asked me about his work. It's obvious that he's a real military nut – he's got a pistol range in his basement and a Sherman tank in his driveway.

'So you were in the special forces, Tom. Do you like guns?' he asks me.

'I haven't thought about it,' I say, thinking it an odd question. I certainly don't go out in the woods at night dressed in camouflage.

In Hereford, I put Clancy's photograph in the downstairs toilet. Until now, I haven't thought about the significance of that, but when I do it makes me smile. It's a crock of shit. He's American, just like Anna, and if there are two opposing sides then he's been sent by the enemy, even if he doesn't realise it, whereas Freddy Forsyth is friendly forces. I'm not frightened of them if the best they can send is Tom Clancy. I take down the photograph and tear it up, dropping the pieces into the kitchen bin.

Another photograph on the wall shows me being introduced to Prince Charles. That can stay up there, because he's friendly forces too. Maybe he is our Commander-in-Chief, although he doesn't know it. Was I recruited then? I wonder.

What other pictures do I have? On the landing wall there's a charcoal drawing of three members of the counter-terrorist team wearing black kit and carrying weapons. It was drawn by a member of the Regiment and underneath is a winged dagger and the words 'standby, standby'. That drawing can stay – I have good feelings about the Regiment.

Wandering into the office, I glance around at the various charts on the walls and papers on the desk. One document is the final specifications for the life-support suit, and there's also a mock-up of a promotional brochure. The desk calendar is out of date and a box of paper-clips has spilled out on to the floor.

Where do I start in here?

There's a filing cabinet directly in front of me, and to the right, tucked in a corner, a large cupboard is stacked with boxes of files held in 'deep storage'. It's too much to look at now, I decide. I'll come back to this room later.

Immediately out the door and to the right is the main bedroom. There's a large photograph of Anna hanging on the wall. She posed for a professional photographer once, who came to her flat in Washington and took a series of artistic nudes, in black and white. She had her favourite photograph blown up, and gave it to me as a birthday present. It shows her semi-naked, partly in shadow, standing beside a black grand piano with one stilettoed foot propped on a piano stool and her breasts in the light. She's quite proud of her chest.

It's not a particularly memorable or romantic picture, and I can't honestly remember the last time I noticed it. Now I reach up, lift it from the picture hook and put in on the floor, facing in to the wall. If I had more energy, I'd carry it outside and find a council skip.

I want no reminders of Anna. I'm going to sterilise and redecorate until there's no trace of her.

*

She tells me she has the chance to study medicine at Bristol University.

'That's quite close to Hereford, isn't it?' she says on the telephone. I know what she's thinking. She's visited me twice since I left Washington and I think she's in love with me. She says we're meant for each other and that fate brought us together in that chance meeting at the wine bar. Her letters are full of stuff like that, as if everything in life has some deep, spiritual meaning.

I've never been quite sure how to handle Anna. I'm not in love with her, but she's good company and I do feel very protective of her because she seems isolated and has few friends. But I've been honest from the beginning about our relationship. She can't accuse me of leading her on, or giving her false hopes.

On her last visit I took her to see the Bolshoi Ballet in London, on one of those special package offers that included a night at the Dorchester Hotel in Park Lane. Anna had danced from a young age, encouraged by her father.

I'd given up smoking and taken to chewing wine-gums until my jaw ached. Pulling up at the front of the hotel, a valet unloaded our luggage and drove the car to the garage. I walked into reception, wearing jeans and training shoes.

'Excuse me, sir,' said the doorman in his green hat. 'You appear to have something attached to your trousers.' Two wine-gums were glued to my right buttock. Picking them off, I popped them into my mouth and thanked him. Anna wanted to disown me.

At the reception desk, I asked about our room. The receptionist checked the computer. 'I'm sorry, sir, but we don't appear to have any record of your booking.'

'We're here to see the Bolshoi,' offered Anna, trying to restore her social cachet.

The receptionist flicked a few more computer keys. 'Oh, yes, here it is. But I'm afraid the reservation is for tomorrow night.'

Anna isn't the type to blush with embarrassment. Instead, she was perfectly calm as she politely informed the hotel that, in that case, we'd be back the following evening.

She wouldn't talk to me at all in the car. We drove down to Aldershot and spent the night in a little hotel. Anna went straight to bed to read her book, while I stayed downstairs and had a few drinks. It took another twenty-four hours – when the curtain came down on the ballet – for her to forgive me.

Now I'm worried about her coming to the UK. She's young and very bright, and I admire the fact that she wants to become a doctor, but our relationship has no future. I hope she's not investing her emotions in me, because the only thing I care about right now is the project.

*

Harry and I leave for Kathmandu in three days. We'll be away for nearly two months, testing a device for NASA that will be on the gondola. It's a Tissue Equivalent Proportional Counter, better known as TEPC, and it monitors the effect of solar radiation on human tissue. They use them on the US space shuttles, but these go aloft at such speeds that the device has barely a fraction of a second to take measurements at any given altitude.

NASA wants to get readings at fixed altitudes for longer periods, and when this was mentioned to Loel Guinness, he offered to take the TEPC on High Adventure's next Everest expedition. That's why Harry and I are off to the Himalayas. It's a kind of *quid pro quo* arrangement. We want NASA to be associated with the Skydive from Space, and by helping them in their research we can use their name on our marketing and promotional material.

In addition, NASA is going to provide a second opinion on the life-support system, bio-medical sensors on the suit and pre-launch weather forecasting. It has also offered us access to its training facilities, such as the swimming pool used by its astronauts to test EVA suits and possibly a flight in a K-135 jet that can simulate zero gravity. The latter has no relevance to the project, but it might beef up the documentary to have me floating inside the plane. In reality, at 130,000 feet the gravity is only reduced by a mere fraction, and there's no chance that I'll drift off into space or somehow miss the planet.

Four of us are going on the Everest expedition – myself, Harry, Brian T., who's ex-SBS (Special Boat Squadron), and Karl Henize, a NASA scientist and astronomer. The plan is to carry the TEPC up the mountain and take measurements at three given altitudes – 17,000 feet, 19,000 feet and 21,000 feet, for a week at each location. We won't be going to the summit.

From a scientific viewpoint, the experiment is important. Solar radiation is normally filtered through the Earth's atmosphere, but what happens when there isn't the same amount of atmosphere, or none at all? The answers are important if humans are going to work for prolonged periods in space.

Harry has arranged for us to link up with an Everest expedition run by a friend of his, John Tinker, who is aiming to get to the summit. We meet up with Karl at Bangkok Airport. He's carrying the TEPC in a metal box. The technology isn't difficult to operate, and so it wasn't strictly necessary for NASA to send Karl, but he volunteered because he's a keen mountaineer and has always wanted to see Mount Everest.

Although he's best known as an astronomer, he's also an astronaut. He flew on the space shuttle *Challenger* two missions before it exploded on take-off. He also served on the support crew for *Apollo 15*, and would have flown on one of the later *Apollo* missions had the programme not been ended. Although now in his mid-sixties, he looks much younger and has that characteristically solid American jaw-line and a healthy suntan.

We spend a week in Kathmandu, making final arrangements and beginning our acclimatisation. It's a fairly typical third-world city, loud and dirty, with more cows and dogs than people. Most of the time it reminds me of a Far Eastern version of the Glastonbury Festival, because there are hippies everywhere with beads in their hair and colourful clothes.

There's nothing much to do except shop for souvenirs and drink cheap beer, although Brian, who's our team medic, arranges for us each to have a physical. Karl, who's almost twice my age, has a lower respiratory and recovery rate than mine.

'I can't believe you're fitter than I am,' I say to him.

Harry pipes up: 'He could be dead and still be fitter than you.'

Harry's an old hand in Kathmandu, and arranges the sherpas to carry our equipment. John Tinker's expedition is already at Base Camp. We load the trekking bags on to trucks and set off on a hair-raising seven-hour drive through spectacular scenery. Karl is like a schoolboy on a camping weekend. As we catch our first glimpse of Everest towering above, with a plume of white streaming off the summit, Karl sighs and says, 'If I don't make it, Tom, leave me here.'

Base Camp is like a makeshift city of multi-coloured tents and flags. There are several international expeditions acclimatising and waiting for a window in the weather. On the moonscape of rock and shale there is nowhere to sink a tent peg, so the guide ropes are weighted down. Harry and Brian are sharing one tent and Karl and I have the other. In addition there is a cooking and dining tent with tables and chairs.

We're at 17,000 feet, and already I have a blinding headache that feels as though someone has let a jackhammer loose in my skull. I've been vomiting, but I don't blame the altitude. I ate some yak for dinner and it's horrible stuff. I wonder if they actually bothered cooking it, or if they just cut it into strips and dry it in the sun like biltong.

From now on I'm sticking to porridge, cereal, pasta and stew. I crawl into a sleeping-bag and fight the headache all night. By morning I'm not vomiting so much, but my head is still hurting so I don't go on the acclimatisation walk. Instead I stay in my tent, trying to sleep and forcing myself to drink plenty of liquid. Harry says most people have trouble breathing at Base Camp, but the headaches usually pass.

Everything gets dirty quickly from the swirling dust and yak dung. Our tent is a mess – or at least my side of it is. Karl is remarkably neat and irritatingly happy. He's had a few mild headaches but is so bloody enthusiastic he ignores them. On our third morning he's up at 5.30, unzipping the tent. 'Hey, Tom, Tom, you gotta see this. It's amazing. The sun is just hitting the mountain.'

I've just spent the last eight hours trying to sleep between bouts of nausea. I'd just managed to doze off. 'For fuck's sake, Karl. Yes, it's beautiful. Now shut the bloody tent, it's freezing.'

There's not a great deal to do at Base Camp except acclimatise, so we read books and tell stories. I ask Karl about space and he tells me about the shuttle voyage and how he orbited the Earth 126 times, covering more than three million miles.

The 1985 mission had replaced a module on the US Spacelab with open pallets containing astronomical instruments. Karl did his best to explain some of the tests, but they were far too technical for me.

'It still feels like only yesterday,' he says, leaning back and glancing up through the unzipped tent. 'I'd been waiting eighteen years to get into space.'

'Were there any problems?'

'We had our moments. The launch was delayed a few times by technical problems, but the take-off went smoothly. Then, five minutes forty-five seconds into the flight, one of the three main engines shut itself down prematurely. We did an "abort to orbit" – the very first by a shuttle. Mission Control thought about recalling us for a while, but we completed the mission.

'Do you know, one of my only regrets is that I didn't get to see Everest from space. The orbits of the *Challenger* weren't stationary, and it moved up and back from the North to the South Pole as it circled. Every time it passed over the Himalayas the mountains were either in cloud or I wasn't at the window. That's one of the reasons I wanted to come with you guys – to see *the* mountain.'

My headaches aren't getting any better, but I force myself to start walking a little, heading up the moraine. On the steep scree slopes there are pillars carved out by water, wind and ice, with huge rocks balancing on them. The nights are clear and cold, and when the stars come out, Karl points out the various constellations and tells me stories about how they were discovered. There are things up there that he found.

After a week we begin climbing towards an interim site known as the British 1922 Camp, at 19,500 feet. I manage to get a few kilometres up the glacier to about 18,000 feet before I start dropping behind. My headaches are even worse, but there's no hurry. I can go at my own pace and meet up with the others at the next camp.

Brian and Harry are experienced climbers – they've been here before – and Karl seems to be okay. It's tough going on the loose shale and rock, with my head pounding and my lungs hurting. By early afternoon the others are long gone, but I have a couple of sherpas looking after me. When darkness falls I camp in my sleeping-bag with a waterproof outer, while they sleep under yellow tarpaulins. It's a lousy night, with fearful headaches and vomiting. My pulse is 100 beats per minute. Tomorrow morning, I'll go back down to Base Camp – it's the only sensible thing to do.

At daybreak I go back down and try to recover my strength. It's important just to breathe comfortably. I'll give it a day or two and then make another attempt to join the others. By then they should have reached Advanced Base Camp, at 21,500 feet.

My resting heart-rate is down to 72 beats per minute, and I manage to eat a decent meal of bread, cauliflower cheese, potatoes and hotdogs. It's disappointing not being with the others, but I can catch up with them because the TEPC has to stay at Advanced Base Camp for at least a week. The path is easy to follow because equipment and supplies are being shifted up and down the mountain in a daily convoy of yaks and sherpas.

After a second night's sleep I decide to try again, and set off early for the British 1922 Camp. My lungs hurt from breathing so hard and I tell myself to go very, very slowly. Even so, my heart rate is soon above 130, and the headaches have started again. I fight for every breath and step as the wind gusts to 60 mph, sending spin-drifts swirling into my face. The yaks are roped together and the sherpas chat among themselves as if we're on a picnic outing. I envy the bastards; they're used to this rarefied air.

Finally I reach the interim camp. I'm exhausted. I drink some tea and eat a few dry biscuits before crawling into my sleeping-bag. This headache feels like a part of me. Early next morning, I set off for Advanced Base Camp, still battling nausea and exhaustion. It's like being on Selection again as I'm drinking out of puddles and eating snow.

A third of a mile short of the camp, at 20,000 feet, I prop myself against a rock and watch the white dots swimming in front of my eyes. Then I hear Harry's voice. He's coming down towards me with Brian and two guys from the expedition. They're carrying Karl between them.

'What's wrong?' I pant.

'He's sick. We've got to get him down quickly.'

Despite my concern for Karl, I feel total relief. I don't have to keep climbing.

Harry tells me what happened after they left me. They made it to British 1922 Camp and the next day pushed on to Advanced Base Camp. Karl had been tired but okay. He got through the first night but started vomiting during the second. Harry says it often takes forty-eight hours for the worst of it to kick in.

'He woke up and said he thought he was going to die. We got him on oxygen straight away and realised we had a problem.'

The expedition has a Gamow bag, and Karl was put inside. This is a barometric device that can artificially lower the occupant by between 6,000 and 8,000 feet. This seemed to help, but they couldn't transport Karl in the bag because it had to be kept inflated. He thought he could walk but they finished up having to carry him, taking it in turns to hook his arms over their shoulders and walk him down.

I look at Karl. He's in a shit state; his lips are blue and his eyes are fluttering.

It's about 10 a.m. as they pass me. I turn and stagger after them. By the time I reach the interim camp, the Gamow bag has been set up and Karl is inside, back on the oxygen. Brian, the medic, has decided that Karl can't endure the trek to Base Camp and has more chance of surviving in the bag. Meanwhile, Harry has radioed down and two doctors are on their way up with more sherpas and fresh yaks.

I take over the foot pump that keeps the Gamow bag inflated while Brian monitors Karl's blood pressure. Harry has gone straight back up to Advanced Base Camp to pick up the TEPC and more oxygen. We have two sherpas with us, one of whom has summited Everest four or five times.

Karl is conscious and coherent, but he looks awful. I can see his face through a window in the Gamow bag and I make sure he keeps the oxygen mask over his mouth and nose.

'My head is killing me,' he says.

'Yeah, well, that'll teach you to go out drinking all night. My old CO used to say that you can't go out at night hooting with the owls and come here in the morning and expect to scream with the eagles.'

Karl smiles.

'When you orbited the Earth, how high did you fly?' I ask, trying to keep him occupied and alert.

'About 200 miles.'

'It makes my 20-odd miles seem like a walk to the local shops.'

'Yeah, but you're going to jump out when you get up there.'

'Do you think I'm crazy?'

'Doesn't everyone?'

'Well, my mate Lurch says he wants my car if I croak.'

Karl smiles again, breathing deeply into the mask.

'You and Harry go back a long way, don't you?'

'Yes.'

'He was telling me you were in Africa together. What were you doing?'

'It's a long story. We were there trying to save rhino and elephants from poachers. It was a task force made up of ex-SAS and intelligence officers, who were identifying dealers, uncovering corrupt officials and training anti-poaching units.'

'Did you see any rhino?'

'Sure.'

Karl wants to hear a story, so I tell him about Ted Reilly, the chief game-warden for Swaziland. He was as tough as teak in his bush hat and trademark shorts, and he loved every rock and blade of grass of his homeland. When Ted looked at you, he seemed to be gazing into the distance as if he'd spotted one of his beloved rhinos. He'd been losing three or four a year to poachers despite the electric fences and thirty-metre watchtowers.

One day a young black lad found me at the main game lodge and said Ted wanted to see me. When I arrived, Ted was loading up the Land Rover at his homestead. 'The bastards have got another one,' he said. Ted would have lined up all poachers and shot them. 'Do you want to come out?' he asked me.

'Sure.'

I slid into the passenger seat and two of Ted's rangers climbed into the back. They were carrying knobkerries, little club-like sticks, and wearing perfectly ironed shirts and shorts. We drove for about twenty minutes on dirt roads and then went bush-bashing. It was the dry season and the ground was firm. Ted's fists were tight on the wheel as he told me about the civil war over the border with Mozambique, ten miles to the north. To the south was South Africa, where the reforms of President F. W. de Klerk were only just beginning to take hold. Swaziland had become a sanctuary for ANC exiles and a stomping ground for South African spies. Ted had watched it grow increasingly lawless and knew it had become a major route for smuggling contraband.

'Sometimes they take it out in fucking diplomatic bags,' he told me. 'The North Koreans and Chinese. How do you stop that?'

I asked him who was doing the poaching.

'They're locals or they're hired from across the border in Mozambique. I know who's putting them up to it – a group of local businessmen. That's what your guys should do – take them out. Go in with one of your teams and just blow them away. It's the only way you're going to stop the poaching.'

I laughed sadly and told him we weren't licensed to kill.

We bounced over rough ground for another twenty minutes before finally emerging into a clearing. A couple of local villagers were crouching in the shade of a tree in scruffy old shorts and T-shirts. They rose from the dust as the Land Rover pulled up. In front of us lay a single rhino, down on its front knees with a bloody hole in its head where its horn had been hacked off. The cavity was infested with maggots and the stench was overpowering. It had been dead for several days.

Ted was on the verge of tears. 'It's Mtuabu,' he said, crouching beside the body. 'She was born here about eight years ago.' He pointed to the bullet holes. 'They've sprayed her with an AK-47. She didn't stand a chance.'

Using a piece of wire, he began showing me the entry and exit holes, while I took photographs. I had to force myself to look through the camera lens. Isn't it strange how I have no trouble killing a man, yet the death of an animal upsets me so much?

Ted took a large knife from the Land Rover and sliced deeply into the rhino's neck. 'I have to get the bullets out,' he said, choking on the words. 'Maybe we can match them to the gun if we ever catch the bastards.'

'Where do they get the guns?' I asked.

'In Mozambique you can get an AK-47 in exchange for a bag of sugar. It's the largest dumping ground for AK-47s in the world.'

After pocketing half a dozen slugs, Ted began walking around the area, examining the tracks. 'They travel in twos and threes, always on foot. It's not hard to track a rhino. They'll follow one for up to a week and then bang! Sometimes they get the baby rhino and deliberately hack it to make it call out to its mother. When the mother comes close enough they kill it. At eight thousand dollars a kilo, it's worth the effort.'

'And then what happens?' I asked.

'The horn will finish up in Manzini [Swaziland's second largest city] and then go out in a diplomatic pouch or be smuggled into South Africa.'

We climbed back into the Land Rover and sat in silence on the drive home to the lodge.

'Are you awake, Karl? Don't fall asleep on me.' I lean over and look down through the window in the bag.

'Yeah, I'm listening.' He slurs the words.

'Your turn, Karl. You tell me a story now.'

He knows that I'm a keen pilot, so he talks about his astronaut training – NASA taught him how to fly military jets and he used to take one home for the weekend. That's a hell of a company vehicle!

Karl wants to go to the toilet. He's quite coherent and insists on getting out of the bag, even though Brian wants him to stay inside. The zip doesn't stretch from end to end and only opens a third of the way down. It makes it difficult to get him out. His blood pressure starts to drop and we immediately rush him back inside.

Brian and I take it in turns pumping the bag and keeping Karl awake. He's remarkably calm but he has no strength or energy. The oxygen mask keeps slipping off his face and he takes an age to put it on again. It's getting dark and the temperature has fallen until frost covers everything. I crawl into my sleeping-bag next to Karl and let a sherpa do the pumping. I'm exhausted and my head is throbbing.

Suddenly, I don't hear the pumping for several seconds. The sherpa has stopped because he doesn't realise the importance of keeping the bag inflated. We're communicating with sign language and it's impossible to make him understand. I go back to pumping.

'My turn for a story, Karl. Then it's your turn again, okay?'

There is silence.

'Karl? Can you hear me?'

'Yes,' he murmurs.

'I don't suppose you've ever heard of Tim Mace. He's a guy I know who trained to be a cosmonaut with the Russians. He was almost the first Briton into space, but they chose his colleague instead, Helen Sharman.'

Tim had been an Army Air Corps pilot and a very good skydiver before he trained as a cosmonaut. I tell the story of how Tim arranged a fifty-way jump, hoping to break the world record. It was a 'military only' attempt, and a lot of my old mates were jumping, including Doug, Sharky and Dick Kalinski. We gathered at the drop zone and Tim was already flapping and barking orders like an RSM.

'I'm going to allocate you all numbers from one to fifty. You have to remember your numbers,' he yelled, waving a clipboard.

'Edwards, one. Johnson, two. Hennessey, three. Donaldson, four . . .'

Standing right at the back, I put my hand up. 'Excuse me.'

'Yes, what is it?'

'You said that we had to remember these numbers.'

'Yes. That's right.'

'Well, number one was Edwards, number two was Johnson, number three was Hennessey, but I'm buggered if I can remember any more.'

The rest of the guys couldn't stifle their laughter, but Tim looked at me in disbelief. He muttered through clenched teeth, 'You only have to remember your *own* number.'

'Oh, I see – that makes it a lot easier.'

I lean over and look into the bag, scraping away frost. Condensation has formed droplets on the inside of the plastic window. I can't see Karl's face in the darkness. 'You're still with me, aren't you mate? It's going to be your turn in a minute.'

There's no answer. I shake the bag. 'Come on, Karl, come on! The doctors will be here soon. Then we'll stretcher you down. Hang in there.'

I don't know if I should open the bag to check if he's okay. I can't see anything through the bloody window. I shake him harder, getting tearful. 'Please, Karl . . .'

Slipping off my gloves, I unzip the bag and press my fingers against his neck. There's no pulse. He's dead. It's one in the morning, and we've been pumping for thirteen hours. I crawl into my sleeping-bag and lie awake until just before dawn. Then I radio Harry with the news. Later in the morning, he arrives with a few others from the expedition.

There's no question about what to do with the body. Although logistically it might be possible to get him off the mountain, it would mean taking sherpas and yaks from the main expedition, which has spent hundreds of thousands of dollars to reach this point. It could also jeopardise more lives.

Karl said he wanted to be buried on Everest if he didn't make it. He's going to get his wish. The sherpas make the grave, fashioning the sides from shale until they look like Cotswold stone walls. We put his body into a sleeping-bag and lay him to rest. Someone recites the Lord's Prayer and the sherpas say their own words. Afterwards, when the stones have been piled on top of the grave, Harry scratches an inscription on a large rock: 'Dr Karl Henize, friend and astronaut, RIP 5.10.1993.'

Three days later, we arrive back in Kathmandu. Harry has Karl's personal effects and is going to take them back to America. He talks to Dr John Stanley at NASA, and one of Karl's friends has to break the news to his wife and grown-up children.

I'm still feeling pretty weak, but the headaches have gone. I decide to stop off in Thailand for a week on the way home, staying on one of the islands to recuperate. Meanwhile, Harry is flying to London and then straight on to Houston for the memorial service.

When I telephone home there is more bad news. Anna has been in a road accident. She's been living in Bristol for about three months, sharing a house with other students. I've barely seen her in that time, but I'd lent her my Ford Sierra while I was away.

She's in tears and I try to calm her down. The story is so convoluted it takes me a while to work out what happened. She'd been driving from Hereford to Bristol, carrying all her worldly possessions in the back. Americans aren't very experienced at overtaking on two-way roads, because they're so used to driving on motorways. Anna had been in fourth gear as she tried to pass slower cars. She didn't have the acceleration and was caught on the wrong side of the road, colliding head-on with another vehicle. A third car then crashed into them.

The Sierra burst into flames, but somehow Anna managed to climb out of the wreckage as the fire spread to the other cars.

'How did you get into my place?' I ask.

'The police gave me a ride. I didn't have a key so they broke a window. I'm sorry. I didn't know what else to do.'

Christ, what a week I'm having!

Anna is upset about the car, but I tell her not to worry. 'The main thing is that you're okay.'

*

All Anna's possessions were destroyed in the flames. She managed to rescue only one item – a wooden jewellery box that was blackened and scorched on one side. The box is now sitting in the storeroom just off the kitchen, resting on a shelf beside the gas meter. It's been there ever since the accident.

I go downstairs and open the door. The light is on a pull-string. A part of me doesn't want to look inside the box. Instead, I have an overwhelming urge to fling it into the garden. I don't want it in my house; I can take nothing from Anna. She is like a virus who contaminates my sterile environment.

No, I must confront this; I must discover the significance of everything.

Picking up the jewellery box, I carry it to the kitchen table and unhook the clasp. Inside is a blackened and twisted piece of number plate from my car. Anna had obviously taken it for posterity, or as a morbid souvenir of the accident.

But why has she left it here? What significance does it have?

I close the lid and put the box back on the shelf. I'm not going to throw it away just yet – not until I discover what it means.

14

The town centre is only about ten minutes' walk from home, but I won't go out by myself. I have a lot of friends in Hereford – drinking buddies, old girlfriends, mates from the Regiment – and I don't want them to see me like this. It's not just the dribbling or the shaking. I'm normally so full of beans, cracking jokes, blaggarding and flirting with the girls. I've lost the spark; my mind is like army porridge.

Hereford is small enough for news to travel quickly, and I know people will be watching me; trying to see if I'm the same old Tom. They'll be whispering to themselves about how much weight I've lost and how yellow my skin is. Worse still, when I'm gone, they'll tell stories about how I used to be the life and soul of the party.

My garden seat in the kitchen has become known as the 'mad chair', and that's where Jackie finds me every morning, staring at the door of the refrigerator and listening to the disembodied voices of breakfast TV hosts drifting from the living-room.

By mid-morning the girls normally arrive – Irene and Fran, identical twin sisters who I've known for a few years. They bring along Jenny, a friend of Irene's who has a wicked sense of humour. They tease me about dribbling on my shirt and never getting up from the 'mad chair'. I'm affectionately called 'the Mong', and they carry on around me, working a rota system to cook and clean up the place while I feel like the family Labrador. I'm glad of their company and they help me through some bad times.

The girls take me out occasionally. We go up to a local wine bar for brunch, and they sit me at the end of the table and every so often pause from their chatting and ask if 'the Mong' wants another coffee.

The drugs make me hungry, and I wolf down steak sandwiches while the girls hand me extra napkins and complain about my table manners. 'Do you think I'm getting better?' I ask Fran.

She smiles. 'Of course you are, Mong.'

'How can you tell?'

'You just seem to be more yourself.'

But the truth is that most of the time I feel worse. The drugs have made me so lethargic and flat that all I do is sit in my chair, smoking and drinking tea. I'm miserable and I want to know why. I want to dissect everything about my life and find a reason for how I'm feeling.

When I left the Charter Clinic, Dr Oz gave me his home telephone number in Somerset and said that I could call him if things got really bad. A couple of times, late at night, when I wake on the sofa and feel desperately alone, I call the number.

'I'm not getting any better,' I say. 'I can't go on like this.'

He tells me to take deep breaths. 'It's going to take time, there are no miracle cures.'

I've been meaning to write letters to Saad and Loel Guinness, thanking them for what they've done for me. Without them I might still be in the asylum in France, and I could never have paid for my treatment or medical bills. It's an enormous effort of willpower to actually sit down with a pen and paper, though. Apart from the indolent effects of the drugs, I haven't written many letters in my life and I want to make sure these are worded perfectly.

Jackie offers to post them, and while she's out I get a call from Anna. It's not the first time she's phoned, but Jackie has intercepted most of the calls and told Anna it might be best if she leaves me alone. She still calls, though.

The conversations seem to always take the same course. Anna will start crying and weaving her magic, playing on my emotions. She has this way of manipulating me which is why, deep down, I'm afraid she may have put a spell on me. I don't mention it to Jackie because she might tell Dr Allman that I'm getting paranoid again.

*

There are faxes going back and forth to NASA and the Russians, as well as to Loel Guinness and Joe Kittinger. The time differences are a nightmare and I've had trouble sleeping since I got back from Nepal.

High Adventure has lost patience with my organisational skills, so I've hired a personal assistant, Jackie Green, a keen skydiver, who started work at the beginning of December. The upstairs office is under control but the living-room is scattered with papers. I'm on the third draft of final specifications for the skydive suit.

There's still a chance, albeit a slim one, that we can be ready for a full dress-rehearsal jump from 85,000 feet in eight months. If all goes well, the mission jump will take place two to five weeks after that.

I can't believe how complicated it has become. Everything has to be spelled out in such clear, concise terms that there is absolutely no chance of misinterpretation. There are annexes, clauses, sub-clauses, parentheses and riders covering every aspect of the mission. Sometimes I think people have lost sight of the prize.

Two high-altitude balloons will be manufactured by one of two American companies, Raven and Winzen. Each envelope will have a capacity of approximately 23 million cubic feet and, when inflated, be about a third of the height of the Eiffel Tower. A Canadian team formerly involved in Canada's fledgling space programme is likely to be the launch team – they come highly recommended by Danny Ball and the National Scientific Balloon Facility (NSBF).

The gondola is to be made by a British company with an on-board life-support system designed and built by Zvezda. After the jump a radio-controlled explosive device, designed by the NSBF, will sever the gondola from the balloon envelope and it will descend via a cargo parachute that should ensure the payload isn't damaged. The same device can be triggered if there is a problem during the ascent and the mission has to be aborted.

A small army of technicians, launch crew and engineers will check and recheck every rivet, cable, circuit and valve. At the same time, meteorologists at the site will liaise with the National Weather Centre and NASA to get a forecast for the jump.

For two hours prior to take-off and during the flight I won't take a breath of ambient air and must breathe only pure oxygen. This will rid my body of any nitrogen which might form bubbles under my skin and expand in the increasing altitude – similar to 'the bends' suffered by deep-sea divers.

During the ascent, the suit will slowly inflate until at 39,000 feet it reaches a pressurised setting of 0.22 kilograms per square inch. It will then artificially hold my body at this 'height' as I continue climbing.

Zvezda has promised a clear frost- and fog-free visor, but thermal protection is more difficult. My body temperature will basically be controlled by the oxygen flow through the suit, with excess heat and humidity dumped during the ascent. However, the cold is certain to attack my extremities and electrical heating elements will be added to the hands and feet.

A specially designed container on my chest will hold the camera avionics, microwave transmitters, batteries and oxygen supply. In addition there will be video recorders as a back-up against microwave link failure. Extensive chamber tests will be done to make sure the various cameras and related equipment can function at high altitude and not interfere with other systems.

Before stepping into the suit, pads will be attached to my chest and arms to monitor my heart and respiratory rate. These will be constantly transmitted to medical staff on the ground. If there is any serious deterioration in my physiological condition during the ascent, the emergency 'cut-down' will release the gondola. At any stage I can unhook my 'umbilical cord' and bail out.

The preferred location for the jump is the south-western US desert, most likely in Texas or New Mexico. The main control centre will be located at the launch point along with a media centre, microwave receivers and a satellite truck to feed the signals to the TV networks. Take-off will be before dawn to avoid ground turbulence and heat haze. Once the balloon envelope has been filled with helium, the rate of climb will be between 700 and 1,200 feet per minute. It will take approximately two hours to reach 130,000 feet.

As the sun rises, I will see it before anyone else on Earth, but the sky above me will be dark because there is nothing for the light to reflect upon except the balloon and gondola. Barring any cloud or haze, I should have an uninterrupted view for 700 miles in every direction, but the Earth will appear as swirls of colour rather than having any definable detail. The only sound I will hear is the air pulsating through my suit.

Once I reach float altitude, I will have several minutes to do any final checks and disconnect from the on-board life-support system. Then I will pull myself up from the stool and shuffle to the edge of the jump platform.

The exit is crucial. I want to fall away cleanly, with my arms angled back behind me, head down in a dive. There will be no sense of falling; I might as well be suspended in space. By the time I reach opening height – 10,000 feet – I will have fallen nearly twenty-three miles in four minutes.

The tandem-style parachute is 415 feet square and takes a little longer to open than a single parachute. It has good steering and is very slow and docile. If something goes wrong, an emergency AOD will open the reserve parachute at 8,000 feet. I should spend approximately ten minutes under the canopy and land within twenty-five miles of the launch site. A helicopter recovery team will pick me up.

As I go through the project specifications, I'm adding details and altering others. Cutting corners to save costs is not an issue, but some of the Russian ideas have questionable value, such as using scaled models in wind-tunnel tests. There is no way to simulate the mission accurately, which is why the test jump from 85,000 feet becomes so important.

There's a Christmas Boogie at Ampuria Brava, which is an annual event where a lot of old mates get together for some jumping and partying. Sharky is going for sure.

Jackie says I need a break from the paperwork, and points out that I can also do some training. I throw a bag into the car and drive down to Spain. It's been weeks since I had a decent sleep and I want to relax, but the best intentions are under pressure once I get among the old crowd. One or two beers a night – with the promise of an early night – just gives me the taste, and I finish up carousing until the early hours and crashing out until mid-morning when the sun wakes me up. Then I'm jumping all day on just a sandwich and bottles of water.

Chris Meacock has flown a big Skyliner over from the Peterborough Parachute Centre to give us an extra plane. I can't believe he's the same lad I used to bounce on my knee as a toddler, and who followed me round like a puppy dog when I did commentaries for the Red Devils. Now Chris is in his early twenties and looks a lot like his dad, John Meacock. He's a civilian pilot, and whenever he isn't flying he has his nose in a book, studying for his commercial licence.

'Come up with me, Tom,' he says, as the Skyliner is being refuelled, ready for another lift.

'Yeah, sure. But let's do it later. I'm off to Barcelona to pick up a mate from the airport.'

By the time I get back, the Skyliner, a big box aeroplane with a tailgate, is on its second last lift before dusk. Sharky has had a chest infection and been in bed for a few days, but he's come to the drop zone to get some fresh air. We can hear Roland, who runs the parachute centre, talking to Chris on the radio. The Skyliner has dropped its load and is standing on its nose, descending quickly.

'Chris, can you do a hot refuel?'

The reply comes back, 'Yes.'

If the engines keep burning and turning while they refuel, they might get another lift in before dusk. A lot of people are jumping, and more lifts means more money. The tanks are never filled completely because a heavier plane takes longer to climb to altitude. Normally they put in just enough fuel to get it up and down a few times, particularly so late in the day.

The radio crackles and I hear Chris say, 'Reference to last: no, I can't do a hot refuel.'

I look up and see him bank the Skyliner for his final approach to landing. He's misjudged it and is off-line with the runway. He's coming in towards the open grass area alongside the runway, where twenty skydivers have just landed and are gathering their canopies.

Unwilling to put it down on the grass, Chris sweeps overhead and I notice one of his engines is feathering. He's got a problem. He banks hard left, turning away from Ampuria Brava because he doesn't want to fly low over the town with only one engine.

'Mayday! Mayday! Mayday!'

The second engine is feathering. He's in a tight turn, losing altitude. The wing-tip catches in a tree and the Skyliner nose-dives. There's a dull thud but no flames. I'm already running, across the runway and the grass. There's a swampy ditch along the eastern edge of the drop zone and the skydivers are trying to find a way to cross. I plough straight through it and keep going in thigh-deep grass. The boggy ground is sucking at my shoes. Ahead of me I can see the tail of the Skyliner. What if it explodes? I have to get Chris out.

The cockpit has been obliterated, and there's wreckage everywhere. Chris is wearing a leather bomber jacket and is still harnessed in the pilot's seat. The metal plate of the seat had snapped on impact and allowed his body to go forward. His neck hit the dash with such impact that it severed his head. There's just a stub, spitting blood.

I lean into the cockpit and turn off the electrics. The turbines are white-hot because there's no air passing through them. There had been no explosion because there's no fuel in the tanks. A short distance from the nose of the aircraft, I find what I've been looking for. I drag a piece of carpet from the wreckage and cover Chris's head.

Sharky arrives close behind me and turns just as Chris's younger brother Stuart arrives. He grabs him around the chest and spins him around. 'There's nothing we can do. You don't need to see this.' Stuart is fighting him, but Sharky doesn't let go. He walks him back to the parachute centre with his arm around his shoulders.

Nobody feels like jumping any more – we've lost a friend. John and Sue Meacock arrive from the UK on the first available flight and I speak to them briefly, saying how sorry I am. It reminds me of talking to Al Slater's father, and how impossible it is to find words that can offer comfort. I've known John Meacock for nearly seventeen years.

Afterwards, as a tribute to Chris, we put a sixteen-way together, a standard formation with four diamonds facing, except only fifteen people jump and we leave one position vacant. It's called 'the missing slot', and symbolises where Chris should be.

As we come in to land beside the runway, I look across to the crash site and see a rainbow arcing up from the trees.

That night, outside the bar of the parachute centre, I ask Sharky if he ever thinks about dying. I know he's surprised – not so much by the question, but the person asking it. Sharky has seen me do some wild things and he's heard stories from the Regiment.

'Not if I can help it,' he says, trying to fathom why I've asked him now. Chris's death had affected all of us, and each person has his own way of dealing with grief. I tend not to let my emotions show or allow things to prey on my mind, yet this time I can't seem to erase the image of Chris still harnessed in the pilot's seat, with a bloody stump where his head should be.

The next day is New Year's Eve, and I decide I've had enough of Ampuria Brava. 'Let's go and have New Year with Harry,' I say to Sharky.

'Where is he?'

'In Chamonix.'

'How long is that going to take?'

'If we set off now we can be there by nine o'clock tonight. We can see in the New Year.'

Sharky shrugs. 'Okay, sure.'

We toss our gear in the car and head north across the border. I drive most of the day and at about seven that night it's teeming with rain when the car breaks down in the foothills of the Alps. The coil is getting wet, but we manage to wrap it up and get the engine started again. It's after ten in the evening by the time we arrive in Chamonix. Higher up on the slopes the rain has turned to snow.

We wander around a couple of bars and nightclubs, hoping to bump into Harry. My desert boots are sodden, and the first thing I eat all day is a hotdog from a stand on the footpath. Eventually I get a barman to turn down the music while I call Harry's house. He and Cath live about seven miles out of town.

'What the hell are you doing in Chamonix?' he asks.

'I've come to celebrate New Year.'

'Well, I'm half cut and it's heaving with snow up here. I can't get down to you.'

There's no way we can get to Harry's place, so we're stuck here, without a hotel, at a quarter to midnight on New Year's Eve and it's starting to snow. I can imagine Hillbilly laughing if he could see me now.

'I'm really sorry, Sharky. It's not what I planned.'

'Forget about it. Let's find a bar before we freeze to fucking death.'

We celebrate two New Year's Eves – a French one and then the English one an hour later. By half past three I'm well pissed, yet I don't feel drunk or tired, even though I've been driving since yesterday morning.

Sharky and I go back to the car and put on layers of clothing, wrapping duvet jackets around us. We keep the engine running all night to stay warm. By morning I have to dig the car out. Sharky is still sleeping. When he wakes we're already half-way through France.

'Where are we going?' he asks.

'Home.'

'Oh.'

Sharky doesn't ask why. I guess he just accepts that I must have a reason. The truth is, I don't know why; I simply woke up and wanted to be back in Hereford.

It takes us less than six hours to get to Calais, doing over a hundred on the motorways. We're back in England at 9.30 p.m. and I let Sharky drive from the ferry terminal in Dover to his place in Aldershot.

I help unload his gear and he says, 'You're staying the night, aren't you?'

'No thanks, Sharky. I'll give you a call.'

'Come on. Look at you – you're exhausted. Chill out for a couple of days. At least get some sleep.'

'No, I have to get home.'

15

I can't bear to be by myself, not even for five minutes, which must drive Jackie crazy. I follow her around the house talking about myself constantly, trying to analyse how I'm feeling and seeking reassurance. 'Am I getting better, Jackie? Can you notice any improvement? Am I shaking as much? Are my eyes still yellow?'

I sit next to her in the office as she makes her calls, occasionally picking up a sheet of paper and forgetting which file it comes from. Jackie doesn't get angry, she simply sorts it out and offers to make us some tea. I'm swimming in tea – drowning in the stuff. It's a wonder my eyeballs aren't spinning like those old-fashioned fuel-gauges, where the petrol made a little ball dance behind the glass.

Meanwhile, the cups are piling up in the sink and I can't motivate myself to wash up. The physical and mental effort required to carry out such a chore is beyond me. Instead I listen to the tap dripping into a saucer, noting how the 'plink' sound slowly changes pitch into a 'plonk' as the water gets higher.

I tried to mow the lawn yesterday. What a joke! You can see it through the window. I managed to get the electric mower out of the shed, plug it in, mow a haphazard-looking square in the centre of the back garden and then I came back inside. The mower is still sitting out there – waiting for the rain and the rust.

Of course, the back fence still hasn't been fixed. It's a solid paling fence that blew down in a strong wind. I want to replace it with railings so it won't happen again, but if I can't finish cutting the grass I've got no chance of building a bloody fence.

Every time I see Allman he asks me how I feel. I rattle off a list of the negatives while Jackie will counter with a more positive appraisal – 'No, it wasn't so bad, Tom. You felt good on Wednesday.'

You see, it's all a matter of degrees. Even my good days are bad. Even the hours are broken up into a good fifteen minutes and a bad fifteen minutes – a good thought and a bad thought. The only consolation is that I'm getting closer to remembering the 'dark days'.

*

There's so much to do and so little time if I'm going to jump this year. The telephone calls take me until late at night, and when Jackie arrives in the morning I've barely slept. There are faxes spilling out of the machine and curling on the floor. She makes me breakfast but I'm not hungry. Without even thinking, I stub out my cigarette in the egg yolk.

'You've got to eat, Tom.'

'Sorry, Jack, I had a midnight snack,' I lie.

'And how much did you drink?'

I pretend not to hear her, and doodle in the margins of the *Daily Telegraph*. Something is happening, but I don't know what it is. It's like having half an idea or the answer without the question. When I do go to bed, I wrestle with problems from the project and make mental lists of what I have to do tomorrow. I doze off for a few hours but it isn't a refreshing sleep. More than once I've woken in a sweat, having seen the image of Chris Meacock strapped in the cockpit seat.

I look at the calendar – Wednesday, 16 January. I'm doing some chamber tests today at RAF North Loughenham near Peterborough. In Air Troop we used to do a decompression test every year as part of our HALO training. During the tests the chamber would be set at about 26,000 feet and about half a dozen of us would sit opposite each other, wearing oxygen masks. Going though the procedures, we'd give a thumbs-up to confirm we were getting oxygen and then the guys sitting along my side of the wall were told to take their masks off.

We each had a clipboard with paper and a pencil, and were told to start counting down from 100 to 0 by multiples of five – 100 . . . 95 . . . 90 . . . 85 – while writing the numbers down. Then we'd have to draw a picture of a bicycle.

Initially, nothing seemed to be different, and I had only a vague awareness of being warm. The lads sitting opposite, still wearing masks, were watching us and beginning to recognise the first signs of hypoxia, like the blueness of our lips and fingertips. That was the main aim of the exercise – to be able to recognise the effects of oxygen deprivation.

Eventually we were told to put on our masks, and immediately I realised what I'd lost. My peripheral vision returned and the light grew brighter. I looked down at what I'd written on the clipboard. My 'bicycle' was ridiculous, and the numbers were all over the place; I'd missed out '75' and '70' and written '45' three times.

This time in the chamber I'm undertaking a special run up to 40,000 feet, followed by a rapid let-down. This will simulate the pressure change I'll encounter during the latter stages of the freefall descent. It's an important altitude because throughout the mission my skydive suit will keep my body at a simulated altitude of 39,000 feet even when I'm three times that high. The suit will only start to de-pressurise when I drop below 39,000 feet during the freefall.

Before the test I have to de-nitrogenise my body by breathing pure oxygen for an hour. I sit in a classroom, reading a book, plugged into an oxygen bottle on wheels. From there I transfer to the chamber and the oxygen lines are plugged into the main console. The chamber is sealed and I sit down on a bench, putting on a headset so I can hear the instructions.

'Okay, we're now taking you up – 12,000 feet . . . 18,000 . . . 25,000 . . . 38,000 . . . 38,500 . . . 39,000 . . . 39,500 . . .'

Anything above this altitude and it becomes difficult to breathe the oxygen being supplied. The lungs expand to the point where even a bandage tightened around the chest will make things easier. That's why a pressure suit becomes imperative at greater heights.

It gets warmer and the mask grips my face tightly. The oxygen seems to be punching into my mouth and I have this sensation of being able to feel the gases and fluids in my body.

'We're now going to begin the let-down.'

There's a sudden rush of air and my ears pop immediately. In effect I'm coming from thinner air to denser air, as they let air back into the chamber. There are two RAF pilots in the chamber also doing the test. A rapid let-down is unusual for them, because normally they practise for entirely the opposite event of an aircraft cabin losing pressure at high altitude, with the pressure inside suddenly leaping upwards from an artificially controlled 8,000 feet to 40,000 feet. It's a hell of a thump.

A new pile of faxes and phone messages is waiting for me back in Hereford. We have problems in Moscow. George Rykoff has resigned from the project for health reasons. He's also had a disagreement with some of his colleagues about work practices and is particularly concerned that High Adventure is being overcharged.

Rykoff is my main contact at Zvezda and he's become a good friend. I trust him implicitly and losing him is a great blow. Every hurdle seems to get higher, and as I solve one problem, another three emerge. I'm bogged down on the budgets and specifications; the draft contract is forty pages long, and I have to check every detail including the insurance, timetables, payment schedules and penalty clauses.

When I telephone Rykoff I can't hide my frustration.

'I just want a four-minute jump. Four years for four minutes – that's not too much to ask, is it?'

'You deserve to get the record, Tom,' he says. 'But sometimes you have to strive for years for just one minute of something very special.'

That night I go to a bar I haven't visited before. I don't want to be distracted by people I know. I just want to think and to knock myself out with drink so that maybe I'll be able to sleep. I take a book with me, but find myself doodling on a scrap of paper, coming up with word associations.

When Jackie arrives in the morning, I haven't slept. I pretend to do the crossword while I write things in the little box they leave for doing anagrams.

'You look awful. Didn't you sleep?' she asks.

'Like a log.'

Anna calls me from Bristol most weeks, but I've only been down to see her once. Occasionally she comes to Hereford. It's Tuesday afternoon and I know she gets an exam result today, so I give her a call. One of her house-mates answers the phone.

'Hello.'

'Hello, is Anna there, please?'

'Is that Tom?'

'Yes.'

'Oh, she's not here. She's gone to see a friend, but she said she's going to call you.'

I smell a lie. I don't know why. Does betrayal have a scent?

Anna calls me about five days later. She's been back to Washington to see her new boyfriend. I know she's telling me this so she can get a reaction.

'That's great. Is he a nice guy, Anna? I hope he's not some weirdo French poet.'

She accuses me of teasing her and says that I don't care.

'Listen, Anna, if you meet someone else that's fine by me. I've told you that. I'm happy for you.'

She might be crying, I can't tell. She's thinking of leaving Bristol and going back to America. I know she wants me to tell her what to do, but I can't because it's her life. I never made her any promises; we said good-bye to each other in Washington.

Anna calms down and I tell her that I'll call her next week. Afterwards, I pour myself a glass of wine and when that's finished I pour another until the bottle is empty. I'm sitting in the kitchen, scribbling words on the MFI table-top with a pencil. There's a wet rag so that if anyone comes in I can rub it off quickly. I'm writing down every emotion I can think of, starting with the letter 'a': affection, adoration, anger, anguish, apathy . . . No, forget about doing things alphabetically, what are the emotions that first come to mind? Love and hate. Fear.

—Okay, let's look at fear. What does that stir?

The image of my father's face bellowing at me. He frightened me.

—No, forget that – I love Dad, I respect him. Don't go into love or respect, we're going to address them later, stick with fear. What else frightened me?

When I think of love I think of Jason and Mum.

—No! Stay with fear.

Crossing the Atlantic? No. Everest? No.

—During the Falklands?

I was excited, not frightened. Put that one over there. I jot down the word 'excitement'.

—When was I frightened?

Sitting in that bloody hospital with broken teeth and a busted kneecap waiting for Dad to arrive.

—Yes, but that wasn't so bad. Move on.

Parachuting? Yes, when I did that first jump I was frightened, but it wasn't terror. Knowledge dispels fear. Should I write terror over here?

—No, just stay with fear.

I was frightened of failure. I thought I was going to fail Selection.

—Yes, but if you knew you weren't going to pass, how could you be frightened of failing?

That's always been my defence – I laugh and pretend it doesn't really matter. I guess I haven't really been frightened that often in my life. In Northern Ireland, as a young paratrooper in a steel helmet, I remember facing a riot knowing the order to charge was coming. But nature had pumped me full of adrenalin – it was an adventure. The older guys were probably frightened, but I didn't know enough.

And in the building site in Cheltenham, under the scaffolding, when my heart was racing and I saw the broken bottle in that thug's hand, I controlled my fear. 'How do I stop being afraid?' I asked myself. 'By escaping from the fear,' was the answer. 'I am going through you.'

Let's move on to another word. At the centre of the table, I've written, 'EMOTION . . . E-MOTION . . . ELECTRICAL MOTION'.

—No, no, don't get side-tracked; we all know what emotion is.

But that's the problem, don't you see? All my emotions are mixed up.

—How did it happen?

Think about it. Somehow we store our emotions, not just what we're feeling now, but the aggregate of all the emotions we experience in a lifetime.

—That must be one hell of a storage system.

Yes.

—What sort of device would be needed to do that?

There's an expression that Des uses when people ask him for something: 'Fill your boots', which means, 'Take what you like.' This line keeps coming back to me like an irritating jingle. Fill your boots. Fill your boots. I'm not sure, but I have this idea that nuclear fuel rods slip into 'boots' at power stations.

I picture a series of 'boots', shaped like test tubes. From the earliest moment of life, as a new-born baby, when we first feel the fear at leaving the womb, the first 'boot' is created and a single drop of fear splashes into the bottom. Then as we experience each new emotion – joy, warmth, security, sadness, love, anger – new 'boots' are created and a drop falls into each of them.

Over my lifetime these boots will slowly fill. As an innocent child the first drops of emotion are 100 per cent pure. Later, as emotions become tainted by cynicism or vanity, they are less pure. Equally, some events cause conflicting feelings, such as joy *and* sadness, and these might be impossible to separate, so that globule of emotion remains a mixture. As time passes, the 'boots' continue to fill, and the weight of the fluid above presses down on those first pure drops of emotion that we experience, so that these become even more concentrated.

What about the soul – can that fit into my system? It's important, because there are only three things that can't be found by an autopsy – the mind, the soul and the spirit.

—No, forget about the soul for now; I want to finish my device. I need to get rid of some shit in my life. What is it that is bothering me? Why can't I be happy and enjoy myself like normal people?

Because you have too many mixed emotions. You have to find a way of getting rid of things you don't need, instead of carrying them around.

—Okay, so let's look at this device. Don't ignore the soul. Where does it fit in? I don't even know where it is in the body. That doesn't matter. I can picture it as basically a dumping ground for all the emotion that we don't need. Yes, that makes sense.

Going back to the 'boots', I invent a little valve on the bottom of each of them. When the pressure builds up, the valve opens and a drop comes out. That drop goes into a sump which is the soul. The first globule released is right at the very bottom. It might be that first bit of joy you felt when your mother held you as a newborn baby. It's 100 per cent pure and highly concentrated – you can't split it, or there'd be a huge explosion.

What if I don't want to lose that joy? Maybe I want to keep the memory of it?

—Ssshhh, we'll come to the mind later. That's the filing system. You have to go through there before you can dispose of things completely. You don't want to dispose of them yet?

No.

—Good. You see, each day we collect a bit of joy, sadness, anger . . . all kinds of feelings, and then at night, as we sleep, these are shuffled around and put into the correct 'boots'. The mind is a filing system that lists it all.

This is all so complicated.

—No, it's not. It's logical.

Fuck it, I want to go for a beer.

—But what about the device? It's not finished.

Finish it later.

When Jackie arrives in the morning, I'm still at the table. I wipe it clean and lie about having gone to bed early.

'You are going to eat something, aren't you?'

'I'm really not that hungry, Jack. I had too many biscuits.'

'I'm going to cook anyway.'

'Okay, just give me something small.'

The device isn't finished. All this information is pouring into my head and I have to keep pushing it aside so I can concentrate on the mechanics. When I come across a problem I add something like another small 'boot' or an extra valve. I need it to be right before I start playing with the information.

There's a phone call from one of Anna's flatmates in Bristol. Anna has taken an overdose and is at the hospital. I get straight in the car and start driving. On the way, I stop at an off-licence and buy a bottle of wine. I ask the shopkeeper to take the cork out and I swig it while I'm driving. I've never done it before.

Anna is home from the hospital and being consoled by a friend. She's been crying and I give her a hug. We're in her bedroom which Anna has decorated nicely with cushions and veils.

'What happened?' I ask.

'I can't take it, Tom, being over here . . . My whole life is a mess. You don't love me.'

'Oh, come on, Anna, we've been through this before,' I say softly, trying to find the right words. 'I'm very fond of you, but I don't think I love anyone. That's just me. I'm just a selfish bastard and I'm preoccupied with the project. You should forget about me. You're young, pretty, with a great future . . .'

'There's so much I need to talk to you about,' she says, and immediately I think back to when we first met and she spent five hours on the telephone telling me her life story.

'Yes, I know.'

And so we talk. Anna says that she loves me and wants us to be together. I try to explain my feelings, but silently I can't stop thinking about the device and my emotions. As Anna calms down, her tears turn to anger and then spite. She tells me about a one-night stand she had with a guy she picked up in a bar and how they fucked for four hours straight.

'Doesn't that hurt you?' she asks.

'What did you do that for, Anna? I thought you wanted to get out of all that crap.'

'But how does it make you feel?'

'I don't really care.'

It's the worst thing I can say, but I don't flinch. I know that she's trying to hurt me, but she can't. I won't let her. I've put on my Para head and she's not going to get through to me.

'Listen, Anna, I don't want any more love. Not from Mum, or Christine, or from Jason or from you. I don't want any more respect, or fear, or joy, because I've filled my fucking boots. Simple as that. There is no more room. Yes, I'm the most arrogant person in the world, the most loved person, the most frightened, but you can't touch me. I've filled my boots.'

There, I've said it! That's why I'm so screwed up; I don't have any more room for joy, or sadness, or love, or fear. That's what I have to change.

We talk for hours and Anna falls asleep on her mattress on the floor. I sit beside her with a piece of paper and a pencil. I haven't slept in three days, but my mind is racing and I'm too busy thinking about my device – the pressures and temperatures.

I write a very sentimental letter to Anna, telling her that she's bright and beautiful, with so much to offer to the right person.

She wakes as I'm about to leave. It's six in the morning.

'Look, I'm sorry, I have to go home.'

'What's that?' she says, looking at the letter in my hand.

'I wrote you a note. Don't read it now.'

On the drive home to Hereford my mind is a blank canvas, upon which I draw my designs, adding refinements and tinkering with components. It's almost ready, but not quite.

Almost as I walk into the house the phone rings. 'I read your letter,' says Anna, getting quite emotional. 'I can tell it comes straight from the heart.'

'I was just trying to be nice.'

'I know there's nothing left between us, but can we please be friends and have a nice time? You helped me a lot, we've addressed it all. Can we please, please just go off for a couple of days? No strings. I'd love to see Wales.'

'I'm really busy, Anna.'

'Please.'

'Okay.'

My thoughts are still accelerating, but I'm past the point of wanting to sleep. I drive back down to Bristol and Anna is waiting outside the house. Her friends are there as I load her bag into the car and we head off to Wales. Anna is conducting the tour, looking at a map and a tourist guidebook, telling me which B-roads to take. I don't have a clue where we're going. I don't care. I just keep talking, telling her stories from my childhood. When we stop at landmarks, Anna reads the history and says how 'Gothic' everything looks. I'm not the slightest bit interested.

That night we book into a Bed & Breakfast in south Wales. We stay at a pub until closing time, but I can't get drunk. I nearly throw up when I try to eat a piece of chicken, so I push it around my plate and order more alcohol.

Anna talks about her father and I tell her about pressures and temperatures and the strange pieces of space debris that have been found in orbit. My mind is unbelievably sharp and my senses so acute that I'm enjoying this experience. It's as if my subconscious has cracked open and all this information that has been stored over a lifetime is spilling out and I can access it all instantly – names, dates, places, facts, figures, you name it.

That night, as Anna sleeps, I lie awake, revelling in my heightened perceptions. The next day is exactly the same, and I spend another night staring at the ceiling being bombarded by past experiences and new sensations. I'm trying to break down my life into its many parts. Who am I? Where did I come from? I don't know a lot about my family history. When I get back to Hereford, I'll phone Mum and ask her.

What about the people I've met and the friends I've made? Where do they fit into my life? What about you, Anna? It hasn't been a very healthy relationship. Look what it's done to you.

I'm starting to recognise the signs now – things that Anna has said to me in the past and the games that she plays to manipulate my emotions.

We're sitting in a café in Bristol, having just arrived back from Wales, when a university student asks if I'll help her with a survey. I take the clipboard and start having fun with the answers, making the girl laugh.

As she walks off, Anna says, 'Can I see what he's written?'

'Yes, sure.'

It seems so harmless, yet there is something in Anna's voice that registers with me. Why does she want to know what I've written? What is she trying to discover about me?

Nothing escapes me. My mind has become a massive melting-pot of emotions and ideas. I'm back at home watching TV, and as soon as I change to a new programme I begin to pick up the signs. It might be a woman giving birth and I absorb every single detail as though it's flowing straight into my subconscious. Afterwards, I can recite them back almost in parrot fashion, but on top of this I've already drawn the parallels, made the connections and recognised the signs that are being transmitted to me.

The channel is important because it doesn't seem to happen with the Discovery Channel, which has documentaries about wildlife or space exploration. Maybe it has something to do with Sky TV. The satellite channels must be okay because I installed the dish myself after I bought it for £80 out of a magazine. I don't trust aerials and cables.

Everything I've done in life and everyone I have come in contact with is significant, be they good, bad, happy, funny, sexual, loving or hateful. Each has played a part in bringing me to this moment. I had to leave school at fourteen. I had to join the Parachute Regiment and the Red Devils. I had to marry Chris and have Jason and then divorce. I had to pass Selection for the SAS and then go on 'the circuit' and finally embark on the Skydive from Space.

The world is made up of two opposing forces, and I am just a pawn like everybody else. But unlike everybody else, I know that I'm a pawn. Yes, I'm sure that's the conclusion.

The Falklands, the flight across the Atlantic, Anna, the burnt-out car, Everest, not meeting Story Musgrave, the man who went into space with Karl Henize and delayed a second mission when Karl died. Story was due to fly on the next shuttle to fix the Hubble Telescope. Hubble? Who is Hubble? An astronomer. Why is that important? Stop thinking about it. Come back. You simply asked the question, have I reached the right conclusion? Is this about opposing forces?

Good and bad. If you take nothing from 'good', you get 'god' and that's 'go on dreaming'. Even Stephen Hawking says there must be a God, but each person's perception of who or what God is varies. Religions can fight about it, but I need to break things down. Go on dreaming. God isn't totally good and the devil isn't totally evil. Both allow things to happen. There is an equilibrium between them, but there can never be total balance or tranquillity.

The game, if you like, is chess. Black and white. White makes the first move. Jason plays chess. He's very good. When I taught him, I told him to be very aware that when you make a move you bear the consequences of that action, just as you do in life. You can lose a game by not moving in time. 'No action is an action', which is another one of Des's sayings.

And in chess it sometimes doesn't matter how important a piece is. Jason once sacrificed his queen and check-mated me within three moves with his knight. Chess, grandmaster, grandfather passing things down. It's just a game, they play it in space to occupy their time.

Sotheby's had an auction in New York selling off Soviet space memorabilia. Loel Guinness wanted to buy a magnetised chess-set that had been used on the Mir space station. It was to be a gift for me but the bidding went too high.

Black and white. Some people are colour-blind. How do you explain to a blind man what red is? My shirt is blue but if I switch off the light there is just blackness. You have to understand the spectrum of colour. Rainbows. There was a rainbow at Ampuria Brava after Chris Meacock died.

—No, no, don't think about rainbows. Stick with black and white.

White is light, the forming of a star, creation, the Big Bang, the black hole; everything is black and white. White is like a sperm drop, white is snow.

—What about black?

Black is oil. Think of the *Torrey Canyon* off Cornwall and the dying wildlife. Oil, Algeria, the Gulf; fighting between Arabs and Jews and the Americans with their money.

—Just shut up! Just shut up!

Oil, what is oil? It's millions of dead beetles crushed over billions of years. What is it for? It's a coolant and a lubricant. The Earth spins at a certain speed, rotating through space like a gyroscope. Precession and rigidity are the two principles of gyroscopic action, so you need the mass on any given side to remain constant, otherwise it goes off balance. But the oil is being sucked out of the ground. It's heavy shit, right near the centre of the mass. What's happening to the weight distribution?

—Forget about oil. Think about something else.

It isn't good or evil. Children are baptised and dabbed with oil. Yes, but some Catholic priests sexually abuse children and destroy their lives for ever. I've seen the destruction; images of burning rigs in the Gulf. Burning rigs and burning men. Men who disappear. Americans and their oil. The Beverly Hillbillies. Hillbilly? Where do you come into it? What were you there for? You were a fucking good agent. No, you weren't, you were my best friend.

I lie down on my bed and tell myself, I just want to go to sleep. It's not that I'm tired, I just want to stop thinking. It might be fascinating, but I need a break. Slow it down. There's too much information coming in.

Has it been four or five days since I last slept? I can't remember. In the kitchen, I make myself a cup of tea and notice the collage of Red Devils photographs on the wall. I put them there. Why did I do that? Because I went to Sharky's house one day and he had lots of photographs on the walls. It seemed like a good idea.

Where do we stand, Sharky? Which side are you on? I know you're harmless, but we're all being used.

I think of other characters in my life. Steve Chandler – the resident comedian in 2 Para who messed up rehearsals for the Queen's visit – where did you fit in? You made me laugh. I remember being shocked when you died, choking on your own vomit in Berlin after a heavy drinking session. You sat bolt upright and said, 'Christ, what a night,' and then flopped back again. End of story.

And what about Ken Yeoman, my old sergeant-major in the Red Freds? You made me go straight back up and perform a CRW stack after I nearly bored a big hole in the ground doing a diamond formation for the first time. I thought Canopy Relative Work was a waste of time, but you made me persist. It might have been the right decision, Ken, but a year later you were crippled doing a CRW stack and will spend the rest of your days in a wheelchair.

Where are the other Red Freds now? Lurch is messing around as a private investigator and doing odd security jobs; Jim Coffey is battling a serious illness; and when I last heard of the FISP he was a bouncer at a club in Glasgow. Dixie ran a parachute centre in Cyprus for a while and John Street is a long-distance truck driver. You all played a part, but which side were you on?

I grab my coat and walk outside to the car. There's something I've forgotten to do. I do it every New Year, but this time I was in Chamonix, trying to find Harry and grieving over Chris Meacock's death. It's cold and the engine protests as I pump the accelerator. I'm in no mood to nurse machines. Parking beside a pub opposite St Martin's Church, I wander inside and order two drinks – a whisky and a White Russian. Watching the barman fill the glasses, I don't even look around to see who else is in the bar. Instead, I walk outside and into the cemetery, carrying the drinks. I stop at Hillbilly's headstone and raise the glass.

'Cheers, mate, this one is for you,' I say, pouring the White Russian on to the earth.

I miss Hillbilly. He could bring out the best and worst in me, but it was always a laugh. I don't blame him for my divorce – that was nobody's fault – but I wish he was here now because I need someone to help me make sense of what's happening.

I wander over to Al Slater's grave and offer up the whisky. 'I don't want you flapping about being forgotten, Mr Grumpy. No one is going to forget you.'

Pinching some flowers from a nearby plot, I arrange them as best I can. 'I can't tell you how many times I've wondered whether I could have done more to save you, Al. If I'd confronted the guy who jumped the gate, would that have made a difference? Would you still be alive?'

As I'm about to leave, I pause at the grave of Vince Phillips. He died in the Gulf on the *Bravo Two Zero* mission. Vince was a fine soldier and a selfless human being. I'd never have passed Selection without him. I might have even perished on the Pen y Fan if he hadn't stopped to help me.

Why did I ever leave the Parachute Regiment? Why did I join the SAS? Why did I pass when I knew I was going to fail? Fit guys, better soldiers than me, twisted their ankles and had to jack it in. I ran through the same grass and didn't twist my ankle. Was that fate or was it luck?

I have so many questions and I don't have the facts to answer them. I need to talk to people like Duke Allen, my old mate from the Recruiting Team. We were born within hours of each other and we can wear each other's clothes. I should have been in the Falklands with you, Duke. You were there in the thick of things with 2 Para, and you were also at Warrenpoint, when the IRA killed eighteen of our comrades.

All of my senses are tuned precisely and I'm totally aware of my environment. In the jungle phase of Selection, towards the end, I began to feel like this. The stench of my body disappeared and the sores and rashes didn't send the same signals of discomfort to the brain. I became almost like an animal that prowled the rainforest.

Masses of information is coming in and I'm trying to make sense of it. Amidst it all I know there's a message for me; for some reason I've been chosen, but I don't know why or what my mission is supposed to be. It's like listening to Morse Code being sent on a bad signal and coming in too fast. Although I can read it, I am only getting the occasional word, never the whole sentence. One of the easiest traps to fall into when learning Morse Code is to become distracted by the message and forget to listen to the dots and dashes. I have to concentrate harder and fill the gaps.

When Jackie arrives in the morning, I'm writing on the table. I don't bother trying to wipe off the words.

'Can't you find any paper?' she laughs. 'There's plenty in the office.'

'I want to show you something,' I say.

She sits down and I start explaining about the 'boots' and our emotions. 'Look at the word "God" – it means "go on dreaming". Words are important – my dad taught me that – but a lot of them have hidden meanings. It's the same with people, some of them aren't what they seem.'

'Like who?'

'Like Anna.'

Jackie shakes her head, trying hard to understand.

'Haven't you ever wondered how she survived the car accident? Three cars burst into flames and she manages to crawl out of the wreckage without a mark on her. Think about it. That's the problem, Jackie. You're probably only a two- or three-move chess-player; that's how many moves you can think ahead, but I'm a twelve-move player. I can think twelve moves in advance and that's why I know what's going on.'

'What *is* going on?'

'Go on dreaming.'

Harry phones a few hours later from Chamonix. I know that Jackie has called him, even though I told her not to tell anyone because they wouldn't understand.

'Listen, mate, I hear you're working too hard and not eating,' he says.

'I'm fine. Right as rain.' I give nothing away.

Harry seems satisfied, but then Jackie calls another mate from the Regiment, Andy D., who comes over to the house. I clear off the table and begin trying to explain my device to him.

'Right, how many emotions have you got, Andy?'

'Shit, I don't know.'

'Just start naming a few.'

I write headings across the top of the table and explain how the system works. 'I haven't finished it yet and most of it is in my mind, but it's a fascinating concept.'

Andy D. turns to Jackie in disbelief. 'He's having me on, isn't he?'

'No, he's serious. Just listen to him.'

I'm thinking out loud, trying to get feedback. 'Everything has a significance; everything I do, or see, or you tell me. Even the words in the newspaper.'

Andy suggests we go for a drink. I think he wants to get me away from the house and the table. We head to a pub, and standing at the bar is Minky, my old DS from Selection, and he's talking to someone else I haven't seen in years. Looking around, I suddenly realise there are dozens of people I know. Just when I've been pondering questions about my life and experiences, it's as if an entire cast of the leading characters has come together.

My mind is accelerating away again, and before I reach the bar I know exactly who is around me and how they fit into my life. Meanwhile, I'm carrying on a conversation with Andy and answering his questions normally.

'Listen, Tom, you look bloody awful and you need a break.'

'I'm fine, really.'

'No, you're not. I tell you what you should do. Why don't you go and see Harry for a few days. Take Anna with you. You can do some skiing and unwind.'

'I've got too much to do with the project.'

'Forget about it for a while. You're going to get sick unless you look after yourself. Jackie is worried, and so is Harry.'

I can't understand why everyone is so concerned. I feel okay; my mind has never been so sharp. Maybe this is like those oxygen deprivation tests where you don't even realise that it's getting darker and your peripheral vision is worsening.

The flight leaves from Heathrow at 8 p.m. I didn't sleep again last night, but it doesn't bother me at all because I don't want to miss any of this adventure. I'm getting closer to the truth. There's a tape running inside my head and each time it plays, I'm picking up a bit more of the message. Unfortunately, every time I try to look at all the information, my attention is drawn to bits and pieces.

Stop digressing. Focus.

On the drive to the airport, I'm waffling to Anna, still going through events in my life and talking about what emotions they produced. We get to a roundabout near Gloucester at about 5 p.m. My brother Andy lives about a mile away and I want to see him. There's something I need to know.

'But we don't have time,' says Anna.

'We'll just pop in for a minute.'

I introduce Anna and the kettle is filled for a cup of tea. Andy says I look like shit. We're in a hurry and Anna keeps glancing at the clock, but

I don't come out and ask him straight away. I wait until the tea is poured and then deliberately manipulate the conversation by inventing a story about an article I'd read in the newspaper about 12,000 grouse having been bagged on one of the big estates in Scotland.

'Andy, do you remember as kids we used to go shooting?'

'Yeah, with our air guns. We shot sparrows and put their heads in a box.'

'You remember that, too. I still feel bad about that. Kids can be nasty creatures.'

It was a macabre, stupid thing to do and I've always felt guilty about it. That's why I wanted Andy to confirm my recollection. Did it really happen? Has it been troubling him, too? It's another piece of my past that I'm squaring away.

Unfortunately, we miss the flight to France by only a few minutes and Anna is furious. I tell her not to worry, we'll book into a hotel at the airport and catch a flight in the morning. Anna is looking for a postcard at the newsagents and she picks up an image of Big Ben. Suddenly I remember having read somewhere that Big Ben had stopped for the first time in decades. What is the significance of that? I stare at the postcard.

—It's time, Tom, it's time.

I have to find out when Big Ben stopped. What was I doing at that moment?

—Tom, it's not important.

TIME . . . EMIT . . . MITE.

—Forget about it. Find a hotel.

We check in and follow our bags to the room. Immediately, I order a bottle of wine from room service. It's ten o'clock and Anna wants to sleep. She's still angry about the flight and says that I've been 'talking a load of garbage' all day.

'What is wrong with you? I've never seen you like this.'

'I'm sorry, I'm just preoccupied.'

I'm sure she's pretending to be asleep when I phone Jason. He tells me about a careers advice project at school, where he had to fill in a questionnaire about his likes, dislikes and ambitions and they put his answers into a computer.

'Guess what mine came out as?' He laughs.

'What?'

'A fish farmer.'

Instantly, I think fish farmer . . . fisherman . . . fisher of men . . . Jesus Christ was called 'the fisher of men' . . . Jason's initials are J.C. – Jason Charles.

—Forget about it, Tom. It's got nothing to do with religion.

We talk about school and exams for a while and then Jason says he has to study.

Anna is listening to the phone call; I'm sure of it. She's part of this, but what is she trying to do?

'Are you still angry at me?' I ask, as I put down the phone.

'I'm livid.'

There's an interesting word. Turn 'livid' around and it sounds like 'devil'. Take away the 'd' and you have 'evil'. Turn it again and it becomes 'live'. Everything has to live. What are you trying to tell me? Give me some more signs. I know I'm getting closer.

At the airport the next morning, 1 February 1994, Anna leaves me minding the trolley as she goes to buy a magazine. Someone asks me for a light and I turn around. The next thing I remember is Anna asking, 'What are you doing, Tom?' I look up and discover that I've wandered away and left the bags unattended.

'I think you're still half asleep,' she jokes.

Sleep? I don't trust you enough to sleep.

We board the plane and I'm sitting by the window. Anna is by the aisle. Most people look downwards when they gaze out of a plane, but I like to look up. At 35,000 feet, the sky above is starting to become inkier. I remember something the astronomer Sir Fred Hoyle once said: 'Space isn't remote at all. It's only an hour's drive away if your car could go straight up.'

I'm not bothered about the device any more; the general design is there and I can make it work given a little more time. No, I'm looking for a conclusion. If there are two opposing forces, good and evil, what do they want with me?

This has something to do with time and space. I've done a lot of research on densities and pressure for the project. I know that light travels at 186,000 miles per second, the same as radio waves. I've read

Stephen Hawking's *A Brief History of Time* and I know his theory on the Big Bang. Where does time begin in the Universe? Is there a beginning and an end? I want to read more, maybe then I'll know the answer.

High pressure moves to low pressure. Why did I learn about that?

—Because you needed to know the principles of flight to be a pilot.

Why is that important?

—Wait for the conclusion.

When do I know that I've reached the right conclusion?

—You'll know.

Is it simply another point in time? An hour from now, will the conclusion be different?

—Don't worry, you'll know.

When Anna had the car accident two policemen brought her home and broke a window to let her into my house. She contaminated my safe haven. She orchestrated everything. When the police phoned me to explain the situation, I recognised one of them as being ex-army. Did we ever soldier together? I wonder. Did he touch my life in some way? No, he was one of her minions. He was working for her. How did you manage to escape from that car, Anna? How did you survive the flames?

I open a magazine and straight away my eyes fall on a full-page advertisement for a Breitling watch. It's exactly the same as the watch I'm wearing. Anna gave it to me for my birthday.

She passes across her magazine. 'This is interesting, Tom.'

I don't look at the first paragraph, but I pick up on the phrase 'trilogy of time'.

'Do you know anything about that?' she asks.

And then it dawns on me. After seven days without sleep, I have my conclusion. Anna is my natural enemy. Fundamentally, I am a good person and she is evil. My mind flashes back through memories of our time together. Not the happy times, but the unhappy ones.

Am I being unfair to her? Beautiful, voluptuous Anna with her dark eyes and delicate features. I think of everything she told me about herself. Her father was in the navy. He doted on her. She did some wild things in her adolescence and has seen a lot of people screwed up by drugs or alcohol.

But is she a good person?

—She likes people to think she is.

So what is she really?

—One of them – an enemy operative.

I'm a soldier and the aim of any soldier is to kill the enemy. I look across at Anna and she brushes hair away from her eyes and smiles. A great weight has been lifted from me and the relief is enormous. I have my conclusion: Anna is evil and she has to die.

16

I'm watching every move that Anna makes – the way she sips her drink; the way she licks her fingertip before she turns the pages of her magazine; the way she crosses her legs and leans then against mine.

When she speaks to me, I keep my answers light, lulling her into a false sense of security.

'I'm looking forward to seeing Harry and Cath,' I say.

'Uh-huh.'

'I missed seeing them on New Year's Eve. Cath is a real darling.'

Anna doesn't lift her eyes from the page. 'I hope they have some fresh snow.'

I lean my seat back and watch her. For the first time in a week I can relax because I know what I have to do. This is my destiny. My path has been laid out for me and I will know the moment. Why have I been chosen?

—Because you passed a very difficult Selection.

What is the significance of Chamonix?

—I don't know. Maybe it's important that Anna dies in the Alps.

So how will I kill her?

Maybe I could get one of those big chair-lifts up the mountain and sling her off the top. Mountains, Mont Blanc, Switzerland, Italy, France, the border; perhaps I'm supposed to kill her where all the countries meet, in the no-man's-land. It's not as if Anna has any strong claim to a culture or national heritage.

If the police find a body on the border of three countries, who investigates the death? What court would try me? I need a cover story.

I'm watching Anna fold the magazine and straighten the pages. She dabs the corners of her mouth with her little finger and says, 'You've been talking non-stop and now you've gone all quiet.'

Yeah, fucking good one, Tom, you've just spent days telling the enemy your entire life story. No, no, it doesn't matter, she knows it already.

If the enemy has all the answers what do they want from me?

I don't know yet.

Hotel Le Touring is like a rabbit warren of small rooms and narrow corridors. Exposed wooden beams brace the ceiling and the doors have old-fashioned latches. I have to duck my head as I step down into the room, which has a double bed, a wooden wardrobe and a small sink. There's just enough space to walk around the bed.

After dropping off our bags, we decide to take the hire car and drive out to Harry's place. Anna says that I look terrible, but she wants me to see Harry because maybe I'll listen to him. She's not the most attentive or nurturing of women. That probably comes from living in Washington, where you learn to mind your own business and watch your back.

Anna offers to drive.

'But you don't know the way,' I say.

'Yes, I do. I've been there before.'

Has she? My mind is racing again, flicking through index cards of past events, trying to establish if Anna has ever been to Harry's house. Oh, that's right, I remember now. We flew from Washington to Europe to do some training jumps.

We drive in silence. The narrow mountain road is full of twists and turns and there are mounds of old snow on either side thrown up by the snow-plough. Pine trees cling to the slopes and sometimes, as we turn a corner, I catch a glimpse over the edge.

Something reaches into my chest and squeezes my heart. She's going to drive us off the road – I'm sure of it. We'll plunge down the mountainside and I'll perish in the flames. Anna won't die – she can survive a burning car without a scratch. My hand grips the door handle; the knuckles are white.

We're on a right-hand bend and I spy a police van that has pulled over a car. Three or four gendarmes are milling around, questioning the driver. I have to get to them. They'll keep me safe.

'Stop the car! Stop the car!'

'What's the matter?'

'I've got to go.'

'Can't you wait?'

'Anna, stop the car!'

I pull on the handbrake and throw the door open while the car is still moving. Then I'm out and running back towards the police. Confronting the nearest one face to face, I push him squarely in the chest, looking at him with mad eyes. He's confused. I'm swearing at him in English, trying to get myself arrested.

I hear Anna's voice. 'It's all right. It's all right. He's with me.'

There's a scuffle and the gendarmes are starting to rough me up.

Anna is screaming, 'Leave him alone! Leave him alone! He's my husband.'

They're putting me in handcuffs and the van door slides open. I'm safe.

Anna is frantic. 'Where are you taking him?'

'*Poste de police.*'

'I want to come as well.'

Instantly, I say, 'No, no, no, *non la femme*. No come.'

The door slides shut and I can still hear Anna arguing with them. The engine has started and we're moving. I don't try to look out the window. I close my eyes and concentrate on getting my heart to stop racing. Stay calm. Relax. I'm safe.

At the police station, I'm put in the waiting room still handcuffed, getting dark looks from the gendarme I pushed.

'What is your name?' asks a senior officer.

'Tom Read.'

'You are English?'

'Yes.'

'Have you any identification?'

I twist on the chair and reach with two hands for my back pocket. Instinctively, I know my wallet is not going to be there. I left it in the car.

'Where are you staying in Chamonix?'

'A hotel, ah . . . What's it called? It has a big wooden door . . .'

He's losing patience with me. 'Why did you push my officer?'

'I'm sorry. I had a fight with a woman. A big fight. You know how it is? She made me angry and I just wanted to get away from her. I didn't mean to push anyone. I just wanted to make him understand me.'

The conversation is going round in circles because I have no answers for them. Finally, they leave me alone for fifteen minutes while they decide what to do. Then the handcuffs are unlocked and I'm told to go. There are no charges. I thank them and walk outside. I don't know where I'm going; I have no money and I don't remember the name of the hotel. As I pass a shop-front, I catch a glimpse of a reflection in the window. It's an old man who's thin, gaunt and dishevelled. His clothes are hanging off him and his eyes have sunken deep into his skull. Surely that can't be me!

There's a restaurant next door and I ask a waitress if she knows Harry.

'*Oui.*'

'*Quel est le numéro* . . . his phone number?'

'*Un instant.*'

She goes to look, but I can't wait; I have to keep moving. If I can just find the clock tower, then I'll find the hotel. I remember seeing the tower when we arrived. I turn left and right through the narrow streets. People are staring at me.

I wave down a taxi and ask the driver to take me to the clock tower. 'No money. Only this watch. Take it,' I say. He shakes his head and drives away, swearing at me in French.

Another police van is parked on the corner. I tap on the driver's window.

'Can you help me? I'm lost.'

'Where is your hotel?'

'I don't know.' I describe it to the gendarme. 'My wallet is lost. I had too much to drink.' I try to sound embarrassed, but I must look manic because he slides open the van door and takes me back to the same police station that released me. As I walk through the front door, I see Anna at the counter. She's holding my wallet.

Harry and Cath take us back to the hotel. Anna has been telling them how irrational I've been. I laugh it off when Harry asks, and pretend it's all a joke on Anna. I think I'm hiding it quite well, but I'm careful not to make eye contact with anyone, because I'm sure they'll recognise that I'm manic. I can see it in my own eyes when I look in the bathroom mirror.

The others are sitting at a table in the bar, but I've been chatting to the barman because that way I can keep my distance from Anna and watch Harry and Cath's reaction to her. She doesn't seem interested in talking to me any more, she prefers telling them about how horrible I've been. Keep watching the enemy. The confrontation is coming. I'll know the moment.

That night – my eighth without sleep – I lie next to Anna, recalling everything we have ever said to each other or done together. She's been reading a book – *The Pelican Brief* by John Grisham. There are millions of books, why has she chosen this one?

I lean over, careful not to wake her, and read the back cover.

Two Supreme Court Justices are dead. Their murders are connected only in one mind . . . Brilliant, beautiful and ambitious, New Orleans legal student Darby Shaw little realises that her speculative brief will penetrate the highest levels of power in Washington and cause shockwaves there. Shockwaves that will see her boyfriend atomised in a bomb blast, that will send hired killers chasing after her . . .

I put the book down, careful to leave it exactly as I found it. I don't want Anna realising that I've sussed her. She could be Darby Shaw. She's a student from Washington. She's had high-flying clients who are probably from the judiciary or government. Look at how much she knows and how she manipulates people.

This is all part of a conspiracy that is greater than any of us can imagine. Right from the beginning, when I first met Anna in Washington, she's been taking me somewhere. I have to admire how relaxed and cool she's been; she's given very little away. But what does she want from me? I've told her everything about my life – she's even been to the house where I grew up. Is it something to do with the Skydive from Space? Does she want to know about 'the device'? Have I accidentally stumbled upon some secret of the Universe?

It doesn't matter. Go on dreaming.

That's it! It's about children – saving the planet for the children. Jason! It's about Jason! Fucking hell, she wants to kill Jason.

My mind flashes back to the image of them dancing on the boat in Washington; Anna has her arms around Jason's neck. Then I think about the flight to Malta when we lost the electrics, and I can picture them playing in the water in Corsica.

If Jason is so important to you, Anna, how did you treat him? You didn't strike me as being particularly protective or nurturing. You're not the maternal type, are you? But why kill him? What has he done to you?

Jason Charles – the initials J.C. I know nothing about Jesus Christ. I'm not a religious person. I neither believe nor disbelieve. I haven't read the Bible. Go on dreaming.

My father always told me I was a dead ringer for my grandfather, who I never met. He died of the effects of gas in the First World War, at the age of thirty-three. 'The same age as Jesus Christ,' Dad would say. He'd also tell me stories about the Middle East, because he was there during the war. He'd visited the Sea of Galilee, and was convinced that Jesus didn't 'walk on the water' as the Bible says, but swam. Dad reckons that very few people could swim in those days, particularly in the desert countries, so when Jesus swam to a boat in the Sea of Galilee to address the crowds on the shore, the people were stunned. Somehow, the difference between 'walking on water' and 'swimming in water' became lost in the translation of the gospels.

Jason Charles – 'J.C.' – who is his mother? Christine . . . Christ . . . Christmas. Christine was born on Christmas Day. Her middle name is Mary. She told me she was pregnant in Berlin. But I slept with her before we married; she wasn't a virgin. Oh, shut up, Tom, this is all bollocks!

Go on dreaming.

None of it matters, I have my conclusion. Anna has to die because she is the epitome of evil. That's why I've been brought to this place, at this time. The ultimate confrontation is coming.

It's starting to get light outside and Anna is beginning to stir. Be careful. She can control everyone's mind, except mine. I am protected by a force that is greater, or at least equal to hers, but I must be wary about what I say and I must not, under any circumstances, take anything from her.

'Words are the tools of thought,' my father used to tell me. 'Always pay attention to the content of the message and, more importantly, how you deliver it.'

As Anna wakes, I hang on every syllable and study the way she delivers it. She can only hurt me if I lie, and once I lie she'll know that I'm against her.

'How are you feeling?' she asks.

'Much better.' (I feel very calm.)

'Did you sleep?'

'Yes, I've slept.' (She didn't ask which night.) 'I must have nodded off at about three o'clock. You nudged me and I was awake for half an hour but I got back to sleep again.'

She's brushing her hair. 'Are you going to eat something today?'

'I'll try to get something down, darling, but you know what it's like when you haven't eaten for days, the old tummy shrinks right up. A piece of toast would probably fill me up.' I'm smiling and trying to be light-hearted and disarming. This battle is mental as well as physical. Only natural forces can kill me, and Anna is unnatural. Good is superior to evil, but only by a fraction. There can never be total balance. White starts on chess, which gives it a slight advantage because black is always reacting to white's last move.

Anna picks up a tangerine and I know that she's going to offer it to me. My thoughts are racing. I read somewhere, or someone told me, that tangerines make you want to go to the toilet. Suddenly, I have this image in my mind of my insides dissolving and rotting, collapsing out of my arse.

'Eat this tangerine,' Anna says. My heart is pounding. She's watching my reactions in the mirror. I pick up the fruit and prepare to break the skin with my thumb.

'Oh, Anna, I can't.' I toss the fruit towards her and her hand shoots up and plucks it out of the air. Yes, she's sharp today. This might be the moment.

The peel comes away easily in her fingers and she splits the fruit into segments, eating several pieces. She hands me the remainder. 'Your turn now.'

I'm shaking. 'Oh, Anna, I think if I eat anything I'll throw up. Maybe I'll get some toast downstairs.'

'No, come on, eat it, it'll do you good.'

'All right, here goes. Do I have to eat all of it?'

'Yes, all of it.'

I relax and put a segment in my mouth. I'm safe because I can't eat it *all*. Anna has already had a few pieces. It may be a play on words, but it's still the truth.

Harry and Cath arrive to go skiing while I'm still getting dressed. The girls go downstairs for breakfast and Harry waits for me in the room. 'How are you feeling?' he asks.

'I'm very frightened.'

'Why?'

'I can't explain, Harry, but there's a lot going on and you have to trust me, mate. Can you do that?'

'Yeah, of course.'

'Do me a favour, Harry, I have to go to the toilet. Will you stand by the door and watch me?'

'What?'

'I can't explain, Harry, but please.' I'm still not totally convinced that my insides won't come flooding out.

'Give me a break, Tom. I don't want to watch you go to the loo.'

'Harry, just stand there. You don't have to bloody argue.'

'What's this all about?'

'It's about Anna.'

'Are you two still fighting?'

'Listen, she's not what she seems. Just be careful. Don't be alone with her.'

How can I explain it to him? Anna and I are the only two people on the planet who know what's going on. But she's far more advanced than me because she ignores all the signs. Either that, or she's controlling them.

Sitting in a café, watching the others eat, I'm acutely aware of everything around me – the conversations, people, movement and background noise. At the same time I'm watching Anna and keeping up a conversation with Harry, trying to act normally. But there are so many signs it's becoming embarrassing. Someone puts a song on the jukebox. Cliff Richard is singing about his 'devil woman'.

Anna is sitting opposite, looking at me, thinking to herself, 'Is he picking up on all this? Is he there yet?'

I will take nothing from her, not even a light for my cigarette. Two French guys are sitting at the bar and I ask them if I can have a light. One of them hands me a book of matches. My hands are shaking as I strike a match against the black strip and suddenly the entire book goes up in flames. I toss it into the ashtray and watch it burn. This is Anna's doing; she has agents everywhere.

Is there anyone helping me? I wonder silently. Anna has a smirk on her face.

There must be, just keep going. She doesn't want you dead, you have something she needs.

As we drive up to the ski area in Harry's car, Anna says disgustedly, 'This is some holiday.' She thinks I'm on drugs, but I've never taken them. Still playing games, aren't you, Anna? Well, it won't work. I know what you're doing.

At the ski-hire shop they're all joking about the size of my feet. I laugh but never take my eyes off her. The confrontation is approaching, I can sense it now. I have to warn Harry and Cath.

Soon we're outside on the lower slopes at the beginning of a T-bar lift. There's a small café with a veranda. Harry and I are sitting on a low stone wall with our skis propped up nearby. Anna and Cath have put their skis on and are heading up the mountain. I'm trying not to lose sight of them.

'Look, Harry, something is happening that I don't fully understand, but it's very big – beyond imagination. You have to trust me, please. I can't explain the details.'

'Yeah, sure, Tom. I told you I trust you. What's wrong?'

'I'm terrified.'

'Why?'

'We've been through a lot together, haven't we? I love you and Cath and I don't want to see anything happen to you. I need you to believe me and not Anna.'

'Why, what's happened?'

'Anna isn't what she makes out to be. Don't underestimate her. She's extremely powerful. She can read your thoughts and influence what you do.'

'Don't be silly, Tom.'

'It's true. Believe me!'

'Okay, okay.'

Glancing down the slope, I see the mist starting to roll up the mountain towards us. It's as though it wants to engulf us in a cold, wet embrace. This is Anna's doing. Where is she? I can't see her. I peer across the upper slopes, trying to find her again. Fear is squeezing at my heart, holding the organ in its fist and strangling the life from it. I can't lose sight of her; Anna knows that I know; she could be anywhere.

'Harry, please don't go skiing. Stay down here.'

'But I've got the lift passes.'

'I don't want you to go up there. Just stay here with me. I want you to be close by.'

'Okay, Tom. Sure. Calm down.'

'If things start happening, don't be scared.'

'Okay.'

While I scour the slopes for Anna, Harry talks to a couple of local girls he knows.

'It's all right, Tom. I've given the passes away,' he says afterwards.

'Who to?'

'Those girls. I know them. They're going up.'

But Anna is up there. I panic. 'No, Harry, stop them! Get the passes back, don't let them go.'

'Why not?'

'Harry, please, just trust me.'

'Okay, Tom, okay.' Looking very embarrassed, he gets the passes back. He's pissed off with me but I don't care. He just has to believe me.

'I'll be back in a few minutes,' I tell him.

'Look, Tom, what is going on? I want you to tell me what's bothering you.'

'I know, but I have to go to the toilet. Just keep an eye out for Anna. Can you see her?'

'No.'

'Well, I'm telling you that when I come back she's going to be here. Be very careful what you say to her.'

I don't want to leave him, but I'm going to look like a raving madman if I piss my pants. I've done things like that on the flight across the Atlantic and in the Regiment, but not here, not now.

The well-packed snow descends slightly and I turn left around the building. I can still see Harry, until I turn left again. There's the toilet doorway and a little concrete ramp. I rush inside, already cursing and fumbling with the catches and buckles on my ski pants. Afterwards I wrestle the pants back on and clomp outside in my heavy ski-boots. Sure enough, Anna is sitting on the wall next to Harry.

'Are you all right?' I ask him as I struggle up the slope.

'Yeah, fine, mate.'

Anna moves away from us, flashing me a poisonous look.

'What did she say?'

Harry shrugs. 'She wants to know what the fuck is the matter with you.'

'So do I,' says Cath, joining us. 'What are you doing to Anna? She's really upset.'

I look from one to the other. 'Listen, Cath, you don't know me very well. Harry and I go a long way back and he understands. Just go along with everything Harry says and does.'

She looks at him and Harry nods purposefully. Then he takes her further down the slope, perhaps to explain. Anna and I are alone together. I'm not frightened. She can't hurt me.

'Well, it's come to this then, Anna. It's going to be one of us. I don't really care about me, but what's going to happen to Jason?'

Her dark eyes are blazing and her jaw is clenched tightly. I can see the tiny veins in her neck.

'What are you going to do to Jason?' I ask again.

She shrugs. 'I don't know. Maybe nothing.'

I'm right – Jason is in danger! I can't let her out of my sight or she'll be back to England to deal with him.

Anna spins on her heels and walks away, storming off to sit alone on the balcony of the café, watching me and seething. Harry and Cath suggest that we all leave.

'Good idea, Harry. We'll take Anna back to your place.'

I've decided how she's going to die. Her period is due and once she starts menstruating it won't stop; she'll bleed to death. Natural forces will do the job for me. I just need to get her back to Harry and Cath's house and tie her down to the bed until her period starts.

Anna is walking ahead of me, pretending to be frightened. She doesn't know that she's going to die. This is the day of reckoning; the right time and the right place.

'Come on. Let's get back to your place,' I say to Harry.

'Okay. It won't be long.' He's loading the skis on to the car roof-rack.

Anna sits in the front seat beside him and I'm in the back seat with Cath. She holds my hand. My eyes are boring into the back of Anna's head. Be nice to her, let nature take its course, I think. Yet in the quiet of the car, I know that Anna is using mental telepathy on Harry and Cath. I have to interrupt her thought processes.

'Fuck off, you evil bitch, you can't hurt them! You're going to bleed and there's nothing you can do about it—'

'For fuck's sake, Tom,' says Harry. 'Cut it out!'

'You're going to die, Anna, it's that simple. I know what you're up to; I know who you are. You're evil.' I'm on the edge of the seat, spitting the words at the back of Anna's head. Cath is trying to stop me. 'No, Cath, don't let her into your mind.'

Harry no longer tells me to shut up. He just shakes his head and keeps driving until we pull up outside a large grey building.

'Why are we stopping?'

'Cath has to drop off some skis.'

'No! Cath, we've got to stay together.'

'I'll only be a few minutes.'

'No, no, we have to stay together.'

'Okay, we'll all go in,' says Harry.

Anna is in front of me as we walk through the doors into a small reception area. There's a couch in the middle of the room and a counter. I see the nurse's uniform.

'Harry, Harry, what have you done?' I turn to him, pleading.

'Look, Cath knows a nurse who works here. She's just going to get someone to have a look at you.'

'No, you don't understand. I must not be separated from Anna. I *must not* . . .'

'Listen, Tom, Anna is not evil.'

'She's got to you! She's got to you!'

Cath is speaking French to someone. Anna decides to go to the ladies' toilet. Suddenly, I realise that she's gone and I start yelling. 'Harry, trust me, she can't be out of my sight!'

'Don't worry. She'll be back in a minute.'

'No, I want to see her *now*.' All the while I'm edging closer to the rest room. I pull away from Harry and launch a kick at the door, trying to bust it open. 'Anna! Anna!'

She comes out in tears and cowers away from me. I edge back across the corridor.

'That's enough, Tom. Just calm down.' Harry's words are soothing, but I don't take my eyes off Anna. 'We're going to get someone to take a look at you. It won't take long. Just talk to the doctor. I'll wait here for you. Cath will go home and get you some clothes.'

'What about Anna?'

'Just trust me, mate. This has got way out of hand. Anna's upset. She'll go home with Cath.' He's close to tears now too.

'No, Harry. Please, you don't understand.'

Anna is in a corner, still wearing her ski-boots on the slick hospital floor. Harry is looking up and down the corridor, waiting for the doctor. I think I've bluffed him. I drift off into an adjoining room, desperately looking for some way out. If Anna leaves here, she's going to kill Jason. She's going to destroy everything that is precious to me; everyone I love.

I spy a pair of long sharp scissors lying beside an examination table. I slip them down the front of my trousers and pull my jacket together. Harry turns at the last moment.

'What have you got there?'

'Nothing.'

'Come on, Tom, what's underneath your jacket?'

'Nothing, I'm just holding my gut. I've got a cramp.'

Anna has followed Harry into the room. She's only about six feet away, standing at the corner of the bed. My fingers close around the scissors. I look up, straight into her evil eyes and then lunge.

In a flash of silver, the first blow glances off her head and plunges into her shoulder. I want to drive the blade through her eyes and kill her quickly. Harry is wrestling with me, grabbing at my arm as it comes down again and I stab her chest. I don't know where the third blow lands. People are screaming and running.

Did I kill her?

Harry is lying on top of me, pressing my face to the tiles. I hear Cath's voice and heavy feet pounding on the floors. Trolleys are clattering through the corridor.

Is she dead?

Harry whispers in my ear, 'Why, Tom, why?'

I didn't want to stab her. I wanted her to bleed to death when her period started. If only they'd taken us home instead of coming here.

'I ca . . . ca . . . can't breathe, Harry.' He doesn't hear me.

Anna's ski-boots have left two snaking red tracks on the white tiles where they dragged her away. I follow the blood slick until it grows faint and disappears at the door. Is it enough blood?

The sedative rushes through me and everything slips into soft focus. People float, voices overlap, colours wash out and my eyelids are so heavy. It's been eight days, please let me sleep.

BOOK THREE

17

There. It's done. I've been through the whole story, and now I'm exhausted. Not one soul has ever heard the full details before, and I'll never reveal them again.

God only knows if I'm any closer to discovering the cause of my problems, but at least I've confronted the consequences. I haven't tried to hide what happened or to make excuses. You won't catch me watering down the truth or shifting the blame. And if I've left anything out then it's not intentional – a lot of things spilled out when my mind cracked open.

Stress seems to be the favourite excuse for my breakdown. People find it easier to accept if they have an explanation – I know I would. I've been at home for almost a fortnight and I still haven't finished 'sterilising' the house.

Jackie is coming in every day and we've started addressing bits and pieces of the project, keeping in touch with people. Although we make only one or two telephone calls a day, I find it a struggle, so Jackie does most of the talking. I brief her beforehand and then she rings Slim McDonald, who's been working on the camera designs, and tells him that the operational side of the jump is on hold while we work on the funding and sponsorship.

Dave Hirst is the next call. 'Tell him I'm sorry I haven't phoned him before now. Say that I'll be in touch in a week or two.'

Jackie passes on the message.

I've seen very few of my friends since the breakdown. One or two have dropped round to see me, including Frank Collins, my old mate from Air Troop, who's now an army chaplain. Frank began to question a lot of things after Al Slater's death, and he found the answers in the Church. He left the Regiment and studied theology, becoming a Church of England minister. Now he has God for a new CO. Good luck to him.

I still miss the Regiment, particularly the camaraderie and the excitement that each day held. There is also something very easy and reassuring about waking each morning and having a uniform to put on and scoff ready in the cookhouse. The boring, mundane decisions of everyday life are taken for you, along with the very big decisions of tasking and deployment. In this way, a soldier can concentrate on making the split-second choices in training or in action that can keep him alive.

*

The ranking system in the SAS is different from the rest of the army. Within the Regiment I'd been a corporal, yet despite having completed all the qualifying courses like drill and duties and Junior Brecon, the rest of the army regarded me as a private soldier, or a 'tom', as they're called. Occasionally, this bothered me, but I knew that it partly came down to the choices I'd made, such as joining the Red Freds.

I have never been particularly comfortable with authority figures, especially officers. Little things have coloured my view. I remember in the Parachute Regiment, the battalion had to provide waiters for the Officers' Mess and Sergeants' Mess. Being a young crow, I finished up at the Army Catering Corps barracks, learning how to serve soup and lay tables.

I hated it! By then I had been to Ireland, patrolling streets that were home to snipers and terrorists, yet found myself waiting on tables and watching officers with upper-crust accents gallivanting around the Mess like rude, spoilt little brats. They would dance on table-tops, play 'chicken' with knives and say things like, 'Oh, I say, bring me some more potatoes – I want to throw them at Cyril.'

'Yes, sir, coming, sir.'

And these are the people I'm supposed to look up to?

My decision to leave the SAS had a lot to do with character clashes with certain superiors. I had just got back from over the water in early

1986 when I learned that a serious allegation had been made against me. An intelligence officer claimed that I had let an unauthorised civilian drop me at our base in Northern Ireland – a serious breach of security.

I had a week to prepare a written statement in my defence before facing the CO of the Regiment. The new boss didn't have an infantry background and had come from the RCT (Royal Corps of Transport). The allegation was ridiculous. The woman concerned had been cleared through proper channels and had previously attended a formal function at the social club at the base. She didn't know I was SAS because I'd given her the official cover story – she thought I was a signaller. On the night she dropped me off, we'd met at a police function and she'd offered to drive me back to base because it was pouring with rain. There had been no breach of security.

A week later, as I stood in the CO's office, he said to me, 'Okay, I've looked at this. Do you stand by your statement?'

'Yes, sir. That is exactly what happened.'

'Okay.' He put the statement to one side and looked up at me from behind his desk. 'But I'm more concerned about your attitude.'

This took me by surprise. 'I'm sorry, sir?'

Suddenly it dawned on me that this was the crux of why I'd been summoned to his office. A clash of personalities had occurred in Northern Ireland and someone had informed the CO. Air Troop was a nice happy family with Dunderhead in charge; we worked hard, played hard and had a good relationship with the police. Unfortunately, during the tour, I had argued several times about tactics with a new officer. Normally the SAS is like a Chinese Parliament where all opinions are welcome, but this officer, despite having very little experience across the water, would not listen to anyone other than himself.

I tried to explain the situation to the CO, but he didn't seem interested in my case and didn't go into specifics. He was an officer defending one of his own. Three times he sent me out of his office and told me to wait in a side-room. Meanwhile, senior members of B Squadron and the Regiment were summoned to discuss my future. I was flattered and touched by the support they gave me, but ultimately the CO decided my fate. He called me back into his office.

'I consider myself to run a team here,' he said, using his favourite football clichés, 'and frankly, you're not a team player. I see myself as the captain of this team – no, more as a manager – and when someone isn't playing for the team, I pull him off the field.'

As he spoke, I couldn't help thinking that a lot of people, like Al Slater, would be quite hurt by the SAS being compared to a football team.

'. . . therefore, I am returning you to your unit for twelve months.'

He was sending me back to the Parachute Regiment for a year. After that time I could reapply to join the SAS.

As I left the office, the adjutant took me to one side. 'What are you going to do, Tom?' he asked.

'I think I'll PVR [purchase voluntary redundancy].'

This surprised him. 'I wouldn't make that decision too hastily.'

'I think it's been made for me.'

Back at the accommodation block, I packed my few possessions, handed my kit into stores and paid the £200 to buy my way out of the army. Isn't it amazing how quickly your whole life can change?

I should have taken more time to consider things. I should have gone for a walk or sat by the Clock Tower, looking up at all the names of those who'd died in the Regiment. Maybe then I would have listened to a wiser counsel or not antagonised the situation.

The sad fact is that from the moment I drove out the gates of Stirling Lines, I regretted my decision. I didn't want to leave the SAS; it was my life and I loved it.

Ironically, among the letters I found as I sorted through my kit was one from the CO, which had been sent only a few weeks earlier on 6 March 1986:

Dear Tom,

As you know we have recently within the space of a week conducted two successful operations . . . My purpose in writing now is to acknowledge formally your contribution to these successes and to the currently encouraging situation . . . You have every right to be fully satisfied and indeed proud of the work you have done. Please accept my personal thanks and, on its behalf, the gratitude of the Regiment. Well done.

From the camp I drove straight down to a local pub in Hereford, where some of the lads joined me for a farewell drink. Hillbilly said I could doss down at his place for a while because I had nowhere else to stay and very little money. The army would keep paying Jason's private school fees for another couple of months and then he'd have to change schools. Then there was the cheque I had to send to Chris every fortnight. I had to find work soon.

*

Ironically, I'm starting to hate this house. It's supposed to be my safe haven, but it brings back too many memories. I know that doesn't make sense; I've spent weeks *trying* to remember things and 'sterilising' this place since coming home from the clinic – taking down photographs and throwing things away. Now I've decided that some memories are best left in dark corners.

I want to get out of here, away from Hereford. I take off in the car, with no particular destination in mind, but a few hours later I find myself in the Rat Pit, a Para pub in Aldershot. I can't recognise a single face or remember anything about the drive. Using the public phone in the bar I call Sharky Sheridan, who's still in the Parachute Regiment and is now the chief instructor of the Red Devils.

'Tom, where are you?'

'In the Rat Pit.'

'What are you doing there?'

'I don't know, Sharky. I've just arrived here.'

'Are you all right?'

'No.'

'Give me five minutes.'

I don't know if Sharky knows what happened in France, but he's probably heard a few things on the grapevine. When he emerges through the pub door, his famous grin disappears immediately.

'Who's died, Tom?' he asks, fearing it might be Jason.

'Basically, me.'

I tell him bits and pieces about what happened in Chamonix and how I finished up in the asylum, but I don't mention stabbing Anna. I doubt if Sharky has ever seen me being serious for more than ten minutes, but already I feel much better.

'So how are things with you, Sharky?'

'Good, good. We're overseas for a month at Easter, team training in Cyprus. Remember last year?'

'Of course.'

The Red Freds go somewhere warm every spring to practise for the up-coming season. I was invited to join them and decided it was a good opportunity for some extra training for the project. I hired a car and tagged along with Sharky and the boys, doing my own thing while they worked on their displays and occasionally performed around the island. It was a great trip.

On the second last day, in high winds, the boss, Captain Terry Carrol, hooked it in and bounced as he hit the ground at a rate of knots, smashing his pelvis. They shipped him off to hospital and that left Sharky in charge. The next day, I asked him if I could organise a skydive.

'Yeah, I got no problem with that,' he says.

'What about a nude jump?'

'Well, I'm not doing it, but if you think you can get enough lads . . .'

Sharky had done one of them before, and took the view that while it may seem all virile and exciting in the aircraft, once you step outside, stark naked at 13,500 feet, no matter who you are, you can't look macho when your manhood shrivels up to nothing.

I put it to the rest of the lads and got ten nude jumpers, including myself. Only the cameraman was allowed to wear a suit because he needed more control in the air to get the pictures. Everyone else on board had to be naked, and that included the pilot, Roger Brown. A gorgeous-looking blonde from Sussex, who worked at a local bar, had come down to the drop zone for the day. She asked if she could come up for the ride.

'Only if you're naked,' I said. 'There are no exceptions.'

'Sure, I'm game.'

Roger's eyes lit up at the thought of having this stunning creature sitting naked next to him.

In a quick calculation, we added up the weight of the fuel, the jumpers, the pilot and the girl. It came up just over the odds, so we had to lose someone. The blonde had to go; Roger was gutted.

We walked fully clothed out to the Islander and, once away from the drop zone, started stripping off in the shade of the wings. Glancing up, I noticed the sponsor's name stencilled on the aircraft – the *Sun* newspaper. What they'd give for a photograph of this, I thought.

One of the guys asked me if I'd ever done this before.

'Once. On a civilian jump in Spain there were two blokes on board who were naked. They talked me into joining them.'

Roger undressed in the cockpit and handed his clothes out the window. The rest of us clambered on board, wearing nothing but parachutes, goggles and grins. The constant stream of banter and blaggarding was eventually drowned out by the noise of the engines. The temperature decreases by two degrees every thousand feet, and it was cold inside the Islander, although nothing like it would be outside in freefall.

When the door opened, we started sliding outside, gripping the hand rail along the side of the fuselage. The jumper in the doorway did a rocking count: 'Ready . . . set . . . go!'

That's it! We're away, accelerating through the deep blue towards the olive groves and whitewashed farmhouses below. I managed to close on the formation – only the cameraman remained outside. We fell at about 120 mph, and around me the grinning faces had concave cheeks caused by the rushing wind and hair that darted upwards. How can people not love this sport?

Cyprus is normally a quiet drop zone in the middle of nowhere, but somehow word had got round about the nude jump and women had come from everywhere – wives, girlfriends and spectators. Showing off, I came in fast and lifted my legs up to slide. Unfortunately, I managed to find the only thistle on the drop zone and turned my backside into a pin cushion.

Later the Freds sent me a video of the nude jump, with a warning – 'For Your Eyes Only'.

'Why don't you come out again?' suggests Sharky, breaking into my thoughts. He has to shout above the noise of the pub. 'You look like you need to get away.'

'Are you sure?'

'Yeah, I'll mention it to Terry Carrol. I'm sure he'll say yes.'

It's getting late and Sharky invites me to kip at his place overnight. In the early hours, unable to sleep, I get up and leave without waking him. On the drive home, I think about Cyprus. Maybe that's just what I need. These drugs have turned me into a zombie, but if I get out there, among the lads, maybe I'll start feeling like my old self again.

A few days later I phone the Red Devils team office, and Sharky has it all arranged. 'The team is gonna be thrilled to see you. After last year you're a bit of a legend.'

Jackie is coming with me – which is great, because she needs a holiday – and so are Fran and Jenny. I can't believe how excited I am. After being cooped up in clinics and imprisoned by drugs, I'm going to take control of my life again. Jackie wants me to wait until Easter Monday and fly out with her and the girls, but I'm so keen that I catch the red-eye flight that arrives on Good Friday. 'Sharky and the lads will be there,' I tell her. 'They'll look after me.'

I arrive at about four in the morning and go straight to bed at the Sussex Apartments, about a mile from the drop zone. A few hours later, Sharky sends a couple of the lads to wake me and ask if I want to come jumping. As I look around the strange room, I feel as if someone has put an enormous weight on my chest that is pressing down against my lungs. 'Take deep breaths,' I tell myself. 'Breathe slowly.'

Where am I? I don't recognise this place. Who are these people?

—Calm down, you're in Cyprus. It's okay – the Freds are jumping.

But why am I so frightened? Feel my heart, it's racing.

—Sshhhhh, settle down. You're on a holiday.

At the drop zone, training has already started. One of the lads runs up behind me and playfully jumps on my back, but I cower away from him. It takes me a while to realise that people are staring at me in shock. Some of them are close to tears. I'm hollow-eyed and gaunt; drugged up to the eyeballs and prone to just staring into space. The voices around me are flat and monotonous. There is no warmth in the sun.

'You don't want to jump yet, do you, Tom?' asks Sharky, very deliberately making me focus on his face and shaking his head firmly.

'No.'

'That's good. Let me just go and talk to the boss, okay? You stay just here.'

He talks to Terry Carrol and then comes back to me.

'Listen, Tom. How about we go and get some breakfast? Someone else can handle the jumping. We'll get a bite to eat, sit on the beach, play a few games of pool . . . anything you want to do. Come on, let's go.'

Sharky spends all day with me, but I can't say more than a dozen words to him without losing track of the conversation. We'll be playing pool and after about three shots, I'll put my cue on the table and wander away, or I'll pick up a ball and stare at it. Sharky tries to get me to eat but I give up after a mouthful and light a cigarette.

My chest is tight and there are butterflies in my stomach. I keep gulping each breath, as if I'm not getting enough oxygen. What is this place? Who are these people? I don't want to be here. I want to be around things and people I recognise.

Sharky takes me back to my apartment and Dixie lets me use his telephone.

'Help me, I have to come back,' I say to Jackie.

She tries to calm me down and says she'll be with me in a day or two, along with the girls. 'We'll look after you,' she says.

'No, no, no. I'm scared, Jack, I have to get home.'

'But there won't be any seats. It's Easter. Just hang on.'

I lie down and close my eyes, trying to sleep. Sharky is sitting in a chair, watching me as I try to control my breathing and relax. When I hear him stand, I suddenly sit bolt upright. Sharky jumps about a foot in the air.

'Where do you think you're going?' I demand.

'I was just going to have a shower, Tom, I haven't got any stuff here.'

'A shower! Why do you want a shower?'

'I need to change, mate, I've been like this all day.'

'No, no, Sharky, we need to go to the airport.'

'What do you want to go there for?'

'I need to check on flights.'

'We're going to do that tomorrow.'

'No, now.'

I don't say a word on the drive to Larnaca Airport. I stare out of the windscreen and try to stay calm. Where is this place? Who are these people?

The main terminal building is teeming with holiday-makers. As we walk through the main doors I take hold of Sharky's hand. Embarrassed, he tries to pull away, but I drag him closer and we walk side by side to the British Airways counter.

'Excuse me, is there a flight to London?' I ask.

The girl misunderstands me and thinks I'm waiting for someone. 'There's one just arrived,' she says.

'When's it going back?'

She looks at me strangely. 'In about half an hour.'

'I'm on it,' I say, letting go of Sharky and turning towards the departure gate.

'Tom, you can't!'

'I'm on it! That's it! No problem! Thank you, Sharky.' I shake his hand.

'But Tom, you've got no money, no passport, no ticket, no kit. You can't get on the aeroplane.' He's pulling me back as I try to walk through passport control.

Suddenly, it dawns on me. 'Sharky, I have to go back and get my passport.'

'Yes, that's right, Tom, let's go back and get your passport.'

On the slow drive back, Sharky chats to me and tries to take my mind off the flight. 'I know you're not well, Tom, and all the lads are really upset. Some of them were nearly crying when they saw you. I know why you want to go home and we'll try to get you there, but no airline is going to take you if you act like this. Look at you!'

We decide that I need something to really knock me out. It's still early in the evening and we go to the Sergeants' Mess, looking for the RAF medic. He joins us in the bar and Sharky explains the problem. 'He needs to catch a plane. What's the heaviest stuff you can knock him out with?'

The medic quizzes me on what drugs I'm taking and checks the manual before giving me the strongest sedative he has. Then Sharky suggests I have something to eat, but I end up staring at the plate. Janie Barnes, the wife of a pilot, starts comforting me and I'm drawn to her, because women seem to be less threatening than men.

Standing up suddenly, I announce to Sharky, 'I have to go to the airport.'

'Okay, Tom, we'll go and book a flight for tomorrow. Then we'll come back and you can get some sleep.'

Janie comes with us because she keeps me calm. She's also a senior air-traffic controller in London, and maybe she can sway an airline into giving me a seat. When we arrive at the airport, she arranges a meeting with officials and then takes me to one side. 'Listen, Tom, if they find out you've got a problem with your head, they'll never let you on board. I'm going to tell them that there's a problem at home. Let me do the talking and don't stare at anybody.'

Janie is gone for fifteen minutes and manages to get me on a flight the following evening. Sharky is going to stay with me until then, and we head back to the apartment. Poor old Sharky – all night long he sits in a chair watching me, and every time he moves, I sit bolt upright and demand to know where he's going.

I don't sleep at all. I lie on my back, with my hands on my chest, and stare at the inside of my closed eyelids. I'm not focusing on any one thing in particular, but millions of thoughts are racing through my mind, too quickly for me to make any sense of them. The only image that comes back repeatedly is one of home. I have to get home.

Next morning, I visit the drop zone and immediately gravitate towards Debbie, the only female member of the Freds. She's injured her back on a heavy landing and won't be jumping again for a few weeks. Initially, she asked the boss if she could go back early, but he wanted to keep the whole team together. I ask Terry Carrol if I can have a word with him.

'Can I ask you for a big favour?' I say, tearfully.

'Whatever you want, Tom. If it's in my power I'll sort it out.'

'Well, I know you told Debbie that she couldn't go back early, but I'm asking you to reconsider. I'm on a flight this evening and I really need Debbie to come with me.'

He doesn't hesitate before saying yes.

It's Saturday at the drop zone and there are lifts going on all the time, with one team repacking while the other team is jumping. After sitting with Debbie in the sunshine for a while, I get up and stretch. I feel much better, and say I might go up for the ride while they're jumping.

Roger Brown starts flapping because he doesn't fancy having a raving lunatic sitting next to him in the cockpit. 'What if he doesn't like it up there?' he whispers to Sharky.

I wander over and climb into the glass bubble of the Islander, but immediately it seems very confined and claustrophobic. Sharky sees my discomfort.

'It's too close,' I say to him.

'That's right, mate. You're not ready yet. Best to get out.'

Debbie stays with me for most of the day and on the drive to the airport that evening. In the departure lounge I swallow a handful of tablets, trying to knock myself out completely. I'm almost rattling with pills by the time I board the flight. Debbie sits in front of me and she leans back occasionally to stroke my brow and touch my hand. 'Not long to go now, Tom. We'll soon be there,' she says.

Mercifully, I manage to doze off for an hour, and I dream about what a difference a year can make to a life. Last time I flew home from Cyprus the lads had had to almost pour me on to the flight because I'd been drinking Harvey Wallbangers all night.

I'd turned up at Larnaca Airport reeking of alcohol and wearing a Red Devils T-shirt with spaghetti bolognese spilled down the front. When I woke up, I was lying across four seats, with chewing gum in my hair and no idea if I was on the right plane. As I sat upright, the stewardess came back to me. 'Ah, Mr Read, you're awake.'

'Yes. Have you seen my teeth?'

'They're on the floor.'

'Oh. Thank you.' I felt like death warmed up. 'Where is this flight going?'

'To London.'

'Oh, good.'

'Do you remember getting on the flight, sir?'

I thought about this. 'Ah, actually, no, I'm afraid not.'

'When you came on board you said, "I need to lie down. You can stuff your scoff up your arse and I don't want to see any bloody films."'

'Oh, God, I'm so sorry. I really am.'

'The chief steward was considering not letting you on board, but one of the girls recognised your T-shirt. She'd been to see the Red Devils do a display in Cyprus. Are you with the Red Devils?'

'I used to be.'

'Well, we weren't that busy and you were reasonably quiet and said you just wanted to sleep, so we asked a gentleman to move down the plane so you could take up the back seats.'

Another stewardess had then come across to us, carrying two Bloody Marys. 'Here, I think this is what you need.' They were packed with ice and just perfect.

'Let me apologise again for my behaviour,' I'd said, starting to feel human again.

'No, don't bother, it was really very amusing. But if you're going to apologise to anyone, you might speak to the male steward. His name is Christopher.'

'Why, what did I do?'

'We were on the tarmac for twenty minutes before take-off and you went to sleep lying down. When he couldn't wake you to fasten your seat-belt, he tried to do it himself, but you grabbed his wrists. You wanted to know if he was a poof *before* he joined British Airways or if he'd joined British Airways and then *become* a poof.'

'Oh, no.' I buried my head in my hands.

Finishing my second Bloody Mary, I went looking for this Christopher. 'Listen, mate, I think I owe you an apology. I've been told what I said and it was totally out of order. I hope you can forgive me.'

He laughed and in a very effeminate voice said, 'Oh, really, that's okay.'

'But just tell me one thing,' I said.

'Yes?'

'What was the answer?'

Debbie stays with me as I collect my bags and walk out of the customs hall at Heathrow. Jackie is waiting for me. God, it's great to see her.

'I should drive,' she says, as we reach the car.

'No. I'll do it.'

'But you're not yourself.'

'I can't sit still, Jack, I have to be doing something.'

She stares out of the window and doesn't say much. I know she's disappointed. She's been so excited about going to Cyprus and really wanted this holiday. She deserves it – I've been hard work. From that moment, we never mention it again – Cyprus becomes the 'C-word'.

As I walk into my house, I feel a mixture of joy and sadness. I've never been so happy to see a place, regardless of its fading wallpaper, leaking taps, brown sofa and the cardboard box that doubles as a coffee table. I'm safe now, and I think I never want to leave here again. I'm going to stay here for ever. Yet at the same time, I know that I have entered a prison.

I thought I'd seen rock-bottom when I felt the cold hospital floor in Chamonix pressed against my cheek; or as I stumbled in a drug-induced haze through the Charter Clinic; or as I lay every night on my brown sofa, unwilling to sleep in my own bed. But I was wrong. Now I know there's still further to fall. There is no redeeming feature left in my life. There is no warmth, comfort or joy in the world. There is no point.

I'm not getting better – I've been deluding myself. I hate this house more than anywhere else in the entire world – this is where I began losing my sanity – yet I'm scared to leave here. This is my sanctuary and my prison cell.

I tell myself that I'm not contemplating suicide, but perhaps the truth is that I lack the means. Maybe if I had a gun it would be different. Then again, I have a cupboard full of drugs, they'll do the job. Is that what I really want? If I stop to consider all the people it would hurt, the answer is no, but I can't think of anything except hopelessness and despair.

I'm sitting on the sofa with my head in my hands, facing the unlit gas fire. There's an old black and white movie on the TV but I don't recognise any of the actors. They're probably all dead. I don't want to listen to what they're saying. I don't want to know about some contrived plot with its manufactured conflict and neatly packaged ending. I'm dealing with a real-life drama; this is life or death:

When I phone Jackie I only have to say her name.

'Hang on, I'll be there in five minutes,' she says.

I go upstairs into the bathroom and wrap a towel around my waist. There's a face in the mirror that I can't recognise; it has bulging eyes that are brimming with torment and fear. It's an old man's face, yellowed by drugs and nicotine. Don't look! Turn away!

Downstairs, I turn on the electric kettle and start washing the dishes. Jackie comes in the front door and looks relieved to see me. Her boyfriend Steve is with her.

'Jackie, I'm not handling it well,' I say. What a massive understatement! She makes me put down the cups and leads me upstairs.

'Okay, this is what we'll do,' she says, in a motherly voice. 'We'll get you dressed and then we'll take you for a drive to the hospital. I'll be with you. I won't leave.'

She helps me to get dressed and sits next to me as we drive to the Stonebow Unit. The duty psychiatrist admits me immediately and gives me enough sedatives to choke an elephant. I don't sleep, but it slows me down. The doctor explains that I'm going to be a night patient for a while, but I can go home during the day. It makes sense, because the nights are the worst.

'You'll still be a voluntary patient,' he says reassuringly. 'You just come and see us every evening – bring your pyjamas.'

Jackie gives me a hug. 'I'll meet you here in the morning, okay? That's a promise. Then I'll take you home and cook you a big breakfast.'

18

What went wrong in Cyprus? I got well too quickly, according to Dr Allman. They decreased the drugs prematurely, when I still had control over them. What he doesn't realise is that I've always had control over them. Now he's increased the dosages again and I'm a dribbling idiot.

Before Cyprus, I saw myself as getting better. Now I know that's a lie. Who am I fooling? I might be on these drugs for years. I might never find myself again.

I haven't been out of the house since then and I'm going crazy staring at the four walls. I won't even walk to the end of the garden. Loel Guinness has invited me out to stay at his estate in France. I'd have the run of the place – hot and cold running servants, the swimming pool, the gymnasium – I could chill out and just get better, he says. But I'm staying at home because I can't risk another Cyprus.

Eventually Jackie gets fed up with me and says, 'Right, we'll find something to do. What about that horrible wallpaper in the back bedroom?'

'Yeah, let's do it,' I say. Ever since I moved in to this place I've been talking about redecorating the spare bedroom, which is papered with red and black racing cars. I've also promised to fix the boiler door and the radiator that leaks rusty water.

Jackie goes to the hardware store and picks up some tools and wallpaper stripper. We carry all the kit upstairs and put old sheets on the floor. Quick cup of tea and we're into it – stripping down the walls. I take off a tiny piece of paper no bigger than a matchbox and say, 'Is that all right, Jack?'

'Yes, fine.'

Then I strip off another small piece and ask the question again, holding it aloft like a trophy. After ten minutes I sit down, exhausted. Jackie does the whole job herself, while I watch and dribble.

With the spare room decorated, I can get a lodger to help pay the bills. Irene's friend Jenny is looking for a place, and she's a good choice because she knows how 'Mong-like' I can be. Apart from being good company, she's also a trained chef and cooks brilliant meals. We even open a bottle of wine occasionally and do things properly.

During his holidays, Jason comes up from Cheltenham for a few days. I can hear him outside in the garden, kicking a ball with a neighbour's kid. The grass is quite long because the days are warmer and I can't motivate myself to get the mower out. I'm in the kitchen, reading my French book. Learning a language is my latest project.

There's a cry and I run outside. Jason is rolling around in agony. He's missed the ball and kicked the ground, dislocating his weak knee. The kneecap is sticking out at an obscene angle. I reach his side but then start backing away. He's screaming and I can't handle it. I crouch next to the wall like a gibbering wreck, unable to help my own son. I can't even look at him, let alone phone a bloody ambulance.

Jenny hears the commotion and rushes outside. She takes control of the situation straight away, getting a blanket to put over Jason and a bag of frozen peas from the freezer. The pain must be agonising, but he's stopped crying and he keeps saying to me, 'I'm sorry, Dad. I'm sorry, Dad.' My heart wants to break.

The ambulance officers put him on gas and take him to hospital. I ride in the back while Jenny follows in her car. She has to keep me calm while we wait in the casualty department because I'm terrified of being there and distraught about Jason. 'Its all right, Tom, he's a strong young lad. It's happened before. It's not a big deal. They're putting it in plaster.'

When they let me see Jason, he tells me not to worry, but I still feel devastated. Back at the house, Jenny pours me a glass of wine and I say,

'That's it! My own son in pain and I couldn't help him. I lost it. I have to get better, Jen. Then I can get off these drugs.'

That's the catch-22, you see. I know that I'll never get better while I'm on the medication because it masks things, but until I get better the doctors won't let me come off the treatment. The truth is I don't need all these drugs. I recognise my illness for what it is and the drugs don't help the problem, they simply hide it away so no one can see. But I can see it; I know it's there.

My nights at the Stonebow Unit become fewer as the weeks pass, although it's sometimes the only way I can guarantee a decent rest, because I sleep so fitfully on the brown sofa. I can't imagine ever sleeping in my room again. No matter how strong the sleeping pills are, I still wake in the wee hours with the duvet wrapped around me and the TV showing rubbish. That's the worst time – the midnight of my soul.

Yet, as the days pass, I slowly start feeling a little sharper and more aware of things happening around me. This is one step at a time, like learning to walk all over again. First I get to the end of the garden, then I make it to the little park at the end of my street, and then to a pub for lunch with the girls, or to visit Irene or Fran for a cup of tea. I still have my moments, though. I'll be riding in the car with Jenny, half-way to Fran's house, and suddenly I'll ask her to turn around and take me home; or we'll have only just arrived and I'll stand up and start getting ready to leave.

'Where are you going, Tom?' Jenny will ask.

'Home.'

'But we've only just arrived. I haven't had my cup of tea.'

'I have to get home.'

Jenny learns not to argue. She knows that I'll stand by the door waiting for her until she picks up her car-keys and says goodbye.

Mum phones me each week and I let the answering-machine pick up the call. Then I'll wait until I'm in exactly the right frame of mind before calling her back. I have to sound as upbeat as possible, because that way she won't worry about me.

'Are you looking after yourself?' she asks.

'Yes, of course. I've got lots of people looking after me.'

'And you're eating well?'

I could run a tape saying, 'Mum, I'm fine.'

This goes on for a while and then I say, 'Hang on, Mum, there's a knock at the door. Oh, it's only Irene, she's come round with some dinner for me. Bless her. Mum, can I give you a call back? I don't want it getting cold. I'll call you in a couple of days. Bye now. Take care.'

There's no one at the door, of course.

Each time she phones, Mum tells me how wonderful Christine has been, calling her every day. The sentimental, selfish side of me still thinks about the possibility of us getting back together. I don't like being on my own and Christine is a wonderfully warm, maternal figure, who will wrap me in cotton wool and protect me.

'I read that book by Jim Davidson,' Mum says, sounding disapproving. My heart sinks and I feel like a twelve-year-old who's been caught with a girlie magazine under his bed.

I'd bodyguarded the comedian for six months after leaving the SAS, and if ever a man needed to be protected from himself, it was Jim.

'He's not a very funny writer, is he?' Mum continues.

'He exaggerates a bit,' I say. 'That's what comedians do.'

Jim had written his autobiography, *The Full Monty*, and included several of our escapades in Berlin involving brothels, alcohol and condoms full of water. When I mentioned the book to Mum, I didn't expect her to go and buy a copy.

Jim loves the Regiment, and makes a point of doing several gigs a year for the lads. That's how I first met him – after a show at the Paludrin Club in Hereford. He was a friend of Hillbilly's, who introduced us at the bar.

'I hear you've left,' said Jim. 'What are you going to do?'

'Go on the circuit. You know, do a bit of bodyguarding.'

'You should give me your number, I might need some protection.' Jim has that cheeky schoolboy grin where you never quite know if he's being serious or not.

A fortnight later, I was soaking in the bath at Hillbilly's when Jim phoned. 'I want you to come on tour,' he said.

'What for?'

'To look after me.'

I laughed. 'You're a big boy, Jim.'

He told me that he had a tour of England and Scotland and then a trip to Germany to film a Christmas TV special for the forces. 'Listen, Tom, I'm a danger to myself. Every time I have a drink I seem to finish up on the front pages of the tabloids. I want you to keep me out of trouble.'

Since the break-up of his second marriage, Jim had gone right off the rails. He'd be out drinking most nights in places like Tramp and Stringfellow's, and I think at one point had even gone to a Harley Street psychiatrist for help.

A week after the phone call, I found myself on tour with Jim, driving through the Midlands towards Birmingham. Jim dozed in the passenger seat, occasionally opening one eye to see where we were. He'd lost his licence for drink-driving and that made me the chauffeur as well as the minder.

We had to leave early to reach the new venue, where Jim checked the sound system and his dressing-room before we booked into a hotel to wait for the evening's show. It surprised me how emotionally fragile Jim became, particularly before a show, when he couldn't go on stage without a few brandies. Yet once he was out there, he acted as though he was born to perform. I watched from backstage and got to know all the routines, although Jim often threw in variations and ad-libbed with the audience.

At the end of the show, Jim went straight to the bar while the roadies and sound blokes packed up the equipment and trucked it to the next venue. After a mystery tour of various bars and night-spots, Jim and I would stagger back to the hotel to sleep it off. Early next morning, we were on the road to somewhere else.

I always used to laugh at celebrities who complained about how tough their lives were – living in nice hotels, earning lots of money and being chauffeured around every day – but now I could see that it was bloody hard work.

For Christmas 1986, Jim was booked to appear in *Cinderella* at the Bristol Hippodrome. We turned up to do some advance publicity, and one of his interviewers was a girl from the local TV station, Alison Holloway. Straight away I knew Jim had fallen for her – he's a sucker for a pretty girl.

'I'm an incurable romantic,' he told me.

'No, you're a horny old goat,' I replied.

Back in London, Jim started writing to Alison, laying on the old Davidson charm with a trowel, hoping to get a date with her when he returned to Bristol for the panto. Later he discovered that she'd been pinning his letters to the office noticeboard and he'd become the laughing-stock of HTV.

But you had to give him credit for perseverance, because come opening night Alison was on his arm as they arrived at the first-night party. He took her out again, with me dropping them at the restaurant and picking them up later. After Alison had been safely delivered to her doorstep, Jim said to me, 'I'm going to marry her.'

'Haven't you learned your lesson yet?' I asked him.

'I don't like being single, Tom,' he said, 'and I always say that if you get married in the morning and it doesn't work out, it won't spoil the whole day.'

Within two weeks they were engaged. The *Sun* newspaper publicly bet Jim a thousand pounds the marriage wouldn't last a year. Jim accepted the bet and married Alison at a register office in Bristol, with the reception at the Clifton Hotel. Dave Emerson from Emerson, Lake and Palmer played keyboards, and a few other celebrities attended. Of course, Jim got totally legless at the reception, and Alison, who'd known him for all of two months, said, 'I can't understand it. I've never seen him as drunk as this.'

Someone replied: 'Stick around, babe. You ain't seen nothing yet.'

In the early hours, I was asleep in my room when the hotel manager woke me. 'Mr Read, perhaps you could help us. There's a spot of trouble in the honeymoon suite.'

I quickly pulled on trousers and a shirt and found Jim sitting on the floor, covered in cake and still dressed in his bridegroom's clothes. Apparently, Alison had locked him out of the room but he'd managed to get inside. A fight had followed and more than cake had been exchanged. Jim had obviously lost.

'Mr Davidson will pay for the damage,' I assured the manager. 'Perhaps you could find him another room.'

By the time the manager returned, I'd talked to Alison and the newly-weds had patched things up. Thankfully, the story didn't make the newspapers, but it didn't bode well for the future. The marriage lasted about a month, and the *Sun* had a field day. Jim was accused of giving Alison a black eye, but he claimed she could handle herself.

'She can punch like a bloke,' he said, explaining how he barricaded himself in the bedroom of their rented flat. 'But she burst the door open like the Incredible Hulk, pushed the weights out of the way and came after me. I slung a dumb-bell her way but she kept coming. I pushed her away, caught her in the eye with my thumb, bruising her eye and dislocating my thumb. I ran off to hide.'

Conceding defeat, Jim paid a thousand pounds to charity after he and Alison agreed to divorce before they killed each other.

I had been out of the Regiment for nearly four months and there hadn't been a day go by when I didn't regret leaving. I missed the lads and the lifestyle, particularly when I talked to Hillbilly and he was full of stories and preparing to head off to somewhere like Cyprus or Botswana for troop training.

When the letter arrived from St James's Palace, I looked at the envelope and thought that one of the lads was winding me up. However, there was no mistaking the message inside: I was to receive the Queen's Gallantry Medal for the mobile intercept job in Northern Ireland. Al Slater was to posthumously receive a Military Medal for the same operation.

The invitation said I could bring two guests to the Palace, so I invited Mum and Jason, who was then eight years old. Mum was thrilled, and I arranged for her to stay at the Special Forces Club in London, where Tankie, who ran the SAS Association, took her on a guided tour, pointing out pictures on the walls of war-time heroes and spies.

The next day they sent a car to take us to Buckingham Palace. I'd been re-issued with a dress uniform for the day, which I had to return to Hereford. Mum and Jason found their seats among the guests and I took my place in a line of about fifty people who were due to receive various awards and honours. I was last in the queue.

The entire ceremony ran like clockwork. The Queen arrived precisely at 10 a.m., smiled at the guests and then waited as names were announced. She chatted for a minute to each person and then politely the ceremony continued.

When it came to my turn, it was unnerving to hear my name mentioned in the same sentence as the SAS because that sort of thing normally never happens.

'Is your family here?' the Queen asked.

'My mother and my son.'

'They must be very proud.'

'Yes, Ma'am.'

She asked me about the area of Ulster where the mobile intercept had taken place, and said she used to go fishing there as a child. They were clearly happy times, and she seemed quite sad that so much had happened to change things. I was astonished at how well she'd been briefed.

'What are you doing now?' she asked.

I hesitated. 'I'm between jobs, Your Majesty.'

'So you are no longer with the services?'

'Unfortunately, no, Ma'am.'

'Are you intending to go back into the army?'

'I seriously hope so, Ma'am.'

We chatted for about five minutes, according to my mum, who had been timing each of the Queen's audiences. 'You were the longest,' she said proudly. As we left, a group of senior staff officers approached me and asked me why I had left the Regiment.

I explained what had happened and one of them said, 'Do you want to go back in?'

'Yes, I do.'

That was the end of the conversation, and I thought no more about it as I drove on to Bristol where Jim had arranged a big party to celebrate. All the dancing girls from the panto were there, and we got smashed on beer and White Russians.

Amid all the revelry, I had a phone call from Hillbilly, saying, 'What the fuck have you done? The RSM is trying to get hold of you.'

'Okay, I'll call him tomorrow.'

'No, he wants you to call him straight away. I've got his home number.'

Half cut, I telephoned Taff and told him about the message from Hillbilly.

'Yeah. I've been speaking to the CO and all that concerns you is one question: do you want to come back into the Regiment?'

I didn't hesitate. 'Yes.'

'Okay, come up and see the CO tomorrow.'

The following day, back at Stirling Lines, I found myself standing in the same office as six months previously. The CO invited me to take a walk with him. I was dressed in civvies and we strolled around the camp, attracting the interested stares of passers-by.

'Have you considered coming back in?'

'Sir, I didn't want to leave in the first place.'

He flinched slightly and kept walking. After about ten minutes, he said, 'I'm giving you the opportunity to come back in and keep your rank without doing Selection.'

Inside I'm thinking, 'Yes!'

Then he gives me the catch. 'You'll be joining G Squadron.'

'But that's not my squadron, sir.'

'It is now.'

'Is there any chance of a transfer?'

'If you do a year, then you can go back to B Squadron.'

At that moment the future was written in his eyes, but I wasn't looking. He didn't want me back in the Regiment – someone higher up the line had no doubt pressured him – and he certainly wouldn't be doing me any favours.

19

The days are growing warmer and I'm feeling better in spite of the drugs. There are even times when the clouds part, as Des would say, and I get a little burst of sunshine. It's like being my old self again. Dr Allman says I'm making good progress – God knows what he means, but he's cut my visits to one a week.

Jenny has moved out and I'm on my own again, but it doesn't worry me so much. I'm still sleeping on the sofa downstairs but I don't wake in the middle of the night as often, because the sedatives are knocking me out until past midday. There's not much of the day left by the time I drag myself up and have breakfast.

Occasionally I have bleak moments when I get terribly depressed, but I blame the drugs for these. Most of the time I'm simply lethargic and out of step with the world. It's an uncomfortable feeling, a bit like watching yourself on video or hearing yourself on tape. Is that really me? Do I really sound like that? That's why I've decided to come off all the medication except for the injections.

It's the height of the skydiving season in Spain, and Sharky and some of the lads are jumping at Ampuria Brava. Jackie and I are going down to join them for three weeks. The trip to Cyprus had been too soon, but now I'm feeling better. I figure that if I can get my old 'party head' on and have a few drinks with the boys, then happy days will be here again.

The holiday is one big drinking session, interrupted by energetic bouts of windsurfing and swimming. Jackie is jumping six or seven times a day, but I don't go up once. At one point, she finds me sitting in the shower, wearing sunglasses and singing Elvis Presley songs, while pouring mouth-wash on my hair instead of shampoo.

When I get back to Hereford, I miss my next appointment with Dr Allman. He leaves messages on my answering-machine but I don't call him. I've decided that I'm coming off the medication completely. In the back of my mind, an idea is taking hold that if I'm truly to understand this chemical imbalance in my brain – or whatever it is – I have to recognise how it affects me and learn how to differentiate between reality and any alternative signals that I pick up. That isn't going to happen while I'm zonked out of my scone on drugs. I have conclusions to come to and decisions to reach, but the chemicals are blocking out the receptors.

Christmas comes and goes; the anniversary of Chamonix passes unmentioned; I'm going to be thirty-nine years old on my next birthday. How long before I declare myself better again?

I'm feeling pretty good, although a little under-utilised. I'd love to lose a few pounds, but that won't take me long once I get back into training. My running gear has been sitting upstairs for months, and every night I tell myself that I'll start my new fitness regime in the morning. Of course, it never happens. That's the same story that half the world will tell you.

The British summer has been lousy and it feels as though it's been raining for months. By November I've had enough of the drizzle and Jackie and I head down to Ampuria Brava for a week. We stay at a mate's apartment, and the last thing Pete's wife Kate says is, 'Make yourselves at home, but don't leave me without any toilet rolls.'

On our last day, we go out and buy a hundred rolls and build a big pyramid of them in the middle of the coffee-table. There are so many rolls that we hide them all around the house, knowing that Kate will be finding them for months afterwards.

More importantly, I manage to do some jumping this time, and put the tandem rig to good use, taking up some friends. I've sold Zephyr to the jump centre and she's being used by student pilots. I can fly her when-ever I'm down here.

I haven't worked since the breakdown and my mortgage is being paid by the DHSS. I hate the idea of relying on welfare, so I'm taking the next job I get offered, even if it means going to Algeria to guard oil rigs. Of course there'll be a question-mark hanging over me, but the only way to prove to people that I'm fully recovered is to show them I can work. Maybe I can even convince Loel Guinness and High Adventure to put the Skydive from Space back on the agenda.

That sounds positive and confident, but deep within I still feel as though I'm not quite in control of my destiny. Perhaps it's because I've never come to terms with what happened in Chamonix, or discovered the reason for what I did there. I know that I'm not the same person I was then. What you see is a brave, confident front, whereas in reality I'm clinging to the wreckage and trying to convince everyone, including myself, that I'm okay.

One night in a bar at Hereford I meet a very attractive lady, stylishly dressed, who holds my gaze when I find myself staring at her. Her name is Olivia, and she's not one of the normal crowd of wives and girlfriends who have some link with the Regiment. She must know that she's attractive, with her striking blue eyes and fantastic figure, but she's also intelligent and strong-willed. She isn't going to fall for smooth talk and boyish charm.

Although it is classed as a city, Hereford is more like a small town, and people tend to congregate in one or two night-clubs. As a result it's almost inevitable that I'll bump into Livvy again. A few weeks pass and I see her on a Thursday or Friday night at a wine bar. Although it's not really planned, each of us knows that the other is likely to be there.

After a few more days I start giving Livvy a call of an afternoon, to ask her if she's going out that night.

'Oh, I don't know. Maybe,' she says.

'Yeah, I'm the same. I haven't decided.'

'Where would you go if you did go out?'

'Probably to the local. What about you?'

'Yeah, the same.'

'Well, I might see you out then.'

'Mmm. Okay.'

When we do bump into each other we feign surprise, although I can't hide the fact that I'm really pleased to see her. We seem to have a lot in common. The evening passes too quickly and is followed by more meetings until we slowly become inseparable. Livvy's mother is French, and her Gallic temperament gives rise to occasional displays of her fiery temper, which I find quite spirited. She becomes very staunch and gestures in her Continental way, particularly if the issue is sensitive or close to her heart.

I don't know how much she knows about my breakdown. Hereford thrives on gossip, so I'm sure someone has told her. At least it hasn't frightened her away. Although she's never said anything, I know she has a busy enough life without worrying about me.

There are so many simple things I struggle to do since the breakdown, yet Livvy takes everything in her stride and confronts daily challenges with ease. She is a very pragmatic lady, and it shows in how well she is bringing up her two daughters. Her eldest, Alicia, is ten years old and very bright, with a passion for horses. Little Georgia, who is to become my god-daughter, is a sweet baby with an irresistible smile. I doubt if any children receive as much love and attention. Livvy dotes on both girls, and at the same time manages to look after a large house and work part-time. She is, not surprisingly, hopelessly late for every appointment, date or meeting, but when she does arrive – breezing in with a warm smile and a kiss for everyone – she looks fabulous.

I've invited her to come to Spain with me at the end of March. We'll drive down through Chamonix and spend a few nights with Harry and Cath, then we'll cross the border and do some jumping at Ampuria Brava. We might even visit Livvy's family in France on the way back.

It's been nearly two years since the attack on Anna. I'm still telling myself that everything is okay, even as I'm holding things at a distance, scared to let them get too close. 'It won't happen to me again,' I say. 'I'll see it coming next time.'

In the afternoon I walk up to the local park and sit on a bench, where I can watch the children running and laughing in the playground. Sometimes I feel self-conscious when people pass by me, because I worry that they'll think I'm a child-molester or a pervert. It's a sad world.

Lately, I've been using my surveillance training to become grey and nondescript, trying to blend in with the background so that no one gives me a second glance. Sitting on my park bench, I don't have a newspaper to read. They taught us to never carry a morning paper after three o'clock in the afternoon, because it shows you're an idle bastard and attracts attention. You can have a newspaper in the morning, but never fill in the crossword puzzle or have it open on the astrology page.

Occasionally, I have a feeling that I'm being watched. Surveillance teams have come into the area and they know that I've gone 'foxtrot' (on foot) from the house. I watch the cars that pass and I imagine that I can recognise the 'enemy' because they use black vehicles. You'd think they'd be cleverer than that, wouldn't you?

Today I saw a black Peugeot near the roundabout, and a dark Audi sedan filling up at the service station. I watched them closely even though my one Para brain-cell was telling me, 'This is all a crock of shit, you're just getting paranoid again.' This is the brain-cell that was disciplined at Depot Para and taught to be logical, practical and scientific. It can accept mysterious things and coincidences, but it doesn't go looking for conspiracies or plots.

Yet I can't stop my thoughts from racing. It's like doing a freefall commentary when you're flashing towards the ground and the words spill out in a torrent. You tell yourself to slow down, speak clearly, don't let the adrenalin take control, but it's hard because everything is moving so quickly.

On the ten-hour drive to Chamonix, I can't stop talking. I tell Livvy my entire life story, letting the words tumble out. She's excited about the holiday and doesn't mind listening.

'I haven't got much time,' I tell her.

'What do you mean you haven't got much time?'

'I haven't got much time for you.'

She doesn't understand me, and I think she's afraid that I'm dying of some terminal illness.

'Do you think I'm evil?'

She looks shocked. 'What do you mean?'

'You don't think I'm evil, do you?'

'No, of course not. Where does that question come from?' She laughs apprehensively. I don't realise that I'm scaring her.

In Chamonix, I overhear Cath telling Livvy about my breakdown. 'He's the last person you'd ever expect it to happen to,' she says. 'But he seems much better now, and you two get on really well together.' Livvy admits to having trouble keeping up with me, I'm so full of energy.

In Ampuria Brava we party every night and I barely get more than a few hours' sleep. I seem to be able to drink and drink without getting drunk. Eventually Livvy starts to flag. 'Don't you ever sleep?' she asks.

'I have these nightmares.'

'What sort of nightmares?'

'Things that frighten me.' Then I start laughing. I can't tell her the truth because I want to make a good impression on her. I want to show her the real me – the party animal who always has a funny story and can somehow get another round of drinks after last orders. At the same time, I know that I'm slowly losing my grip on reality; the truth is leaking away through the 'cracks' in my head. A part of me is fascinated by the sensation, but at the same time it appals me.

When we get back to Hereford, this whole process seems to accelerate. One night I go out and on the spur of the moment I walk into a strange bar. Immediately, I feel as though it has been preordained and I'm simply following my destiny. Every person in that bar is supposed to be there; every fixture and fitting has been carefully prepared. No one knows this except me.

It's getting worse. I'm not sleeping or eating; I'm smoking three or four packets of cigarettes a day, lighting one before another is finished; ideas are flashing through my head at a phenomenal rate.

There are men from the Water Board working over the road. Earlier they knocked on the door and asked if they could fill their kettle with water. They're not really from the Water Board, of course. They're watching the house from their van – waiting for me to make a move.

20

I'm in hospital again. I don't recall exactly how I got here, but my memory is slowly coming back, one piece at a time. The problem is that I can't tell if they're my memories, or if I'm just remembering what people are telling me about what happened. For instance, the nurses say I've been here for a fortnight, but it seems like only a few days. Most of that time I've been drugged to the eyeballs and dragging my knuckles along the ground. That's how they handle a problem like me – hit me with the old rhino dart in the arse and pump me full of medication.

What can I remember? What have people told me? Livvy knew something was wrong. Since getting back from our holiday, I'd grown more and more manic. I'd turn up at her house and tell her I was frightened and she'd spend hours trying to comfort me. She wanted me to see a doctor but I was afraid they'd put me in hospital.

'Shhhh. Calm down. I'll come with you. I'll look after you.'

'Will you, Livvy?'

'Of course I will.'

I'm still sleeping on the sofa, with the TV blaring, drowning out my thoughts. Except I'm not really sleeping. I'm trying to make sense of all the information I'm picking up from around me.

What can I remember? Livvy says I called her a witch and growled like a wild animal. I don't remember that. She came around to my house because she was worried about me. It was late, nearly ten in the evening, and I was dressed in a pair of underpants and a dressing-gown, looking yellow and gaunt. I hadn't slept or eaten and I'd been smoking one cigarette after another and drinking pots of tea.

Livvy says that I had this mania about washing, taking one bath after another, as if I wanted to cleanse myself. I don't remember. She says we climbed the stairs and I ran a bath. I sat in there, looking pathetic, in three inches of cold water, scooping it over my shoulders and down my arms, while I rocked back and forth. I don't remember.

'You're not a witch, are you, Livvy?'

'No.'

'You're not evil, are you, Livvy?'

'No.'

Then I stood up in the bath and began speaking as if addressing a crowd. It was all about good and evil, God and the devil. Livvy was good because she was standing by God. So what am I? Am I good? Am I evil? Livvy is with me and she's an angel, so I know that I must be good.

'Olivia . . . Livvy . . . live . . . but your name spells "evil" backwards.' What is evil? Jeffrey Dahmer ate people, does that make him sick or evil? And what about Adolf Hitler?

Everything is a play on words and each question leads to another. Words are extremely important – that's my father talking again. I could never say to him, 'No, I don't mean exactly that.' He'd lean close, stare at me with his piercing eyes and sneer, 'Well, say what you mean.'

For forty-five minutes I addressed the bathroom wall. Livvy calls it a 'masterpiece' and swears she's never heard anybody speak so eloquently about good and evil. She wishes she could remember more of the details. I wish I could remember any of them.

'Do you want me to give you a cuddle, Tom? Do you want me to touch you?' she asked me.

'Touch . . . touch me . . . why do you want to touch me?'

'To comfort you. Because you're not well, are you? You don't feel well, do you?'

'What's wrong with me?'

'I don't know. Tom, you're shivering. You've been standing in that bloody bath for ages. Please get out. Let's go downstairs and have a cup of tea.'

Livvy says I terrified her, and she kept trying to find a way to get out of the house and away from me. If she made a dash for the door, she feared that I would throw my hand out and slam it closed. I was standing naked in the kitchen when I called her a witch and began growling. My eyes were like dark holes and she thought I was possessed. I wish I could remember.

Eventually, Livvy managed to get out of the house and go for help. She drove towards Andy D.'s house, but her car broke down on the way. That car is always breaking down. Earlier in the evening, she'd phoned another mate of mine, Cammie Spence, who is also ex-SAS. She left a message on his answering-machine saying that I was acting strangely.

I can remember Cammie coming round and standing in the front doorway, trying to calm me down. He kept one foot outside the house as a precaution and listened to me rant about Livvy. 'You've lost it, Tom,' he kept saying. 'You've got to get to the hospital.'

'In the morning,' I tell him. 'Not now. I won't do anything stupid. I'll be okay tonight.'

I don't remember what happened next, although at some stage during the night, I looked in the bathroom mirror and didn't like what I saw. I rabbit-punched the glass and it smashed, but I didn't cut my hand. Afterwards, lying on the sofa, I heard the back door slide open. Andy had come to check up on me. I pretended to be asleep until I heard the door close again and his footsteps growing fainter down the side-path.

That's what I mean about things coming back to me bit by bit. Next morning, Cammie called the doctor, who arrived with two policemen. I remember being very calm, lying on the sofa in tracksuit bottoms and a T-shirt. Dr Edwards, a local GP, was speaking softly: 'Listen, Tom, have you been sleeping?'

'No.'

'Okay, look, you're having a bit of a bad time.'

'Yeah, I agree with that.'

'Well, I want you to go to the Stonebow Unit. Don't worry about it. It's for the best. Can you get yourself there?'

'Yeah.'

'Are you sure? I can arrange to get you there, but you know what that will mean?'

'No, I can do it.'

I see it as a challenge and put on my running kit, lacing the shoes as I sit on the stairs. If they are watching the house, I want them to think that I'm just going for a run and I'll be back soon. That way, they might not follow me.

The Stonebow is only half a mile from my house. I turn right out my front gate and then right again past all the terraced cottages with their neat little front gardens. I can hear my training shoes slapping on the footpath and I'm thinking about white cars and black cars; good forces and enemy forces. My lungs are full of garbage and I'm already puffing. Don't look back. Just act normally. You're going for a morning run.

There's a car yard at the T-junction and I know I'm almost at the hospital. Dr Edwards must have phoned ahead because Allman is waiting for me. 'Right, we're going to admit you as a voluntary patient,' he says. 'Are you happy with that?'

'Yes.'

I don't want doctors taking the decision for me. Once that happens, everything will change. If I'm sectioned, then my life will always be in their hands, but as a voluntary patient, I still have some control over my destiny.

'Right, Tom, we're going to start you on the medication.'

'Okay.'

'This is Stephanie. She'll be your key nurse. I want you to go with her.'

'Can I go for a walk before I come in?'

He looks concerned. 'I'd rather you didn't.'

'Don't worry, I'm not going to do anything stupid. I just want to go for a walk.'

'Do you want someone to come with you?'

'No, I'd rather be on my own.'

As I leave through the front doors and cross the car-park, I feel absolutely terrified. I'm hyperventilating and struggling to control the urge to run. I don't know what frightens me most – what's out here, or what's waiting for me inside the Stonebow.

I walk past the car yard and then circle the block very slowly. Panic grips every fibre of me and each step is sheer bloody-minded defiance. There is no other reason for it. I simply want to show that I am not beaten yet.

At the Stonebow they hit me with the rhino dart and I remember very little of the next two weeks. I sleep most of the time and they feed me when I wake. At some point, I tossed my false teeth out the window – don't ask me why. That's why I have this big gap in my mouth. Another time, a fire alarm went off in the middle of the night and I remember the firemen and police arriving. There were uniforms in the corridors. I recognised one of the policemen and was suddenly convinced that they'd come for me.

Initially, they put me in an observation room where the night staff could keep an eye on me through peep holes, but now they've moved me to a shared ward. It has a little patio, with a view over a courtyard and I can see the spire of Hereford Cathedral, with the golden cockerel weather-vane gleaming in the sunshine. It's quite comforting because that used to be Frank Collins' church.

There are three other patients in the ward, two alcoholics and a bloke who sleeps all the time. Perhaps he's dead. Mainly I talk to Mick, an unemployed builder in his early forties who, like me, has terrible problems sleeping. At night we sit up together in the smoking room, listening to the radio. The songs have messages for me, but the chlorpromazine is beginning to block out the signs.

Mick's wife divorced him and his sister died of cancer. He tells me his life story and fondly describes his beloved red car, which seems to be the main reason why he wants to get out of here.

A young lad comes into the smoking room, wearing summer shorts and wraparound sunglasses as if he's just back from Hawaii. He takes one of the chairs and faces the window, with his feet on the windowsill. He's listening to a personal stereo and every so often he gets up and offers me a sweet from a brown paper bag. To begin with, I wouldn't take one because I thought they were poisoned, but now I've got him pegged as just another loony. I guess that's a sign that things are beginning to calm down.

Dr Allman comes in about twice a week, but my key nurse Stephanie is available most of the time. She's young, with a pleasant, warm face. Stephanie isn't part of the conspiracy – she's on my side – but there's another nurse who knows Livvy and I'm being careful around her. She might be talking to Livvy on the outside.

Livvy has been phoning the Stonebow every day, asking about me.

Initially, they wouldn't release any details about me other than to say that I was 'comfortable'. Nor would they let her visit me or speak to me on the telephone. I guess they figured she could make things worse.

Now they've relaxed the restrictions and Livvy is coming to see me. When I first catch sight of her in the corridor it is like a breath of fresh air. I know she's shocked when she sees me because she strokes my cheek and there are tears welling in her eyes. I'm so dosed on medication that I must look like a bloody vegetable.

'What have they done to you?' she whispers, her cheek pressed against mine.

Later, we sit side by side in the smoking room and she strokes my hand. 'It's really nice to see you,' she says.

'It's nice to see you, too.' My voice is dead.

'You're going to be all right, Tom.'

'Will I, Livvy?'

'Yes, you'll come out of it. I know you will.'

'I'm glad you said that.'

I'm slurring the words because my tongue is swollen and I don't have any front teeth.

Livvy is only supposed to stay for twenty minutes, but spends nearly an hour with me. As we leave the smoking room, my two 'chaperons' immediately stand to follow me. I want to go downstairs to say goodbye in the foyer, but they won't let me. I have to stand at the double doors and wave.

Next morning, one of the male nurses, John, helps me look for my teeth. He works out which window I threw them from and we go downstairs and start searching through the rose bushes and shrubs. I find them in the leaf litter, but the plate is broken so it means a trip to the hospital dentist to have a new set made up and fitted.

I must be getting better because I'm starting to recognise how crazy people are in this place. Some patients are only in for a week or two, which makes me feel like a veteran. Mick is my pacing partner because we're both so restless. We walk the corridors at night and eventually circle back to the smoking room, where the walls are painted mustard-brown to hide the nicotine stains.

There's a little gang of us who smoke. There's one chair that no one is allowed to use because it belongs to Rosemary. She's a fully fledged loony in her mid-fifties, and the most foul-mouthed woman I've ever met. I'm not exaggerating when I say that she could out-swear any paratrooper. She has long matted hair like a street person, filthy toenails and a huge paunch. She smokes about 100 cigarettes a day and there's a mess of burn marks on the carpet around her chair because she's always dozing off with a fag hanging out of her mouth.

It's taken me a while, but I'm starting to recognise her massive mood swings. When the 'darkness' descends she becomes abusive, and will launch into a tirade if anyone so much as looks at her. 'What are you looking at, you cunt?' she'll say, grabbing her crotch. 'You wanna lick this, eh? Is that it?'

I ignore her and find a chair further away.

At other times Rosemary talks about particular male nurses and the crude things she wants to do with them. Then, a few days later, if you mention the same nurses, she acts like a doting aunt, and I can almost imagine her knitting them sweaters and bed socks.

When the foul-mouthed Rosemary disappears, the nice Rosemary tells me about her family. She's been married and has a couple of children and a grandchild. None of them visit her. I can see the tears in her eyes as a match flares and she lights another cigarette. The staff won't talk about the other patients, but apparently Rosemary has been in and out of institutions for nearly thirty years. I call her 'the wise woman of the Stonebow' because she's been here so long that she knows everybody's story.

The 'nice' Rosemary hangs around for a few days, but then she'll switch. It usually happens in the morning, just after the night staff hand over. I might say something like, 'Good morning, Rosemary. Sleep well?' and she'll reply, 'Fuck off and leave me alone! Just fuck off!'

It might seem callous, but being around Rosemary actually cheers me up because I start to count my blessings and realise how much better off I am than some of the others. I have Livvy coming in to see me every day, as well as Chris and Jason and friends like Andy D., Irene and Roy T., my old SSM from the Regiment. Rosemary has no one.

21

I've been in the smoking room since three this morning. Mick joined me
at about four and Rosemary surfaced at seven, when the day shift arrived.
She sat in her chair, tucked the ends of her floral dressing-gown between
her knees and lit up. I watched the white ash get longer until it dropped
between her fingertips.

Some days are better than others, and I manage to get out of my pyjamas and put on a shirt and a pair of jeans. I try to wash and freshen up
for Livvy. She always brings a bowl of fruit because she thinks I need
something to combat all the chemical shit they're pumping into me. The
bowls are nicely arranged and I eat the fruit while we talk, shovelling it
into my mouth like a bloody monkey because the drugs make me hungry.
Half the time I don't even know what I'm eating.

'I thought you didn't like cherries,' Livvy says.

'I don't.'

'Well, you've just eaten a whole bunch of them.'

'Oh.'

When I run out of fruit we go to the canteen, where I eat strange com-
binations in no particular order – starting with yoghurt, maybe, then
eating mashed potato, then soup. I'm not even concentrating – it's just
food.

People are in and out of the Stonebow all the time, and it's quite sad to find out in the morning that someone has left. Mike and Pete are two newcomers. They're nineteen years old – heroin addicts who have reportedly done some terrible things to feed their addictions. One of them, I can't remember which, wrecked the town one night, smashing shop windows until the police arrived. The police recognised him straight away and brought him into rehab.

I'm interested in how they got started. What makes someone try heroin in the first place? Even as a child, Jason would never pass me an ashtray or fetch me a packet of cigarettes because he loathed smoking. Now I can't look at Mike and Pete without comparing them to Jason and counting my blessings. It's the same when I watch their parents come in to visit them, and I think to myself, 'You poor sods – it must break your hearts.'

Early one morning, an old bloke arrives in the smoking room, crawling on his hands and knees. Mick and I aren't too bothered because the place is full of strange behaviour. 'Come in, have a cigarette,' I say.

'Please don't hit me.'

'I'm not going to hit you.'

The bloke is totally out of his head. I calm him down and get him a cup of tea. His name is Roger.

'Do you mind if I stay here?'

'No, not at all. On one condition: you tell us your story.'

Roger finds a chair and tucks his knees against his chest, clutching them tightly. He keeps glancing nervously at the door.

'So why are you here?' Mick asks.

'I tried to commit suicide.'

He mumbles it at first and I can't hear him. 'You did what?'

'I tried to hang myself off the staircase, but the rope broke the banister.'

'Why did you do that?'

Roger shrugs and explains that, twelve years previously, he'd been ill and had been prescribed drugs that were highly addictive. By the time anyone realised the mistake, he was hooked. They tried to wean him off, but he finished up on heroin to feed his craving. 'I'm a 65-year-old junkie,' he says, almost spitting out the words in self-loathing.

'Have you got any family?' I ask.

'A son and a daughter. They live in London, but I never see them. I used to get a Christmas card, but that stopped a few years ago.'

I'm fascinated by what pushed him over the edge. It's one thing to contemplate suicide and another entirely to actually tie the rope around a banister and then around your neck.

'I've been suicidal, too,' I tell him.

'Oh yeah? Did you try to do it?'

'Nearly. I came close.'

'What happened?'

'I thought of my son. I couldn't do it to him.'

Roger nods and asks if he can have another cigarette. He's frightened about leaving the smoking room. He says that one of the night staff had called him a 'druggie bastard' and given him a hiding.

'We have to write out an official complaint,' I declare.

Roger goes white. 'No, I don't want to make trouble. Things will only get worse.'

'We'll help you. We'll start by writing a full statement of exactly what happened,' says Mick. We scrounge up some paper and start writing, careful to get down all the right times and places.

Later, I corner the male orderly in an empty ward. 'Just a quiet word,' I say, staring him down. 'You're a big lad, and you ought to keep your hands in your pockets.' He starts trying to explain, but I stop him. 'I'm not interested. You're way out of order.' Three days later, he's transferred to another wing of the hospital.

Whenever there's a new patient at the Stonebow we hear about it pretty quickly on the ward grapevine. If they've been in before, Rosemary will know all about them and hold court in the smoking room.

Max is a first-timer who is suffering from trauma after witnessing a road accident. The police have been told to leave him alone for a week before they come and get a statement. Meanwhile the doctors are treating him. I get chatting to Max in the canteen and I can see he's pretty vulnerable.

'Tell me what happened,' I say, hoping it might help.

Max describes how he was driving behind a lorry which ran right over the top of a van. The van then burst into flames as it appeared from under the lorry. The driver had been trapped and perished in the blaze. Max could smell the flesh burning and thinks he heard him screaming.

'That does sound pretty awful,' I say, 'but the best thing you can do is tell yourself that he died on the first impact. He didn't feel a thing. He was dead before the flames, believe me. All the police want is a witness statement – the van went under the truck, burst into flames, the bloke died – end of story.'

Max nods his head in agreement, but I can see he's struggling with something more. I light a match in front of his face. 'Does that bother you?'

'No, not really.'

'What's the worst thing that ever happened to you?'

'My father committed suicide when I was twelve.'

The disclosure shocks me, yet Max delivers it in such a matter-of-fact way it seems commonplace. Then I notice the tears in his eyes.

'That's a terrible thing to do to a child,' I tell him, thinking of Jason. Nothing is ever clear-cut. We all have so much emotional baggage to carry around with us it's a wonder we can move.

From then on, I try to keep Max's spirits up. Mick and I are blag-garding him with black humour. 'First thing you should do when you get out of here, Max, is have a barbecue,' I say.

'Yeah, put some chicken on and burn it to hell,' choruses Mick. 'Better still, roast pork and crackling.'

Max is laughing.

I make a point of finding Roger. 'There's someone I want you to meet,' I say. 'He's in here because he saw a bloke burn to death.'

'What's that got to do with me?'

'No, you see, that's not his real problem. His father committed suicide.'

I want to show Roger that killing himself isn't a solution, because it can screw up the lives of innocent people. Think of the poor train-driver who has nightmares about running you down, or the fisherman who finds you at the bottom of a cliff, or the police officers who have to find the smoking gun and leaking body.

Terry wanders in, wearing his trademark summer shorts and wrap-around sunglasses. His personal stereo must be blasting his eardrums because I can hear the bee-like buzzing from across the room. He takes a chair, faces the window and puts his feet on the windowsill, legs apart. From there he can see nothing but sky. After fifteen minutes, he gets up and goes around the chairs, offering everyone a sweet. My paranoia has gone now and I know he's not trying to poison me.

As he's leaving the room, he stops me and whispers, 'The invasion has happened, but I'm wondering how they got their spaceships through. I'll bet that's what they're wondering in America.'

I tell him, 'Terry, you're off your fucking head. That's why you're in here. Have a lie down, mate.'

We're all trying to survive in here, and at times that means helping each other. Part of any battle against the demons of drugs or addiction has to be a personal struggle – one against one. But there is also a support network at the Stonebow, based on shared experiences and common ground. This is our home away from home.

I play chess with Angela, an anorexic who throws up at the sight of food; while Tony, a new-age traveller who has sailed around the world, is teaching me a few songs on the guitar. Julie is a Yoko Ono type who dresses in a kimono and slippers. She must be about fifty years old and is into all that new-age stuff like healing crystals and auras. When I wear a yellow shirt she says it has a great spiritual significance. She has a room downstairs but comes up to our floor to use the smoking room.

Every few days Julie's husband comes in to visit, and I watch their behaviour, just like I watch all of the visitors. I can see when the patients are putting on their best show: 'Yes, I'm much better now . . . I'll be out of here soon . . . When I get home I'll . . .' Meanwhile, their relatives are sitting there, listening patiently but sneaking glances at their watches because they don't want to stay a minute longer than they have to.

I thank my lucky stars that I have people who care enough to visit me, to say the right things and come back again. Chris and Jason have been in twice, and I've put on my best show. I've also seen a lot of Andy, even though the Stonebow makes him nervous, and Frank drops in for a chat.

Livvy comes in every day, without fail, and always with a smile. She has even been accepted by Rosemary, and they chat to each other like old girlfriends. On Wednesday I'll have been here a month, and the dosages of the drugs have been scaled down to the point where I'm beginning to feel less like a Mong.

Dr Allman says it's okay if Livvy takes me for a walk outside. Hand in hand we leave the front doors and slowly follow the footpath around the block, past the cinema and the garage. I'm ready to turn and run straight back again, but Livvy's voice sounds so reassuring as she chats generally about what she's been doing. She used to be a beautician and ran her own business, but now spends her time looking after Georgia and Alicia.

There's a Safeway's supermarket a few blocks away and it has a coffee shop attached. We sit down and stay all afternoon, drinking coffee after coffee. Sometimes I talk a little but mostly I just listen to Livvy, who concentrates on subjects she knows won't unnerve me.

'Why me, Livvy, why me?'

'I don't know. No one knows.'

I feel as though I've let everyone down, including myself – all the people who got me out of France and arranged the clinic in London. I wanted to be my old self again; I wanted to show them I was better and how much I appreciated them.

'Will I ever get better?'

'Of course you will,' she whispers.

There are two reasons why I don't get terribly low, and Livvy is one of them. I look at her and wonder why on earth she has anything to do with me. It's not as if we have known each other for very long, and I must have scared her half to death when I called her a witch and started growling like an animal. Most women would have run a mile, but not Livvy. And it's not as if she doesn't have enough to worry about, being a single mum with two daughters. Why add to the burden by taking on a problem like me?

The other reason I don't get terribly depressed is because I've met people at the Stonebow who are worse off than me. I don't want to finish up like Rosemary, spending my life in institutions. I don't want to be like Max, or Roger, or Mick, or Terry, or Angela, or Tony. I listen to the stories of their damaged lives and console them where I can, but secretly I'm thinking, 'It won't happen to me. I'm going to be cured.' Is that selfish?

Sometimes they ask me, 'Well, what's *your* story?' and I get frustrated because I haven't really got one. I don't know what to make of what happened to me – I haven't reached any conclusions. What do I say? I had a psychotic breakdown and began believing in good and evil.

'Yeah, I've done that, too,' says Mike.

'Absolutely,' echoes Pete.

They're serious and they start telling me about their experiences. I can relate to things they say, but I also know that they're describing psychotic delusions and behaviour that are drug-induced. They were taking LSD and it kept them awake for days on end.

Dr Allman has already asked me if I've ever taken drugs, because apparently I display the classic symptoms of amphetamine psychosis.

'No, never. Why? What effect does it have?'

'The most dangerous aspect is that certain drugs deprive you of sleep. Have you ever been without sleep for an extended period?'

Of course, the answer is 'yes' – during the dark days.

'How long did it last?'

'Eight days.'

Then I think back even further. On Selection, during 'interrogation' – I'm against the wall, blindfolded, wearing pyjamas and plimsolls. White noise is blaring in my ears. I've been days without sleep. Question after question – don't crack now – number, rank, name, date of birth – on it goes, taking people to the verge of breakdown.

Thinking back, further again, I remember a sleep-deprivation exercise in 2 Para. Scientists were trying to find out how much sleep a soldier needed to be effective. Three platoons were chosen – 10 Platoon was allowed two hours' sleep a night, 11 Platoon had half an hour and 12 Platoon had no sleep at all.

During the day we trained in the field and at night they gave us tasks to keep us alert. We played games, watched TV, read books, chatted, or exercised. When people started to flag, the scientists wheeled out the static push-bikes and wired us up. Lads were pedalling away until they began to nod off. 'Wake up, Private. Keep going.'

'Yes, sir.'

The lads given two hours' sleep a night lasted the whole week. Of those who were allowed half an hour, approximately half managed to get through, but they were totally chin-strapped with exhaustion. None of 12 Platoon lasted the week. Scouse Toole was the final one to succumb. He was a stocky little bloke, with missing teeth and an aggressive manner. Towards the end, he was pedalling the static bike and desperately trying to stay awake. His eyelids were fluttering and his head started double-tapping as his chin bounced against his chest.

'Are you asleep, Private Toole?'

'No, sir!'

His chin dropped again and they jabbed him with their fingers. Scouse started to get aggressive and dispensed with the 'sir'. Then they used a stick to prod him awake and he swiped it away. 'I fucking told you I'm awake!' he bellowed. The stick got longer and longer, and finally they just let him sleep because nobody was game enough to wake him.

Allman is staring at me. 'You were going to say something.'

'I don't use drugs. I never have.'

'Okay.'

I'm not playing games with him any more – Doctor knows best. He explains to me that I shouldn't see myself as being alone – psychotic breakdowns are quite common, and he has other patients who suffer from paranoid delusions. People imagine that someone is trying to poison them, or that some secret organisation is conspiring to kill them. Others think that the TV is broadcasting messages only for them, or that the Bible is written in a code only they can understand. Believing your girl-friend is the epitome of all evil is apparently right up there among the top ten delusions.

It's ironic, because whenever I used to read about people who claimed temporary insanity or diminished responsibility when charged with a vio-lent crime, I used to think they were guilty as hell and just trying to cheat justice. Now I know it's possible for the mind to create an alternative 'reality' that is so vivid and believable that it over-rides logic and reason.

Rosemary is taken ill with some form of bronchitis, and they transfer her to the medical wing of the hospital. We all go down to visit her, taking some flowers and chocolates. She's allowed out of bed to join us in her nearest smoking room, where she passes around the chocolates as if her family has arrived.

There's talk of letting her go home again, and Rosemary is excited because she misses her cats. She goes off and gets her hair done one day and comes back looking much better. Unfortunately, she lives on her own, and they're afraid that without proper supervision she'll burn the house down. Even so, she does seem to be getting better and her dark days are less and less frequent.

A new patient has arrived – a Jock who's apparently an alcoholic, but I think he's only here to exploit the system. I can't believe anyone could have so little self-esteem as to *want* to be in this place. He goes from town to town, gets on the dole and then orchestrates things so he gets put into a place like the Stonebow, where he gets free bed and board. Then he goes out on the piss every day and comes back stinking of booze and abusing the staff. One night in the toilets I tell him to wind his neck in or I'll split his head open. I must be getting better – that definitely sounds like the old me.

None of us is supposed to drink, which can be hard when you walk past an off-licence or a pub, particularly for someone like Mick. 'How does that make you feel?' I ask him one day.

'Bloody thirsty.'

'Come on, let's go inside.'

I order two orange juices and I say to Mick, 'Do you want a dash of vodka in yours?'

'No, thanks.'

'Good, that's a start. I could bloody kill one, but I'd better not.'

We feel as pure as choirboys, sipping our juice. Irene and Gerry are there, having a drink with a bloke I don't know. He seems to know a lot about drugs, and asks me about my dosages. '*How* much chlorpromazine are you taking?' He exhales with a soft whistle.

As I'm leaving, I hear him say to Irene, 'How the fuck is that guy walking?'

22

Dr Allman is allowing me out of the Stonebow to spend a night at home. Then I'll go back to the clinic for another three nights. If the experiment works, we'll gradually extend it. That's what I want, even though I hate being in this house.

'Where are all the sharp knives?' I ask, looking at the empty wooden knife-block in the kitchen.

'Um, well, Andy took them away as a precaution,' says Livvy. I can just imagine Andy doing that. Sharp knives and mad people – a bad combination.

Dr Allman has told me that the depression is going to come, just like it did when I got home from the Charter Clinic and then from Cyprus. I think I can handle it this time because I keep telling myself it isn't going to last for ever.

The last couple of days have been fine, although I struggle to remember them. The worst times are when I have my big injection for the fortnight. That's when I start to plummet downwards. 'Depression is just a state of mind,' I tell myself. 'Think of how lucky you are.' I close my eyes and pretend to be blind and block my ears pretending to be deaf. Why am I complaining? I've had an exciting life, I have a bright, intelligent son, I have a roof over my head and a woman who has seen the very worst of me and is still here. Sure I have money problems, but who hasn't? I have nothing to be depressed about.

There's a young guy who wanders around Hereford, dressed in patched-up clothes, having imaginary conversations with himself. Although he's a harmless loony, people still cross over the road to avoid walking past him. He's been around for years but I've never taken much notice until now. The poor sod has nobody. I have friends and family to look out for me, but to be totally alone would be terrible. I have no right to be depressed.

It's the same when I walk into town to meet Livvy – along the way I pass the local blind college. There are people coming out the door with their white sticks, and as they hear me approach they look up and smile. It puzzles me. How can they be so happy? Why am I so miserable?

The nights are the worst. That's when I start thinking about suicide, because it's the only solution I can arrive at. I break down the pros and cons, like a chess player contemplating the consequences of any given move. I think of Roger trying to hang himself and Max losing his father. No, it's just too horrific; I could never hurt Jason like that. But I *want* to think about suicide because it's the only escape available to me. I'm sorry, Jason, for being so selfish.

I remember reading stories about people killing themselves – like the Buddhist monk who doused himself with petrol and lit a match – and I think to myself, I couldn't do that. I also knew a bloke in the Parachute Regiment who, on his last day in the army, handcuffed himself to his car and set it alight. How could he do that?

Yet the truth is that when you decide that you *will* commit suicide, believe me, you *can*. And you don't think about finding a way that won't be messy to clean up, or traumatic for someone discovering the body. None of that matters, because you simply want to escape.

How am I going to do it? I look at my watch, it's 10 a.m. I'm going to walk around to the local garage, wait for someone to come in for petrol and I'll just tie myself to their rear bumper bar with the rope around my neck. I won't scream; I'll gag myself and let them drag me up the road.

There's a knock on the door and it opens before I can answer. Livvy smiles at me and then looks worried. 'You've had a bad night.'

'Uh-huh.'

'You're not going to do anything silly, are you?'

'No.'

Livvy gives me a lot of hope because she doesn't let things get her down. I think religion has a lot to do with it. Despite her disappointments and the hard knocks, she has always been able to thank God for what she has and to accept that things could always be worse. I wish I could do that.

I have enough trouble just getting through each day and concentrating on one thought – getting better – yet Livvy has to look after a family, a house, her finances, cooking, cleaning, washing . . . At the same time she manages to visit me every day and to sit and listen while I complain about feeling terrible.

I'm lousy around the house. Cups are piled up in the sink, the frying-pan is coated with grease, I haven't got a clean knife or fork in the place. Livvy sorts it all out, chiding me gently about having spent too long in the army where things were done for me.

Before she goes to bed at night she always says a prayer for me. Then she phones to say goodnight, and can always tell if I'm really depressed. At about three o'clock one morning she woke and decided to check on me. Her car wouldn't start so she climbed on a bicycle and pedalled for four miles through the rain-glossed streets.

She opened the front door quietly and peeked inside. I was lying on the sofa, on my left side, with the TV blaring and a crumpled cigarette packet in the ashtray. She quietly closed the door and left. She didn't leave a note because she didn't want me to think that she'd been spying on me. On the way home the police stopped her because she had no lights on the bike.

'Aren't you old enough to know better?' a smart-arse young constable said. Livvy just told him to go and catch some real criminals.

Anna is still phoning occasionally, and has sent me some material through the post. It's about three pages photocopied from a medical journal, and she's highlighted various bits. The article is entitled 'Bipolar Disorder', and it details the symptoms of manic depression – basically extreme highs followed by extreme lows.

Isn't it nice that she thinks of me now? During the dark days, when I wasn't sleeping and I'd lost so much weight that my clothes were hanging off me, I don't remember her asking, 'What's the matter, Tom? You really should see a doctor.' Anna is not that sort of girl.

I leave it for a while before I show the article to Dr Allman. 'Listen, Tom, we've considered every possibility,' he says. 'Believe me, it's quite typical what you're going through.'

'So you have considered this bipolar disorder?'

'Yes, early onset of psychotic depression may be related to bipolar disorder, but your problem emerged later in life. I don't think you're a manic depressive – I think it's far more complex than that.'

'So what do I tell people is wrong with me?'

'You have a psychotic disorder with extreme depression.'

'And these drugs – how do you know if I'm receiving the right dosages?'

'That's why I have you come and see me,' he explains. 'Psychological and physical examinations are the best way to tell if a person is receiving the right amount or the right kind of drug.'

'So it's all mark-one eyeball stuff?'

He chuckles. 'I'd argue that it's more technical than that. You see, the amount of drug a person needs varies over time. Certain factors can affect it, such as weight gain or weight loss, sickness, stress, exercise, alcohol.'

I've become very interested in what they're pumping into me, and have started buying and borrowing psychology and pharmaceutical books. They make my bookshelf even more eclectic when a history of the Red Devils sits alongside a copy of *Coping With Mental Illness*.

I read in short bursts, noting how schizophrenia and psychotic depression tend to develop in late adolescence and rarely after the age of thirty-five. The cause is biological; some sort of chemical imbalance in that part of the brain that regulates thinking and feeling. Environmental factors like stress, lack of sleep and alcohol abuse can be a catalyst or increase the severity.

The brain is composed of billions and billions of nerve cells, called neurons. These neurons are densely packed and are distributed throughout the entire brain. All neurons contain chemicals called neurotransmitters which act as messengers communicating information from one part of the brain to another. If there's an imbalance in these chemicals, it screws up a person's ability to think, perceive and act in a planned way.

This is all good information, but what I'm really looking for is a root cause; the bang-on-the-head explanation for all my problems.

'Hey, Livvy, listen to this,' I shout, reading out loud. She's in the other room.

' "Family members of psychologically depressed patients have a higher rate of major depression and specifically of the psychotic form than the relatives of other depressed patients; they also have a six times higher rate of bipolar disorder." '

'Uh-huh.' Livvy is only half listening.

'It also says here that some researchers think it might be caused by influenza if a child is exposed to the virus in its mother's womb. Maybe that's what happened to me. What do you think? I should ask Mum.'

'Maybe.'

'And there's another expert who says it might be caused by birth trauma, you know, forceps delivery and other complications. I was a pretty big baby, you know? Eleven pounds two ounces.'

Every book I read has a new theory, although the genetic link is pretty much accepted. Some psychiatrists think that psychological and social factors, such as disturbed family and interpersonal relationships, may play a role. There are also studies looking for a link with oxygen deprivation (hypoxia), which makes me think about the expedition to Everest and my blinding headaches, as well as the pressure-chamber tests in the Regiment.

I've done so much reading that I'm becoming an armchair expert and can recognise symptoms in the loonies I've met. Rhaffi was probably suffering from *grandiose delusions* and Jimmy is a possible *catatonic schizophrenic*, although thinking you're a bird is pretty rare – most people opt for dogs. God knows about Maria, I think she's a one-off. Maybe Dr Beirut should write a paper about her.

I keep looking for information about how long the illness might last. I know that schizophrenia is a life sentence and sufferers can be on medication for ever. The National Foundation for Brain Research in America says that roughly one third of patients who have a psychotic experience recover completely with no residual symptoms. Another third will have several episodes during their lives and may have residual symptoms in between. The last third have psychotic symptoms indefinitely and often have to be permanently hospitalised. At least there are signs that the severity of the psychosis might level off later in life.

Occasionally, Livvy comes with me when I have an appointment with Dr Allman. She hardly says a word as I fire off lots of questions. Allman suggests trying a few alternative treatments. 'Would you consider electro-shock therapy?'

Livvy's gasps, 'Oh God, they don't still do that, do they? I thought that went out in the 1950s. Tom, you're not having that.'

'I don't know, Liv. Who knows, it might help.' I turn to the doctor.

'No, not that!' she says. 'You're not a monkey; they're not giving you shock treatment.'

Dr Allman then suggests putting me on Lithium for a while. It can have some difficult side-effects, but it may stop my roller-coaster ride of highs and lows.

'How long will I have to be on it?'

'Five years.'

'You're joking!'

'And you'll have to carry a card with you everywhere, explaining that you're on Lithium.'

He starts me on the tablets, but within a fortnight I'm back in his office. 'Why don't you just hang a sign around my bloody neck?' I say. 'I'm not going to carry a card around and I'm not going to wait five years to get better. It's going to happen well before that.'

Whenever I'm at the outpatients' clinic at the Stonebow, I try to drop in and visit Rosemary. We sit in the smoking room and she fills me in on the gossip and talks about how they are going to allow her to go home.

She's telling the truth, and a week or so later Rosemary is reunited with her beloved cats. A nurse supervises for a few hours every day and Rosemary has to look after herself the rest of the time. One evening, I suggest to Livvy that we should visit her.

'Okay, we'll pop round tomorrow,' she says, pleased that I'm sounding much better.

But come the next day, I don't want to leave the house. It's been another bad night. When I'm next back at the Stonebow Unit for my injection I say to a nurse, 'Anyone heard from Rosemary?'

'Yes, she's back in, Tom.'

'Oh, no.'

'She just couldn't look after herself.'

In a way I'm kind of pleased, because after thirty years in institutions, perhaps the best place for Rosemary is in here. At the same time, I know that I don't want to finish up like that – unable to survive or operate in the real world; incapable of comforting my own son when he's in pain;

spending my nights planning my own suicide. I want my life back.

Livvy and I go looking for Rosemary and we find her downstairs. I sit next to her and pat her knee.

'Fuck off and leave me alone!' she says. 'Just look after yourself.'

'Come on, Rosemary, it's me – Tom.'

She glares at me accusingly and then her shoulders droop. 'Just get on with your life. Look after yourself.'

There are other patients sitting around us, most of them strangers to me, some of them knitting, writing, doodling or just staring into space. They don't even bother looking up as I leave. A fortnight later, my key nurse Stephanie pulls me to one side as I arrive at the hospital. 'Rosemary is dead,' she says. 'She had a chest infection. I'm sorry.'

23

Is that what will happen to me? Will I have my own chair in the smoking room, surrounded by cigarette burns in the carpet? Will I wait in vain for visitors or have them sneaking glances at their watches, wondering why the hour is taking so long? Will I be the 'wise old man of the Stonebow' who knows everybody's story?

I've been fooling everyone since Chamonix, including myself. I came off the medication and people talked about 'the same old Tom', but that was bullshit. The truth is I've been psychotic for the past two years, and had simply learned to control it and keep it secret. The drugs helped by blocking out thoughts and letting me sleep, but they made me feel like shit. Livvy is adamant that I stay on them now, at least for a year, but they don't solve the problem, they simply mask it.

For a while now I've been interested in hypnosis. My dad used to tell me stories and I've seen some of the stage acts. In Washington, Anna and I went to a professional hypnotist who said he could stop us smoking. He put Anna under, but I couldn't relax. Eventually I pretended, and as soon as I walked outside, I lit up a cigarette. What a waste of $200.

Now I'm beginning to think that self-hypnosis might be worth a try. Maybe it could unlock memories and help me understand what's happened.

Jackie found an advertisement in a magazine a few months back: 'Become a Member of the British Hypnosis Society', it declared. For

£300 you got a package through the post every month that taught you hypnosis and also explained the legal situation and how to set up an office.

I applied for the course and photocopied the chapters because Jackie also wanted to learn. Straight away they tried to sell us more stuff. For an extra fee I could have a session with the guy who ran the course which included an afternoon on his luxury boat. No thanks!

When I told Dr Allman about trying hypnotherapy he wasn't impressed.

'No, your problem is a chemical imbalance. You need drugs,' he said.

'Okay, so it's not a cure, but maybe it can help me get a good night's sleep. If it can do that I'll be happy.'

The basis of hypnosis is intense relaxation, and allowing the subconscious and conscious mind to interact. It takes me a long while to build up the confidence and energy to give it a try. I lock the doors and windows, unplug the phone, close the curtains, lie on my brown sofa and begin the process of trying to relax. The only sound I hear is the ticking of my wooden clock, with its false brass pendulum. I turn it off, but the silence irritates me because I'm so used to the noise. I set it going again and imagine that it represents perpetual motion.

There are quite a few methods of going into a state of deep relaxation, where the mind becomes remote and detached from everyday concerns. It's not a case of being asleep or unconscious, but rather an altered state of consciousness.

The notes suggest that I picture myself in a lift. I get on at the fourteenth floor and watch the lights count down. It's a slow lift . . . 13 . . . 12 . . . 11 . . . down, down . . .

What bollocks! The door is going to open any minute because someone will want to get on and then they'll ask a stupid question like, 'Is this lift going down?' I can't think of anything worse than going up and down in a box tied to a cable.

Okay, let's try walking down a spiral staircase.

No, that won't work either.

I'll think of my own scene. A place where I felt safe and secure; a place where I can clear my mind and relax.

I'm lying in a hammock in the jungle. It's seven o'clock at night and I have a candle so I can read a book. I'm watching the insects climbing up the poles and the mosquitoes landing and trying to find a way through the netting. It starts to rain and I can hear the heavy drops hitting the poncho strung over my hammock. Yes, I love the jungle.

How about sitting on stag in Norway, staring down the barrel of a gun for two hours looking for the slightest movement in the darkness? Nothing interrupts my concentration, nothing enters my head; my only concern is to cover my arc.

Where else did I feel safe and secure? I want to put myself there. I'm in a meadow on an undulating hill and at the bottom there's a stream with clear water bubbling over rocks and a willow tree dipping its branches into a pool. I know this place – it's in the woods at Holsworthy Beacon in north Devon. I used to go there as a child when I wanted to escape from home. I can picture myself sitting with my back to the tree, dangling a fishing line into the pool but not wanting to catch anything. It's a secluded spot, concealed by the natural contours of the land, and I can hear if anyone approaches. I love this place.

Hold on! It's probably changed by now. The meadow will be a building site, covered in houses, and the stream will be polluted by old paint tins and garden refuse. All the fish have died and the willow tree has been hacked down.

No, I've been back there – with Anna – and it's still the same. Last summer I drove her down to Devon and we found my old house, below the farm. The garden looked spectacular, in full flower as I walked up the little front path, past the tree stump that I tried to dig out when I was younger. I knocked on the door. An old man answered. 'Can I help you?' He had a local accent.

'I'm sorry to trouble you, but I used to live in this house.'

'Did you, now. And what is your name?'

'Tom Read.'

He scratched his chin and I saw the flicker of recognition cross his face. 'I used to be a teacher in Holsworthy Beacon,' he said. 'I remember your family. Didn't you have a brother who went into the circus?'

'Yes, that's right – Vince, he's a trick rope star in America.'

'Look, why don't you come in.'

The house was exactly the same as I remembered. Anna walked around and kept gushing things like, 'Isn't this extraordinary. This is where you slept and this is where you ate . . .'

I interrupted her, 'And this is the window I used to escape through.

My parents thought I'd become interested in gardening, but I used to the earth up outside the window so it was a softer landing when I jumped and disappeared into the woods.'

Outside again, I started to walk down through the woods on a path that had become overgrown. I didn't go right down into the valley to the stream because along the way I got chatting to a local farmer. He remembered me as a little boy when I used to help out on his farm. 'No, the stream is still there,' he said. 'Nothing much has changed around here.'

It takes me weeks of practice to get myself into a state of deep relaxation. On the first few attempts, I manage to get part of the way there before something breaks my concentration like a car horn or voices from the street. Often it's my own fault because I can't stop an unwanted thought from intruding into my mental idyll.

It feels like a positive experience so I try again and again, exhaling all the tension out of my body and relaxing. I'm in my special place. I can feel the breeze on my face and the dappled sunshine . . .

Hold on! What am I going to wear in my special place? Well, I've always been comfortable in an army-issue uniform. I'll wear a jumper, shirt and green fatigues. Okay, that's sorted.

I try again, putting myself back beside the stream where the sunshine is coming through the leaves and playing on my closed lids and the water is bubbling over rocks. There are no conscious thoughts – nothing to worry about. I go deeper still, carried downwards. I can feel myself crying and at the same time I'm watching myself crying. I don't know why.

—Don't dwell on it, just go deeper. Access whatever is in there.

But I'm not a very good climber, I might not get back up.

—Shhhhh. You're somewhere safe. Just relax.

I've accepted that life's experiences have damaged me. Now I have to tie up the loose ends and make sense of what happened.

Looking deeper and deeper into my subconscious, I look for the damaged piece of the 'machine'. I can actually picture what my mind looks like because no one else has ever seen one. To begin with, I imagine a locked door, but I don't know what's behind it. It's a fire door and the lock has five levers, anti-picks and tumblers. Don't worry, I've been prepared for this; I was trained to pick locks by the Regiment.

...fts off and I remember the course, it reinforces my ... my life's experiences have been preparing me for this ... the lessons learned from my father; other people's stories, ... eriences and mistakes. I have been given the tools to get ... e door and address what lies behind it. But what could that be?

Behind the door is a raging inferno, like a star collapsing or the centre of the Earth. I can feel the heat when I press my hands against it and it makes me want to cry. Surely I can't have gone down that far.

I remember being on a signals course with the Regiment up in Scotland, when an old wooden NAAFI building caught fire. A few of us rushed across and decided that we'd save the pool table. I looked through the window and saw a few flames but mainly smoke. I knew nothing then about the flashover effect of a fire suddenly fed on oxygen.

I pushed at the door and as it opened there was a huge yellow roar and a wall of flame exploded outwards through the doorway. I dived out of the way and covered up as it hit me, singeing my eyebrows and hair. I was lucky.

Now I face a different type of 'door' and a fiercer heat. My mind has been damaged or cracked open and the contents are spilling out. There's a frightening mixture of experience and emotions. A part of me wants to keep the fire door shut in case the heat destroys me. Another part of me asks: 'Do I want to go inside?'

The answer is, 'Yes, I do.'

It has taken me weeks and weeks to get this far, and I've been building up my strength and confidence. I created the door and I decided it was locked, but I've been given the tools to open it and to deal with what lies on the other side.

Whatever it is, it has to be *my* creation. I don't want any surprises. There is no fire – I put that there to frighten me. Instead, I imagine finding a white room – as white as the snow holes we used to dig in Norway before we crawled into our sleeping-bags.

In the centre of the white room, I imagine a filing cabinet, tipped over on to the floor, with files spread everywhere and pieces of paper spilling out. The first thing I do is stand the filing cabinet back up and kneel down amidst the folders. Each of them has a heading such as 'Fear', 'Love', 'Hate', 'Joy' – all those emotions that I once tried to fit into my device. There are loose pieces of foolscap paper and I have to decide which folders they belong to, so I sit on the floor and start picking them up.

The first one is the story from my childhood about shooting the sparrows. That probably fell out of the file marked 'Excitement', because as a child I must have enjoyed it, or I wouldn't have repeated the experience. Now I feel ashamed. Where is the 'Shame' folder?

Here it is! There's a piece of paper in there already. It's about Duke Allen, my old mate from the Recruiting Team. While I was in Washington, indulging in flying and earning a good salary, Duke had been having a terrible time. He was living in a shack, guarding a scrapyard with a couple of dogs for company, and the truck he used for shifting gravel had broken down. He was on his uppers and I had the money to be able to help him, except I was too busy enjoying myself to send him any. Yes, that deserves to be in the 'Shame' folder.

Nothing is allowed into this 'white room' unless I know it to be a fact. I tell myself, 'Go all the way back – what are your earliest recollections of childhood?'

Vaguely I remember the Isle of Wight, messing around and going boating with Dad. We had a lot of fun together. I come across a piece of paper and start reading. It relates an incident that happened when I was a child. Dad and I had been invited down to the Isle of Wight to go on a friend's boat, but when we arrived the vessel was on dry land, being cleaned and painted. The owner asked us to give him a hand and I had a great time scraping and painting the hull. Quietly, he slipped a couple of pound notes into my hand. I'd never seen so much money.

Meanwhile, Dad went off to the pub and didn't get back until late. When he arrived, he started bellowing at his friend: 'How dare you invite us down here and have my son working like a navvy! You build up his hopes about going out on a boat and then you do this to him.'

I'd never seen Dad like that before. People were watching and moving away. My hopes hadn't been built up. I loved working on the boat.

I turn over the page. There is no more of the story.

So how did I feel about that incident? Deep embarrassment.

Okay, let's find the 'Embarrassment' file and put it in there.

What else can I remember about Dad? He's one of those people who has tapes in his head, and if you trigger him by mentioning certain things then the tape will start and he'll tell you the story even if you've heard it a dozen times before.

As children we weren't allowed to watch TV unless it was something that Dad wanted to see, like some old honourable and romantic film. Often we didn't see the end because Dad would find something about it he didn't like and announce: 'This rubbish is going off!'

What's next? Look, here's a folder for 'Regrets'. I've always said that I don't believe in having regrets – maybe that's why it's empty. No, here's something (I pick up a piece of paper). I regretted leaving the Regiment the first time. I was too hot-headed and impulsive. The second time didn't matter because I was ready for it then and it was my decision.

I spent two years with Air Troop, G Squadron. They were a good bunch of lads but I was always going to be the outsider, and for all my hard work I knew I'd never be promoted. The CO did not keep his word about allowing me back to B Squadron after a year.

I don't feel bitter because at least when I left the SAS I did so on my own terms rather than being returned to my unit. I didn't want that on my record.

And so it continues. I'm reviewing my entire life, incident by incident, relationship by relationship. Sometimes I need more information, so I telephone people or visit them, to ask questions. Then I rest up for a couple of days before I lie down and go back into the 'white room' furnished with the new information.

During one weekly phone call, Mum asks me if there's anything I need. I tell her, 'Mum, all I want is a big cuddle.'

'Oh, darling, I'm sorry I can't be there,' she says. 'But I can't leave your father, you know that.'

Straight away, I regret having said it. 'No, I'm all right, Mum, really I am.'

I visit the graveyard to see Hillbilly and Al Slater again, gathering details to take back into my 'white room'. We fucked up Al's job. If only we'd been able to call on reinforcements. If only we'd had a gun on that bend where we could have taken out the enemy. If only I'd confronted the dark figure who jumped the farm gate. If only . . .

The same is true with Hillbilly. If I'd just wound my neck in and hadn't shown disrespect I would have stayed in B Squadron with Hillbilly. Who knows, I might have been on the job with him in the Far East.

It's likely that I would have stayed with him before coming back – both of us being single – and maybe I could have saved him.

And what about Chris Meacock? There's another big 'if'. He invited me to go up in the Skyliner with him. If I'd been in the co-pilot's seat I might have stopped him making a wrong decision. He knew he was in trouble at 10,000 feet – he must have done. 'Admit our mistake,' I would have told him. 'Get on the fucking radio. Tell them to clear everybody off the taxi-way and put down on the grass, because you don't have enough fuel to go around again.'

Each time I open a folder there are more things that I have to address. Each separate incident, emotion, character and outcome has to be sorted and filed. 'Tie up the loose ends,' I tell myself. 'Bundle them up neatly.'

I've never been a very good administrator – I've been trained to destroy things, or at least to change them – but now I have this filing cabinet and a mess of folders and paper. I feel like saying, 'Jackie, get in there, sort it out, find the right files.' But this is up to me.

I reflect back on the dark days before Chamonix and every perceived sign and 'message'. What about the device? I tried to create something that could explain my unhappiness and sort out my emotions. The 'boots' and valves were part of an irrational, psychotic, paranoid invention, but I still have to address these thoughts like every other part of my life.

I can't change what's happened or throw things away. I have to come to terms with each event and put them in a file. Only then can I consider getting rid of memories that aren't so important.

So what happened to me? I ate too little, drank too much and slept not at all. I got involved in an unhealthy relationship, full of stress and turmoil. Perhaps the chemical imbalance had something to do with Everest, or the pressure-chamber tests. Who knows, maybe I've suffered the humdinger of all mid-life crises.

Don't ask me for an answer now. I'm still sorting out the scattered files in my 'white room'. If I'm not happy with something, I change it. If I can't change it, I accept it. Maybe when I've sorted out this mess and filed it all away, the answer will be waiting for me.

Epilogue

My biggest mistake was accepting that there is good and evil and not going deeper than that.

I know that now. During the dark days I didn't question the idea of opposing forces, black and white, good guys and bad guys, just like in the Saturday matinees when you knew which side to barrack for because of the colour of the cowboys' hats.

If I'd gone deeper I would have realised there was something wrong with me. Instead, I carried on freefalling into madness.

I'm here in Cadaqués, finishing this book. Livvy is with me and we're sitting on a balcony, looking out over the clay-coloured rooftops and whitewashed church to the Mediterranean. A village has been clinging to these rocky cliffs since before Christ was born.

I first mentioned the idea of writing a book when I was in the Stonebow Unit, but that was partly just a line to get people to tell me their stories. I had no intention of actually doing it. The idea didn't arise seriously until Andy McNab visited me and we talked about old times in Air Troop. By then he had written *Bravo Two Zero* and *Immediate Action*, triggering a real industry in SAS books.

I was struggling to make ends meet and unable to work, but Andy kindly gave me some money and offered to put me in touch with somebody. I told him I didn't want to write a book about the Regiment. It saddened me that some authors had taken awful liberties with the truth with their books. I know, because I was there or because they told me what really happened.

Equally, some of these ex-soldiers had chosen to put themselves on operations that they played no part in, stealing someone else's glory, just to please the reader or enhance their reputations.

'I don't want to write a book about the SAS,' I told Andy.

'Okay, just write about what happened to you,' he said. 'It's a hell of a story.'

I've been off the medication for four months, which doesn't please Dr Allman, but if I can go a year without a relapse, he'll give me the all-clear. 'We have to take the risk that it won't happen again,' he said.

Everybody has a threshold for a psychotic breakdown, and from now on I am much closer to mine because I've been there and come back. I know what it takes. But I do believe that I have the strength and inner objectivity to recognise it if it happens again. Then I'll use the old Para solution and get my shit together. I'll eat well, drink lots of fluids and get training until I'm so tired at night that I have to sleep. That's the plan, anyway.

'What are you going to do in that year?' Dr Allman asked.

'I don't know. Maybe I'll try to make some sense of what's happened and write a book.'

It's the height of the holiday season, and the cobblestoned streets of Cadaqués are crowded. Beach towels and bougainvillaea drape over the balconies and the outdoor cafés are buzzing with laughter and music.

Sharky is down here with his girlfriend and another couple. They're here for the summer and perhaps even longer. Sharky has left the Paras and has settled into civvy street better than most career soldiers.

Although we don't talk about it, Sharky would probably say that the seed for my breakdown was sown when Chris Meacock died in the plane crash. Others will tell you I've always been 'mad' and prone to doing crazy things. The chemical imbalance might be genetic or it could have been triggered by oxygen deprivation or a cellular metabolic defect. I don't know and I don't care any more.

I have reached a conclusion about what happened to me – a conclusion that might not be perfect, but I can live with it. In the eighteen months since my second breakdown I've spent a lot of time lying on my sofa, using self-hypnosis to look deeper and deeper into my subconscious, searching for the damaged piece of the 'machine'.

I remember a story my father told me when I was a young lad. We tend to assume that mathematics is unshakeable in its truth, and that numbers cannot lie. Dad wanted to show me differently.

'What are three times nine?' he asked.

'Twenty-seven.'

'Are you sure?'

'Yes.'

'Okay, remember that.'

Then he told me a story.

There were three people sharing a house, and they agreed to divide all the expenses evenly. They each paid a third of the rent, a third of the telephone bill and a third for all the groceries.

One day they decided to buy a television, and they went down to the second-hand electrical store where there was an old black and white set in the window for £30. They each handed over £10 and carried it away.

As they left, the salesman went to his boss and said, 'I just managed to get rid of that old TV in the window.'

'For how much?'

'Thirty pounds.'

'Oh, no. It's on sale for only £25. Catch up with them and give them their change.'

The salesman took five £1 coins out of the till and ran down the road. On the way, he thought to himself, 'Well, these guys split everything between them; how am I going to divide five £1 coins between three people?'

He decided not to bother. He'd give them each a £1 coin and would pocket the other £2 for himself. Who would ever know?

He caught up with them and gave each of them a coin.

Dad stopped his story at this point and asked me: 'How much did each of the flatmates pay for the TV?'

'They paid £10 each and they each got £1 back, so that makes it £9,' I said confidently.

'And what is three times nine?'

'Twenty-seven.'

'How much did the salesman keep?'

'Two pounds.'

'And what is twenty-seven plus two?'

'Twenty-nine.'

'So where's the other pound?'

I went over and over that story, jotting down the numbers and trying to break down every little part of it, but I still couldn't explain where the missing coin had gone. It defied logic and all that I knew about mathematics, but eventually I had to simply accept that there was no explanation.

After eighteen months of reviewing my life and everything that has happened to me, I have come to a very similar conclusion. Even in my madness, if I could bring the good and enemy forces together and have them do battle, the ultimate result would be a stalemate. I have accepted that fact and there is no point in me continuing to look for an explanation. Arthur C. Clarke was once asked about his views on extraterrestrial life and he said that he'd given up researching it. 'Why should I spend all my time researching UFOs when I'll turn on my TV one day and CNN will tell me that an alien spaceship has landed in Central Park? What good is all my research then?'

I feel the same way about what happened to me. I don't want to know any more, I'm not interested. I don't want any more information. It's not important. I have accepted that 27 + 2 = 29 and not 30. I have broken down my life with great clarity; I have looked separately at each part, trying to make sense of it before I put them back together again. And I realise now that there isn't always a magic solution or a hidden secret. There are some things that can never be explained and we simply have to accept them and get on with our lives.

Sitting at an open-air café last night, Sharky was wearing his old hippy-head and he said to me, 'The problem with you, Tom, is that the planet is transmitting in colour but you're only receiving in black and white.'

Not so long ago I would have picked up on the 'black and white' as being a classic 'sign' – in the psychotic mind there is no such thing as a coincidence. Now I can smile and let it go.

I like Cadaqués – it has a nice feel about it. Livvy and I are thinking
of spending the summer here, and perhaps longer. Apart from that I don't
know what the future holds for us. The Skydive from Space is an unful-
filled ambition, and even if I don't make the jump, I would love to be part
of the attempt. One day the record *will* be broken – that's what records
are for – and I still dream of being up there in that hostile yet beautiful
place, accelerating away from the balloon on a four-minute freefall that
seems like for ever.

'You're not still thinking about that bloody jump,' says Sharky, shaking
his head.

'I don't know. Things have moved on. You once told me that I would
have to be mad to do it. Well, I've been through a lot of pain to get *that*
qualification.'